Order the *Building Local Area Networks* disk today!

The disk for *Building Local Area Networks* is a toolkit of public-domain and Shareware utilities that have proved to be of particular value to LAN managers and users.

Because the files are compressed, you actually receive several disks worth of programs, including the latest compression/decompression utilities.

To order, return this postage-paid card with your payment to: **M&T Books**, 501 Galveston Drive, Redwood City, CA 94063-4728. Or, call TOLL-FREE 800-533-4372 (In CA 800-356-2002). Ask for **Item #026-5**.

YES! Please send me the *Building Local Area Networks* disk for $20 __________

California residents add applicable sales tax ____% __________

TOTAL __________

Check enclosed. Make payable to **M&T Books**.

Charge my ____ VISA ____ MasterCard ____ American Express

Card # ______________________ Exp. date ______________

Name ______________________________________

Address ____________________________________

City ______________________ State __________ Zip __________

7030

NO POSTAGE
NECESSARY
IF MAILED
IN THE
UNITED STATES

BUSINESS REPLY MAIL

FIRST CLASS PERMIT 871 REDWOOD CITY, CA

POSTAGE WILL BE PAID BY ADDRESSEE

M&T BOOKS
501 Galveston Drive
Redwood City, CA 94063

PLEASE FOLD ALONG LINE AND STAPLE OR TAPE CLOSED

Building Local Area Networks with Novell's NetWare

Building Local Area Networks with Novell's NetWare

Patrick H. Corrigan
and
Aisling Guy

M&T Publishing, Inc.
Redwood City, CA 94063

M&T Books
A Division of M&T Publishing, Inc.
501 Galveston Drive
Redwood City, CA 94063

M&T Books
General Manager, Ellen Ablow
Editorial Project Manager, Michelle Hudun
Project Editor, David Rosenthal
Editorial Assistant, Kurt Rosenthal
Cover Art Director, Michael Hollister
Cover Designer, Joe Sikoryak

Printed in the United States of America
First Edition published 1989

Library of Congress Cataloging in Publication Data
Corrigan, Patrick H.
Building Local Area networks with Novell's NetWare / Patrick H. Corrigan and Aisling Guy.
p. cm.
Includes index.
1. Local area networks. 2. NetWare (Computer program) I. Guy, Aisling. II. Title.
TK5105.7.C68 1988 88-26781
004.6'8—dc19 CIP

ISBN 1-55851-010-9 (book) $24.95
ISBN 1-55851-025-7 (set) $39.95
ISBN 1-55851-026-5 (disk) $20.00

93 92 91 90 89 5 4 3 2 1

Trademarks

Coordinator and Message Handling Service (MHS) are trademarks of Action Technologies
Macintosh, LocalTalk, and Macintosh II are trademarks of Apple Computer, Inc.
SQL Server is a trademark of Ashton-Tate/Sysbase/Microsoft
VINES, Mail, and StreetTalk are trademarks of Banyan Systems
Paradox is a trademark of Borland
Sitelock, PS-Print, ANET NetWork Utilities, NETmanager, NETMAN, and PS-Batch are trademarks of Brightwork Development
cc:Mail is a trademark of cc:Mail, Inc.
Monitrix and NetBack are trademarks of Cheyenne Software
Network Courier is a trademark of Consumers Software
OmniShare is a trademark of Corvus System
Office Works is a trademark of Data Access Corp.
ARCNET is a trademark of Datapoint Corp.
eMail is a trademark of Da Vinci Systems Corp.
VAX and All-in-1 are trademarks of Digital Equipment Corp.
ASCOM IV is a trademark of Dynamic Microprocessor Associates
Higgins is a trademark of Enable Software
XTreeNet is a trademark of Executive Systems, Inc.
FOXBASE is a trademark of Fox Software
Printer Assist, LAN Assist Plus, and Map Assist are trademarks of Fresh Technology Group
G-Net is a trademark of Gateway Communications
SQL Windows and SQR are trademarks of Gupta Technology
PC LAN Program, NETWORK, SNA, LAN Server, Network Manager, PROFS, DISOSS, AS/400 Office, Application Program-to-Program Communications (APPC), DB2, Systems Network Architecture (SNA), Service Message Block (SMB), PC-XT, and PC AT are trademarks of IBM Corp.
Chatterbox is a trademark of J&L Information Systems
Network Management Report Utilities is a trademark of J.A. Lomax Assoc.
LAN Spool and Reference Point are trademarks of LAN Systems, Inc.
LifeNET is a trademark of Lifeboat Associates
Automenu is a trademark of Magee Enterprises, Inc.
MCI Mail is a trademark of MCI
Carbon Copy Plus is a trademark of Microcom Software Division
MDBS III is a trademark of Micro Database Systems
LAN Manager andWindows are trademarks of Microsoft Corp.
Workgroup is a trademark of Ncompass Software, Inc.
Close-Up and Close-Up/LAN are trademarks of Norton-Lambert Corp.
NetWare, NetWare SQL, SQL Requestor, Btrieve, Transaction Tracking Sysem (TTS), NetWare XQL, NetWare Access Server, NetWare Care, NetWare 386, NetWare Streams, NetWare Core Protocols (NCP), Apple File Protocols (AFP), Transmission Control Protocol/Internet Protocol (TCP/IP), and NE-1000 are trademarks of Novell, Inc.
PC-Net is a trademark of Orchid Technology
Document Manager is a trademark of Persona
Intelligent Wire Centers MAUs, Advanced Network Manager, and ProNet are trademarks of Proteon
LANPAC II is a trademark of Rancore
RetixMail is a trademark of Retix
Revelation is a trademark of Revelation Technologies
Saber Meter and Saber Menu System are trademarks of Saber Software
NWRANGER is a trademark of SARBEC
Mailbridge is a trademark of SoftSwitch
Linear Bus ARCNET is a trademark of Standard Microsystems Corporation (SMC)
Trancendental Network Operating System (TOPS), TOPS FlashCard, and Network File System (NFS) are trademarks of Sun Microsystems
Telemail is a trademark of Telenet
EtherShare, 3+, CIOSYS, 3+ Open, and 3+ Mail are trademarks of 3Com Corporation
Wang Office, Mailway, and Office Network are trademarks of Wang
WordPerfect Office and WordPerfect are trademarks of WordPerfect Corp.
dBXL andQuicksilver are trademarks of WordTech
Xerox Ethernet, WP, Xerox Network System (XNS) are trademarks of Xerox

Limits of Liability and Disclaimer of Warranty

How to Order the Accompanying Disk

The disk for **Building Local Area Networks** is a toolkit of public-domain and Shareware utilities that have proved to be of particular value to LAN managers and users.

Because the files are compressed, you actually receive several disks worth of programs, including the latest compression/decompression utilities.

To order send a check, or credit card number and expiration date, to:

M&T Books
501 Galveston Drive
Redwood City, California 94063-4728

Or, you may call our toll-free number: 800/533-4372 (in California: 800/356-2002) between 9 a.m. and 5 p.m. Pacific Standard Time. Ask for **Item #026-5.**

Contents

Acknowledgments

Special thanks to Karen and Patrick, Jr., and to Joseph.

We would like to thank Warren Stallings of The Software Training Group for his assistance throughout this project, as well as Jerry Wirkus of LAN Con, Dan Sanguinetti of PC Professionals, Ellen Ketelsen, and Noelle Guy for their contributions.

We would also like to thank Michelle Hudun, Ellen Ablow, Dave Rosenthal, Kurt Rosenthal, Ann Roskey, and Michael Kure of M&T Books; Mike Judson, Susan Lider, Pattee Heiser, and Keith Faust of Novell, Inc., Renee Wildman of Regis McKenna, Inc.; and Kris Drewry of ADIC.

Finally, thanks to Tom Woolf of *LAN Technology* magazine and Susan Kelly and Carolyn Jorgensen for their early encouragement, and thanks to the technical support staffs of Novell, Inc. and Costa Distributing, Inc., and thank you to all the companies that provided products for review.

Introduction

The many books available on the topic of local area networks (LANs) range from detailed descriptions of communications protocols to the theory of LAN architecture design. Little is available, though, to assist in the process of selecting from available LAN parts and pieces and assembling them into a working, functional, productive LAN. We hope this work will help to fill that void.

This book is a guide to selecting and installing PC LANs. The focus is on Novell's NetWare LAN operating system. NetWare is the most widely used operating software for PC-based LANs, and its use is rapidly growing in Macintosh and minicomputer environments, too.

This is not an exhaustive source of information about LANs, nor is it meant to be. It is, foremost, an overview of what goes into building LANs and what they can be used for. Secondly, it is a practical guide designed to aid the user in designing and building effective multiuser, multiprocessor, distributed-processing computer systems based on LAN technology using NetWare.

This book is designed to help you through the whats and whys of putting a LAN together, from selecting LAN components through installing the LAN operating system and applications, to on-going administration.

We hope this book will provide you with a background that helps you in making LAN design, purchase, and operation decisions.

1

What is a LAN?

In simplest terms, a local area network (LAN) is a high-speed communications link for data processing equipment in a limited geographic area. LANs can connect PCs, terminals, mini- and mainframe computers, printers, voice data systems and other devices together.

Just because you can connect devices together, however, doesn't mean they will work with each other. Appropriate operating software is required for effective communication between different systems. One of the fundamental jobs of LAN operating software is to provide this communication.

The rules of communication—how a system talks and expects to be talked to—are called *protocols*. Systems are said to be similar if they use the same protocols. If they use different ones, they can still be made to communicate with each other through software that translates from one protocol to another.

LANs can be used to connect more than PCs. They can connect video systems (cable television is based on "broadband" LAN technology, which will be described later), telephone systems, alarm systems, manufacturing equipment, and almost anything that requires high-speed data exchange. Multiple LANs can be interconnected through local and remote links to create larger internetworks.

In the personal computer environment, some of the major reasons for using LANs include sharing programs, sharing data files, sending messages (electronic mail), and sharing resources (printers, modems, and gateways to other systems) between PCs.

LANs: The New Highways

The advent of the microcomputer, and perhaps more importantly, the advent of the PC LAN, is creating a fundamental change in the data processing world. Like most significant historical changes, the implications are not always immediately apparent.

Up until the early eighties, the data processing environment was totally dominated by mainframe and minicomputers surrounded by armies of programmers, analysts, managers, and Management Information Services (MIS) professionals. Most users had little knowledge of the secret mysteries of data processing protected by this priesthood.

In most organizations, the data processing staff rarely spoke to the administrative staff about their systems, and vice versa. The people who designed systems didn't consult with the people who would have to use them. The people who needed specific computer tools didn't make design requests that could be acted on, and rarely educated themselves about the systems that had become critical to success in their jobs.

To effect any changes in systems or applications, department managers faced an expensive and time-consuming process of reviews and needs analysis. A manager could consider himself lucky if proposed software changes could be implemented in as little as one to three years. By the time such software changes were made, department needs had also changed, and the process would have to start all over again. This system was very effective for keeping programmers and analysts employed, but it was not so good for providing useful systems.

When microcomputers began to appear in corporate offices, department managers (and end users) found that they could often use inexpensive, off-the-shelf software to implement systems in weeks or months that would take years to implement on a mainframe.

The microcomputer brought more control to the department manager, and, as importantly, to the individual user. (This change was not without problems. Systems designed by end users were often hard to maintain and poorly documented. Users lost some of the benefits of the expertise the MIS department could have offered.)

Initially, although microcomputers provided many benefits for the non-MIS users, they had little effect on data processing departments. Early stand-alone PCs could not begin to challenge the power of larger systems. The early PC only had as much as 64K in memory and a few hundred thousand bytes of storage—no hard disks, no expandable memory, and the word "connectivity" had yet to be coined. There were lots of PCs all of a sudden, but with few experts and no support.

Early PC users found the PC world very disorganized. They needed tools that had yet to be invented, maps that had yet to be drawn.

As the industry matured, vendors became aware that their clientele were business people, not "techies." These users were not particularly interested in why something wouldn't work and what wasn't available; they wanted working products and systems now.

The vendors began to provide better mechanisms to support their products. As business users became more experienced, better informed, and better supported, they began to be interested in doing more on their own and for themselves.

Software tools to help the users proliferated. At last you didn't have to be a programmer to put together computer systems that worked. Then two things happened: PCs got a lot more powerful, and users began stringing them together in networks.

In 1984, the idea that networks of microcomputers could replace minicomputers or even mainframes was laughable. Most networks were primitive and unreliable, and users were naive and (so MIS professionals believed) even dangerous around computers. But today, many mini-computer and mainframe applications are being off-loaded to the accessible PC LAN environment. Users are beginning to think of mainframes and minicomputers as just more nodes on the network, and of MIS departments as services providing support instead of authorities controlling access and dictating direction.

If the emergence of PC LANs meant only the replacing of a few big expensive boxes with a lot of small cheap ones, the change would not be very significant. This is not the case, however. The very fabric of the data processing environment is being altered in the process.

Users now have a greater degree of knowledge about their computers and software than in the past. With the advent of the PC, users have become more familiar with the workings, operation, and terminology of their systems. There are hundreds of publications available to users dealing with various microcomputing topics. In fact, in many companies, the users know more about their PCs and software than the MIS people.

Compared to mini- and mainframe software and hardware, microcomputer software and hardware is cheap. Applications that cost $50,000 to $100,000 or more on a mini- or mainframe can often be implemented on PCs (and PC LANs) for a few hundred to a few thousand dollars. Also, available PC development tools are generally much easier to use than their large system counterparts, bringing software development capabilities to the user. There are now thousands of high-quality, off-the-shelf applications available for microcomputers.

The cost equation between "system resources" and "human resources" has changed dramatically. It now makes sense to fit the system to the person, rather than fit the person to the system.

PC LANs are creating turf battles in many large companies, with MIS and telecommunications departments fighting over who should have control over LANs (most of which were successfully implemented without the help of either group). The assumption here is that LANs are like mainframe computers that require centralized management and control.

With small computers and LANs, we are developing a heterogeneous computing environment. More and more we have the ability to interconnect dissimilar systems and share data between them. LAN software, such as TOPS from Sun Microsystems or NetWare from Novell, allows us to effectively connect IBM-type PCs, Apple Macintoshes, Sun workstations or DEC VAXes into the same LAN, while LAN gateways and protocols such as TCP/IP (Transmission Control Protocol/Internet Protocol, a protocol created for the department of defense to interconnect dissimilar computer systems) allow us to access larger systems.

Something entirely new is emerging, not just in technology but in social and organizational systems and management styles as well. The word "network" has come to mean not only a piece of hardware but a way of doing business. The kind of organization that emerges in this process is less heirarchical and less authoritarian than its mainframe counterpart. By the same token, it is more team-spirited, with a greater degree of shared work than its stand-alone counterpart.

Changes in social and management style have spurred the development of appropriate technology, and changes in technology have spurred changes in social and management style.

It can be difficult for department managers to foresee the changes a new tool like a network will bring and what the changes will mean to them, because they will change, too. There's an old saying: "When the only tool you have is a hammer, everything looks pretty much like a nail." What does work look like if you change the hammer?

If centralized mainframe processing is our hammer, what will changing to networks do to our nails?

A fundamental aspect of business practice, perhaps more basic than the sharing of information, is manifesting itself in a new class of software, a new kind of hammer constituitive of the shared LAN environment. It is software that enables groups to coordinate their actions to work together effectively toward group goals. Software of this kind enables electronic mail (E-Mail), group scheduling and calendaring, project management, and electronic meetings. Called *groupware,* these tools provide for more than the sharing of information; they provide a structure to facilitate the ways in which people naturally work well together.

For example, groupware enables people to work closely together from separate places and at different times. Software of this kind can have an enormous impact on where and when people work, which can affect who can work together and where they can live, and the implications of *that* are best left to another book.

Networks are dynamic, not static. Because results at work inevitably derive from the give and take of people working together, information seeks always to be shared. At the same time, information is a valuable commodity that companies look to protect. LANs are the data highways, providing effective paths for sharing and protecting information.

Consultants will tell you that you should plan exactly what you will use the network for, how you will share resources, who will have access to what, and all the software you will use. This planning can help give shape to your initial installation—it gives you a place to start. Rarely will your plan much resemble the network you and your people will actually use. In fact, the network will change your business and your thinking, and, in the process, change itself.

2

LAN Components

Making Choices: The Good News and the Bad News

In 1983, Novell set a milestone in achieving connectivity when it started writing versions of its operating software to run on other vendors' LANs hardware. Other LAN software vendors, including Banyan Systems with their VINES operating system, and Lifeboat Associates with LifeNET, soon followed suit.

At the same time, many LAN hardware vendors began making their hardware available for multiple LAN communication specifications (protocols) and operating environments. Currently, many vendors of PC LAN hardware make sure that their equipment is available for NetWare, the IBM PC LAN Program, MicroSoft's LAN Manager, and other LAN operating systems and protocols.

Network purchasers could finally choose LAN hardware separately from LAN operating software. For example, today both Novell's Netware operating software and IBM's PC LAN operating software could run on the same physical network.

When IBM came out with its PC Network, hardware vendors scrambled to provide software emulators for IBM's communication protocols, to allow the IBM operating software (and applications written for it) to run on their hardware.

In the early days, although various PC LAN operating systems provided PC to PC, PC to disk server, or PC to file server communications, they did not generally provide for such things as LAN to LAN communications, LAN to mainframe communications, or integration with wide area networks, etc. Other vendors quickly moved in to try to fill these voids, which created a plethora of translation/communications products with varying degrees of sophistication and workability.

Current LAN technology allows you to use different kinds of cables within a single network, as well as to bridge transparently among different LAN hardware types like Ethernet, ARCNET, and Token Ring in one network.

This ability to mix and match, and the increasing reliability of LAN components on the market, makes it harder to make a "wrong" LAN purchase decision. You will find yourself faced with a multitude of valid choices, millions of words of marketing and media hype, and very little reliable information about what really works. This cornucopia is the good news and the bad news .

You can find yourself caught up in a hunt for an illusory "best" LAN, and while you search, the technology changes. It has become cliché that all systems are obsolete by the time you buy them. At some point the time spent searching for the perfect system becomes better spent optimizing one of many good combinations available. If you're installing a small (ten to twenty workstation) departmental LAN in an average office environment, most of the popular LAN hardware will probably prove more than adequate.

The best rule of thumb seems to be to plan the LAN for optimum performance given your present needs (and budget). At the same time, plan for your LAN to expand, because it will. Finally, keep things as simple as you can.

If you wade through the alternatives carefully and tirelessly, you are more likely to find the precise combination of components that will give you the highest degree of performance per dollar invested, but the research process can be a long and frustrating one. In the end, you may overlook some incompatibility anyway, and then, when you find some way around that problem, your solution will create more problems. Nevertheless, when you are building true multivendor, multiproduct systems you do need to find out as much as you can about what works or what works with what.

You will also need to deal with the unknown. When a vendor says that a product is "network compatible," you don't always know what that means. Is it compatible with your LAN hardware and operating software? Is it compatible with other products that make up your system? Has it been tested in a similar configuration? Will it work the way that you envision or expect it to work? These are questions for which you can't always get good answers. You need to be prepared to solve problems others may not have yet encountered.

You can expect that everything in a new system won't always work correctly at first. Problems inevitably arise, and you learn to plan for disaster control and recovery. Of course, the more practical knowledge and experience you can bring to resolving problems, the better. For example, you will learn not to change too many aspects of an operating network at once. When several aspects of a network are being upgraded, implement the upgrades one facet at a time, and test for unexpected incompatibilities, hardware failures, and software limitations.

LAN Standards

The thing I like most about standards is that there are so many of them.

— Quote from an industry commentator

The array of LAN choices can be daunting to manufacturers as well as users. No component manufacturer can afford to make unlimited variations of a product to fit all the other possible components and protocols. Nor can a manufacturer afford to make a product that works with only a very limited number of LANs. Instead, a number of standards have emerged that manufacturers and purchasers alike can use to organize LAN choices.

What are Standards?

Standards are agreements, pure and simple.

Standards in the LAN and data communications world are usually a way of promoting connectivity between products from different manufacturers. Theoretically, any device adhering to an industry standard should be able to communicate with any other device adhering to that standard. Unfortunately, this is not always the case. Standards do not always specify all aspects of products or systems. LAN standards, for example, often specify only certain aspects of a system, leaving the specification of other, possibly critical, aspects to the product vendors. In addition, vendors often implement nonstandard enhancements to their products. To get the enhancement, you may have to accept noncompatibility with other vendors' products.

De Facto and De Jure Standards

There are two primary categories of LAN standards, de facto (industry) and de jure (official). The names refer to who develops the specifications, and how they become standards.

De Jure Standards

De jure standards are nonproprietary, which means that no one company makes them or owns rights to them. They are developed with the intent of providing for greater connectivity and interoperability by making public specifications, so that independent manufacturers can build to them.

Several permanent committees of industry representatives develop de jure standards. While they are supported by manufacturer subscriptions and by major company end users, they are supposed to remain independent of any particular manufacturer's interests, representing the interests of the entire community. Unfortunately, it doesn't always work out that way.

Subscribing to de jure standards reduces the risk and cost of developing hardware and software for manufacturers. Once a standard has been finalized, a component manufacturer subscribing to it can develop products with some confidence that they can be made to operate with the other components.

Standards-making bodies and some of their published standards include:

The International Standards Organization (ISO)

An important milestone in the development of LAN standards was ISO's publication in 1977 of the Open Systems Interconnection (OSI) model, which specified communications functions in seven layers of hardware and software. The OSI model represents how ISO would like to see LAN products developed, but LAN vendors do not necessarily follow the model in designing products. Industry analysts and writers try to map products to the model for the sake of coherence, but since the products don't fit the model, such comparisons actually add to the confusion.

Most LAN systems are layered in some hierarchy similar to the OSI model. The layers usually divide the network into its physical media, the low-level communication protocols, and network/application services. References to the OSI model are further confused because vendors often use the same terms to identify very different specifications.

Communication protocols are precise rules for communication between two devices, or two software programs, or a device and a software program.

Lower-level protocols specify, for example, exactly how data packets to be sent across the network should be organized and labeled, what route the data should take, and what to do when the data does or doesn't arrive. Part of the specification of a protocol is how it communicates with the layers above and below it.

For most LAN administrators, it is not necessary to know the technical details by which each layer does its job, but it is useful when working with LANs to know the names of the various protocols and their various incompatibilities.

Figure 2.1: The OSI Model

APPLICATION
PRESENTATION
SESSION
TRANSPORT
NETWORK
DATA LINK
PHYSICAL

The functions of the layers in the OSI model are a rough, general description. These general functions are described in the section, *Parts of a LAN.*

Within the OSI model (and other models) is enormous room for variation. Specific standards based on the model (or other models) may or may not interoperate.

The American National Standards Institute (ANSI)

ANSI published the Fiber Distributed Data Interface (FDDI) standard for 100 megabit high speed fiber-optic LANs. ANSI is expected to publish a standard for ARCNET LANS in 1989.

The Institute of Electrical and Electronic Engineers (IEEE)

The IEEE has published and continues to publish its set of LAN standards through its 802 Committee. The 802 standards include 802.3 for Ethernet-type LANS, and 802.4 and the 802.5 standard for token-passing LANs. The IEEE standards are based on the OSI model, but make distinctions within its layers that allow for variations.

Comité Consultatif Internationale de Télégraphique et Téléphonique (CCITT)

The CCITT has published various standards, including a WAN packet switching standard called X.25, and an electronic mail interchange standard called X.400. The X.25 standard governs much of the public access bulletin board industry.

By virtue of mutual industry consent, standards developed by these institutes are "official."

Developing a standard can take several years. Sometimes manufacturers, faced with the reality of a demanding marketplace, are impatient to begin production before the specifications of a standard are finalized. Their product may not be fully compatible with the final standard. Then the manufacturer may or may not bring the product into line and/or provide software or hardware work-arounds to the incompatibility.

Manufacturers further complicate matters by implementing new, nonstandard enhancements to their products, hoping that their innovation will be so wildly successful that it will force an evolution of the industry standard.

De Facto Standards

De facto standards arise in the industry itself. ARCNET, a LAN originally developed by Datapoint Corp., is now a de facto LAN standard. Datapoint retained rights to the ARCNET name, but made the specifications available to other manufacturers. Manufacturers are required to adhere to Datapoint's specifications, however, which has resulted in one of the highest degrees of standardization in the industry.

Far from promoting interconnection of different manufacturer's systems, some de facto "standards" can actually impede it. Some believe, for example, that IBM's complex SNA was designed to inhibit the connection of non-IBM equipment to the IBM LAN, so that buyers are forced to purchase all devices from IBM. Whether by design or mere happenstance, many non-IBM systems (other than terminals and a few IBM look-alike systems) have been effectively locked out of SNA.

De facto standards are often proprietary. MS-DOS, UNIX, and NetWare are all proprietary and de facto standards.

Propriety standards are sometimes unpublished and unavailable to outside vendors. These standards are called *closed architecture*. De jure committee standards that are published and available are called *open architecture*.

Not all proprietary standards are closed. Some manufacturers' market strategy is to publish open standards. Novell and Microsoft both publish information on the Application Programming Interfaces (APIs) of their operating systems, providing "proprietary" but open standards.

How are Standards Developed?

Even official standards are almost always created by vendor clout. The 802.3 Ethernet standard was adopted by the IEEE primarily due to the combined clout of Xerox, DEC, and Intel. The 802.5 Token Ring standard was adopted due primarily to IBM's influence.

De facto standards can arise by consensus and established practice by way of their success in the marketplace. An example of a de facto standard is the PC/AT expansion bus. Another is the "Hayes-compatible" modem, an industry standard by user consensus because the Hayes modem was so popular. De facto standards can arise by the mutual agreement of vendors. For example, products compatible with ARCNET are produced by more than 140 manufacturers worldwide.

Although it rarely happens, standards can also be created by user groups. The Manufacturing Automation Protocol (MAP) standard, which defines a standard interface and protocol for manufacturing control systems and was spearheaded by General Motors, finally may be gaining acceptance by the manufacturing community after many setbacks and delays.

The Department of Defense's Transmission Control Protocol/Internet Protocol (TCP/IP), which has been in existence for many years, is rapidly gaining acceptance as an effective way to interconnect dissimilar LANs and computer systems. This acceptance has been primarily promoted by users, not vendors.

Which Standard is "More Standard"?

You will find arguments about which standards, de facto or de jure, are "more standard." For example, the de facto LAN standard ARCNET is one of the fastest growing network standards outside of Fortune 1000 companies. Most of the published surveys and studies concerning installed LANs, however, poll MIS directors and data communications managers in large companies, who are primarily aware of the larger Ethernet and Token Ring installations in their companies. This means that ARCNET, as well as LocalTalk (Apple's Macintosh LAN hardware) and others are usually grossly under-represented.

The more established standards aren't necessarily the best performing or most cost-effective, but the connectivity gained by their universality lends them an added appeal to manufacturers and users.

Standards have little to do with quality or functionality. In fact, subscription to a standard deliberately impedes innovation, by definition. Developers are hobbled not only into sideways compatibility with other components, but also into a certain degree of backward compatibility (with previous iterations of hardware and software).

This continuity may be frustrating for developers, but it is crucial for end users and manufacturers who cannot afford to constantly upgrade every component every quarter.

Because there are so many standards of both the official and de facto variety, another problem arises. "Standard" products do not always work effectively with other "standard" products. In addition, products employing the same standard may not effectively work together. For example, Ethernet interfaces for dissimilar computers connect effectively at the hardware level, but without effective communication software they will not be interoperable, and communications software specifications were not included as part of the Ethernet standard.

Using Standards Effectively

LAN standards are tools designed to allow the easy interconnection of components from different vendors. Unfortunately, especially in a corporate environment, they can become a means of avoiding responsibility for decisions and actions. ("It can't be my fault it doesn't work! I implemented an industry standard system!") Standards should be used to promote functionality, not impede it.

Standards change and evolve. Many products, systems, and standards employed today will be obsolete in three to five years. Change occurs so rapidly in this industry that it is important to plan for it, even when (especially when!) you don't know what the next change will be. How do you plan for what you don't know about? Mostly, it means keeping abreast of changes in the industry even after the LAN is installed.

It is important to employ systems and standards appropriate to the environment in which they are being used. There are many standards to choose from, but not all are effective in all environments. For example, it is currently much easier to connect DEC systems with Ethernet than with Token Ring. On the other hand, because of the way a Token Bus network controls access, it may be more appropriate for critical manufacturing control than the contentious first come/first serve Ethernet scheme.

Parts of a LAN

LANs connect computers and other devices, such as printers, terminals, and modems, using some type of cabling system, network interfaces, and appropriate network communication and operating software.

The OSI model divides LAN responsibilities into seven different layers, and provides for communication between the layers.

In simplest terms, the hardware provides and manages the connections among devices, the communications software determines where data is directed, and the operating software (and application software, or programs) determines what is done with the data once it gets to its destination.

Summary of OSI Level Responsibilities

Layer 1 is the physical level. This is the cable type (for example, coaxial, twisted pair, fiber optic), and the signal strengths and distances. The cabling system is the data path between network devices. Cabling can consist of various types of copper wire, fiber optics, and other media such as microwaves and radio waves.

Layer 2, the Data Link layer, specifies the strategy and mechanisms for accessing the cable, the form of transmitted data will take on, and how it is reassembled at its destination.

Layer 3, the Network layer, specifies how data is routed from one node to the next.

Layer 4, the Transport layer, specifies how to handle errors (collisions, for example) and retransmission of data.

Layer 5, the Session layer, specifies the maintenance of data links between nodes.

Layer 6, the Presentation Layer, specifies code and data conversions for application programs

Layer 7, the Application layer, specifies file service protocols used directly by an application.

Layers 1 and 2 of the OSI model constitute the physical LAN hardware: the cable, the hardware that accesses the cable, and the software managing the hardware. Usually this hardware is a board installed in a PC, but it can be implemented in other ways, for example, in a chipset. Examples of LANs are Ethernet, ARCNET, Token-Ring, LocalTalk (subscribing to an Apple standard, rather than IEEE). The network interface (or NIC, for Network Interface Card, often called the LAN "hardware") provides the physical connection between the cabling system and each computer.

Besides housing the physical connection to the cable, the NIC can also contain some of the software that manages the lowest level of communication between the workstation and the network.

The kind of NIC in use defines the method used to send and receive data between the computer and the cabling system, the rate of data transmission, the size and make-up of the message unit packets, and how multiple station access to the cable system is arbitrated. The kind of NIC selected constrains, to a large extent, the cable layout, called the topology, and the type of cable that can be used.

Layers 3 and 4 are generally called the communications protocols. Examples of communications protocols are TCP/IP and Netware's Internetwork Packet Exchange/Sequenced Packet Exchange (IPX/SPX).

Layer 5, 6, and 7 are generally thought of as the operating system functions that provide services to applications.

APIs provide optimized communication between the communication protocols and application program requests for services.

Some interfaces bypass intermediate levels. Bypassing levels is usually done to increase performance by allowing for more instruction specificity and cutting out a layer of code translation.

In the case of a LAN using Novell's Advanced NetWare, the operating software for user PCs is usually DOS, but can also be OS/2. The communications software consists of two parts: the program IPX.COM and the program NET3.COM (for use with DOS versions 3.xx. NET2 or NET4 would be used with other DOS versions). These two programs comprise what is called the NetWare Shell.

IPX.COM communicates directly with the particular NIC in the PC. It implements the low-level protocols that allow basic communication between different stations and devices on the network.

NET3 is the software that establishes a dialogue with the file server PC (via IPX/SPX); the file server manages shared files and provides controlled access to them to other devices on the network.

The operating software for the file server (in this case, Advanced Netware) includes the functions to establish communication with the network hardware, then with user PCs and other file servers.

Data is moved from one device to another in stages. Using a NetWare system on an ARCNET model, here is an example of how the software layers function together:

1. An application program on a user PC sends a request to DOS for a file (using standard and extended DOS 21H calls).

2. NET3 examines the 21H call to determine if it is a local or network request. If it is a local request, the workstations DOS Basic Input/Output System (BIOS) handles the request.

3. If it is a network request, NET3 redirects the request to IPX, telling it to send the request to the file server.

4. IPX, in turn, passes the request to the NIC in the user PC.

5. The NIC puts the request into one or more data packets and passes the packets to the cable system. The NIC includes certain information with each packet, including source address (from where the packet came), and destination address (where the packet is supposed to go). Every NIC in a network has a unique address.

6. The NIC in the file server receives the packet(s), and passes the data to the server's memory.

7. The file server NIC sends an acknowledgement to the user PC NIC for each packet it receives.

8. The file server operating software (NetWare) examines and processes the request.

9. The file server operating system must now issue a disk read request to the *disk channel.* The disk channel consists of the disk drives and any interface and controller hardware and software.

10. The disk channel executes the read request.

11. As the data is being read from disk, it is transferred to memory in the file server.

12. The network operating system passes the data from memory to the NIC in the file server.

13. The NIC "packetizes" the data, then passes the packets, one at a time, to the cable.

14. The NIC in the user PC receives the packets, one at a time, "depacketizes" the data, then puts the data into the user PC's memory.

15. The user PC NIC sends an acknowledgement to the file server NIC for each packet it receives.

Remember, this is all taking place while other users are using the LAN and making requests of the file server.

NetBIOS

Some fundamental communications between applications and the network are handled through other paths than the pattern just described. For example, a common API on PC LANs called NetBIOS receives requests for the network from NetBIOS-aware applications and hands them off to the network.

The original NetBIOS, developed by Sytek and IBM for the IBM PC NETWORK, was a ROM-based protocol located on the NIC adapter. It intercepted network resource calls and passed them across the network. IBM's NetBIOS was soon accepted as an industry standard, and many applications are written that make resource calls to NetBIOS.

Manufacturers then wrote software NetBIOS emulators so that NetBIOS-dependent applications would be able to run on their networks. Even IBM itself had to come up with an NetBIOS emulator for its networks that no longer use the ROM NetBIOS.

Each manufacturer's NetBIOS emulator passes requests either to the NIC directly, or to the communication protocol. Hardware vendors write NetBIOS emulators that talk directly to the NIC; network operating system vendors write NetBIOS emulators that talk to the communication protocol they use. What distinguishes the NetBIOS emulator on a Novell network, for example, is that the protocol it passes requests to is Novell's proprietary IPX protocol.

In the NetWare model, applications developers have several choices. They can use DOS BIOS requests as if the PC were a stand-alone and let Net3 intercept network requests, or use NetBIOS requests that will be intercepted by the NetBIOS emulator and passed to IPX or make requests to IPX directly.

Many application developers want to be able to write programs that can make remote requests the same way on all networks, instead of having to write protocol-specific (or even proprietary API-specific) requests; hence, the popularity of NetBIOS and NetBIOS emulators. Unfortunately, all NetBIOS's are not alike. For example, two different versions of NetBIOS that both work on the same physical network may not be able to speak to one another if they use different communication protocols. This might be fine, when one application will use one version and another application a different NetBIOS version. It becomes a problem only when two different versions are supposed to provide the connection between applications or between LANs.

Because NetBIOS lacks tools needed for distributed processing, programmers have to do a lot of network housekeeping themselves when using NetBIOS. While continuing to provide support for NetBIOS, both IBM, in its newer OS/2-based LAN Server, and MicroSoft, in LAN Manager, provide services which replace NetBIOS as their standards.

Unlike IBM's PC LAN operating system, Novell NetWare is not NetBIOS-dependent. Its NetBIOS emulator is provided only as support for third-party applications that require it. As with NetBIOS, Novell provides emulators for these new IBM and MicroSoft APIs.

The importance of this discussion of NetBIOS for LAN implementers is to find out what support the software you want to use requires. If it does require NetBIOS or other support, make sure that the version provided for your LAN will operate with your application by verification with the application dealer.

The Network Interface

The kind of network interface being used determines the method used to send and receive data, the rate of data transmission, the size and make-up of the data packets, and the Cable Access Method, as well as the network topology and cable type(s).

NICs can be designed and built to conform to one of the accepted industry standards, or they can use proprietary designs.

The LAN standard the NIC subscribes to generally specifies such things as packet structure, cable access method, signal strengths, cable types, allowable cabling distances, etc. The standards do not usually specify the hardware and/or software interfaces to particular computers or operating systems. Therefore, there can be vast differences between NICs that conform to the same standard. These differences account for the wide price range of NICs, and can have a big impact on performance. For example, NICs vary in whether they have an onboard processor and whether (and how much) buffering of I/O from the PC and the network is provided. In general, NICs manufactured to conform to accepted standards provide for connectability of NICs from different manufacturers, while proprietary NIC designs sacrifice that compatibility for optimized performance, extended cable length, lower cost, and the like.

The Big Three: Ethernet, ARCNET, and Token Ring

There are three primary standards for NICs in the PC environment: one is de facto, and the other two are de jure. They are ARCNET, 802.3 Ethernet, and the 802.5 Token Passing Ring.

ARCNET is a de facto standard: there are currently over seventy manufacturers of ARCNET NICS and over 1.5 million installed nodes. (Again, ANSI is expected to sanction ARCNET as an official standard through publication sometime in late 1989.)

802.3 Ethernet and 802.5 Token Passing Rings conform to the standards created by their respective subcommittees of the 802 LAN standard committee of the IEEE.

The 802.3 subcommittee specifies standards for networks using the Carrier Sense Multiple Access with Collision Detection (CSMA/CD) access method, while the 802.5 subcommittee specifies standards for ring networks using the token passing access method.

802.3 Ethernet

The 802.3 standard grew out of the original Ethernet designed in 1980 by Bob Metcalf at Xerox Corporation. Metcalf, often called "The Father of Ethernet," went on to found 3Com Corporation, a major LAN hardware and software vendor.

Through the joint efforts of DEC, Intel Corporation, and Xerox, the IEEE 802.3 subcommittee was formed and in January 1985, the first 802.3 LAN specifications were released. Technically, Ethernet refers only to the network specification created at Xerox (and later modified by DEC, Intel, and Xerox), and not the 802.3 specification. The Ethernet name, however, is still used (when we say Ethernet in this book, we are referring to 802.3 networks, unless otherwise noted).

Ethernet uses a cable access method called CSMA, for Carrier Sense Multiple Access. CSMA is often called a "contention" access method, because network stations compete for cable access.

When a station on the network is ready to send a packet of information to another station, it listens to the cable to see if another packet is currently being transmitted by another station. If it does not hear another signal on the line, it will transmit its packet of information. If it does hear another signal it will wait, check the line again, and send when the line is free.

An analogy can be drawn to a telephone party line. On a party line, if you pick up the phone and hear someone talking, you know that the line is in use, so you hang up the phone, wait a few minutes, and try again. If you then hear a dial tone, then you know that the line is free, so you make your call.

With Ethernet LANs, packets are broadcast across the entire LAN, but only accepted and acknowledged by the station they are addressed to.

There is always the possibility of two or more stations attempting to transmit at the same time. On a party line, for example, two people can pick up the phone and dial at the same time, not realizing that both are on the line. Because of this, 802.3 LANs utilize a method for collision detection (/CD). On detecting a collision, workstations involved wait a random period of time (to reduce re-collision) and than transmit again.

Network access is random, not guaranteed. Because of the contention for access, CSMA is *probablistic*, meaning that a station has a certain probability of access to the network at any one time, but never a guarantee.

In an extremely busy and/or malfunctioning network, performance degradation can increase rapidly as data collisions increase and the network approaches a *saturation* point. This is rarely a problem in a properly designed and functioning network, however.

A major benefit of Ethernet is its broad industry acceptance and support. If there is a computer of major business, government or (higher) educational significance, there is probably an Ethernet interface available for it. In addition, most major LAN operating software is available for Ethernet LANs.

Cabling for Ethernet

The original cable used by Ethernet is a thick, 50 ohm impedance coaxial cable (roughly equivalent to the RG-8 cable). According to the specifications, this cable could be up to 500 meters long, with a 50 ohm terminating resistor at each end. This cable, which is usually yellow or orange, is often referred to as *The Yellow Cable.*

Attachment to this cable is by means of a transceiver. The transceiver functions as both the connection device and the portion of the network interface that performs the collision detection function. Attachment between the transceiver and the network interface is by means of a four-pair shielded Attached Unit Interface (AUI) cable.

A second cable specification is called Thin Ethernet, or sometimes "cheapernet," due to its lower cost in relation to The Yellow Cable. Thin Ethernet is 50 ohm RG-58 coaxial cable. According to the specifications, this cable can be up to 185 meters long.

Although transceivers are required to attach to this cable, most PC NICs have a built-in transceiver. Generally, the cheapernet cable is attached directly to the internal transceiver of NIC with a "Tee" fitting.

Figure 2.2: PCs Cabled with Thin Ethernet Cable

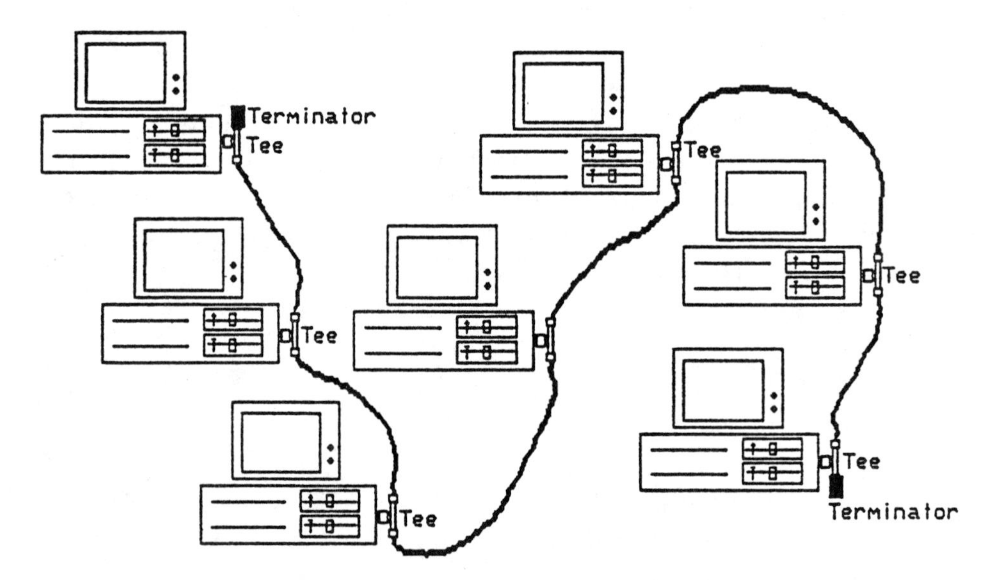

Although the basic Ethernet cabling specification is linear, Ethernet can provide a great deal of cabling flexibility by using various devices such as repeaters, multiport repeaters, and fan-out units.

In addition, although not yet part of the Ethernet specification, fiber-optic links are easily available, providing for extended distances and electrical isolation of sections of the network.

A new specification for Ethernet over unshielded twisted-pair (UTP) wire is currently being drafted by the 802.3 10baseT subcommittee. In the meantime, many not-yet-standard UTP implementations are available.

A major drawback to Ethernet is the difficulty in diagnosing hardware problems, especially in a strictly linear network. Because signals are broadcast across the entire network, a problem at one location may be reflected at another location. Generally speaking, however, this will not be a problem in a properly designed and installed LAN.

NICs for Ethernet vary in how "smart" they are, depending on such factors as whether there is an on-board processor and how much on-board buffering is provided. Major manufacturers of Ethernet NICs for PCs include 3Com, Interlan, Excelan, Western Digital, Novell, and Gateway Communications.

802.5 Token Passing Ring

802.5 is a specification for networks using a physical token-passing access method.

A ring network is a closed loop in which data travels in one direction. Each LAN station is cabled to the next station and the previous station in the ring. It receives data from the previous station and transmits data to the next station.

Figure 2.3: Ring Data Path (without MAU)

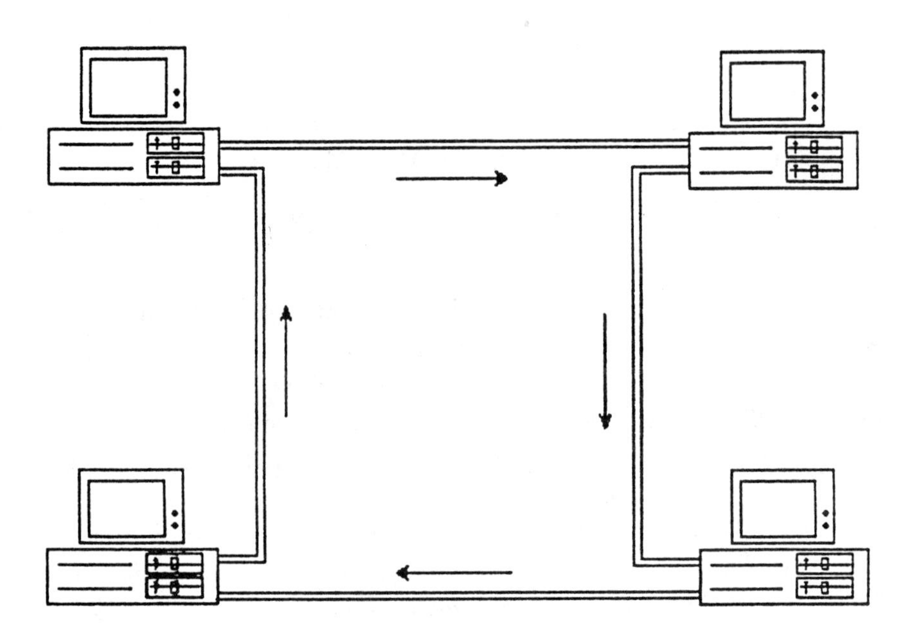

To allow easier connection and disconnection of stations, all cables go through one or more central hubs. At the hub, each station is connected to its next and previous stations. These hubs, called *Multistation Access Units* (MAUs), automatically bypass disconnected or powered-off stations, maintaining the integrity of the ring. Because all cables fan out from the MAUs, this is called a *star-wired ring topology*.

Although the 802.5 specification was heavily influenced by IBM, other manufacturers, including Proteon, were also responsible for the specification. Because of IBM's dominance of 802.5, the network specification is often called the IBM Token Ring, although that name really only applies to products from IBM.

Figure 2.4: Star-Wired Ring Topology

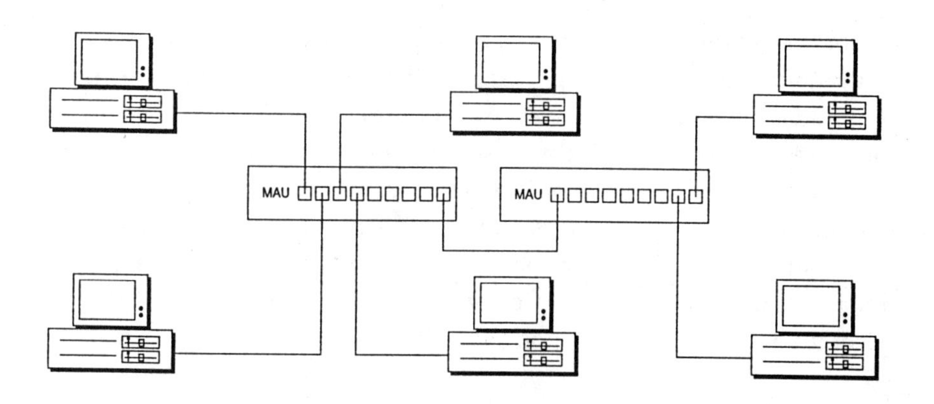

Figure 2.5: Star-Wired Ring Data Path through MAU

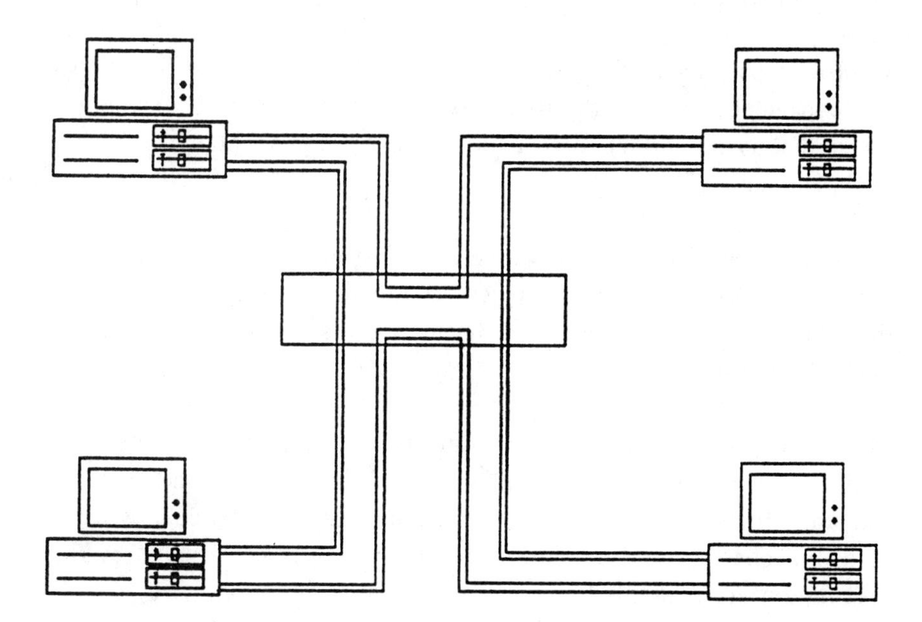

Token Passing Access Method

Token passing systems pass an electronic signal called a *token* from station to station in a predetermined order. If a station has possession of the token, it can send a packet of information. If it does not have possession of the token, it must wait until the token is passed to it before it can transmit. Basically, token passing systems are "contention-free" systems. Instead of contending for network access as in CSMA systems, each station waits its turn until it receives the token. In token passing systems network access is guaranteed, while access is random in CSMA systems. Performance in heavy traffic situations is generally better than contention systems.

In a token passing ring, the token is generated by the first station to attach to the network. That station becomes the *active monitor*, and makes sure that no other station generates a token. The token is passed from each station in the ring to the next station in succession. Each station receives the token, then regenerates it and passes it to the following station.

The token passing method used by 802.5 token-ring networks allows one packet per token. If a station receives a "free" token, meaning a token that is not attached to a data packet, it may attach a packet to that token.

The packet, which contains source and destination address information as well as data, must be received and retransmitted, along with the token, by each station on the ring in succession until it reaches the destination station.

The destination station reads the data from the packet, changes one attribute on the packet (called the *acknowledgment bit*), and then retransmits the packet and token to the next station. The acknowledgment bit tells the sending station that the packet was received by the destination station.

When the sending station receives the packet and token again, it strips off the packet and only retransmits the token. The token is now "free" for the next station to use.

A major advantage of the 802.5 token passing ring is the token passing access method, which *guarantees* access to the network. The overhead could make this scheme less effective than CSMA in lightly loaded networks, but as traffic increases, the lack of contention, collisions, and retries makes this a more efficient access method.

A major drawback to ring networks is the fact that every station acts as a repeater. Since each packet is received and retransmitted (repeated) by each station in the ring, any malfunctioning station has the opportunity to corrupt any packet, regardless of its destination or source. Although MAUs are designed to minimize problems by automatically removing downed stations, MAUs cannot always detect malfunctioning stations.

In addition, if the network is down due to a malfunction, network diagnostics, including IBM's network manager, cannot diagnose the problem. This can be alleviated by using Proteon's Intelligent Wire Centers MAUs and their Advanced Network Manager, which use an out-of-network data path for diagnostics and management. This can add to the cost of the network. Furthermore, such non-IBM equipment may not be acceptable in some "True Blue" shops.

The current 802.5 specification provides a data transmission rate of 4Mbps. IBM, as well as other vendors, is currently shipping a 16Mbps version of the ring. Although this is not an 802.5 specification yet, it is expected that the committee will bless the new system.

In addition to the higher speed, the 16MB version provides for an *Early Release Token*, which allows two packets (from different stations) to be attached to the token. This should provide more efficient use of the network, adding to overall throughput.

The 16Mbps system is not designed to use UTP cable; it will require shielded twisted pair or fiber optics.

The Token Ring is primarily designed to use shielded twisted pair cable, although UTP is supported for shorter distances. In addition, companies such as Proteon are providing other types of links, including fiber optics, microwave and infrared.

ARCNET

ARCNET is one of the oldest existing LAN systems, originally developed in 1977 by John Murphy of Datapoint Corporation. Since then, ARCNET has become one of the most popular LAN hardware systems in the world, comprising an estimated 25 percent of new LAN installations. This figure includes all LAN types; the estimate for PC LANs is much higher. For example, based on information from Novell distributors (and others) more than half the installations of Novell NetWare are using ARCNET hardware.

Why is a LAN system that does not bear an IEEE stamp of approval so popular? There are several important reasons: namely reliability, flexibility, performance, ease of installation, and ease of fault diagnosis. The consensus among LAN resellers and installers is that ARCNET is the easiest LAN to install and troubleshoot. Once installed, ARCNET controllers rarely cause trouble, and, due to the "star cluster" topology of ARCNET, isolating sections of the network for diagnosis is quite easy.

While ARCNET, at 2.5MB/sec, is not the fastest LAN around, its token-passing protocol provides reasonable performance that does not degrade quickly under load (as opposed to Ethernet's CSMA/CD scheme, where in heavy traffic collisions increase, leading to more retransmissions that lead to more collisions).

ARCNET also provides a great deal of cabling flexibility. Additionally, virtually any manufacturer's ARCNET hardware (NIC) will function properly in the same network with any other manufacturer's hardware, providing a degree of standardization not always available in the rest of the LAN world.

The major manufacturers of ARCNET currently include SMC, Pure Data Corporation, Thomas Conrad Corporation, and Tiara Computer Systems.

Figure 2.6: Standard ARCNET Topology

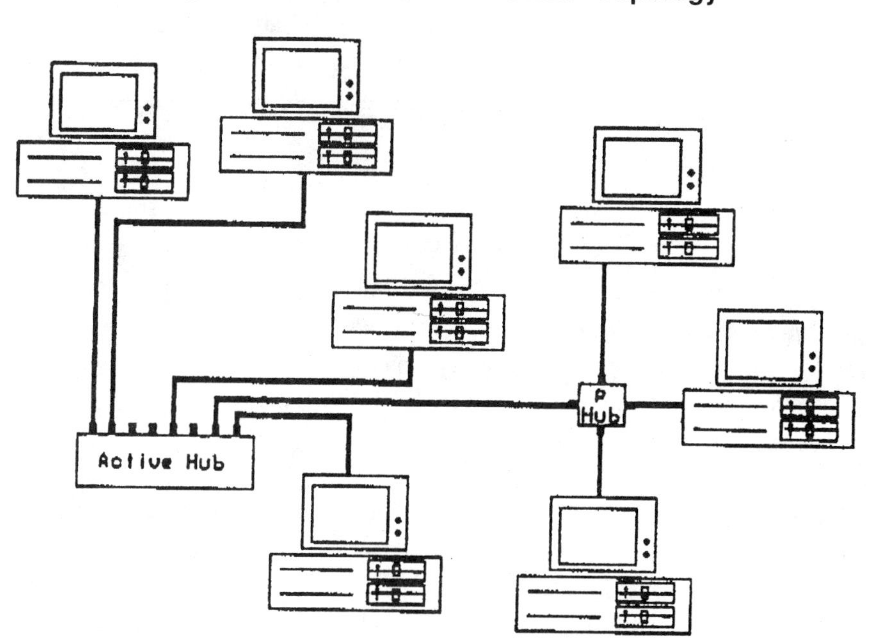

The standard topology for ARCNET is a star-cluster scheme, with ARCNET stations attached to distribution devices called hubs. There are two types of ARCNET hubs: active and passive. An active hub is a powered unit that acts as a distribution device and signal amplifier, while a passive hub only distributes signals over short distances (without amplification). Active hubs may have between four and 64 ports, while passive hubs have four ports. By using multiple hubs, an

ARCNET can have a diameter as large as 20,000 feet, meaning a maximum cabling distance of 20,000 feet from any node on the network to any other node. Standard ARCNET cable is RG-62 coaxial cable with an impedance of 93 ohms.

With ARCNET, all signals are broadcast across the entire network simultaneously. This is possible because ARCNET uses a *bus* topology, where all LAN devices share the same cabling set, making it possible for every LAN device to talk to and hear every other LAN device, which is not possible in the Token Ring design, where stations can only talk to directly connected stations. By using the broadcast transmission method, ARCNET eliminates the need for each station to act as a repeater, as is necessary in the Token Ring design. When each station can listen for messages addressed to it and ignore everything else, the savings in overhead are considerable.

ARCNET uses a Logical Token Passing scheme to control cable access. As in the Token Ring system, a token is passed from station to station in a predetermined order. If a station has possession of the token, it can send a packet of information. If it does not have possession of the token, it must wait until the token is passed to it by the previous station before it can transmit. The ARCNET token passing systems guarantees regular network access.

Each ARCNET station has an address from 1 to 255, set by a switch on its card. Each ARCNET station puts the address of the next highest station in its Next ID (NID) register. With ARCNET, the token, which acts as permission to transmit, is passed by each station to the station whose address is in its NID register. When a station has possession of the token, it can elect to send a data packet to another station. After it sends a packet (and receives acknowledgment) or if it elects not to send a packet, it broadcasts the token across the network to the station whose address is in its NID register. The addressed station acknowledges receipt of the token and begins the process over again. ARCNET dynamically and automatically reconfigures every time a station is added to or removed from the network.

Figure 2.7: ARCNET Logical Token Passing Method

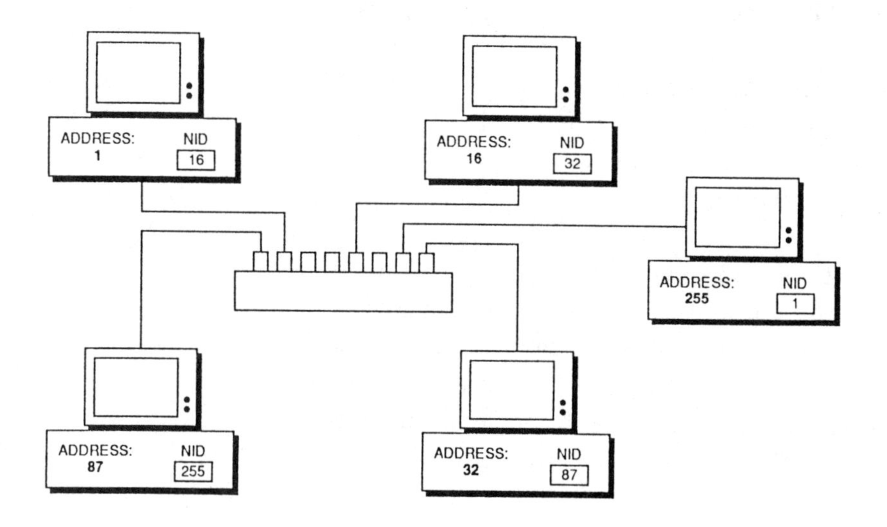

Although ARCNET has a slower transmission rate than 802.5, actual throughput on ARCNET LANs can often be greater than 802.5 Token Ring throughput because the token passing overhead is so much less. Token Ring networks require the token to be passed, processed, and regenerated by every workstation between the sending and receiving stations; ARCNET networks broadcast data packets, which are ignored by all but the addressed destination.

Fault diagnosis on ARCNET is usually quite easy. Because of the star cluster topology, it is easy to disconnect whole sections of the network for fault isolation. In addition, there are several inexpensive software products that aid in fault location and diagnosis.

Many extensions have been added to ARCNET since its original development. Some of these are:

1. **Fiber optics**. The maximum distance between standard active ARCNET devices (ARCNET controllers and active hubs) is 2,000 feet. With fiber optics, that distance can be extended. With single fiber optic controllers and links, that distance can be extended to 4,000 feet, while dual fiber systems can extend the distance to 11,500 feet.

2. **Linear Bus ARCNET**. Another relatively recent development is the Linear Bus ARCNET card, originally developed by Standard Microsystems Corporation (SMC) and now produced by several manufacturers. This card uses special circuitry to allow up to eight cards to share the same linear cable. This cable can have a length of up to 1,000 feet. Attachment is made using the same type of BNC "T" connector used with thin Ethernet cable. One end of this cable may be connected to an active hub, allowing interconnection with the star-cluster topology.

3. **Twisted-Pair ARCNET**. ARCNET boards and hubs designed to use UTP phone wire have been developed by SMC (and, again, now manufactured by others). These twisted-pair boards may be cabled up to 400 feet to special twisted-pair active hubs and up to 10 boards may be daisy-chained. Only a single-wire pair is required.

4. **16-Bit AT and Microchannel Interfaces**. First released by Thomas Conrad Corp. (16-bit AT) and Pure Data (microchannel), similar controllers are provided by other major ARCNET manufacturers. These boards generally provide better performance due to the 16-bit data path and improved packet buffering.

5. **Nodal Priority**. SMC now manufactures a 16-bit board designed especially for LAN servers. This board, the PC500FS, can send multiple packets each time it has possession of the token. This

means that it can respond to pending requests from multiple workstations on the same round trip of the token.

While some of the enhancements described above contribute to increased performance, ARCNET is still crippled by two factors: its relatively slow 2.5 megabit transmission speed (by today's standards), and its inefficient 508-byte data packet size. Several groups are attempting to correct the situation.

The ARCNET Trade Association is currently setting the specifications for an enhanced ARCNET that will initially provide a 20-megabit-per-second transfer rate, and a larger packet size, probably 2,048 bytes, possibly 4,096. The advantage of this specification is that it will be supported on existing coax cabling (and possibly UTP) and will maintain full downward compatibility with current ARCNET products. The design will allow 20-megabit boards to communicate with 2.5-megabit boards at the slower speed. While the current specification calls for 20 megabits per second, faster speeds are planned in the future of up to 100 megabits per second.

3

Shared LAN Resources

Disk Servers and File Servers

Early microcomputer LAN operating software, such as Orchid Technology's PC-Net, Corvus Systems' OmniShare, and 3Com Corporation's EtherShare, allowed multiple computers to share a common hard disk. These early systems would allow you to partition a disk into read-only shareable volumes and read/write nonshareable volumes.

Called *Disk Service,* this was the most common approach to resource sharing on microcomputer LANs for several years. If two or more users attempted to write to the same volume, the disk's File Allocation Table (FAT) could easily become corrupted (the FAT tells the operating system where to find files on a disk). Each PC using the disk attempted to control it as if it were a local drive. This is the primary reason most early PC LANs were trouble-prone.

Another approach, called *File Service,* also provides for shared access to a common hard disk, but maintains central control of the FAT. File servers provide access control at the file level, not the disk level. File Servers are much less prone to FAT corruption than disk servers. In the PC LAN world, this approach was pioneered by Novell Data Systems (now Novell, Inc.) in 1982. Today, virtually all PC LANs are based on file-server technology.

Besides protecting the shared disk's FAT, file servers generally provide file and record locking schemes, some measure of security, print spooling functions, and more. The sophistication of today's high-end file server systems rivals that of the best minicomputer or mainframe operating software.

Unlike such multiuser computer systems, however, file servers do not process the data they retrieve. The data is requested by and delivered to devices on the LAN. Processing occurs independently, on the individual workstations. Modified data that is returned to the server is then updated on the disk.

Central Server and Distributed Systems

Most high-end LAN systems use a central file server approach. One or more computers on the LAN are specifically designated as file servers and generally run software specifically designed for file service tasks.

Distributed LAN systems provide for the sharing of all or most resources on the network. This means that each user can offer his or her disks, printers, etc., for use by others. Most current distributed LANs, like the central server LANs, use file server technology.

In general, distributed LANs are potentially more cost-effective, but central server LANs provide for easier manageability and greater security. Currently, the most effective PC LANs employ a central server approach.

File Servers

What makes a computer function as a file server is software. The particular machine that is used for a file server might be a standard PC or AT-type machine, a minicomputer, or a specialized proprietary computer designed specifically as a file server. In any case, it is the software running in that machine that defines it as a file server.

The primary purpose of file server software is to synchronize access to shared resources. This means the server software, in cooperation with applications programs, makes sure that users have simultaneous file access where appropriate, while preventing simultaneous access where it is inappropriate.

File servers can also provide various levels of security and access control, allowing a system manager to designate who has access to what resources. In this area there are vast differences in capabilities between different file server systems.

The efficiency and sophistication of a file server's data management and retrieval vary widely from one network operating system to another. High-speed disk access techniques, use of disk *caching* (keeping recently requested data blocks in server memory), and use of proprietary disk file structures are among the methods used to increase data retrieval speed.

File servers fall into several (sometimes overlapping) categories:

- **Generic Servers** are usually industry standard mini- or microcomputers. For PC LANs, 80286- and 80386-based PCs are commonly used as file servers. Generic servers often offer greater flexibility than proprietary servers.

- **Proprietary Servers** are machines designed specifically to be used as network servers. They often provide higher performance than generic servers because of features tailored to a server's needs. To their disadvantage, they usually operate only with a specific vendor's LAN hardware and operating system.

- **Nondedicated Servers** function as user workstations as well as file servers. Although most manufacturers provide for nondedicated servers, performance and system integrity issues can make this a risky approach. Users and applications can easily "lock up" a nondedicated server. Nondedicated servers can sometimes provide cost savings.

- **Dedicated Servers** function strictly as servers, and are not available as user workstations. Dedicated servers generally provide better performance and system integrity than nondedicated servers.

Other Server Types

File servers are the most common kind of servers on networks, and frequently, the phrase "file server" is shortened to "server." This can be misleading, because file servers are only one of the resources that a network can share. Other server types include print servers, communications servers, database servers, FAX servers, batch process servers, and others. Network operating systems can provide many of these services from the file server without the need for designating separate machines for each service. Usually, extra, separate servers are set up for two reasons: 1) to lighten the load on the file servers, and 2) to optimize the performance of the particular service by dedicating a processor to it.

Print Servers

Most file server software includes shared print service functions for printers physically attached to the file server machine. Other machines on a network, however, can also provide shared print service. Some LAN operating systems, such as 3Com's 3+, provide this capability directly. Others, like Novell's NetWare, support it through third-party utilities.

Print servers are often used to physically distribute shared printers, to support specialized printers that require specific control hardware and/or software, and to add printers when a file server's printer attachment capability has been reached.

Depending on the print server software, a print server machine can be dedicated, functioning only as a print server, or nondedicated, functioning concurrently as a user workstation or other server type.

The disadvantages of using print servers as workstations are similar to the disadvantages of using file servers as workstations: the workstation may run a little slower when print services are being used, and/or a user or an application could "lock up" the server. The consequences of a lock-up on a print server, however, are usually less severe than on a file server.

Specific requirements for print service at the file server and/or at print servers on other workstations depend on the LAN operating system. For NetWare LANs, there are several third-party print server packages available. (See *Appendix B—Network Utilities* for product profiles.)

Batch Processing Servers

Batch processing servers allow time-consuming tasks, such as reports, to be off-loaded from a user's machine or from a database or file server, allowing the user to continue working while the batch processor handles the off-loaded tasks.

Several third-party packages are available that provide batch processing services (See *Appendix B—Network Utilities* for product profiles.)

FAX Servers

FAX Servers provide all workstations on the LAN with access to a single FAX service. The server can be a workstation PC with an installed FAX board, or a special device designed for FAX service.

Choosing Applications Software

Selecting software for use on a LAN is like selecting software for use on stand-alone PCs, with some extra factors that need to be considered.

- Will the application run on a PC on a LAN? Most software will run on a PC that is attached to a LAN, but not all. An application that requires in excess of 512K of memory (or less with some LAN operating systems) may not be able to run with LAN workstation software loaded in a PC.

- Is there a special network version available? Network versions often offer features and benefits that stand-alone versions do not. These could include licensing for multiple users, separate configurations for each user, LAN printer support, record/file locking, etc.

- If there is no LAN version available, is the single-user version compatible with the above network operating system? Are there any special problems to be addressed when using the single-user version on a LAN? Is there a network or site license agreement available and what are the terms?

- Is the application compatible with your selected LAN operating system? Some applications will work with certain LAN OSs and not others. While some applications may run on different LAN OSs, they may have special features that are only supported on specific LAN OSs.

- What is the basis for LAN pricing? Many software vendors have not figured out how to price software for LANs. Here are some variations:

  Server-based pricing. You pay a single fee for each file server that has the program loaded on it, regardless of the number of people using the software.

  Active application-user pricing. You pay for the maximum number of users who will access the program at a time.

  Total application-user pricing. You pay for each user that will use the application.

  Total number of LAN users pricing. You pay for each user on a LAN, regardless of the number of users who will actually use the application.

  Some combination of the above. For example, some vendors charge a base price, plus a surcharge for additional users over a certain number. The permutations are seemingly endless.

Working with Existing Applications

When existing PCs are being networked, it can make your job easier if you make the new LAN environment look as similar as possible to the users' familiar stand-alone environment. By making sure that familiar applications and peripherals are still available, you can lessen the trauma of change engendered by the LAN installation. If users are already using WordPerfect, for example, make it available on the network, too.

Moving as many applications as possible from PC workstations to the file server can simplify support and maintenance, but you might consider doing this on a gradual basis as users become familiar with the LAN.

When users are moving to PCs on a LAN from terminals on a mini or mainframe it is not as easy to emulate their environment, but it is important to provide as much continuity as possible.

Software Licensing

You may be violating licensing agreements if you allow more users to concurrently access a program than you have program licenses for. As pointed out above, licensing practices among software vendors vary widely.

Utilities such as Saber Meter from Saber Software and SITELOCK from Brightwork Development will "meter" software access, allowing only the number of users to access an application that you have licenses for. (See *Appendix B—Network Utilities* for product profiles.)

Record and File Locking

LANs allow multiple users to access the same data files. Because of this, some method must be employed to either prevent multiple users from writing to the same file concurrently, or to synchronize concurrent access to allow one user to change part of a file while allowing other users to change other parts of the same file.

The two methods used are called *file locking* and *record locking*, respectively.

File locking lets an application program "lock" an entire data file while it is in use by one user so that other users may not modify or delete it. File locking is used with word processing programs, spreadsheet programs, graphics programs, etc.

Record locking allows a specific portion of a file to be locked by one user, but allows other users access to other portions of the same file. Database management and accounting programs designed for use on a LAN usually employ record locking.

Locks can be employed on exclusive or nonexclusive basis. Exclusive locking means that when one user has a file or record locked, other users are denied all access to that file or record. Nonexclusive locking means that multiple users can read a file or record, but only the user who has locked the file or record can write to it. Applications can employ variations of these locking methods (see *Chapter 4—LAN Databases*).

LAN Software Types

There are several classes of software used by PCs on LANs, including:

Single-User Software

Single-user software is software designed to be used by a single user on a single computer. Although single-user software is usually not designed to allow for data or file sharing, most can be installed on LAN file servers. Licensing issues aside, single-user software can usually be used by multiple users simultaneously, but the data files usually cannot.

Most network operating systems allows you to prevent multiple users from concurrently accessing files that should not be shared. Novell's NetWare provides for default file locking for most single-user applications automatically locking data files in use by another station.

Multiuser Software

Multiuser software provides for concurrent sharing of data files by multiple users (where appropriate). Multiuser software provides simultaneous shared access to the user while maintaining data integrity with file, record, or field-level locking. Software of this type includes multiuser DBMS and accounting systems.

Software Enhanced for Networks

Software enhanced for networks is software that is designed to take advantage of network resources such as shared printers, modems, or host gateways. For example, a word processor enhanced for networking, such as the network version of WordPerfect, generally provides transparent access to shared printers, multiple configurations for multiple users, and file locking.

Groupware

A relatively new category of software called *groupware* has begun to emerge in LAN environments.

Although definitions vary, essentially groupware is software that enables individuals to work together as a group, or software that facilitates group goals. The definition stretches as vendors try to position themselves under groupware's popular umbrella. (Vendor hype notwithstanding, all multiuser software is not groupware.)

Groupware mirrors the current trend of management organization by workgroups. Members of workgroups might, for example, work in the same department, or be engaged in a particular project. Workgroup members might work in the same building or be separated geographically. They might be on the same or different schedules. They might even work for separate companies, and individuals will often belong to more than one workgroup.

Obvious candidates for groupware include software for electronic mail, electronic meetings, group scheduling and calendaring, and some project management tools. Examples include WordPerfect Office by WordPerfect Corp., Office Works by Data Access Corporation, Higgins by Enable Software, and the Coordinator by Action Technologies.

Choosing the right groupware for your organization may well be more a matter of tailoring to your organization's way of doing business than of finding some "best" product.

So far there are no industry standards about what groupware is, let alone how it should operate. There are, however, emerging standards for communication exchanges that can serve as platforms for present and future groupware products. Many products that include the ability to exchange messages, such as the Coordinator, FrameWork III, and Da Vinci eMail, for example, make use of Action Technologies Message Handling Service (MHS) as a platform. Novell now bundles MHS with NetWare, presumably to promote it as a standard and encourage more development based on it.

Early groupware efforts have generally been thought a bit cumbersome and "unfriendly." For example, while electronic mail (e-mail) is much more efficient than the telephone for many communications, the loss of human contact bothers many users.

The success of even the best designed groupware product depends on user acceptance, and the commitment of the organization needs to be strong enough to make sure that users continue to use the product during the early stages.

To implement electronic mail and other groupware successfully in an organization everyone has to use it regularly. If you can't count on Fred to read his mail when he comes in, you'll call him instead. When e-mail is successfully implemented in an organization, its use becomes a standard business practice, not a personal choice.

Users who need to work together may need to use different mail systems. This is especially true in large organizations and between different organizations. Some of the problems and solutions involved in this process are discussed in the following section.

Electronic Mail

As standards for electronic mail develop (and as products that communicate among the various standards also develop), we are rapidly reaching a point where virtually any computer user with a modem or LAN connection can be made to communicate with any other user.

While electronic mail is one of the more important tools to emerge from LAN and WAN technologies, the exchanging of messages between users is not its only implementation.

Although some local and wide area network databases require high-speed, constant, and immediate communications, such contact can be expensive and is not always necessary. An alternative is a "store and forward" scheme where communications are initiated only under specified conditions. The specified conditions for data transmission could be, for example, when there is data to transmit, when there is a certain amount of data to transmit, at timed intervals, or under a defined combination of conditions. The connection media is often by modem and telephone line. The most common implementation of this kind of system is electronic mail, but can include other kinds of transaction-based distributed data systems.

X.400

The CCITT international standard for electronic mail and messaging interchange is called X.400. Messaging products developed to this standard can speak to one another transparently. Although not yet widely implemented in the United States, many vendors have announced support for it, including IBM, Telenet, Hewlett-Packard, DEC, and Data General. At the moment, X.400 is an important link to international systems, and may provide an unparalleled level of connectivity as acceptance and implementation of the standard grows.

X.400 specifies data transmission in the form of messages and the information that can accompany a message (the envelope). X.400 is "peer-to-peer," which means that nodes on the network can send and receive information from one another without depending on a central, or master, host computer.

Information that can be included on the message envelope are the hooks that enable programs based on the standard to provide services. The list of services below, while not exhaustive, gives the flavor of message services specified by X.400:

Basic Services	Including message identification, submission time-stamping, content type indication, access management
Submission and Delivery	Nondelivery and delivery notification, multidestination delivery, grade of delivery

User Agent Services	Importance and sensitivity indication, primary and copy recipients indication, subject indication, reply request indication, encryption indication, multipart body indication

The X.400 standard allows for multimedia messages, including FAX, voice, Telex, and graphics as well as text.

Other Messaging Standards

Many network vendors and third-party companies provide proprietary standards for message handling and/or e-mail. Some then provide translation utilities to the outside world via gateways to other proprietary systems, to X.25, and to X.400. Proprietary systems tend to offer customized enhancements applicable to the needs of particular users. These special enhancement features are generally lost in translation to products based on other standards.

MHS

MHS, like X.400, is a platform developers can use to build electronic mail packages of their own, or to interface with other MHS applications.

Like X.400, MHS creates an envelope that fits around a message. The envelope contains address and origin information. It also provides hooks that sending and receiving applications can use to manage what should be done with the message when it arrives. Because of this organizing feature, electronic mail based on MHS can contain rich tools for organization and structuring. MHS uses also extend beyond e-mail, however, since MHS does not care what the content of a message is.

Application developers can use MHS to transmit and process data in distributed databases of many kinds. Further, MHS can initiate action at the receiving computer. For example, an MHS application could update a central database with contact and sales orders from salespeople in the field. At present, though, most commercially available MHS applications are electronic mail.

MHS uses a store and forward scheme for delivering mail. If the message is addressed to a user on another LAN, the message is forwarded to that computer or to an intermediary *hub* computer via, for example, a dial-up modem. Using hubs frees users to call in to pick up and drop off mail whenever they like. In most cases, the hub consists of MHS software, a modem, and either a stand-alone PC or a workstation on the LAN. Using an intermediary hub frees users from having to communicate in real time.

If the intended receiver uses a different mail package, the message can still be deliverable as long as both electronic mail packages use MHS as the underlying message-handling API. For example, users of Framework III and the Coordinator can send messages to one another transparently. It will not be apparent to either that they are using different packages to communicate.

If the underlying message service is different, then the message will have to pass through an e-mail gateway that translates from one protocol to another.

MHS is an "open" standard. Specifications are available from either Novell or from Action Technologies (the original writer of MHS).

X.400 is addressing universal messaging exchange for the entire computer community, where MHS is PC-LAN specific. At the same time, MHS can provide most of the services available in X.400, and it is less complex to program.

Choosing between X.400 and MHS is not a problem systems implementors face today. Few X.400-based products exist, and while more will be appearing in the LAN environment, so will gateways allowing communication among X.400, MHS, and other proprietary systems.

Some in the industry predict that proprietary standards will all but disappear as X.400 takes over. If industry trends mean anything at all, then X.400 will probably knock out most—but not all—proprietary contenders. In the meantime, third parties will continue to develop communication gateways for the systems that are around today.

Making Connections

Many companies find themselves trying to link dissimilar e-mail systems, including IBM PROFS, DEC All-in-1, Wang Office, e-mail on PC LANs, and e-mail on public data networks such as MCI and Telenet.

Some PC LAN e-mail packages provide gateways to certain mainframe, minicomputer, and public data network e-mail systems. For example, cc:Mail provides PC LAN users with links to IBM PROFS, Telenet Telemail and MHS, and a link to DEC All-in-1 is promised by mid 1989. Network Courier provides gateways to PROFS, All-in-1, MCI Mail, and X.400, while Higgins has links to PROFS, MHS, and others.

Another approach is the Mailbridge family of products from SoftSwitch. Mailbridge translates routing information and message formats for a large number of e-mail systems, including:

IBM PROFS	Wang Office Network	Framework
DEC All-in 1	IBM DISOSS	3+ Mail
Higgins	IBM AS/400 Office	HP Desk Manager
NBI WP	Banyon Mail	Network Courier
Wang Mailway	MCI Mail	Data General CEO
cc:Mail	SM/TP (TCP/IP)	The Coordinator
Xerox WP	PC/TSO Mail	

Mailbridge requires an IBM mainframe as a host. All of the routing and address information has to be entered in advance of any exchange between users, and has to be manually maintained and updated.

User addresses in most systems cannot be addressed in the addressee format; most must be addressed in the native users' format, then translated by software at a central host into the proper address for the receiver.

For example, say one package requires the address in the form:

```
//jrobinson/sales/sf
```

The receiving package requires:

```
US @ CA @ SF @ SALES @ ROBINSON @ JACK
```

It isn't only that one address has to be translated into another; that would be a trivial mechanical exercise a gateway could perform. The problem is that the second address requires information that is simply not available in the first address. If the first address is at maximum size already, extra information cannot even be appended by a processing gateway at the first system.

There are several methods for this kind of translation:

- An administrator might build a map "by hand" of each user address in each mail system form. In this kind of system, users that change addresses frequently generate a huge administrative overhead.

- Another approach is to have the first user type a generic or "dummy" address in the address field, and the real address as free text in the message. Say, for example, a user wants to communicate with MCI Mail. The user would enter in the address field a name like //MCI/. Then the user puts the real MCI address on the first text line of the message. When the user's mail package sees MCI in the address field, it hands the message to the MCI gateway. The MCI gateway reads the MCI address from the first line of the message, prepares a message in MCI form, and sends it out.

Some "smart" gateways can do some limited best guess matching of user names from one standard to another. If the gateway is too generous in matches, too much mail will be delivered to the wrong people. If the guessing is too narrow, too much mail will be returned as undeliverable.

Choosing an Electronic Mail Package

Some network operating systems, like 3+ and VINES, come with built-in electronic mail. Others, like NetWare, come with a message handling platform that will run several different third-party e-mail and groupware packages. Either way, you don't have to use the mail system that comes with your LAN. Third-party packages are available for most LANs.

A number of factors determine whether you need electronic mail or which system you should get.

1. With what other mail systems will you want to communicate?

2. Does the package allow mail to be prioritized?

3. How extensive are the tools for indexing and finding messages?

4. How private are your communications? Are archives made of mail you send on a central computer?

5. Can you use your own word processor to compose? Can you send attachments from other programs, like Lotus 1-2-3, WordPerfect, or SuperCalc?

6. How much RAM is required at each workstation? How much disk space do the program and mailboxes take up on the server? What kind of software is required in the workstation and on the server? What kind of modem is required?

7. Do you want any of the extra features some packages offer? These include calendars, group meetings, reminders and alerts, built-in word processing, automatic forwarding, etc.

8. How much will it cost? Is there an additional fee for each user? Are there hub charges?

9. What are the additional phone costs going to be, and how does this compare to the decrease in phone communications the mail system should cause?

10. How hard is it to learn, to use, and to administer? This is partly a question of good design. You should also look for a package that uses an interface your people are used to, or that at least has a familiar "feel." On the other hand, this can be a matter of the same old trade-off: the more choices you have, the more you have to learn.

11. Does the package let users talk to one another by aliases or familiar names, even across different LANs?

12. Can LAN users check their mail from remote computers (for example, when they're traveling)?

For profiles of several e-mail and groupware packages, see *Appendix B—Network Utilities*.

Shareware and Public Domain Software

Shareware and public-domain software circulate among users, and gain acceptance largely through user consensus. Shareware is different from public domain software: Shareware is distributed on a "try before you buy" basis; if you like the product, you send the publisher money, and if not, you discontinue using it. The most common sources of shareware are computer bulletin boards. Public domain software is software that the author has provided for free to anyone who wishes to use it, usually with the stipulation that it not be sold or used for direct financial gain.

The most useful shareware programs in a LAN environment are utilities that take up where the network operating system leaves off, providing resource management tools for printers, file handling, and the like. Some of the most popular programs around, for example, are archive programs such as ARC and PKZIP. Archive programs archive multiple files into a single file, usually compressing them by 40 percent to 50 percent or more. Archive programs are used to save disk space, to archive historical material, and to facilitate faster data transfers by modem.

Viruses

There has been considerable concern lately about the appearance of the computer virus and worm. The virus and worm are computer programs that invade computers and replicate themselves until they are removed or until they exhaust the computer's resources. A frequent source of contamination is software downloaded from bulletin boards or passed hand-to-hand on disk.

An infectious virus makes good copy. After the worm infection of the Department of Defense's ARPANET network in 1988, the media overindulged in hysteria. Exterminators were coming out of the woodwork. Judging from press coverage, you would think infections had reached the final stage of fatal epidemic. The truth is, infections just aren't that common, especially in the PC LAN environment.

Still, it doesn't hurt to protect yourself. By following a few commonsense guidelines, such as only downloading software from known sources, avoiding the loading of new shareware directly on your LAN until it has been thoroughly tested, and performing regular rotational backups, you should avoid or prevent most problems.

4

LAN Databases

What to Look for in a LAN Database

Not too many years ago, the only Database Management Systems (DBMSs) that existed ran on large mainframe computers and were maintained by a multitude of programmers. In that environment, needs were usually thoroughly assessed before any software was purchased or code was written.

In today's PC environment, however, users often do the bulk of database design and programming themselves. This approach, while perhaps workable on a stand-alone PC, can be a problem in the LAN environment, where different levels of users may need access to the same data. A DBMS designed to be used by an occasional user for simple list management would probably be completely unusable for someone trying to create a complex inventory and invoicing application. In addition, a DBMS optimized for free-form query of data stored in table form may not be the best for some data entry and transaction processing systems.

LANs have extended the usefulness of database software by allowing a whole department or company to have access to the same data concurrently.

Before deciding what database system will fit your needs, you need to examine what your needs really are and in what direction they are likely to go. You should realize that the system you design includes the computer system, but must be designed in the context of the larger system that constitutes the office. System design identifies the work that an office as a whole must accomplish, the people who will participate and what each will do, and the tools they will use and the precise steps to be taken by whom, when, where, and with what.

The system you design will change the work flow in your department or company, so the stakes can be high.

For example, you will be choosing the degree of centralization for your system. Some advantages of a more centralized system are that it can be easier for all users to access all data (the "big picture") and it can be easier for you to enforce data standards and security, and the hardware costs can be less.

On the other hand, a more distributed system encourages people to manage the information relevant to their jobs themselves. This helps avoid keeping information for its own sake. Distributed systems give remote users more immediate access to the computer as a dynamic tool of use to them in accomplishing work, rather than as a system for reporting work that is already done.

A system approach that fails miserably in one office might work perfectly well in another. Factors that influence the success of the approach include the fit of the software to the users' needs, the degree of training and support, and the "fit" between the company's management style and the system's style. For example, a system that enables salespeople in the field to use the computer for managing their contact schedules, writing orders, and communicating with customers directly will work well only if management supports that degree of independence. If communication with customers (mail contact, invoicing, and the like) is mainly conducted by the central office, the salesperson "ownership" and maintenance of customer names and addresses can impede customer communications. If sales are tightly controlled by the central company, this software system will frustrate salespeople and management alike, and will eventually go unused.

The system implementor rarely gets to start from scratch, nor design in a vacuum. Usually a system is being designed in reaction to the failures of the current set up. System designers often fail to take into account user attitudes shaped by previous systems, but the strength of strong negative assessments of certain programs or styles may preclude obvious solutions.

The section which follows reviews the kinds of database software from which you can choose, and issues surrounding their implementation and use.

What is a Database Management System?

The label DBMS is applied to a wide range of software products, from simple filing systems to complete applications development environments. A DBMS is basically composed of two parts:

1. A file management system
2. A user and/or programmer interface to the filing system, often including complete application development tools

Both functions of the DBMS are important, and one or both may help determine the suitability of a DBMS for a particular situation or need.

What are You Using the DBMS for?

To help determine what DBMS is appropriate, you need to ask some questions:

1. Who is designing the database files and applications? If all or many users in an organization are creating databases and applications for their own use, you may want to place your emphasis on design tools that require little if any programming. If a group of database programmers or developers are creating applications to be used by others for data entry and retrieval, flexibility and programmability may be primary concerns. Although many products claim to fill both needs, few, if any, really do.

2. Who is using the database? Are the users knowledgeable about PCs and software? Can they handle queries and ad hoc reports, or do they need well-defined, easy-to-use, preprogrammed applications? Generally the latter preprogrammed and easy-to-use systems are relatively inflexible. Can users live with a limited selection of preprogrammed reports? The more choices the user has, the more flexibility there is, but more choices make a system harder to use.

3. What is the orientation of the DBMS? Some DBMS systems are oriented toward the data structure, while others are oriented toward the user interface. For example, the table orientation of Paradox' data structure is very apparent to the user while the data structure is transparent to a user of a DataFlex application. The table orientation of Paradox is usually better in situations where data will often be retrieved in an ad hoc, nonstructured way, while the screen orientation of DataFlex is often better for creating highly structured data entry and retrieval applications.

4. How is data retrieved? Sorting is fine for small files, but indexed retrieval and reporting is a must for efficient use of large

databases. Although many database systems provide for indexing, they don't all do it the same way. Some, like DataFlex, DataEase, and dBASE, allow virtually unlimited multifield indexes. Others, like Paradox, are more limited. The method of index updating can be important for performance as well. Some programs update indexes immediately on-line, which can slow performance but which makes fully updated data available to multiusers sooner. Some programs allow batch keying and update, which is much faster for the data entry person, but which delays data availability for others. Batch data entry of some sort allows for off-site keying.

5. Can data be entered into multiple files (tables) through the same screen? While most sophisticated DBMS systems allow data to be entered into multiple files through the same screen, many require that each file have its own separate data window. This makes design more complex.

6. How much control does the applications designer have over the appearance of screens and output? Can the programmer completely control the screen design? Is this control available through the easy applications generation tools? Can the programmer design custom report formats?

7. Are users locked out of records in use by others, or is there some method to provide concurrent access? This is not important in all environments, but it can be critical in others.

8. Can reporting and updating be performed concurrently by different users? If the database has to be "locked" to run a report, valuable time may be lost.

9. What about access to and from other applications and files? Does the database have file import and export capabilities? Are there interfaces for programming languages?

10. Are applications and files easily transportable? Is it difficult to move a specific set of files and/or applications from one database to another?

11. What does it really cost? The cost per user on a LAN database varies greatly from product to product. Vendors have different pricing and licensing schemes. Some systems are priced by user and some are priced by file server. Within these schemes there are variations. With Advanced Revelation, for example, you buy a single-user package at a retail of $950, then add users with "bump disks," which allow four additional users for a retail price of $495. With R:BASE you have a three-user license initially ($725), then you may add six users at a time for $695 retail, or you can buy a single-server license (unlimited number of users) for $2,695.

    Many DBMSs provide run-time systems that allow you to distribute applications at a nominal fee. Others allow you to distribute compiled code at little or no charge. The costs vary: The DataFlex multiuser run-time for DOS LANs retails at $300 per server, and provides the full DataFlex Query system. For a mere $9.95 you can buy a license to distribute an unlimited number of your Paradox applications. For $200 you can buy an Advanced Revelation run-time version for one user. Additional users are added using the Revelation bump disks at $495 for four users.

12. What about performance? Performance and response (data retrieval, saves/updates and reports) of LAN databases can vary from relatively fast (DataFlex) to relatively slow (Advanced Revelation). In general, several factors can affect performance of all DBMSs, including LAN speed, workstation processor type and speed, file server type and speed, etc. With some DBMSs performance can be affected by available workstation RAM and/or the size of the database. DBMSs that use sort routines will generally slow down as the database gets larger, while DBMSs that

use indexed retrieval will generally offer fairly flat performance regardless of database size.

13. What about security? Depending on your particular LAN environment, a DBMS that has its own security system may be important, or the security may just be redundant and get in the way. With NetWare LANS, the latter is often true. If it is important, make sure that the implementation works in your own environment. Different vendors have different ideas of what security should be, and those ideas may not necessarily coincide with yours.

14. What operating environments are supported? With the advent of OS/2 and the increasing interest in UNIX and XENIX, this question becomes more important. If you are planning to move to another operating environment, it would be nice to move your DBMS—lock, stock and data file—with you. If the vendor supports multiple environments, you might want to find out if the applications that you have written are transportable.

15. Can applications interoperate over multiple operating systems? This is a question that wouldn't have been asked much a few years ago, but LANs are increasingly connecting systems that use different operating systems. Data Access says that the same DataFlex files can be concurrently accessed by LAN users using MS/DOS, OS/2, UNIX, XENIX, AIX, and VAX VMS. In addition, they say applications written in DataFlex can be transported within the same processor family (8086, 286, 386, and the VAX as one family; 68000-based systems as another) without recompiling. Fox Software, the publishers of FOXBASE, says that Macintosh users on the upcoming Macintosh version of Novell NetWare will be able to concurrently share database files transparently with PC users on the same network.

16. What about support? Support plans vary as much as DBMSs do. Some examples: Users of DataPerfect receive unlimited installa-

tion and configuration assistance (no design support, however) and a toll-free number to call; R:BASE users receive thirty days free support, then can buy a one-year contract that can cost $175 to $600 for a single user, depending on the products being supported; DataFlex users receive unlimited support on a toll line, a monthly newsletter, and monthly bulletins on known bugs, patches, and work-arounds. Many vendors offer different kinds of extended support programs for groups such as software developers, major accounts, etc.

Database Service and Server-Based Applications

Software for DBMSs is undergoing rapid evolution in the industry. Database Service and server-based applications are currently hot topics of discussion. Many writers and industry pundits assume that database service is inherently better and faster for shared database access than file service, and that file server-based database servers are better than other approaches.

Currently, the standard approach to retrieving data from a networked database is file service. With file service, a database program running on a workstation PC requests blocks of files from the file server. With most database files, for example, only the file blocks that contain the requested data records and associated indexes, if any, are downloaded. In most cases that portion of the database is then locked to other users. The workstation PC can modify and/or update the specific locked records, then upload the file blocks containing them back to the server, at which time they will be unlocked to other users. With file service, database processing takes place at the workstation.

Database server systems split up the job of database processing: each user's workstation PC runs the "front end," or user interface software, while another machine on a network processes the database requests.

This "back end" processor is called a *database engine* or *database server*. With this approach, only individual records are transmitted from the database server to a workstation. Because individual records are being sent to and from the workstation, traffic on the network may be lessened.

On the face of it, it sounds as if database service should be faster and more efficient for database processing than file service; yet this may not always be the case.

A database server can be implemented in several ways:

1. It can be a separate, secondary process on a network file server
2. It can be a Value-Added Process (VAP) on a file server, working as part of the LAN operating system
3. It can employ a coprocessor in a LAN file server
4. It can use a dedicated PC on the LAN
5. It can be a separate background process on a designated LAN workstation
6. It can employ a coprocessor in a LAN workstation

All of these approaches can be considered server-based applications, and each has its own advantages and disadvantages. Remember, server-based does not necessarily mean file server-based, although that is still the current prevalent usage of the term.

1. *Database Service as a Second Task on a File Server*

This is the approach that is currently receiving the most attention by the press. The CPU of the server divides its attention between its file server function and its database server function.

For example, Microsoft's network operating system LAN Manager runs the database service as a secondary, separate process on the network file server (that should be using the OS/2 PC operating system). The basic idea is that the file server machine is the "logical" place for database service to take place. What is not often considered sufficiently in this implementation is the degradation on overall performance that can result. With a slow network, a fast server, and little traffic, this approach may not worsen performance at all. But on a fast, busy network, sharing the server CPU between file service and database service can create a performance bottleneck at the server while workstation processors lie idle.

2. *Database Service as a Value-Added Server Process*

A Value Added Process (VAP) is an extension to the file server software. A VAP performs tasks whose results are then integrated with the file server work. Although tighter integration of tasks could result in less overhead, this approach can have the same potential bottleneck performance problems described above when the database service is performed directly by the file server resources.

3. *Application Coprocessor in the File Server*

With this approach, a separate processor board is installed in the file server. Workstation database requests are routed to the coprocessor. This eases the load on the main processor while eliminating the LAN traffic that would ensue if database requests had to be sent across the cable to individual workstations for processing.

All other things being equal, using an application coprocessor in a file server probably provides the best performance of the database server designs available. It does not use file server CPU time for database processing, it does not add to traffic on the LAN cable, and it minimizes the time files or records are locked by workstation requests.

4. *Dedicated Database Server*

   By using a dedicated database server, (that is, a second PC separate from the file server and used only for database processing), you can reduce traffic on the LAN cable and free workstations from lengthy database processing.

   You can store database files on the hard disk of the database server PC or on the file server. (For security and backup reasons, it can be desirable to store the files on the file server. In that case, the database server has to update the files on the file server, which increases LAN traffic that was supposed to be avoided.)

5. *Background Database Server on a Workstation*

   Under OS/2, you can use a workstation PC as a database server, where the server functions are performed as background tasks. This would have most of the attributes of a dedicated database server, but would provide lower performance due to the sharing of the workstation CPU, bus, and network interface.

6. *Application Coprocessor in a Workstation.*

   A coprocessor in a workstation PC would probably have about the same overall effect on performance as a separate database server. Because the expansion bus and network interface are being shared, performance of the host workstation could be affected in a heavy-traffic situation.

One additional performance factor to consider is the database server itself. Multiple requests and updates must be queued by the database server, while update processing with file service is provided by the workstation PC. With a busy system, the database server itself can become a bottleneck, while DBMSs that do not employ a database server distribute the workload to each user's workstation.

A serious potential problem with distributed database processing is that each of the workstations has the power to corrupt the entire database. With database service, since all database processing is being handled by a single dedicated CPU, there is less chance of file corruption.

System integrity is another factor to consider, especially with applications and/or coprocessors running in the file server. What if a server-based application "hangs up" the server? Applications have been known to hang single PCs, and they could also hang a file server running a server-based application.

One primary advantage of the database server approach is that a "client" workstation can access multiple database servers, so that physically separate databases can be treated by the user as one logical distributed database. A user can request data without necessarily knowing or caring where the data is physically located; the database software locates and delivers the requested data.

With this distributed database approach, available databases could include a PC database server on the local LAN, a mini- or mainframe computer on the local LAN or accessed through a gateway or bridge, or a remote database accessed through a remote gateway or bridge.

Because you are generally not moving vast amounts of data across a LAN when accessing a database server, low-speed remote LAN bridges (say, 19.2 Kb/sec. or lower) may become more viable. With database servers, you are only sending requests and retrieving records, not massaging large blocks of data at the client PC.

Distributed databases enable you to retain central control AND empower remote users and offices.

While many database server systems have been announced, few are actually available for PC LANs, and very few benchmark tests have been published.

Most of the forthcoming database server systems are based on Structured Query Language (SQL). SQL is an ANSI standard for data retrieval based on IBM's design and specifications. Most announced SQL servers are based on the ANSI standard.

Even after the SQL database servers reach the market, it will take time to create or modify applications to make use of them.

In the long run, standardization on SQL servers will probably mean interchangeability of various vendor's DBMS front ends and applications generators with various database servers.

The big advantage of this approach is that users can get many different views of the same data, using familiar front-end DBMS interfaces, like Lotus 1-2-3, Paradox, DataFlex, DataEase, and dBASE.

Initially, however, DBMS vendors may have to choose sides, as each database engine developer attempts to lock front end developers into their "enhanced" standard SQL servers. This would in turn force users to choose the SQL server that runs their favorite interface, and that SQL server might not run other interfaces that they need. Eventually, however, front-end developers will provide their interfaces for all the SQL servers that survive the initial market struggle. They will have to in order to survive themselves.

Some DBMS vendors have already announced alliances with particular SQL database server vendors. For example, Borland's Paradox, Micro Database Systems MDBS III, and Ashton-Tate's dBASE IV will front-end the Ashton Tate/Sybase/Microsoft SQL Server for LAN Manager. Paradox and WordTech's dBXL will work with Oracle's database server, while dBXL and Gupta Technology's SQL Windows and Oracle's front end will work with Novell's NetWare SQL.

On the downside, expect the first generation of SQL database servers to be slow performers. There will inevitably be problems to solve, incompatibilities and unexpected bottlenecks. As SQL database servers are optimized, performance will improve. Like the database machines used in mainframe and minicomputer environments, later generations of database servers may well use specialized operating software (and possibly even specialized hardware) optimized for database service.

As the technology matures, however, SQL (or whatever it may evolve into) and database servers will come into their own. Faster hardware, including machines optimized for database service, more sophisticated server software, and optimized applications, could all contribute to the process.

Much of the commentary about SQL database servers by the press and by vendors is speculative. It is too early to tell which products will prevail and what their practical shortcomings will be, since so few have actually been released.

SQL DBMS Servers

Novell Netware SQL

Novell is offering NetWare SQL as their back-end database "engine" for Netware 2.1 and above. NetWare SQL runs on a file server or NetWare External Bridge as a VAP. The workstation runs only the front-end application and the NetWare SQL Requestor, which takes the front-end application requests translates them into SQL requests, and transmits the SQL requests to the database server for processing. NetWare SQL relies on NetWare's System Fault Tolerance (SFT) for error recovery, but it continues transaction recovery and record locking within itself.

NetWare SQL uses the NetWare Btrieve record manager to access the database files. The NetWare Btrieve server program consists of two VAPs: BSERVER, which directly accesses database files on the server, and BROUTER, which routes requests to other servers. When there are multiple database servers on the network, BROUTER determines which server the data is on and routes the request there. BSERVER uses NetWare's Transaction Tracking System (TTS) to provide file roll-back and recovery.

NetWare XQL is Novell's application program interface to SQL. XQL provides access to the SQL database through ANSI-standard SQL statements and other, lower-level function calls. Using XQL, a C, BASIC, Pascal, or COBOL application can pass requests to the NetWare SQL database.

Third-party front-end programs for NetWare SQL include WordTech's dBXL and Quicksilver, Gupta Technologies' SQL Windows, Revelation Technologies' Revelation, Borland's Paradox, and others. Novell will itself provide a "blueprint" driver for Lotus 1-2-3 users.

Fox Software FoxServer

Fox Software will soon provide a version of Novell's NetWare SQL called FoxServer. It incorporates dBASE language functions into NetWare SQL. This means that front-end applications can use SQL, XQL, Btrieve, and/or dBASE commands to directly access the database server. According to Fox the product is expected to ship in late 1989 or early 1990.

Ashton-Tate/Microsoft SQL Server

Another example of SQL server software is Ashton-Tate/Microsoft SQL Server, developed jointly by Microsoft, Ashton-Tate, and Sybase as their database engine for OS/2 servers. SQL Server can run as a task in an OS/2-based file server, or on a separate machine running OS/2. Network operating systems supported by SQL Server include Novell NetWare, IBM LAN Server, and networks based on Microsoft LAN Manager.

SQL Server is compatible with Sybase's minicomputer-based SQL server.

SQL Server provides on-line, write-ahead transaction logging. This means that transactions are written to a log file before the database is updated. In the event of a system failure, database changes can be recovered from the transaction log.

SQL Server incorporates a set of extensions (nearly all SQL databases have their own nonstandard extensions) called TRANSACT-SQL that can store commonly used group of commands at the database server and execute them with a procedure call. This means that a "client" workstation can send a single command to the server to execute complex transactions.

Among others, products that will "front-end" SQL Server include Borland's Paradox, Revelation Technologies' Revelation, Ashton-Tate's dBASE IV, and WordTech's dBXL and Quicksilver.

Gupta SQLBase

Gupta Technologies is a pioneer in SQL database servers. Gupta shipped the first SQL database server for PC LANs. Its SQL back-end engine offerings are SQLBase and SQLBase for OS/2, both of which work on any NetBIOS compatible LAN.

Gupta produces a powerful, event-oriented application program developer called SQLWindows. SQLWindows is a Microsoft Windows-based application generator that supports graphics, menus, dialogue boxes, and mice. Although SQLWindows only works with SQL-Base now, Gupta plans to allow it to interface with other SQL DBMSs including ORACLE, Novell's NetWare SQL, Lotus's forthcoming DBMS product (based on Gupta's software), and Microsoft's SQL Server.

SQLWindows currently runs under DOS Windows and will eventually run under the OS/2 Presentation Manager. Since SQLWindows does not (yet) have a built-in report writer, Gupta has licensed SQR, a report writer produced by SQ Software originally intended to enhance the report writing capabilities of the ORACLE DBMS.

Gupta also supplies versions of WordTech's DBXL and Quicksilver dBASE-like products that will access the SQL-Base server.

SQLNetwork is a series of products that provides connectivity between Gupta's SQL products and IBM's mainframe-based DB2. SQL-Network uses IBM's Application Program-to-Program Communications (APPC) to provide this connectivity.

ORACLE

Oracle Corporation, one of the largest independent vendors of DBMS software, currently provides a XENIX-based SQL database server for use with PC LANs. This means that PCs on NetWare LANs and others, must used network interface cards that support NetWare and the TCP/IP protocol concurrently, or a TCP/IP gateway to access the database server. Users on MS-Net and LAN Manager-based LANS and others must use similar methods.

A primary advantage of ORACLE is the fact that it currently runs in a wide range of operating environments on microcomputers, minicomputers, and mainframes. Like Gupta Technologies, ORACLE supplies versions of WordTech's DBXL and Quicksilver dBASE-like products that will access its SQL database server.

5

Internetworking and Connectivity

A LAN, like a stand-alone PC, can eventually communicate with other computers and/or other LANs. There are several types of communication approaches that may be important to you:

- LAN to LAN repeaters, bridges, routers, and gateways
- Remote LAN to LAN bridges and routers
- WAN gateways
- Host (mini- or mainframe) gateways (local or remote)
- Asynchronous communications servers

LAN to LAN Connections

The four primary ways to connect LANs together locally (as opposed to remotely, which is a separate issue) are: repeaters, bridges, routers, and gateways.

Repeaters

Of the four methods, repeaters are the simplest. Repeaters are simply devices that amplify and reshape the signals on one LAN and pass them to another. Repeaters can be used to extend LAN cable distances.

Repeaters connect identical LANS together at the lowest hardware level: Ethernet to Ethernet, StarLAN to StarLAN, Token Ring to Token Ring, etc.

Because repeaters simply repeat signals and do not provide any *filtering* capability, all traffic on all LANs connected by one or more repeaters is propagated to all others, which can have a negative effect on LAN performance.

Bridges

Bridges, like repeaters, connect LANs together at the hardware level. While repeaters connect LANs at the lowest physical hardware level, bridges connect at the higher hardware level, called the Media Access Control (MAC) level. (The MAC is a subdivision of the hardware level).

In general, bridges are hardware specific: Ethernet to Ethernet, Token Ring to Token Ring, etc. An Ethernet bridge, for example, would allow two or more Ethernet LANs to be connected and to interoperate regardless of the protocols or LAN operating systems being used.

Theoretically, bridges can be used to connect any LAN that conforms to IEEE 802 standards; in practice, however, it has proven difficult to implement Ethernet to Token Ring bridges because of differences between the two standards.

Bridges use routing tables to determine which traffic to forward to devices across the bridge. This means that local traffic stays local, while internetwork traffic can cross the bridge. Local network traffic on one LAN will not affect performance on another bridged LAN.

Figure 5.1: LAN Bridge

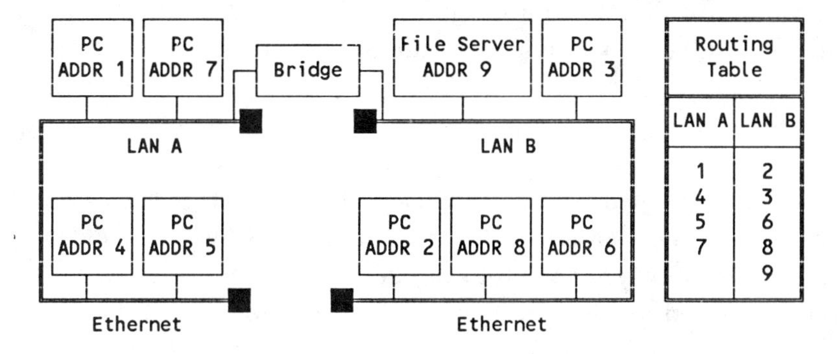

A bridge uses its routing table to determine if traffic must cross it. Traffic from PCs 1, 4, 5, and 7 to the file server will cross the bridge, while traffic from PCs 2, 3, 6, and 8 to the file server will not. Local traffic on LAN A will not affect performance on LAN B and vice versa.

In order to function, a bridge must know the addresses of all devices to which it will forward packets. With early bridges, system administrators had to manually build a *routing table* to tell a bridge which addresses were on which side of the bridge. Most current bridges are *learning bridges* that build their own routing tables. Learning bridges learn the locations of all network devices that are sending and receiving packets.

Bridge performance is usually measured two ways: the number of packets it can *filter*, or examine, and the number of packets it can *forward*, or pass to another LAN. Filter rates of current products fall between 2,000 and 25,000 packets per second, while forward rates fall between 1,500 and 15,000 packets per second.

Bridges can be proprietary devices, or they can be software and hardware residing in a general purpose computer, such as a PC.

When used properly, bridges can increase overall network performance. By sectioning a large LAN into smaller LANs linked together with bridges, local transmissions can be kept in the local area, and only traffic addressed to another LAN will need to cross a bridge. In this way, overall LAN traffic can be reduced. If used improperly, however, bridges can become bottlenecks, impeding the flow of data.

Routers

Routers operate at the protocol level, and are therefore hardware independent. Instead of forwarding packets, routers forward the data in the packets. Routers are protocol specific: a router must know the protocol(s) used for the data that is being forwarded.

For example, Novell's NetWare uses protocols called Internetwork Packet eXchange (IPX) and Sequenced Packet eXchange (SPX), while 3Com's 3+ operating system uses the Xerox Network System (XNS) protocol. A router that only knows the IPX/SPX protocols will not forward XNS data, while a router that only knows XNS will not forward IPX/SPX data.

Figure 5.2: LAN Router

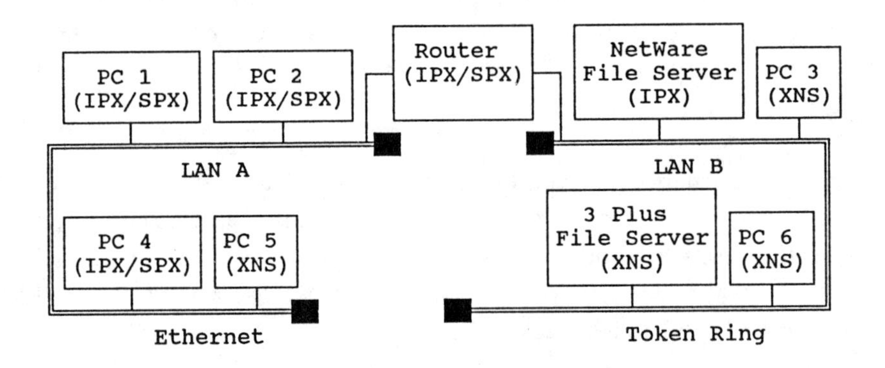

A router must know the protocol(s) being used in order to forward data. In this illustration, the IPX/SPX router will forward traffic between PCs 1, 2, and 4 and the NetWare File server, but will not forward traffic between PC 5 and the 3 Plus file server.

Because routers operate at the protocol level, they can be used to link dissimilar LANs, such as ARCNET and Ethernet, Ethernet and Token Ring, etc. The "bridging" capability of Novell NetWare file servers, for example, is really a routing capability. NetWare "Internal Bridges" allow the interconnection of different LAN hardware types using Novell's IPX/SPX protocols. NetWare "bridges" do not support other protocols, however.

Some routers, such as those from Proteon, Inc., support multiple protocols. These have the advantage of supporting connections between multiple protocols on multiple types of LAN hardware.

Like bridges, routers only forward traffic addressed to the other side. This means that local traffic on one LAN will not affect performance on another. Again, like bridges, routers can be proprietary devices, or can be software and hardware residing in a general purpose computer, such as a PC.

Routers are useful for interconnecting both similar and dissimilar LANs, as well as limiting overall LAN traffic.

Remote Bridges and Routers

Bridges and routers are available that link LANs together remotely through a variety of means. To be effective, remote links need to be very fast or must be used very efficiently.

Like local bridges and routers, remote units can be proprietary "boxes" or hardware and software that installs in a PC or AT type computer.

Remote bridges and routers can use several methods for data transmission, including asynchronous dial-up, synchronous dial-up, synchronous leased line, and X.25 public or private data networks.

Asynchronous Bridges and Routers

In asynchronous communication, or *async*, as it is usually called, data is transmitted as characters in a continuous *bit stream*. Before and after each character is sent, *start bits* and *stop bits* indicate the beginning and end of each character. When transmission errors occur, entire streams of data need to be retransmitted.

Async communication can take place in either a half duplex or full duplex mode. Half duplex means that only one side can send data at a time, while full duplex means that both sides can send data simultaneously. To be effective, LAN bridges and routers require full duplex communication.

Compared to synchronous communications, async is relatively inefficient, because it has a high operational overhead (the start bits and stop bits, etc.) and error recovery generally prolongs response times. Async has the advantage of easily operating over standard, voice-grade, dial-up telephone lines.

Synchronous Bridges and Routers

Synchronous bridges and routers transmit synchronization characters before each block of data sent. After the synchronization characters are sent, the receiving bridge accepts all bits transmitted until new sync characters are sent, indicating the end of that transmission and the start of a new one.

In general, synchronous protocols provide greater throughput and better error recovery than asynchronous protocols. In addition, some synchronous protocols, such as the international standard for wide area networking X.25, provide for multipoint links. Bridges and routers using X.25 protocols can be linked across public and private wide area data networks.

In the past, synchronous protocols could only be used with specially conditioned data grade links and phone lines. With the advent of relatively inexpensive, high speed (9.6 Kb/sec) synchronous modems, synchronous communication over voice-grade dial-up lines is becoming more common.

Synchronous bridges and routers are available that transmit data remotely at speeds up to 9.6 Kb/sec. using dial-up lines, up to 56 Kb/sec using conditioned data-grade lines, and up to 1.544 Mbits/sec over high-speed T-1 lines or satellite links.

Lower-speed remote bridges and routers (19.2 Kb/sec and below) are going to seem very slow for those used to LAN speeds. In fact, for many applications, these speeds are nearly unworkable.

One of the most common uses for remote bridges is database access. With most database products, however, massive amounts of data must be moved across the LAN (and, in this case, the remote bridge) to sort and/or select records. Database servers, which do much of the data processing themselves rather than sending the data across the network to the workstation, can mean a lot less traffic, making lower-speed bridges and routers a more viable solution.

With higher-speed bridges and routers, the major cost is not the bridge hardware and software, but the remote link itself. The monthly cost of a 56 Kbit/sec leased line, a T-1, or satellite link can be very high.

LAN to LAN Gateways

LAN to LAN gateways, like routers, work at the protocol level. Unlike routers, however, gateways provide "protocol conversion." For example, the Interlan/Novell TCP/IP gateway provides protocol conversion between the Novell IPX/SPX protocols and the TCP/IP protocol. The TCP/IP protocol is widely used for communication between dissimilar computer systems.

The TCP/IP gateway allows NetWare users to route data from PCs on any NetWare-supported LAN to an Ethernet LAN supporting TCP/IP. PC users on an ARCNET, for example, can transfer files through the gateway to a UNIX computer on Ethernet.

LAN to WAN Gateways

Like LAN to LAN gateways, LAN to WAN gateways provide routing and protocol conversion. The most common LAN to WAN gateways convert from a PC LAN protocol, such as Novell's IPX/SPX or IBM's NetBIOS, to the X.25 protocol.

X.25 Gateways

The X.25 international standard for wide area network communication is the protocol used on most of the public data networks in the United States, such as Tymenet, Telenet, and Accunet.

Like a LAN, an X.25 network is a *packet switching* network. Data is put into packets before being transmitted across the WAN. Packets can be routed to and from one X.25 Packet Assembler/Disassembler (PAD) to and from other PADs, providing a "one to many" communications capability.

In addition, X.25 is a "transparent" protocol; it doesn't care about the content or structure of the data in the packet. As long as the receiving computer can understand the data sent by the sending computer, communication can take place.

X.25 packets can encapsulate other protocols, which allows diverse systems to use the same WAN. In contrast, IBM's Systems Network Architecture (SNA) requires adherence to strict formatting rules for data to be transmitted across its networks. Even so, an X.25 PAD can encapsulate SNA data in X.25 packets and send them to another PAD for retransmission on an SNA network.

An X.25 gateway on a LAN allows multiple users to access a public or private WAN through one connection or modem. Different LAN users can simultaneously access multiple services on the WAN.

Most X.25 gateways for PC LANs consist of a PC or AT type computer, a wide area communications board, communications software, and a high-speed, synchronous modem. Current gateway technology allows for communications speeds of 9.6 Kb/sec to 56 Kb/sec.

LAN to Host Gateways

Another type of gateway used on a LAN is a LAN to Host gateway. This is a gateway designed to allow multiple PC users on a LAN to communicate with a mainframe or minicomputer that is not locally connected to the LAN.

The two most common types of LAN to Host gateways are 3270 SNA gateways for communicating with IBM mainframes, and 5251 gateways for communicating with IBM Systems 34, 36, 38, and AS400. In addition, gateways designed to communicate with computers from UNISYS and others are available.

Usually, a host gateway requires a PC on the LAN that is dedicated to the gateway job, but some gateways also work in a nondedicated mode.

The gateway computer usually contains a special communications board and runs special communications software that allows it to communicate with the host computer as well as other PC workstations on the LAN. In addition, PCs using the services of the gateway must usually run communications software that enables communication with the gateway, and terminal emulation software to talk to the host computer.

In general, the terminal emulation software running on workstations using the gateway must be designed so that each workstation appears to the host computer to be one of its standard terminals. For example, an SNA gateway to an IBM mainframe must appear to be an IBM 3278 or 3279 (or equivalent) terminals. A gateway to an IBM System 36 must appear to be a group of 5251 terminals (or equivalent).

SNA Gateways

IBM's SNA is a relatively complex, hierarchical standard for connecting IBM terminals, printers, etc., to IBM mainframe computers (There is more to SNA, but this description is sufficient for our discussion).

In order for an IBM terminal to communicate with an IBM mainframe it must generally be connected by a coaxial cable to a Cluster Controller (CC), which is then connected, usually through a modem, to a Front End Processor (FEP), which connects to the mainframe.

A mainframe can support a number of FEPs, which can support a number of CCs. In turn, a CC can support a number of terminals, usually in multiples of eight.

In order to communicate with the mainframe, the gateway must attach to the CC or emulate it. Gateways that attach to the CC are called *Coax Gateways*, while gateways that emulate the CC are called *Remote Gateways*.

Depending on the specific hardware and software used, gateways can be dedicated, providing gateway services only, or nondedicated, running as a workstation as well.

Remote gateways attach to the FEP (again, usually through a modem) and emulate a CC. Depending on a number of factors, including the gateway communications hardware and software, the PC in which the gateway resides, the speed of the modems, etc., remote gateways can support from eight to 128 simultaneous users.

Because they eliminate the cluster controller, remote gateways can be very cost effective.

Coax gateways are very useful for supporting a small number of users where a cluster controller is available. The low-end coax gateways use a low cost 3270 emulation board, such as the IRMA board from DCA or the PCOX board from Novell. These gateways can support up to five simultaneous users.

Another type of coax gateway supports up to forty simultaneous users. This type of gateway usually requires a board with an on- board processor. In addition, it must attach to a special port on the cluster controller called the 3299 port. When this port is enabled, seven other CC ports must be disabled.

The biggest advantage of coax gateways is that they can be attached to existing cluster controllers. This can be an advantage when a small number of LAN users need to access the mainframe, or when cabling issues, internal politics, or other factors make attaching directly to the FEP difficult or inconvenient.

Selecting a Host Gateway

The issues involved in selecting gateways go beyond the scope of this book. It is important, however, to be aware of some of the possible pitfalls.

In a recent "NetWare SNA Gateway Laboratory Report," Novell outlined some of the potential reliability problems with SNA gateways.

The report emphasizes that an SNA gateway can put greater stress on LAN software drivers (communications software for specific LAN interface boards) than PC workstations or file servers. In addition, problems with PC compatibles, such as BIOS compatibility, bus timing, etc., which may not show up under normal operation, can be magnified when such a machine is used as a gateway.

The report also suggests that gateways that use IBM's NetBIOS protocol are prone to errors and slower throughput due to the limited buffering capability of NetBIOS. Gateways send and receive data in bursts, and buffering is important to prevent lost packets and retransmissions.

The report goes on to caution that these problems may not show up in a testbed environment, but could show up in production situations where the gateway is operating at or near full capacity.

In addition to the potential problems outlined above, LAN to Host gateways can differ vastly in the areas of performance, screen display, keyboard mapping, graphics support, and overall functionality. A gateway product that is appropriate for one company's environment may not work well in another's.

Probably the best source for accurate information about gateways is other users. Network users' groups, seminars at trade shows such as Networld, and on-line forums such as the Users' Forum on Novell's NetWire service (accessed through CompuServe) are all possible sources of information. Working with a knowledgeable dealer, VAR, or consultant can also help, but remember that consultants will tend to have unbalanced experience. They tend to have in-depth knowledge of certain products, but no real breadth of practical experience or theoretical background.

In any case, be prepared to spend some time tuning and tweaking the product you end up selecting. Try to locate someone who has experience with it, and make sure they are sufficiently available to support you. Finally, make sure that any purchase contract has escape clauses.

Asynchronous Communications Servers

An Asynchronous Communications Server (ACS) is designed to allow LAN users to share asynchronous modems across a LAN. The ACS is usually a dedicated PC with one or more multiport communications boards and several attached modems.

Async servers are designed to provide either dial-out services (modem pooling), dial-in services (remote LAN access), or both.

Dial-out Services

Dial-out services allow users on a LAN to access remote services (bulletin boards, on-line databases, etc.) by using available modems attached to the ACS, rather than attached to their own PC.

A major advantage of using async servers for this is the reduced number of modems and telephone lines required—a large number of users can use a small number of modems on an as-needed basis.

This scheme can entail several disadvantages, however. The cost of the ACS hardware and software can often end up being greater than the cost of locally attached modems. Communications software choices are usually limited; with most async servers, specially modified software is required.

Until recently, most approaches to modem pooling required specialized hardware either in the ACS or the user PC. Novell's NetWare Asynchronous Communications Server (NACS), for example, requires one or more relatively expensive Wide Area Network Interface Module (WNIM) boards in the ACS. The NACS uses a specially modified version of Dynamic Microprocessor Associates' ASCOM IV communications and terminal emulation software.

More recently, several companies have developed communication server software that runs on PCs without any special hardware (apart from the modem, of course). J&L Information Systems and Network Products Corp. provide software that allows the use of generic hardware in the ACS and no specialized hardware in the user PC. This approach requires communications applications that use DOS interrupt calls rather than direct I/O to a COM port. Several vendors of communications software are modifying their packages (such as Crosstalk and Procomm) to work with this new breed of ACS.

As mentioned above, the J&L Information Systems Network Communications Server (NCS) can use the software-only approach, but can also be used with communications software that makes direct I/O calls. J&L supplies a Network Communications Adapter (NCA) card that is installed in a user's PC. The NCA is a serial redirector card that redirects I/O from a COM port across the network to the NCS. This allows programs that use hardware I/O (including CAD programs and communications software) to access a port on the NCS.

Although these latter approaches can allow for nondedicated operation of the ACS, so that it can function as a workstation as well, it is usually not recommended for critical or high-traffic situations.

Dial-in Services

One of the most common LAN user needs is the ability to dial in to their LAN from a remote PC. There are several ways that this can be approached:

1. LAN software vendors, including Novell, often provide for remote access through a serial port on a file server. This approach has three disadvantages:

    A limited number of serial ports are available on a file server.

Because of the nature of asynchronous communications, the serial ports used for dial-in continually interrupt CPU processes, severely affecting server performance.

Because applications processing takes place on the remote dial-in computer, program and data loading from the file server takes place at async speeds, usually 9,600 bits/sec. or less. Many users will find this unacceptably slow.

2. Instead of dialing directly into a file server, remote users can dial in using an ACS. In this case, applications processing is still done at the remote PC, but communication to the file server is through the more efficient LAN channel, rather than serial ports. This eliminates the first two problems listed above, but not the third.

   This approach usually requires special ACS hardware and software, increasing overall cost.

3. A third approach allows remote users to dial into the LAN through an ACS and use the resources of an unused LAN PC. Remote users load specially modified remote control software (software that allows one PC to control another) and dial in through the ACS to the LAN PC that has corresponding software loaded. Novell's ACS provides this option using a modified version of PC Anyware, a popular remote control package.

   The advantage with this approach is that all application processing takes place on the PC attached to the LAN, not the remote PC. Only screen and keyboard information cross the modem link.

   The major disadvantage to this approach is the cost of the LAN PC running PC Anyware, on top of the cost of the ACS. Also, screen updates on the remote PC can be somewhat slow, but this is usually a far more workable solution than the remote program execution approach.

4. A similar approach to the one above eliminates the ACS. Instead, LAN PCs with directly attached modems are made available to remote users. These PCs can run any of the popular remote control software packages such as PC Anyware, Close Up, Carbon Copy, and others.

   With this approach, PCs are usually dedicated to communications functions, but this does not have to be the case. LAN PCs could be used on an "as available" basis, as long as users remember to reload the communications software when they finish using their PCs (so that they become available to outside callers).

   Diskless LAN workstations, without screen or keyboards, are often used as dedicated ACSs. These have the advantage of taking up very little space, and can also be stacked on top of each other.

   Products such as the Chatterbox by J&L Information Systems can also be effective. Chatterbox is actually multiple PCs residing in a single box, and can be very economical in terms of cost and space.

   The major disadvantage of this approach is the cost of hardware. Each remote connection requires a local PC and LAN hardware.

5. A fifth approach uses a single PC and LAN connection to support multiple dial-in users. The approach requires an 80386 PC, multiport communications boards, and multitasking communications software. The software allows multiple remote control sessions on the same CPU.

   Novell has recently announced the NetWare Access Server, which uses this approach.

The NetWare Access Server uses a specially modified version of Quarterdeck's DESQview, a modified version of DMA's PC Anyware, and one to four of Novell's wide area network interface module WNIM+ boards. In addition, each user requires 640K of RAM and, of course, an available WNIM port and modem. Up to fifteen remote users are supported per server at speeds up to 19.2 Kb/sec.

The major advantage of this approach is the lower hardware cost. A potential disadvantage is lower performance with a large number of remote users attached.

6

Network Operating Systems

The network operating system (NOS) is the central nervous system of a PC LAN. The NOS is the software that manages shared LAN resources. The NOS provides file service (synchronized access to files), print service (shared access to printers, usually with spooling), and usually some level of security that controls access to shared resources.

Currently, Novell's NetWare is the industry leader in PC LAN operating software. Estimates of Novell's market share vary from 50 percent to 75 percent of the PC LAN market.

As of February 1989, Novell has been shipping approximately 17,000 copies of NetWare per month (one copy is required per file server). By contrast, the entire population of MS-Net-based LAN file servers is about 50,000. (MS-Net is the basis of LAN software from IBM, 3Com, Ungermann-Bass, and others). As of February 1989, reportedly fewer that 5,000 copies of Microsoft's OS/2-based LAN Manager operating system—including 3 Com's 3+ Open had been shipped, and many of those were still not delivered to users.

When selecting your operating system, consider the following:

- **Application compatibility**. If your applications are not effectively supported in the manner in which you need to use them, look elsewhere.

- **Manageability**. What tools are available to effectively manage the system? You should be able to create new users, create directories, add and remove applications, and upgrade or reconfigure the system without major trauma.

- **Ease of Use**. When installed properly, the system should be easy for users to navigate. This could mean a limited number of new procedures and/or commands to learn, or an effective menu system, etc. The key phrase here is "when installed properly."

- **Reliability**. LANs that are prone to crashing are worse than useless. If you can afford no downtime, consider an operating system that provides redundancy, such as Novell's SFT NetWare.

- **Security**. A LAN OS should provide the levels of security needed for your situation.

- **Performance**. Of all the factors affecting PC LAN performance, the LAN OS is probably the major one. Having all of the latest, greatest, and fastest hardware rarely makes up for an OS that is a dog when it comes to performance.

- **Expandability**. A four-user LAN may fit your needs today, but you should be able to expand your system if necessary without having to retrain your staff.

Although NetWare is the current leader, it is not the only NOS available. Since it is the focus of this book, it will be dealt with in some detail, but some of the other operating systems available will also be profiled.

MicroSoft MS-Net

MicroSoft does not sell MS-Net as a completed product. It is sold to software hardware vendors, who must provide significant modification and enhancement. This means that every LAN OS based on MS-Net is somewhat different.

IBM uses MS-Net as the core of its PC LAN Program, and 3Com Corporation uses it as the core of its 3+ LAN OS. Other companies supply MS-Net under the MS-Net name.

The MS-Net file server software runs as a task under MS-DOS and provides file and printer services. MS-Net allows for multiple file servers on a network. MS-Net uses the DOS file and directory structure, and server volumes are limited to the DOS 32 MB size, but multiple volumes per server can be supported.

At the workstation, the MS-Net Redirector accepts network calls passed from DOS and reroutes them to the file server.

MS-Net security is device-oriented, not user-oriented. Passwords are placed on directories, which means that users must enter passwords for all directories to which they need access. This method is somewhat more cumbersome and difficult to administer than the one password per user method used by other network OSs.

SNA, Bisync, X.25, and Async gateways to MS-Net LANs are available from several manufacturers.

3Com 3+

3+ is 3Com's MS-Net-based LAN OS. The 3+ server uses a proprietary emulation of DOS called Concurrent Input/Output SYStem (CIOSYS).

Unlike DOS, CIOSYS can process multiple requests at once. Like NetWare, the server provides memory caching for files and directories. Because the server's memory can easily be filled, 3+ also allows workstation caching (which also reduces traffic on the network).

One important difference between 3+ and NetWare is that NetWare user information is file-server dependent, while 3+ uses a global naming scheme—that is, each NetWare file server knows only about the rights of users created on it. 3+ uses a name-server function to track users access rights to all network resources. This means that as long as a user has the right to a resource, they can access it from anywhere on the network without having to specifically attach to a particular file server. 3+ allows only a single name server on a network. This makes occasional bridging of networks that have their own name servers difficult.

In addition to MS-Net file services, 3+ provides elevator seeking and disk caching functions in the file server.

Microsoft LAN Manager/3Com 3+ Open

LAN Manager is MicroSoft's OS/2-based network operating system. Developed in conjunction with 3Com, LAN Manager runs as a task under OS/2. Because LAN Manager runs on top of OS/2, a file server may concurrently be used for other tasks, such as database services. LAN Manager, like MS-Net, is an Original Equipment Manufacturer (OEM) product, which means that Microsoft sells it to other manufacturers who enhance and modify it. 3Com calls their version 3+ Open (not to be confused with the MS-Net-based 3+, as confusing as that may be).

Workstations can be OS/2- or DOS-based; although DOS-based workstations won't be able to take advantage of certain OS/2-specific features or perform some LAN management functions.

Like OS/2 itself, LAN Manager is a product of evolution, and shows some of its DOS and MS-Net roots. The fact that it is based on the multitasking OS/2 operating system gives it a greater ability to handle multiple requests than the single-tasking, DOS-based MS-Net. It offers a significantly richer set of APIs than MS-Net, and greatly enhanced security and management functions and features.

LAN Manager contains security features such as support for password management, and controlled access to network devices that, like NetWare, function by assigning users to groups. Again, as in NetWare, access to a resource can be restricted at the group or user level.

LAN Manager provides error detection, notification, and logging. Each server maintains an audit trail of statistics, log ons, resource use, and security violations. LAN Manager provides spooled print management. LAN Manager provides application services through OS/2 APIs and its own additional network APIs.

LAN Manager, like MS-Net, is sold to other vendors (such as 3Com, IBM, Interlan, Excelan, DCA, HP, and others) who then create a finished product. In addition, Microsoft has published the driver specifications, and NICs from many vendors are currently supported.

IBM LAN Server

IBM's LAN Server is based on Microsoft's LAN Manager. LAN Server, like LAN Manager, runs as a task under OS/2. Also like LAN Manager, workstations can run DOS or OS/2, but DOS stations will not be able to take advantage of certain features.

Although LAN Server is based on LAN Manager and has many similar features and functions, it also has several significant differences. Microsoft and IBM have publicly disagreed about the level of interoperability between LAN Manager and LAN Server. It appears, however, that the two systems are somewhat interoperable.

The security structure of LAN Server differs greatly from that of LAN Manager. While LAN Manager servers maintain their own security tables, LAN Server uses a global Domain Controller—one server that controls security for all file servers on a network. Users must first log on to the Domain Controller to access resources of any other server. This is very much in line with IBM's traditional top-down system management philosophy.

LAN Manager and LAN server both have full-screen interfaces (menus), that are visually similar but somewhat different in function and slightly incompatible with each other.

Instead of using LAN Manager's built-in print spooler, LAN Server uses an extended version of the OS/2 Presentation Manager spooler.

For various reasons, many of the commands of LAN Manager are different from those of LAN Server, making it more difficult for a user or administrator to deal with both operating systems.

Banyan VINES

Banyan Systems' VINES, (which stands for VIrtual NEtwork operating System), is touted to deliver "universal connectivity." VINES includes file and print service, a global naming and access system called "StreetTalk," and built-in connectivity to SNA, TCP/IP, and X.25 networks.

VINES file server is based on UNIX, and files are stored in UNIX format. Network services (file service, print service, etc.) are basically UNIX applications. VINES file server software uses enhanced disk access techniques, including elevator seeking, directory caching and file caching to improve performance. In addition to the DOS 3.x record and file locking functions, VINES also incorporates semaphore (logical) locking capabilities, including those used by Novell and 3Com.

VINES communications and gateway functions are integrated into the operating system. Banyan says this "saves users from choosing and integrating a mind-boggling array of point products designed to address individual or discrete interconnect problems." This approach simplifies things for the systems integrator and administrator, but also limits choices.

VINES security is user-based rather than device-based. Access rights are based on user and group profiles. VINES uses StreetTalk to make user profiles available to all network file servers, providing users with global access to internetwork resources with a single login. This approach makes for easier centralized multiserver administration.

VINES LAN hardware support includes Ethernet from 3COM Micom/Interlan and Ungermann-Bass, Omninet, IBM PC Network, IBM Token Ring, ProNET 4, 10 and 80, ARCNET and Allen Bradley Vista LAN-PC.

TOPS

TOPS from Sun Microsystems/TOPS Division provides distributed file service for PCs, Macintoshes, and UNIX-based systems. TOPS lets any LAN station act as a file server.

The physical connection for TOPS is Apple's LocalTalk, which is built into the Macintosh, or Ethernet. TOPS supports several LocalTalk cards for PCs, including their own TOPS FlashCard. TOPS also runs on PCs with 3Com Ethernet cards and on Macintoshes with Ethernet cards or adapters from Kinetics, Apple, and 3Com.

Any station can become a file server by "publishing" one or more "volumes." You can publish one or more disks or directories as volumes available to other users. When you publish a volume you can restrict access to it by assigning it a password. TOPS security also allows you to declare that a published volume is read/write or read-only. Macintosh users can add an additional level of security to their volumes published as read/write. Mac users can specify "one writer only" or "many writers." If "one writer only" is specified, the first user to access the disk will be able to write to it, while subsequent users will only be able to read.

TOPS allows any station to share Apple printers on the network, and also allows PC users to publish their local printers for use by other PC users. TOPS provides print spooling to shared and nonshared printers.

Novell NetWare

Novell's NetWare was the first true file server system available for PC LANs. Originally written for Novell's proprietary S-Net file servers and network interface cards, NetWare now runs on a number of file server platforms, including IBM XTs, ATs, PS/2s and compatibles, and Digital Equipment Corporation's VAX minicomputers. Other minicomputer platforms will be supported by Portable NetWare.

NetWare drivers are available for nearly all network interface cards currently available for PCs. This includes nearly all brands of ARCNET, Ethernet, Token-Ring, and proprietary LANs such as Proteon's

ProNet, Gateway Communications' G-Net, Racore's LANPAC II, and others.

NetWare currently supports DOS, OS/2, and Macintosh workstations, with support for UNIX workstations forthcoming.

NetWare was designed and optimized as file server and network management software, and uses a proprietary directory and file structure that is designed for quick file access. To PC users, however, it appears as a DOS structure. NetWare file servers and volumes have names, not drive letters. "Logical Drive Pointers"—alias file servers, volumes, and directories as DOS drives—provide easy, transparent access to any attached file server, volume, or directory. NetWare allows volume sizes up to 255MB, and up to 2GB storage per file server.

NetWare enhances file server disk access by using the following techniques:

- **File Caching**. Files read from disk are retained in server memory for future access until the memory space occupied is needed by newly-read data.

  NetWare sets aside a certain number of 4K blocks of server memory for file caching (the number of blocks depends on the amount of available server RAM). As blocks of data are read from disk, they are placed into the cache area. Each time a block is read from disk into cache, it is time stamped. Each time a "cache block" is accessed by a read or write, its time stamp is updated.

- **Directory Caching**. NetWare directories are kept in memory in the file server, eliminating the need to access disks for directory lookups.

- **Directory Hashing**. NetWare builds and maintains indexes or "hash tables" in file server RAM for all directory entries. When a file is requested, NetWare looks up the requested file in a hash table, rather than sequentially searching the directory.

- **Elevator Seeking**. When multiple requests to read data from a file server disk are pending, NetWare sorts the requests and prioritizes them based on the current read/write head position. Data is then retrieved based on the disk track and sector location, relative to the current head position, instead of the order in which the data was requested.

  For example, with three requests pending, if data for the third request is closest to the current position of the disk's read/write heads, and in the current direction of travel, that data will be retrieved first. If data for the second request is the next closest in the direction of travel, that data will be retrieved next, etc. Elevator seeking optimizes head movement and results in high throughput with multiple disk access requests.

- **Hot Fix**. If a bad block is detected on a file server disk during a write operation, Hot Fix moves the data to another area of the disk, then records that block's location in the disk's bad block table.

NetWare Security

NetWare provides very high levels of security and access control. File server access is controlled by a user name and password. The system keeps a security profile of each user and only allows access to directories at security levels assigned by the system supervisor.

Passwords on NetWare file servers are encrypted. This allows a user to have the same login name and password on different servers (with different supervisors) without compromising security. The system supervisor can require users to have passwords, specify a minimum password length, and require users to change their passwords at given intervals. NetWare provides an optional intruder detection and lockout function. When a specified number of incorrect login attempts are made with a given user login name, the user account is locked for a specified period of time.

Internetworking

Using NetWare's bridging functions, similar and/or dissimilar networks can be connected in a single file server or through external bridges. Up to 100 file servers can be used in a network or internetwork, and a user can attach up to 8 at a time. SNA, Async, 5251, X.25, and other gateways are provided by Novell and other manufacturers.

NetWare does not currently have the type of global naming capabilities available in Banyan's VINES or 3Com's 3+, however Novell has committed to providing this capability, probably in late 1989 or early 1990.

Network Printing

NetWare provides extensive support for using and managing shared network printers. Each NetWare file server supports up to five attached, spooled printers. As of version 2.1, NetWare supports third-party print server software that allows network stations to be used as print servers (See *Appendix B—Network Utilities*). NetWare for Macintosh allows AppleTalk printers to be used by NetWare PC users. (See *Appendix C—NetWare for the Macintosh*).

NetWare supports multiple print queues, and multiple queues can service a printer (even at different priorities), and multiple printers can be serviced by a single queue. The system supervisor can designate who can use a particular queue or who can manage a queue.

NetWare provides extensive printer and print queue management capabilities. The PrintDef and PrintCon utilities allow you to create print job definitions so that printer initialization and reset strings can be sent with each print job.

Additional Features

The NetWare 2.1x operating system and workstation shells keep track of a wide range of information concerning network traffic. Tools such as NetWare Care from Novell, Monitrix from Cheyenne Software and NWRanger from SARBEC can monitor or report much of this information. (See *Appendix B—Network Utilities*, for more information).

System supervisors and other designated users can file server resource usage, including disk space and memory usage, file server traffic information, disk caching statistics, and much more with the FConsole utility. FConsole also allows console operators to perform certain management operations at their desk that once had to be performed at the file server.

NetWare Versions

As of this writing, the following versions of Netware are available:

Advanced NetWare 286 requires a 286 or 386 AT compatible PC as a file server. Advanced NetWare can be used in dedicated or nondedicated (file server as workstation) mode, and it supports all available features and functions listed above. Advanced Netware supports 1,000 open files per file server, 100 concurrently attached users, 15MB of file server RAM and 2GB of disk. As of this writing, the latest version is 2.15.

In addition to the features and functions provided by Advanced NetWare 286, SFT NetWare 286 adds disk mirroring or duplexing and, optionally, transaction tracking.

Disk mirroring allows one disk drive to duplicate another. All data is written to both simultaneously. If the first drive fails, the second drive takes over with no loss of data. The defective disk can then be removed for repair or replacement.

Disk duplexing is similar to disk mirroring, except the entire disk channel, including controller(s), is duplicated. Duplexing is usually implemented using two of Novell's disk coprocessor boards (DCBs). The DCB is an intelligent disk interface that off-loads many disk access tasks from the file server's CPU. A DCB can improve overall disk access performance.

SFT also allows you to implement the Transaction Tracking System (TTS). TTS, when properly implemented, will back-out uncompleted database updates in the case of an accidental shutdown of a workstation or file server. This means that only the update will be lost, and the integrity of the database will be maintained.

SFT NetWare will not run in a nondedicated mode. As of this writing, the latest version is 2.15.

Advanced NetWare 68 is for Novell's proprietary 68B file server. In other ways similar in capability to Advanced NetWare 286, NetWare 68 supports up to 4,000 open files, 254 concurrently attached users, and up to 8MB file server RAM. The current (and probably last) version is 2.1. Novell will be discontinuing direct support of the 68B, and has licensed the technology to another company.

ELS NetWare 286 Level I is a four-user version of NetWare (ELS stands for Entry Level System). ELS I requires an AT-compatible 286/386 file server in nondedicated mode, and does not support bridging or internetworking. ELS 286 Level I supports a limited number of network interface cards. Since ELS I is a version of NetWare 2.0a, many of the features and functions outlined above are not available. (See *Appendix D—Installing ELS NetWare.*)

ELS NetWare 286/2 Level I is a version of ELS Level I that requires an IBM PS/2 model 50, 60 or 80 as a file server, and only supports IBM's PCN II network cards.

ELS NetWare Level II is similar to Advanced NetWare 286, but does not support bridging or internetworking, and supports a maximum of eight concurrent users. ELS level II can be installed in two modes:

> In dedicated mode, ELS II will run on an 8088/8086 file server supporting a maximum of 640K RAM. This effectively limits file server disk space to about 70MB.
>
> In nondedicated mode, ELS II requires a 286/386 file server, supporting up to 15MB of file server memory and 2GB of disk.

Level II is currently shipping version 2.12, with a 2.15 version expected in mid-1989.

NetWare for Macintosh is a VAP that allows Apple Macintosh computers to access a NetWare server as if it were an AppleTalk server. Netware resources appear to Macintosh users as AppleTalk server resources. NetWare for Macintosh adds NetWare security, fault tolerance and print spooling functions to Appletalk networks and also gives PC users access to Apple printers. NetWare for Macintosh requires NetWare version 2.15 or above.

NetWare VMS runs on a DEC VAX minicomputer as a task under DEC's VMS operating system and uses the VMS file system. PCs on a LAN can access VMS files as if they are DOS files. This means that some applications running under DOS and VMS can access the same data files.

NetWare VMS provides software that emulates DEC terminals. Users on a NetWare LAN can access the VAX as a NetWare file server with DOS or OS/2 or as a VMS user through terminal emulation.

The major purpose of NetWare VMS is to provide connectivity between the NetWare DOS and OS/2 environments and the VAX/VMS environment. NetWare VMS runs as a task under the VMS operating system, and therefore does not communicate directly with the VAX hardware. In effect, NetWare is a guest operating system. In comparison to NetWare on a 286/386 file server, performance will be slow due to the additional overhead that the VMS operating system adds.

NetWare VMS, currently shipping as version 2.01, does not include all of the features of other current NetWare versions, such as Macintosh support and some of the enhanced print spooling functions.

The following versions of NetWare have been announced but are not yet available:

NetWare 386

NetWare 386 3.0, announced by Novell for release in the third quarter of 1989, is a 32-bit network operating system designed to take full advantage of the 80386 processor. NetWare 386 will support up to 250 concurrent users, 100,000 concurrently open files, 32TB (terabytes) of disk space per server, 32 logical drives per volume, 4GB maximum file size (for a single file spanning multiple physical drives) and up to 4GB of RAM. NetWare 386 is said to provide two to three times the performance of previous versions.

NetWare 386 introduces fundamental changes to NetWare's structure. Among these changes is the introduction of an open software bus to which server applications can be dynamically linked to provide added services. These NetWare Loadable Modules (NLMs) include the NetWare core services, file and print service, as well as database services, communications services, messaging, etc. NLMs also replace the VAPs found in current NetWare versions. Novell is making the interface specifications for NLMs available so that third parties can write applications.

Although not fully implemented in the initial NetWare 386 release, NetWare Streams will provide support for multiple concurrent protocols running as NLMs, including Novell's own NetWare Core Protocols (NCP), Apple File Protocols (AFP), Transmission Control Protocol/Internet Protocol (TCP/IP), Sun Microsystems Network File System (NFS), Trancendental Network Operating System (TOPS), and IBM's Service Message Block (SMB) protocols for OS/2. This will allow direct file server access from Macintoshes, UNIX workstations, etc., instead of the gateway approach currently used. (With the current NetWare for Macintosh, Macintosh users access a NetWare server through a translator called the Service Protocol Gateway. See *Appendix C—NetWare for Macintosh.*)

Other enhancements include:

- New print services, with support for up to sixteen shared printers attached to the file server and workstations, enhanced print queue management from any workstation, and notification of print job completion.

- Passwords that are encrypted at the workstation so that they cannot be intercepted on the cable.

- The ability to assign access rights to individual files as well as to directories.

- Multiple file names, allowing files to be named appropriately for each environment (DOS, Macintosh, UNIX, etc.) that might access them.

NetWare 386 introduces the ability to alter the server's configuration without taking the server down and reinstalling it. Addition disk drives can be installed on-line, and even added to existing volumes. Many file server parameters that used to be set during installation are dynamically adjusted according to network usage. Such dynamic resource configuration includes memory allocation for file and directory caching, file handles, and routing buffers.

A second release—version 3.1—is scheduled for the spring of 1990. Version 3.1 includes a number of enhancements, including:

- support for multiple concurrent protocol stacks running as NLMs, including AFP and optionally TCP/IP

- support for multiple inter-process communications protocols, including Novell's Sequenced Packet Exchange, (SPX), NetBIOS, Named Pipes and Transport Level Interface (TLI)

- enhanced file system support, including OS/2 1.2 and CD ROM and WORM drives

Novell also announced a collection of development tools for 3.1, including a native-mode 386 C compiler and the NetWare RPC (remote procedure call) software. The native-mode compiler allows development of server-based applications that are not constrained by the memory segmentation requirements of 8086 compilers. NetWare RPC generates source code for both the client and server portions of a server-based application.

Portable NetWare

Portable Netware, which is based on NetWare 386, is designed to run as a task under other operating systems, such as UNIX. It will be sold to other manufacturers, who will then "port" it to their own operating systems. A number of minicomputer vendors, including Prime and UNISYS, have announced that they will provide Portable NetWare to their customers. Novell has indicated that a version of Portable NetWare will probably be made available for the IBM AS400, and future releases of NetWare VMS will be based on Portable NetWare.

7

Choosing LAN Hardware

Choosing a network and its components is a balancing act. You will have to weigh the factors of performance, cost, compatibility, adherence to standards, reliability, etc.

You, as system integrator and designer, must balance the components of the system to achieve optimum performance for your investment. Choosing low-performance workstations, for example, could cancel out the benefits that a high-performance file server could provide. The world's fastest LAN hardware will rarely, if ever, compensate for a poorly written application (although faster hardware is usually the way people try to solve this particular problem).

The many factors to consider when selecting LAN hardware and software can probably be summarized in the question: "Will the system you select provide the functionality and performance you need cost-effectively now and in the future?"

Which Comes First?

You have three primary choices to make for a PC LAN: cabling, LAN hardware, and LAN operating systems. There is no hard and fast rule about which you must choose first, and with today's mix and match environment, it is getting more difficult to make a serious mistake.

In many cases, your specific requirements will help make choices for you. Internetworking requirements, the use of specialized equipment, company standards, etc., can all dictate your choices.

If you need a particular application, your other choices need to support that application. With PC LANs, applications software will rarely dictate cabling or LAN hardware, but might dictate a particular LAN operating system, which might in turn dictate your hardware and cabling choices.

If you need to use existing cabling, or if the physical layout of your building(s) makes a particular cabling type or topology more appropriate, choose cabling first, then find LAN hardware that supports your other needs. Sometimes making use of existing cabling can save money, and it might guide your choice of network hardware. Existing cabling, however, is not always appropriate for networking and it can deteriorate over time.

If your chosen LAN operating system supports multiple hardware types, such as Novell NetWare, Banyan VINES or CBIS Network OS, and you are not constrained by other factors, you have the freedom (or the problem) of multiple choices when it comes to LAN hardware.

Particular communications needs may guide your choice of LAN hardware. A need to support UNIX workstations or DEC minicomputers may steer you toward Ethernet, while connectivity with IBM mainframes may steer you toward the Token Ring.

If there currently are (or will be) other LANs installed in your organization you can assume that they will someday be connected. Maintaining consistency where that is feasible can often prevent interconnection problems later on.

Budget constraints are often a major factor in LAN selection. One warning: avoid the temptation to "get by" with less than what you really need. This approach can result in disastrously unworkable systems.

Company policies or standards can sometimes dictate specific cabling, LAN hardware, LAN operating system(s), or applications. If this is the case, your job just got easier (or harder). It got easier because your choices are limited, but it got harder if the company standards do not allow you the flexibility to get the job done. If the latter is true, you have two choices: find a way around the standards, or don't get the job done.

LANs almost always grow, and as they grow they change. Changes in the LAN will change the way you and other LAN users work, again changing the LAN. You need to be ready to deal with change as it comes by making choices that allow for expansion, upgrades, and modification as your needs change.

Performance

Many factors affect LAN performance, and proponents and vendors of leading LAN hardware and software products all claim best performance for their favorite systems or products.

The performance focus is most often on the LAN network interface hardware, but LAN hardware is only part of the overall performance issue, and in many cases not even a major part. Nearly any of the popular types of LAN hardware will provide more than adequate performance in a typical office environment.

Factors that affect LAN performance include:

- **Cable Access Method**. The cable access method used by the LAN hardware will affect performance. All other things being equal (which, of course, they never are), contention methods are more effective on lightly loaded networks, while token-passing methods may be more appropriate for high-traffic situations. Both methods are consistently reliable and perform adequately in the average office environment.

- **Raw Data Transfer Rate**. Although the raw data transfer rate is the most often quoted performance factor, it does not always reflect the actual throughput of the network. Other factors such as board design and LAN operating system are equally important.

- **Network Interface Card (NIC) Design**. Various factors affect the performance of network interfaces, including:

  Onboard Processors. Although it would seem that onboard processors would necessarily improve NIC performance, this is not necessarily the case. In fact, with many of today's faster CPUs, some onboard NIC processors cannot keep up with the speed of the host machine. In addition, poorly written firmware (software in a ROM chip on the NIC) can create extra overhead. The mere presence of an onboard processor does not guarantee higher performance, although some boards do use them effectively.

  NIC to Host Transfer Method. One of the most critical factors in NIC performance is the method used to transfer data to and from the host computer. There are three methods used to transfer data between a NIC and PC; shared memory, direct memory access (DMA), and a shared input/output (I/O) port. The details of these methods are beyond the scope of this book, but in general, DMA is the slowest method, shared memory is the fastest, and using I/O ports is somewhere in the middle.

Bus Interface. The physical interface of the NIC is important. A 16-bit, PC AT-type interface, for example, can potentially transfer data at twice the rate of an 8-bit PC-type interface. This could be important for file servers, database servers, graphics workstations, etc.

Priority Schemes. Priority schemes allow certain nodes on the network to have more access than other nodes. The 802.5 Token Ring specification, for example, includes provisions for a priority scheme. Standard Microsystems currently provides an ARCNET board with "Nodal Priority," which can send packets to more than one station before passing the token. File servers and database servers in busy networks might benefit from this.

LAN Driver Software. Poorly written LAN drivers can destroy the performance of the fastest boards.

Consider the use to which the board will be put in evaluating performance. The NIC in a file server, bridge or gateway will generally handle much higher traffic loads than the NIC in a user's workstation. Factors such as larger RAM buffers, on-board processors, wider data buses (16 bit vs. 8-bit) and *nodal Priority* (a priority scheme used on some ARCNET boards) can be important here.

- **File Server Performance**. In the past, file server performance has been over-emphasized. However, with the advent of file server-based applications and secondary processes (such as Novell's Value Added Processes), file server performance is becoming more of a real issue.

- **Disk Channel**. This consists of file server hard disks, controllers, interfaces, coprocessors, etc. With the advent of faster server hardware and more efficient LAN operating systems, the disk channel is becoming more of a performance bottleneck.

- **LAN Operating System**. In a PC LAN, this is one of the most important performance factors. A LAN operating system (OS) needs to be optimized to allow multiple users quick, concurrent access to shared resources.

- **Workstation Performance**. Application processing takes place at workstations on a PC LAN. A high-speed 286 CPU will definitely outperform a low-speed 8088 CPU.

- **Application Software**. In the short history of computing, millions and millions of dollars worth of faster hardware have been purchased in attempts to solve problems caused by poorly written application software. Unfortunately, the only major benefit this approach usually has is to put a few extra million dollars in the pockets of hardware vendors.

Perhaps the best way to benchmark LAN performance in an office environment is to measure productivity gains. This means seeing how you work with your PCs and how much LAN performance will affect productivity. Some examples:

1. A secretary spends an average of thirty minutes editing a six-page document. With a "faster" LAN, the document can be saved in five seconds. With a "slower" LAN the document can be saved in eight seconds. On balance, does the faster LAN provide any real productivity gain?

2. A clerk enters an average of 100 transactions into an accounting application. It takes approximately thirty seconds to enter each transaction. On a "faster" LAN, it takes five seconds to save each transaction, while it takes eight seconds on the "slower"

LAN. The whole process on the faster LAN would take 58-1/3 minutes, while it would take 63-1/3 minutes on the slower LAN. That's a time savings of five minutes per 100 transactions. If we extended this to a full eight hour day, that is approximately forty minutes per day saved.

3. A researcher needs to run several database queries a day, using a number of selection and sorting criteria. The average query takes approximately ten minutes on the "faster" LAN, and approximately fifteen minutes on the "slower" LAN. In an eight hour day the researcher could run forty-eight queries on the faster LAN, but only thirty-two queries on the slower one.

These are hypothetical examples. While they don't reflect real performance measurements, they should serve to illustrate the point that the effect of LAN speed on real productivity depends significantly on other factors. The issue of performance is sometimes complex, and LAN hardware may or may not be a significant factor in any given situation.

Selecting Specific LAN Components

Besides choosing types of cabling systems, LAN OSs, and hardware, you will still have to choose specific components. These components include network interface cards (NICs), hubs, repeaters, bridges, etc. You will also need to select power backup systems, tape drives, and the computers that will become file servers and workstations.

For the major LAN types, similar components are available from numerous manufacturers. There are currently over forty manufacturers of 802.3 Ethernet products, over fifteen manufacturers of 802.5 Token Ring products, and over 100 manufacturers of ARCNET products. Within the various product categories you must select products from specific vendors, and you may find differences in price, performance, LAN software support, etc.

A Note on LAN Market Share

There is vast disagreement in the industry about the installed base of various LAN types. Most of the studies quoted in the press seem to suggest that Ethernet currently leads the pack, followed by 802.5 Token Ring, with everything else lumped into a distant third.

The problem with most of the studies is that they are based on interviews with MIS directors and data communications managers in Fortune 1,000 firms. Unfortunately, data communications and MIS directors in large corporations are often completely unaware of LANs that are not directly connected to their mini- and mainframe computers.

In addition, not all LANs are installed in large companies. In smaller firms ARCNET and Ethernet seem to predominate.

Why is market share important to LAN purchasers? Popularity provides a degree of insurance. Popular LANs attract numerous manufacturers, increasing the available choices: more bridges and gateways, more protocol and hardware support, etc. Popular LANs will get more media attention and more documentation. Experienced consultants are more prevalent. Even cost can become a factor since in more competitive markets product prices tend to drop.

Selection Criteria

Factors to consider when selecting LAN hardware include:

- **Performance**. While LAN performance isn't the only factor to consider, it is in many cases an important one. Various factors contribute to LAN Hardware performance, including cable access method, data transfer rate and NIC design.

- **LAN OS and protocol support**. If the LAN hardware doesn't support your chosen OS and/or protocols, it is useless to you.

- **Adherence to standards**. Standards are important, but should not be allowed to get in the way of getting the job done. In most cases, the popular "standard" LAN systems will suffice, but don't rule out proprietary approaches to meet specific needs. Often proprietary LAN implementations, such as Proteon's Pronet 10 and Pronet 80, or Racore's LANPAC II, can provide far greater performance than their "standard" counterparts.

- **Vendor stability**. It is important to have some method of dealing with warranty and/or nonwarranty repairs and support. If the manufacturer goes out of business, this may prove difficult.

ARCNET

ARCNET is inexpensive, easy to install and easy to troubleshoot, and it provides a great deal of cabling flexibility, supporting a broad range of cable types (coax, UTP and fiber optics), and a choice of topologies (star cluster, linear, daisy-chain). Because of its logical token-passing access method, ARCNET provides consistent performance under load. Because of its lower overhead, ARCNET performance at 2.5 Mbits/sec. compares favorably with Token Ring at 4 Mbits/sec.

Although ARCNET interfaces are available for various mini- and microcomputer expansion buses (including the PC and AT bus, Microchannel, Multi-Bus, STD bus, and the NUBUS used in the Macintosh II and SE), very little, if any, operating software is available to connect non-PC type systems to your PC ARCNET LAN.

One advantage of ARCNET is that virtually all manufacturers' products work with each other. Most currently available ARCNET products seem to be very reliable and the performance of most standard PC bus ARCNET boards seems to be about the same. In fact, most ARCNET boards are so close in design that they even use the same software drivers.

With over a hundred vendors marketing ARCNET products, competition is fierce, and ARCNET boards have dropped dramatically in price in the last few years.

If you are planning to use plain 8-bit coaxial cable (coax) ARCNET boards, use the general criteria above. There are some unique ARCNET boards to consider as well, including:

- High Impedance ARCNET boards that are designed to be used in a linear bus configuration. Up to eight of these boards can be connected in a linear bus with coax cables and "Tee" connectors. The bus must either be terminated at both ends with 93 ohm terminating resistors, or on one end with an active hub and the other with a terminating resistor.

- UTP ARCNET that is designed to use standard telephone wire. UTP ARCNET is cabled in a combination star-cluster and daisy-chain configuration, allowing a great deal of flexibility. Up to eight boards can be daisy-chained together. Like high impedance coax boards, UTP ARCNET buses must be terminated at both ends, either with two 100 ohm terminating resistors or one resistor and a UTP active hub.

In addition to flexibility, UTP ARCNET seems to be very forgiving about nonstandard cable types (not recommended or guaranteed, however).

- Sixteen-bit ARCNET cards that can sometimes provide an increase in performance due to the wider data bus.
- Nodal priority boards installed in file servers, routers, and gateways that can sometimes improve overall performance. A nodal priority board can send packets to multiple stations before passing the token.

ARCNET can use a variety of hubs and links for coax, UTP, and fiber optics:

- Standard coax active hubs usually have eight ports, although some manufacturers provide 16-port hubs. The newer hubs from Standard Microsystems and others include a special, separate RJ-11 port for linking adjacent hubs together. This not only saves a port on each hub, it makes for easier connections between coax and UTP hubs.
- Several vendors, such as Network Innovations Corporation, supply four-port active hubs that are inserted into a PC bus and use the PC's power supply.

  These hubs generally cost less than standard hubs, but the host PC must be turned on for them to function.

  Network Innovations supplies a chassis that will hold up to eight hubs linked together internally, effectively providing up to 32 ports in a single box.

- UTP Active Hubs generally have eight RJ-11 modular connectors. They function just like their coax counterparts.

- Passive hubs have four ports and can be used with standard coax boards for limited distances.

- Active provide connections between coax, UTP and/or fiber optic ARCNET products. Coax-to-coax active links can be used to extend a network.

- UTP-to-coax baluns (cable matching devices) designed for use with IBM 3270 terminals are a very effective way of using standard ARCNET coax products on UTP cable. The baluns should be of high quality, and should never be connected to UTP hubs or boards.

802.3 (Ethernet)

The 802.3 Ethernet-type network probably has the widest industry support. If there is a computer of significance to business, industry, government, or science, there is probably an Ethernet interface for it, and software to allow it to interact with other, similar and dissimilar computers. Ethernet currently provides a wide range of cabling options, including coax, UTP, and fiber optics. Depending on cabling type, Ethernet can be cabled in a variety of topologies.

Ethernet currently provides the widest support of any LAN type for multiple protocols, including Sun's NFS, Xerox's XNS, TCP/IP, and Novell's IPX/SPX. In addition, nearly all major PC LAN operating systems support Ethernet.

The data transfer rate is a relatively fast 10 Mbits/sec.

Because of Ethernet's CSMA/CA access scheme, the network has the potential of reaching a saturation point in high traffic situations. In real life, however, this is rarely a major problem.

Locating faults with the standard linear Ethernet topology can often be difficult, It can be somewhat easier, however, with the star cluster topology used in most UTP implementations.

Ethernet Hardware

There is wide variation in Ethernet boards from different manufacturers.

Hardware differences include the NIC-to-host data transfer method and the use of onboard processors. Board makers can use Ethernet chip sets from several different manufacturers, and they all have different performance specifications.

While most current Ethernet boards for PCs have both an internal transceiver with a BNC coax connector and a DB 15 connector to attach to an external transceiver, some boards only have one or the other, providing less flexibility. Boards are also currently available with a built-in UTP transceiver.

Some manufacturers provide software drivers for only one or two LAN OSs or protocols, while others supply drivers for many. Some manufacturers supply multiple-protocol drivers, allowing the use of two or more LAN OSs or protocols simultaneously on the same station.

Most Ethernet boards require their own specific software. Many of the boards built using the National Semiconductor chip set are virtual clones of Novell's NE-1000 Ethernet card, and can use Novell's drivers.

Ethernet Connections: Transceivers, Repeaters, Bridges, and Routers

A transceiver is required to connect any device to an Ethernet cable. Most Ethernet boards for PCs have built-in transceivers for thin coax.

Repeaters are used to extend Ethernet networks. Separate network segments connected with repeaters in effect become one physical network, with all traffic, including collisions, being broadcast to all network nodes. Bridges and routers filter traffic, only passing data from one LAN that is addressed to another. This means that local traffic stays local, providing for less overall traffic on each bridged LAN. As discussed earlier, bridges generally work at the hardware level (Ethernet to Ethernet), while routers work at the protocol, or low-level software level (IPX to IPX, XNS to XNS, etc.).

Ethernet Repeaters generally fit into two categories: single-port, which connect two LAN segments, and multiport, which connect multiple LAN segments in parallel. In addition, repeaters are available with Attach Unit Interface (AUI) connectors, fiber optic connectors, and connectors for thin coax (RG-58). When selecting repeaters, consider your probable expansion needs.

Consider bridges and routers when most LAN traffic can be confined to logical sub-nets, such as workgroups. In general, consider bridges when multiple protocols are in use on the LAN, and use routers to connect dissimilar LAN types (such as ARCNET to Ethernet) with a specific protocol.

Since many LAN operating systems, such as Novell's NetWare and Banyan's VINES, have built-in routing functions, routing can be a very cost effective approach to internetworking. NetWare even includes software to allow PCs other than a file server to function as a router (this is called the *External Bridge* software).

By segmenting traffic, routers and bridges can improve overall LAN performance, but they can create bottlenecks if they are used improperly.

Protocol support, performance, cost, and vendor support are some of the major issues to consider when you are selecting these products.

UTP concentrators (sometimes called hubs) connect multiple UTP Ethernet transceivers or boards to a coax or fiber-optic "backbone" network, and/or to other concentrators. As of this writing, the IEEE has not adopted a standard for UTP Ethernet, so check with the manufacturers to make sure that the boards or transceivers that you plan to use will connect to your selected concentrator(s).

802.5 Token Passing Ring

The 802.5 Token Passing Ring, usually called the IBM Token Ring or just the Token Ring, is becoming widely implemented in Fortune 1,000 companies. Because of IBM's support of the system, this is probably a good choice for companies with IBM mainframes and minicomputers.

A major advantage of Token Ring is that its token passing access method provides consistent performance under load. Although the raw data transfer rate is a relatively slow 4 Mbit/sec., IBM and other vendors have announced a 16 Mbit/sec. version.

On the down side, the Token Ring is relatively expensive, and the fact that every node on the LAN acts as a repeater means that there are multiple points of possible failure or data corruption.

Most 802.5 Token Ring boards (except IBM's) use a chip set manufactured by Texas Instruments. Nearly every manufacturer's Token Ring board requires its own driver software. Some of the primary differences in PC token ring boards include the bus interface (8-bit, 16-bit, etc.), the quality of the driver software, and the cost. Some boards, such as those from Gateway Communications, include a built-in media filter and RJ-45 connector for use with UTP cable.

Token Ring MAUs

Stations attach to the Token Ring through the Multistation Access Unit (MAU). The MAU is a connection device that automatically adds stations to the ring when the power up, and automatically bypasses them when they power down. The MAU is really a relay box: when a station powers up it sends a DC signal to the MAU, tripping a relay that attaches that station to the ring. When the station powers down, the DC signal stops and the relay bypasses that station.

IBM's standard MAUs have eight ports and are designed to be mounted in a rack. Other vendors provide both stand-alone and rack-mountable MAUs. Rack mounted MAUs are generally preferable when all cabling goes to a central wiring closet, while stand-alones are most often used in a distributed-star arrangement. In addition to eight-port MAUs, several vendors supply four-port models.

MAUs are available specifically for use with UTP cable. Instead of the bulky IBM "hermaphrodite" connector, these MAUs have an RJ-45 modular connector.

Other Choices

The most popular LANs are not necessarily the best performers, especially given special needs. Other LAN types could still prove to be the network of choice to meet special compatibility or performance needs of your environment.

Broadband Networks

There are situations in which broadband networks are more appropriate than the baseband networks we have discussed. Baseband networks allow for a single signal on a LAN cable at a time. Broadband provides the ability for multiple logical networks to share the same cable set at different frequencies, much like cable TV allows multiple TV channels to share the same cable set. In fact, this analogy is a good one because broadband networks use cable TV technology.

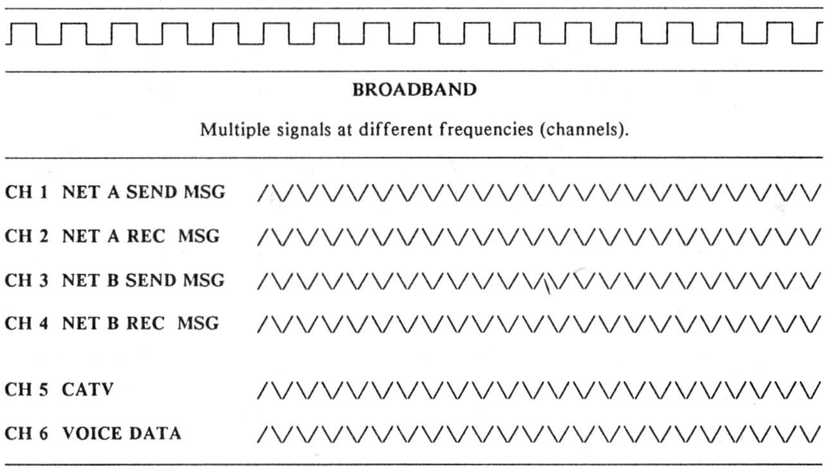

BROADBAND

Multiple signals at different frequencies (channels).

CH 1 NET A SEND MSG

CH 2 NET A REC MSG

CH 3 NET B SEND MSG

CH 4 NET B REC MSG

CH 5 CATV

CH 6 VOICE DATA

Because of the high initial design, and engineering and installation costs, broadband networks are primarily used in large buildings or campuses. College campuses, large manufacturing facilities, and large, single-company office buildings are candidates for broadband LANS.

Broadband networks usually require administrators with a high degree of technical skill, and the network will usually require more maintenance and attention than a baseband LAN.

Cabling Choices

Your choice of cabling is going to be determined by your choice of LAN hardware, or vice versa. Some of the tradeoffs of various cabling types are outlined below.

Unshielded Twisted Pair (UTP)

Unshielded Twisted Pair cable is probably the least expensive cable type available. UTP, generally refers to standard telephone wire that conforms to AT&T's specification for "D Inside Wire" (DIW).

UTP has a number of advantages: it is already installed in buildings, it is inexpensive, and it can be used for many different voice and data communication needs. UTP is currently supported by Ethernet, ARCNET, Token Ring, Apple's LocalTalk, and other LANs. Because of the standard star-wiring scheme of UTP (all lines usually go to a central wiring closet), fault isolation is relatively easy compared to linear topologies.

On the down side, it is relatively susceptible to interference (from, for example, fluorescent lights, electric motors, etc.), it does not support some of the higher data rates of coax or shielded twisted pair, and will generally allow shorter cable runs.

Advantages of UTP include:

- low cost
- easy to install
- allows for flexible configuration (when star-wired)

- same cable type supports many LANs and other data and voice communications systems.

Disadvantages include:

- greater susceptibility to noise than coax or shielded twisted pair
- may not support higher data transmission rates
- length of runs limited

Shielded Twisted Pair

Shielded Twisted Pair cable consists of one or more wire pairs surrounded by a foil or mesh shield, then surrounded by a vinyl or teflon jacket. A shielded, dual twisted-pair cable is the cable usually used with Token Ring networks, will support higher transmission rates than UTP, and generally runs longer distances.

Advantages of shielded twisted pair include:

- less susceptibility to noise than UTP
- supports higher data transmission rates than UTP
- easier to work with (sometimes) than coax

Disadvantages include:

- expensive to purchase
- expensive to install

Coaxial Cable

Coaxial cable is usually referred to as *coax*; until recently this has been the most common cable type used for LANS. Coax is less susceptible to interference than UTP, can generally be run for longer distances, and can support higher data transmission rates. In general, coax is required for broadband networks.

Due to the high cost of the concentrators and transceivers needed in UTP networks, coax networks can prove to be less expensive than UTP networks, even though coax cable is more expensive than UTP cable.

Coax cable is physically more difficult to install that UTP, and different LANs require different types of coax, which makes moving from one LAN type to another difficult.

Advantages of coax include:

- supports higher speeds at greater distances than UTP
- less susceptible to noise and interference than UTP
- thin coax (RG-58, RG-59, RG-62) is usually less expensive than shielded twisted-pair data cable.

Disadvantages include:

- easily damaged
- difficult to work with
- more expensive than UTP
- specific coax types required by different LANs

Fiber Optics

Fiber optic cable has several advantages over copper cable, including support of vastly higher data transmission rates, no susceptibility to electrical interference, and support of longer cabling distances.

Fiber optics is currently one of the most expensive cabling choices, and is generally more difficult to install.

Advantages of fiber optics include:

- no susceptibility to electrical interference
- difficult (but not impossible) to tap
- potentially very high data rates

- supports longer cabling distances than copper

Disadvantages include:

- expensive
- difficult to install, easy to damage

Selecting File Servers and Server Components

The file server is the heart of your PC LAN. It provides controlled access to files, shared printers, and other LAN resources. File servers can be specialized, proprietary computers designed to work with a specific manufacturer's hardware and software (such as Novell's former 68B server or 3Com's 3Server), or a general purpose computer, such as a 80286 or 80386 PC. A minicomputer, such as a DEC VAX, can also be used as a file server in many situations.

General-purpose personal computers are most commonly used as file servers in PC LANs. A general purpose microcomputer usually costs significantly less than a proprietary system, and has the added advantage of not locking you in to one vendor's hardware and software.

If you are going to use a general-purpose computer as a file server, there are some basic rules to follow:

- The server must be compatible with your selected network operating system. LAN OSs like Novell's NetWare 286 use the "protected mode" of an 80286 processor. Machines that have no problem running DOS applications may not be able to handle your chosen LAN OS.

- The server must have sufficient processing power to handle the tasks required by your LAN. In the past, fast file servers for small LANs were often unnecessary. With the advent of file servers running multiple tasks, however, fast file servers are becoming increasingly important.

- The server must have sufficient expansion capability to handle any required network interface cards, RAM expansion boards, and other required hardware. Trying to put four boards into three slots can be a somewhat frustrating problem.

- File server hard disks must be supported by your chosen operating system. Not all LAN OSs support all disk drive/disk controller combinations.

File Servers for NetWare

Most current model 286/386 PCs and compatibles seem to function as NetWare file servers. Some may not, however, and some may have limitations. So don't assume that a particular machine is suitable for your needs. If you are in doubt, Novell has a certification program for file servers. Just because a particular machine is not certified, however, does not mean that it is incompatible. Many vendors have chosen not to pay for the certification. If you are planning to use a non-certified machine you should attempt to obtain a written warranty from the manufacturer or dealer stating that it will function as intended in your system.

Many 286 compatibility problems are due to ROM BIOS code. Sometimes exchanging the original ROM BIOS chips for new ones from vendors such as Phoenix, Award, or AMI can solve a compatibility problem.

For most smaller offices, 80286-based servers are usually more than adequate. If you plan to install a number of VAPs in your server, or you have a large system with lots of traffic a fast 80386-based server would probably be a better choice.

VAPs are becoming increasingly common. Each active VAP uses server CPU time and can affect overall server performance.

A file server running NetWare 2.12 or later with 70MB of disk has the following minimum expansion requirements (*Note*: these are general guidelines):

- At least 2MB of RAM, or 2.5MB with a nondedicated server. If you are planning to use VAPs, or add more disk capacity, you will need additional RAM. Reserve enough expansion slots for future needs.

  Note: NetWare servers require Extended Memory, not Expanded Memory. Extended memory is 80286 "protected mode" memory, or memory above 1MB, and expanded memory, often refered to as EMS or LIM/EMS memory, is "bank switched" memory used by Lotus 1-2-3, SuperCalc, and other programs.

- Expansion slots for hard disk and floppy disk controllers. If you are using a Novell Disk coprocessor or other specialized disk interface, this means at least two slots. If you are planning to implement SFT NetWare with disk duplexing, you will need another slot for an additional disk coprocessor.

- Expansion slots for each NIC required. Depending on your configuration, you can use up to four NICs per file server, where each NIC attaches the file server to another physical network.

- Expansion slots for video board and printer ports.

- If you are implementing UPS monitoring, you will need a slot for the UPS monitor board (unless you are using a disk coprocessor, which has a UPS monitor port, or Elgar's VAP implementation of UPS monitoring).

Drives for NetWare File Servers

A NetWare file server requires at least one floppy disk drive. NetWare supports the following types of drives attached to a file server:

1. IBM PC-XT or 100 percent compatible drives and controllers. This option is only available with NetWare ELS Level IIs, and only in dedicated mode. In this configuration, the XT server is limited to 640K of RAM, and only supports drives up to approximately 70MB.

2. IBM PC AT or 100 percent compatible hard disk controllers and drives. This refers to drives and controllers supported by the drive table in the computer's ROM BIOS.

   By using replacement ROM BIOSs from Storage Dimensions, On Track Systems, and others, many types of drives and controllers can be supported this way, including MFM (Modified Frequency Modulation, the standard hard disk format), RLL (Run-Length Limited, a format method that provides expanded disk capacity), ESDI (Enhanced Small Disk Interface, often pronounced "ezdee"), and SCSI (Small Computer Systems Interface, usually pronounced "scuzzy").

   You are still limited to a single controller of this type, and usually limited to two hard disks on the controllers.

3. IBM PS/2 controllers and drives, including MFM and ESDI drives.

4. Drives supported by the Novell Disk Coprocessor Board (DCB). The DCB is an intelligent SCSI host adapter designed to be used with Novell external disk subsystems. The DCB can also support external subsystems from ADIC, Storage Dimensions, and others, as well as internal drives with embedded SCSI controllers.

The DCB supports certain specific drive and controller combinations. In addition, a generic SCSI option is available that will work with many drive/controller combinations not supported directly.

5. Drives using third-party Value Added Disk Drivers (VADDs). Many third parties, including Storage Dimensions and On Track Systems, have written disk drivers to support other, nonsupported adapter/controller/drive combinations.

NetWare 286 File Server Maximum Capacities:

Number of hard disks per file server	32
Number of volumes per file server	32
Maximum volume size	255MB
Total disk storage per server	2GB
Total file server RAM	15MB
Number of concurrent users	100
Number of concurrently open files	1,000

Selecting Workstations

NetWare supports all DOS- or OS/2-based IBM PCs, XTs, ATs, and PS/2s as workstations. Nearly any IBM-compatible PC will also work.

Because application processing takes place at a user's workstation, performance should definitely be considered when selecting workstations. For most applications workstation performance is more important than file server performance.

A workstation for a NetWare LAN should generally meet the following minimum expansion requirements:

- At least 640K RAM (Novell says 384K, but very few programs will run within that amount of RAM).

- Expansion slots for floppy and/or hard disk controllers, unless you are implementing diskless booting (see note below).

- Expansion slot for your network interface card.

- Expansion slots for video board, printer ports, COM ports, and other peripherals as required.

A Note on Diskless Booting

Most NICs have a socket for installing a Diskless Boot ROM. Diskless boot ROMs eliminate the need for boot disks by reading a special disk image file off a file server. There are advantages and disadvantages to diskless booting.

Advantages:

- **Lower Cost**. Diskless boot ROMs usually cost less than floppy drives.

- **Higher Security**. Users cannot copy files to local drives.

- **Higher reliability in "dirty" environments**. Floppy drives and disks can be easily damaged by airborne debris in manufacturing plants, etc.

Disadvantages:

- **Potentially higher upgrade cost**. Major revisions of NetWare have often required upgrades to boot ROMs. You must consider the cost of new ROMS as well as the cost of opening each PC to replace them.

- **Greater complexity for installations and upgrades**. Special disk image files for booting must be created, and different files must be created for each different workstation boot configuration. Each NetWare shell upgrade requires new image files to be created. If you want to change a CONFIG.SYS or AUTOEXEC.BAT file for one or more users, a new image file or files must be created.

- **Limited workstation capability**. Diskless stations make it more difficult for users to take work home, transfer files to other systems via floppy, etc.

Backing Up Data

The primary benchmark for a tape backup system is "Can I get my data back?" Speed of backup and restoration is also important, but meaningless if you can't restore.

The value of the data is usually far greater than that of the server hardware, and often greater than the value of all LAN components combined.

Most people realize the value of their data only when they have lost it. Recent studies have shown that most companies that experience a data disaster that lasts ten days or more either get acquired by another company or file bankruptcy within a year.

The main reason for backing up is to restore after a data loss. Many people assume that the primary cause of data loss is a hard disk crash, but most data losses that require restoration from backup are the result of operator (or application) error, not disk crashes. Unfortunately, this assumption has led to two major problems:

1. A lot of backup systems make it easy to restore all files, but make it considerably more difficult to restore only a few specific files.

2. A lot of computer users feel safe keeping one set of backup disks or tapes that they reuse daily. These users often discover the hard way that many errors get discovered only after a previous day's backup has been over-written.

Backup Devices

For small PC hard disks, floppy disks can often be an effective, if time-consuming, backup medium. When the disk to be backed up approaches even moderate sizes (20MB to 30MB) however, using disks becomes tedious and cumbersome. For LAN server drives, which typically start at 80MB and currently go up to 650MB or so (for a single drive!), disk backups are out of the question. The most common and popular means of backup for LAN drives is tape.

Other devices used for backup include removable, high-capacity disk drives and optical drives.

Tape

Most tape backup systems use the 1/4" data cartridges designed by 3M. There are two primary types of 1/4" data cartridges: the DC 300/600 type, which can hold between 20MB and 150MB of data, and the DC2000 type mini cartridges, which hold between 40MB and 150MB of data.

Several vendors, including Mountain Computer and ADIC, provide a means to daisy-chain tape drives to provide higher capacities. ADIC has a changer mechanism that will automatically change up to ten tapes in a backup session.

Figure 7.1: ADIC Tape Changer

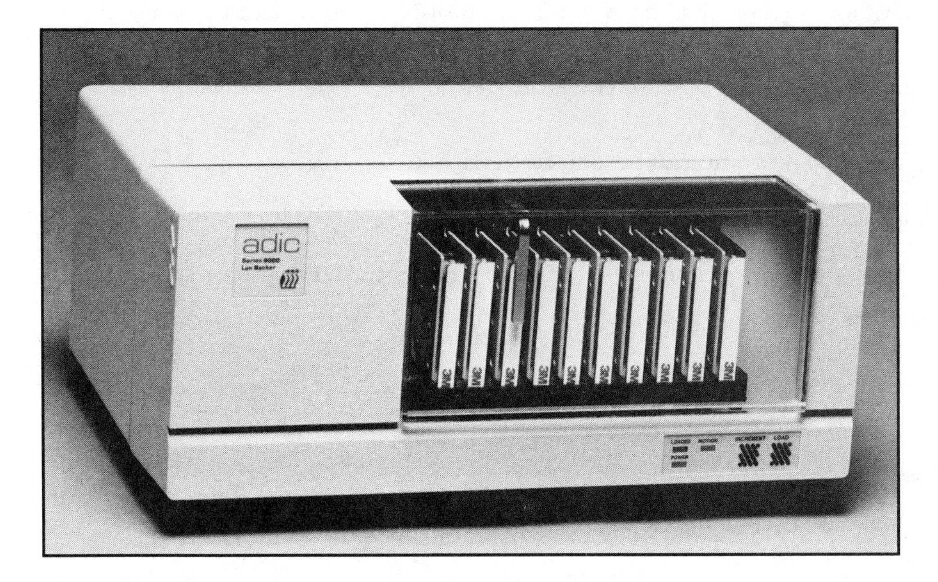

A third type of tape that has gained recent popularity is the Super8 Video cartridge. One Super8 cartridge can hold up to 2.2 gigabytes of data.

Critics of Super8 technology say that it has two critical faults: Unlike data cartridges, the tape has to be pulled out of the cartridge for recording and playback. When pulling the tape, it is possible to bunch or tangle the media in the drive, as happens in home VCRs. Unfortunately, the loss of 2.2GB of data is usually a bit more disastrous than losing a copy of *Police Academy 2*. Also, Super8 read/write heads rotate against the tape, causing increased wear. This could mean shorter tape life.

Currently, workstation-based tape drives provide more flexibility than file server-based tape backup systems. Workstation-based tape drives can be used for unattended backup, while the server must be downed and booted under DOS to use the current file server-based systems.

Although there has been some attempt at standardization, do not expect a tape drive from one manufacturer to be able to read a tape created on another manufacturer's drive.

Tape drives should be selected with care, and should NEVER BE TRUSTED. Any time there is a change that could affect the functioning of a tape drive—such as a change in DOS or network OS versions, or a hardware change in the tape drive's host PC—the drive should be tested.

Problems with Tape

Tape is probably the most effective means available for backup, but even it is often very unreliable. There are several reasons why data backed up to tape may be unrecoverable, including:

- **Media defects**. Tape media, like disk media, can have defects. Nearly every tape cartridge has imperfections.

  Defects in audio or videotape can affect sound or picture quality, but with data tape defects cause lost data. If the backup software does not find and map out those defects (like low-level disk format programs do, for example) data written to the defective areas will be unreadable. Like disk defects, tape defects can also develop over time.

- **Debris on the tape (soft errors)**. Tapes, unlike hard disks, are not sealed; they are subject to dust, smoke particles, etc. Debris can get caught on the tape read/write head, where the tape is dragged past (the tape head, in effect, acts like a plow, pushing the debris along the tape). This can scratch or damage whole sections of tape. This type of damage can occur during the restore process, so read-after-write verification performed after or during a backup session backup cannot prevent it.

If a large enough section of tape is damaged, the software supplied with many tape systems will not be able to read past the damaged section, effectively making the tape unreadable from that point on. Not only is the damaged section lost, but every thing beyond it! This is often true of tape drives that cannot read in a "block addressable" or random access mode.

- **Mechanical failure**. Tape drives, like all mechanical devices, break and wear out. Wear of mechanical components can change the alignment of the tape and the read/write head over time. There are many stories of people replacing worn-out tape drives with new ones of the same model, only to find that tapes recorded on the old drive are not readable on the new one!

  There are primary methods used for tape-to-read/write head alignment:

  1. **Fixed position—alignment to cartridge**. When you insert a tape in the drive, the read/write head aligns itself to the bottom of the tape cartridge. The drive cannot adjust for variations in tape cartridges, or adjust for wear of the tape drive mechanism itself.

  2. **Servo-track alignment during restore**. As the drive is reading a tape, it electronically locates the recorded data tracks on the tape and aligns the tape read/write heads to the tracks. This works well with new, high-quality, properly recorded tapes. Over time, however, tape loses magnetic flux, or the ability to hold data, and the strength of the recorded signal on the tape gets weaker. If this happens, the tape drive may

not be able to align the heads properly and may not be able to read the tape.

3. **Automatic tape-edge alignment during record and playback.** When a tape cartridge is installed, the tape drive locates the edge of the tape (not the cartridge) and aligns the read/write head to it. Because the drive maintains alignment to the tape edge during both archiving and restoring, variations in tape cartridge, wearing of tape mechanisms, or loss of magnetic flux will not affect alignment. This is probably the most effective alignment method.

The read/write heads in a tape drive are subject to wear also. Ferrite ceramic heads can last up to one hundred times longer than the more common brass heads.

- **Error correction/detection.** Most, but not all, tape systems provide some form of error correction and/or error detection. The most common method is the Reed-Solomon Correction Code.

  Designed for disk drives, Reed-Solomon can compensate for the omission of single bits or bytes in a data block. It cannot compensate for the loss of a large number of contiguous bytes, something that is very common on tape. The more sophisticated Exclusive/Or method, used by HP, 3M, ADIC, and a few others, uses a redundant recording method that allows for recovery in these situations.

  Many tape systems provide for automatic read-after-write verification during backup, while others provide for a manual verification process. This can detect errors during recording, but can do nothing about soft errors (debris), which occur during restore.

Tape Drive Performance

Tape drives, compared to disks, are slow. There are vast differences in performance specifications for drives from different manufacturers. There are also usually vast differences in quoted speeds and actual backup times.

Effective backup and restore should be your primary concern. Consider high performance a bonus.

You can minimize the impact of slow performance by performing unattended backups in the middle of the night.

Digital Audio Tape (DAT)

A new standard for high-capacity tape is emerging called Digital Audio Tape (DAT). The recording industry in the United States has attempted to ban DAT because of its potential for creating high-quality copies of CDs, records, and tapes. As a backup medium, DAT is receiving support from many vendors, including Sony, Hitachi, HP, and others.

The emerging standards appear to incorporate very effective error correction and detection. Combined with the high capacity of DAT (approximately 800K to 1.3MB per tape), this should assure a market niche for DAT as a backup medium.

What to Look For in a Tape System

Consider the following features when evaluating a tape backup system:

- The tape drive should provide file by file backup and restore. It is inefficient (and sometimes impossible) to restore an entire tape to retrieve one lost file, yet this is what "streaming," or disk image tape drives, require. Disk image restoration is often fine when restoring data after replacing a defective hard disk. Most restorations, however, are the result of lost or damaged files, not damaged disks.

- The tape software should provide multiple methods of selecting files for backup, including exclusion/inclusion by file and/or directory specifications, date and time, unarchived files, etc. Restore options should include selection by file specification and/or directory, selection of specific files during restore (as opposed to a preset list), and date and time.

- The tape system should be able to back up and restore a file server's security and system files. It should also be able to exclude them.

- The tape drive and software should allow for unattended backups. If this function is not included, using keyboard macros and public domain programs "WAITUNTL.COM" (available from most bulletin boards) will often do the same thing.

- The tape drive should provide error detection and correction during backup and during restore. Error detection should be automatic, not an option to be performed after backup. (Optional tasks, especially if they are time-consuming, are rarely performed.) If the tape software provides a manual verification process, add the time required (usually the amount of time required for a backup) to the backup time.

- The tape drive should be able to maintain constant speed to compensate for variations in tape tension. Some tape systems require regular retensioning of tapes which rarely, if ever, gets done.

- Mechanical wear should not affect tape-to-head alignment. Recording head misalignment due to wear often means that a tape recorded on one drive will not be readable by another similar drive.

- If unrecoverable errors on the tape should occur, the tape system should provide a means to bypass defective sections of tape to continue restore.

- The vendor should guarantee tape cartridge interchange between the same model tape drive.

- The vendor should provide recovery services to attempt restoration from damaged tapes. (ADIC provides this type of service, for example.)

Other Backup Systems

While tape is the most common media for backup, it is not the only one. High-capacity removable floppy disks can be used as well as optical drives.

High-Capacity Floppy Disks

High capacity floppy disks, such as the Iomega Bernoulli cartridges, can be very effective for backup. The high cost of the cartridges generally discourages users from backing up as often as they might otherwise, which makes the system less desirable as a primary backup method. It is a good way to provide secondary backup, or "insurance," during potentially dangerous system upgrades and modifications.

Optical Drives

Optical drives use lasers to read and write data on a plastic disk.

There are two types of writable optical drives: Write Once, Read Many (WORM), and read/write. Currently, WORM drives are plentiful, and read/write drives are mostly still under development. Currently, writable optical drives have capacities between about 200 and 800 MB per disk.

Read/write optical, however, shows great promise as backup media. The high capacity and high speed (when compared to tape) may make read/write optical a very effective backup system. In addition, optical drives are less susceptible to damage from debris than tape.

The cost of media for optical drives is still very high, but expect that to change as usage becomes more common.

Power Backup and Conditioning

Like other computer equipment, LAN file servers and workstations are subject to damage and data loss when subjected to electrical problems. There are several kinds of power problems that you may have to deal with, including:

> **Blackouts**. The power goes out entirely. This can cause data loss, corrupted database index files, and physical disk damage. A NetWare file server is particularly vulnerable to power outages because FATs and directories are held and updated in memory.

Brownouts, Dips, and Sags. The power dips below normal. Persistent brownouts can cause data corruption and loss, and a brownout can cause a computer's internal power supply to overheat and burn out.

Surges and Spikes. Momentary increases in voltage. These can be from a few volts to over 1,000 volts. Surges of 50 volts or more are common, sometimes occurring several times per hour, while surges of over 1,000 volts are infrequent.

Even without surge suppressors, most computer equipment is designed to handle low-voltage surges. Higher voltage surges, however, can cause a PC to shut down and can potentially damage it.

Noise. Generated by copy machines, air conditioners, elevators, refrigerators, switching power supplies of the types used in PCs, newer florescent lights, etc. Noise can cause sporadic disturbances, such as incorrect characters appearing on a screen. In LAN environments, noise has been blamed for mysterious glitches, such as a workstation losing communication with a file server for no apparent reason.

Power Conditioning and Backup Equipment

Power conditioning equipment generally falls into the following categories:

Surge Suppressor. This is the most widely used type of power protection device. Surge suppressors are designed to protect against momentary voltage surges and spikes. Surge suppressors divert high voltages (generally over 200 to 250 volts) to ground.

Isolation Transformer. Isolates equipment from the power lines, eliminating much of the noise and power spikes which occur in commercial buildings.

Power Line Filter. Power line filters remove extraneous low voltage impulses and noise. Some surge suppressors and isolation transformers provide filtering.

Voltage Regulator. Maintains a constant voltage to the equipment. Generally designed to accept power input between approximately 100 and 130 volts and provide a constant 120 volt output. Most computer power supplies don't require voltage regulation (brownout protection, where voltage falls below these levels, is usually provided by backup power systems described below).

Backup Power System. Backup power systems, often called Uninterruptable Power Supplies (UPS), provide emergency power in case of a commercial power outage or interruption. Many backup power systems also provide surge protection and noise filtering. These systems are designed to provide backup power long enough to shut down a system in an orderly fashion, usually ten to twenty minutes.

Backup power systems can of two main types: full-time or stand-by.

A stand-by UPS contains batteries and a power "invertor," which can take the batteries' DC output and convert it to 120 volt AC output. Under normal power conditions, a stand-by UPS delivers power from the incoming commercial power lines. If incoming power drops (usually below approximately 100 volts), the UPS switches from the commercial lines to the batteries and invertor, supplying power to the devices plugged in to it. A stand-by UPS continually recharges its relatively small batteries, which can last for several years.

An On-Line (or full-time) UPS differs from the standby units in that its battery and invertor are constantly powering the attached equipment. An on-line UPS only resorts to AC power when the battery power is interrupted or fails. Although full-time UPS batteries are re-charged continuously, the batteries do not last nearly as long as stand-by UPS batteries.

Vendors of both types of systems will argue the merits of their respective approaches. There are good quality units in both categories, and unfortunately, poor quality units as well.

UPS Output Wave Form

The wave form of the current supplied by the backup power system is very important to the longevity of your equipment.

Backup power systems usually generate current in sine wave or square wave form. Commercial AC power is delivered in the form of a sine wave.

With a sine wave, power changes gradually from a low of 0 volts to a peak of approximately +170 volts, falls gradually back to 0, then changes to a peak of -170 volts. The 120 volt figure that is quoted for commercial AC power is an average value, called the RMS value.

The 120 volt RMS value determines the brightness of light bulbs and affects transformers. Computer power supplies, however, generally use the 170 volt peak value.

Unlike the gradual change of a sine wave from a positive to a negative voltage, a square wave switches instantly from a positive to a negative voltage. With a square wave, the peak voltage and RMS voltages are identical.

Because the internal power supplies in computers use the peak voltage, and lights and transforms utilize the RMS voltage, backup systems that have a square wave output usually compromise between 120 and 170 volts, commonly at 140 volts.

This means that the voltage is too low for computer power supplies, potentially causing overheating, yet too high for transformers, light bulbs, etc., potentially causing shortened life or burnout. This kind of compromise could be classified as the worst of both worlds.

UPSs that generate square wave output are generally less expensive than systems that generate sine waves.

A third wave form, called *quasi-sine wave*, outputs a square wave that is "stepped" (see illustration) to approximate a sine wave. Generally, this kind of unit has most of the benefits of sine wave output, but can be produced at a lower cost.

UPS Monitoring

Many backup power systems include the capability to send messages to attached equipment, such as a network file server, to indicate when commercial power is interrupted, when the UPS battery is low, etc. This function is called *UPS monitoring*. UPS monitoring allows a file server or computer to initiate an unattended orderly shut down procedure.

Network file servers running Novell's NetWare can be provided with UPS monitoring by using a cable connected between the UPS and a special UPS monitor board, Novell's disk coprocessor board, or the mouse port of an IBM PS/2 file server.

If commercial power to the UPS goes out, the UPS sends a signal to the file server (via the UPS monitoring hardware) indicating a power outage. The server then sends a message to users that the power is out and that the server will shut down in a specified number of minutes. At the end of the indicated time, the server will close all open files and "down" itself. If the power should be restored before the indicated shutdown time, the process will be aborted and users who have not logged out will be notified that power has been restored.

One vendor of backup systems, Elgar Corporation, provides the option of using a NetWare VAP to implement UPS monitoring. The Elgar VAP uses a cable that connects to a serial port on the server (this port can also be used for a network printer). This approach has two advantages: it eliminates the need for a UPS monitor card, potentially freeing an expansion slot in the server, and it provides LAN users with the name of the server experiencing the power outage, which can be important in multiserver systems. A disadvantage is that one of the available 100 user attachments is used by the VAP.

Rated Power Capacities

Power capacities of UPS systems are rated in Watts or Volt-Amps (V-A). Larger UPSs are always rated in V-A, while smaller systems are often rated in either Watts or V-A. The two measurements, which are often used interchangeably, are in fact quite different.

For one type of electrical equipment, the Watt and V-A ratings can be the same, while for another type of equipment, they can be different. For example, for light bulbs and electric heaters, Watts and V-A are equivalent values. For computers, however, the Watt rating is approximately 60 to 70 percent of the V-A rating.

To add to this confusion, many manufacturers actually mean V-A when they say Watt.

The confusion of these terms can make it difficult to "size" a UPS for your network. Probably the best approach, short of learning more than you want to know about power, is to rely on the UPS manufacturers' recommendations with respect to size. Most manufacturers provide charts showing recommended units to be used with particular computers and/or peripherals.

Testing a UPS

A common test for a UPS is pulling its plug from the wall socket while it is powering equipment. This method creates an open circuit across the plug of the UPS. When power goes out in real situations, however, the load of all the other devices attached to the power lines creates a short circuit, rather than an open circuit, across the plug. Many UPS systems will pass the pull-the-plug test, only to fail when a real power outage occurs.

One manufacturer, American Power Corporation, provides a test switch that simulates power outage conditions. Unfortunately, for most other backup units there is no good test that we know of to determine how a UPS will respond to an actual power outage (short of cutting the building's main circuit—something that others in your building may not appreciate).

Static

Static discharges are measured in the thousands of volts, and can destroy electronic equipment. There are several methods available to combat static:

> **Anti-Static Chair Mats**. Designed to ground the user, eliminating static discharge. Conversely, standard plastic chair mats can actually increase a static problem.

Anti-Static Equipment Mats. Designed to ground the equipment. Operators should touch the mat before touching the equipment.

Grounding Straps. These go around an operator's wrist, and attach to a static pad under the equipment.

Touch Pads. These sit on a desk or table next to the equipment. An equipment operator is supposed to touch the pad to discharge static before touching the equipment.

Anti-Static Carpet. Specially designed and treated carpet that eliminates or minimizes static charge buildup. This is probably the best overall solution, but can be very expensive for existing buildings.

Anti-Static Spray. Used to treat carpets. Although a very good temporary or short-term solution, it is probably the least effective long-term method because it requires constant retreatment.

How To Determine if You Have Power-Related Problems

If you are connected to commercial power lines, you have power problems. The question isn't if a power surge, power outage, or line noise is going to cause a problem, but when it's going to do it.

Many problems are caused by improper grounding. Ground problems are far too commonly caused by improper building wiring, even in newer buildings. A simple circuit tester, the type with three LEDs, can help locate some of these problems.

Power in industrial areas is especially prone to noise, surges, and low voltage conditions.

If you are in a location where line noise is prevalent, such as a medical office, an industrial area, etc., consider some type of noise protection.

If you have problems that seem to be power-related that you can't solve, look for a company that specializes in solving power problems. These companies can often be found in the Yellow Pages under the heading "Electrical Power Systems—Testing." Comprehensive electrical testing can be expensive, but worth it if it solves your problem.

LAN Component Protection

Minimum protection for specific LAN components should include:

File Servers: Ideally, a file server should be plugged into a dedicated electrical circuit. If a dedicated circuit is not available, make sure that noise-producing equipment, such as copiers, air conditioners, fans, and refrigerators, are not on the same line.

File servers should at least be protected by surge protectors to guard against power surges and spikes, and power backup systems, to protect against power outages and brownouts. The power backup systems used with file servers should include a UPS monitoring function (if it is supported by the LAN server software) to properly down the server in case of a power outage. If static electricity is a problem, static mats or other static control equipment should be employed.

Workstations: At the very least, workstations should be protected by surge protectors. If line noise is a problem, line filters and/or isolation transformers should be considered. If static electricity is a problem, static mats or other static control equipment should be employed.

Certain applications require that LAN workstations be equipped with power backup systems in order to allow for the orderly closing of files.

Selecting Surge and Spike Protectors

There are several important factors to look at when selecting surge protectors, including:

Response Time. This is measured in nanoseconds (billionths of a second) or picoseconds (trillionths of a second). The faster the response time, the better chance of protecting equipment.

Clamping Level. This is the voltage protection level. A surge protector with a rated clamping level of 200 volts, for example, would keep the voltage from rising above that point.

Power Dissipation. This refers to the amount of energy a surge protector can absorb. Power dissipation is usually measured in joules. A higher rating means better protection.

Noise Protection. Some surge protectors provide filtering of electrical and radio frequency noise, some do not. Noise can cause spurious data errors.

Fail-Safe Circuitry. A damaged surge protector should indicate that it is not functioning or power off if it cannot protect your equipment.

Warranty. The warranty should be longer than that of the equipment that is being protected. Ideally, the warranty should cover the surge protector and the protected equipment. One manufacturer, Panamax, provides a lifetime warranty for their surge protectors that also covers damage to protected equipment.

Selecting Backup Power Systems

As noted above, there are good quality stand-by UPSs and good quality on-line UPSs. In most circumstances, both will perform adequately. Some guidelines on selection:

- For computer applications, a UPS should have a sine wave or quasi-sine wave output.
- For file servers, the UPS should provide UPS monitoring capabilities.
- The UPS should be rated by the manufacturer to be of sufficient capacity to support you equipment.

If you are in doubt, Novell has certified several brands and models of UPS for use with NetWare file servers. This information is available from Novell dealers and from Novell's on-line database, NetWire, which is accessible through CompuServe.

8

Configuring the NetWare Operating System

Before you can install the NetWare operating system, you must customize it for your particular LAN hardware configuration. In this process, you will select the various file server components that you will be using (network interface cards, disk drives and controllers, etc.) and then create a version of NetWare specifically for those components.

The NetWare Generation program (NetGen) gives you two working options: *Default* and *Custom*. The Default option is for simple, straightforward installations, where you are installing one network card in the file server and one or two printers. The Custom installation is for more complicated implementations, where multiple LAN cards, printer ports, and other options are being installed in a file server.

There are four methods you can use to generate the operating system.

1. The Floppy Disk Method reads information from a set of copied NetWare disks and writes back to them directly, without storing on an intermediate location. This is time-consuming method, since a lot of disk swapping is involved.

2. The RAM disk method uses RAM as if it were storing to a disk. It is an enhanced version of the floppy disk method. It is faster than using floppies, but you will need at least 1MB of RAM.

3. The hard disk method reads all of the needed information to a hard disk and then writes the generated system to floppies. The advantage of this method over methods one and two is that the generated system remains on the hard disk. If for some reason the process is interrupted or aborted you don't have to start from the beginning; you simply resume where you left off (more or less). Also, if for some reason the generated system doesn't work, you can revise it and generate the revision without starting over.

4. The File Server method uses one file server to generate the system directly for another server. This is the fastest method, but you have to have a NetWare network already running to use it.

NetWare, with all of its support files and utilities, comprises nearly forty 5-1/4" disks (the 3-1/2" version uses fewer). If you plan to use the hard disk configuration method you need to make working copies of the following disks:

GENDATA
SUPPORT
NETGEN
UTILEXE-1
UTILEXE-2
OSEXE-1
OSEXE-2

The PC you use during the generation procedure must have at least 640K RAM and at least one floppy drive. For the sake of speed it should also be an AT class machine or better. If you plan to use the hard disk configuration method, you need at least 8MB of available disk space.

The PC's boot disk should have a CONFIG.SYS file that opens at least twenty files and fifteen buffers.

Configuring NetWare Using the Hard Disk Method

Important note: These instructions are for running NetGen the first time. To run NetGen subsequent times, go directly to the \GENERATE\NETWARE directory on your hard disk and type NETGEN.

This chapter illustrates the hard disk configuration method. To be consistent with Novell's documentation, create a directory on your hard disk called GENERATE. If your hard disk is C, for example, type:

```
C:<Enter>

MD\GENERATE<Enter>

CD\GENERATE<Enter>
```

Put the working copy of the disk labelled NETGEN in drive A and type:

```
A:<Enter>

NETGEN<Enter>
```

You will be prompted to swap out diskettes with messages similar to:

```
Insert disk SUPPORT in any drive.
        Strike a key when ready . . .
```

```
NetWare Generation And Installation  V4.00

System Configuration Level

Default Configuration
Custom Configuration

Use the arrow keys to highlight an option, then press the SELECT key.
```

Using the Default Configuration Method

```
NETGEN Run Options

Standard (floppy disks)
RAM Disk
Hard Disk
Network Drive

Drive: C
```

Choose the Hard Disk method, then enter the drive letter for your hard disk.

If you are running NetGen for the first time, you will be prompted to insert disks. You may be asked for certain disks more than once. NETGEN checks other drives for disks, so don't be alarmed if disk access lights on other drives come on from time to time. When the required disks have been loaded, you may be prompted with:

```
Upload Additional Diskettes?

Yes
No
```

The software drivers for many LAN NICs are provided by Novell with the NetWare disks. Some NIC manufacturers, however, provide the drivers for their boards separately. For these drivers, follow the instructions included with the drivers. They may instruct you to answer YES when NETGEN asks if additional disks should be uploaded, or provide other instructions for copying the drivers and returning to the NETGEN process. If you need to upload additional diskettes, select "Yes," otherwise select "No."

Selecting the NetWare Configuration

At this point, you may continue or exit. To leave NETGEN (to load other drivers or for any other reason) choose exit NETGEN here:

If you exit, when you are ready to resume NetGen, go to your hard disk and type:

```
CD\GENERATE\NETWARE<Enter>

NETGEN<Enter>
```

Choose the default configuration again, then choose the Hard Disk Method and enter your drive letter again.

To continue, highlight Select Network Configuration, then press <Enter>.

```
Available Options

Set Operating System Options
Select LAN Drivers
Select Disk Drivers
Select "Other" Drivers
Save Selections and Continue
```

Here you will select the drivers for the file server NIC(s) and type of hard disk(s) and controller(s). Unless you have a Novell internal tape drive, you can ignore "Other" Drivers.

Setting Operating System Options

Your operating system options depend on the version of NetWare you are installing. They are:

Advanced NetWare 286
  Advanced NetWare 286 / Dedicated
  Advanced NetWare 286 / Nondedicated

SFT NetWare 286
  SFT NetWare 286 with TTS (Transaction Tracking System)
  SFT NetWare 286 (without TTS)

For Advanced NetWare 286, dedicated file servers are almost always preferable to nondedicated file servers.

For SFT NetWare 286, Novell recommends choosing the TTS system even if you do not have applications that currently use it, since does not detract from performance of applications that are not tracked.

Selecting LAN Drivers

```
Selected LAN Drivers

A: Standard Microsystems ARCNET/Pure Data  V1.00 (881010)
```

```
LAN Driver Options

Select Loaded Item
Load and Select Item
Deselect an Item
```

Advanced NetWare 286 and SFT NetWare 286 allow you to install up to four LAN drivers and corresponding NICs of various types in a file server. The number of a particular type of NIC that can be installed varies from one to four, depending on the particular NIC.

When selecting LAN drivers, be careful to select exactly the right driver for your hardware. For example, two boards of different models made by the same manufacturer may require different drivers.

Each time you select drivers, conflicting drivers will be removed from the "Available LAN Drivers" list. (Conflicting drivers are drivers that use the same interrupts, DMA channels, etc., as drivers already selected.) When no nonconflicting drivers remain, your options are to accept your selected drivers or deselect one or more drivers and try other combinations.

If you cannot select the LAN drivers that you need, you can exit NetGen and retry using the Custom Configuration method.

Selecting Disk Drivers

```
                    Select Disk Driver Type

IBM AT hard disk controller or compatible  (881012)
IBM PS/2 Model 30 286 MFM disk controller  V1.01 (881028)
```

When you select a Disk Driver, NetGen will ask for the channel number. Channel 0 is used for AT and PS/2-type drives and controllers, while channels 1 through 4 are used by Novell's Disk Coprocessor, Value Added Disk Drivers (VADDs), etc.

The Disk Driver Options window (not shown) will show one or more of the following options:

Select Loaded Item—Allows you to select drivers from a list that is already loaded into the NetGen utility.

Load and Select Item—Allows you to load disk drivers from one or more disk files and then select the newly loaded driver(s). Drivers not supplied by Novell (VADDs) would generally be loaded in this manner.

Deselect an Item—Allows you to remove a previously selected disk driver.

The Selected Disk Drivers window contains a list of all previously selected disk drivers. You can add or delete drivers from this list. Disk drivers may be selected from a list already loaded into NetGen or from one or more lists that may be loaded from disk.

The Select Disk Driver Type window will display available drivers for the selected channel. Only drivers that are compatible with previously selected hardware will be displayed on the "Select Disk Driver Type" list.

After all of the network configuration options have been specified, select Save Selections and Continue.

Entering File Server Information

```
                    File Server Information

A: Standard Microsystems ARCNET/Pure Data  V1.00 (881010)
     Network Address:
Communication Buffers: 40
```

Setting the Network Address

Each network in a NetWare internetwork must have a unique address. This address is assigned at each file server to the NIC attached to that physical network.

This is different from the physical hardware address that every NIC on a network must have, otherwise known as the Node address.

This address must be:

- a hexadecimal number between 1 and FFFFFFFF.

- different from the address assigned to any other NIC installed in this file server.

- different from the address of any other physical network connected to any file server in an internetwork, and it must be different than the addresses of any remote NetWare bridges and/or remote networks in the internetwork.

  If a NIC is attached to a network that has another file server on it, both servers must assign the same address to the NICs attached to that network.

For example, if you are connecting a second file server to an existing network the LAN Driver in the second server must be assigned the same address as the LAN driver in the first server. If the LAN driver in the first server has been assigned the address 1, the LAN driver in the second server must also be assigned the address 1. In addition, LAN drivers for any other network attached to any connected servers must not be 1.

Communication Buffers

The communication buffers are file server memory blocks set aside to hold data packets arriving from the network until the file server is able to process them. NetWare assigns a default value to communications buffers of 40. You can increase this to as much as 150, or decrease it to as low as 10. Novell recommends the following formula:

> Determine the maximum number of workstation shells that can be connected at one time. Multiply by 2. Add 10 for each LAN driver installed in the file server.

Say that twenty workstations will connect directly to the file server. Multiply by 2 and get 40. There are three LAN drivers in the file server, so that's 10 x 3 = 30. 40 + 20 = 60.

After you server is up and running, you can monitor daily buffer usage using the FConsole utility and then make adjustments accordingly.

```
                    Selected Configurations

LAN A: Standard Microsystems ARCNET/Pure Data  V1.00 (881010)
       Option 0: IRQ = 2, I/O Base = 2E0h, RAM Buffer at D000:0
       Network Address: 1

OS Type: SFT NetWare 286 with TTS

Communication Buffers: 40

Disk Chan. 0: IBM AT hard disk controller or compatible  (881012)
              Option 0: AT controller  I/O base = 1F0h, Interrupt = 14
```

After you have selected and configured the LAN Drivers, Disk Drivers, Resource Sets, and "Other" Resources, you are ready to generate the operating system. The "Choose LAN Driver Configuration" option is replaced with the option "Review Selected Configurations."

You should record the information on the configuration review screens for future reference. If you have a printer attached to your PC you can do this with the <PrtSc> key.

Generating the System

```
Continue Network Generation Using Selected Configuration?

No
Yes
```

When you are satisfied with your configuration parameters select "Yes" to generate the network operating system. The process takes several minutes. A series of messages will be displayed similar to the following:

> Novell Linker, Version 2.0
> Linking OSEXE-1:NET$OS.EX1.

If the GENDATA disk is not in a drive you will be prompted:

> Insert disk GENDATA in any drive.
> Strike a key when ready . . .
>
> Configuring OSEXE-1:NET$OS.EXE
>
> Novell Linker, Version 2.0
> Linking UTILEXE-1:COMPSURF.EXE.

Novell Linker, Version 2.0
Linking UTILEXE-1:DISKED.EXE.

Novell Linker, Version 2.0
Linking UTILEXE-2:VREPAIR.EXE.

Novell Linker, Version 2.0
Linking NETGEN:INSTOVL.EXE.

Novell Linker, Version 2.0
Linking NETGEN:INSTOVL.EXE.

Configuring NETGEN:INSTOVL.EXE

```
Download Needed Files To Floppy Disk?
-------------------------------------
Yes
No
```

You now need to download the required files to the working disk copies that you made earlier. NETGEN will request each disk as it is needed. When the copying is complete, you can proceed to generating your workstation shell(s) in Chapter 9.

Using the Custom Configuration Method

The Custom Configuration option of NetGen allows you greater control in situations where there is a high probability of hardware conflicts between boards and other components in the file server.

The Custom Configuration option allows you to:

- Select the configuration(s) of your LAN driver(s). You can select the interrupts, DMA channels, I/O addresses, etc., used by your LAN drivers and NICs.
- Select the configuration of your disk drivers.
- Account for possible conflicts with other file server (see below).

Common reasons for using the Custom Configuration option include:

- You are installing more than one LAN NIC in a file server (creating an internal bridge).
- You are installing more than one disk controller (an AT controller and a Novell Disk Controller Board [DCB], for example).
- You are installing other devices or device controllers (Novell's internal tape drive, for example).

The Custom Configuration option can be used before you install server hardware, so that if you need to make any changes to switch or jumper settings, you can avoid removing boards from your file server. You can even use the Custom Configuration method to help choose the hardware you will purchase, allowing you to predict and avoid conflicts from the beginning.

One of the most valuable and most misunderstood features of the Custom Configuration option is the ability to use resource lists and resource sets.

Resource Lists and Resource Sets

Resource Lists and Resource Sets are simply a means of avoiding hardware conflicts before they happen. By using them, NetGen becomes an evaluation and decision assistance tool.

For NetGen, a resource is any hardware device that could potentially conflict with a NIC, disk controller, or "Other" device in a file server (a Novell internal tape drive is the only "Other" device currently defined).

A selected resource does not have to be installed in your file server (This is not true of disk controllers and NICs, however). You can use the resource lists and sets to help you plan for future server expansion.

NetGen comes with a list of predefined resources, which you can add to and/or modify (See Appendix A of the Advanced NetWare 286 Installation manual for details on creating and modifying resources). Here is a partial resource list:

```
                         Resources
AT Auxiliary ROM
COM1
COM1 (No Interrupts)
Enhanced Graphics Adapter (No Interrupts)
Hercules Mono Adapter
LPT1
LPT1 (No Interrupts)
LPT2
```

Each resource has a definition file that lists the interrupts, DMA channels, etc., used for each possible configuration of that resource. For example, here are the configurations for printer port LPT1:

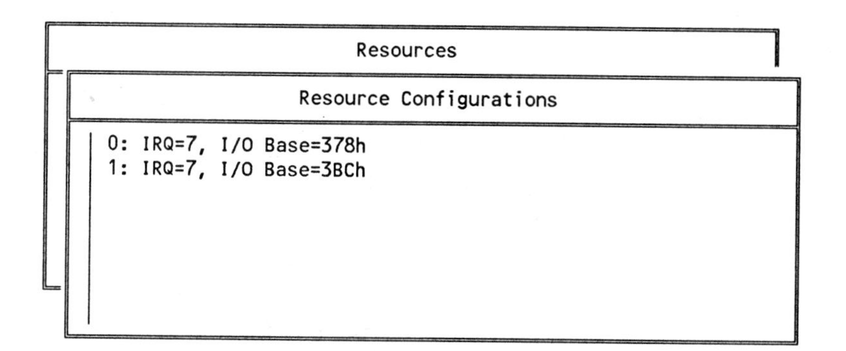

This screen only displays the descriptions of the configurations. Each configuration can be entered or displayed on a configuration screen that looks like this:

```
Configuration Information                              (Mode: Hex)

Number of I/O Address Ranges:     1   Bus: Standard
  Starting Address #1:   378         Range (bytes):              3
  Starting Address #2:               Range (bytes):
Number of Memory Address Ranges: 0
  Starting Segment #1:               Range (Paragraphs):
  Starting Segment #2:               Range (Paragraphs):
Number of Interrupt Lines:        1
  Interrupt Line #1:       7         Interrupt Line #2:
Number of DMA Lines:              0
  DMA Line #1:                       DMA Line #2:
```

In order for NetGen to use a resource, you must put the resource into a resource set. A resource set can consist of one or more individual resources. For example, the resource set for printer port LPT1 consists of a single resource:

```
LPT1
```

The resource set for the Novell 286B file server consists of several resources:

```
AT Auxiliary ROM
Monochrome Adapter
Novell 286B Floppy Controller
COM1 (No Interrupts)
LPT1 (No Interrupts)
LPT2 (No Interrupts)
```

Using Resource Sets

When you select resource sets, NetGen reads the configuration file for each resource selected. Once a resource is selected, NetGen will not allow you to select another resource, LAN driver or disk driver that will conflict. If fact, NetGen will not allow you to select any driver or resource that will conflict with another. NetGen will also not allow you to select any configuration option that will create a conflict.

Creating a Custom Configuration

To create a custom configuration, follow the generation instructions to the point where you choose the System Configuration Level.

From the System Configuration screen choose Custom Configuration.

For the Hard Disk method, choose the Hard Disk Run Option and the drive letter for your hard disk.

```
Network Generation Options

Select Network Configuration
Link/Configure NetWare Operating System
Configure NetWare Operating System
Link/Configure File Server Utilities
Exit NETGEN
```

Highlight the Select Network Configuration option, then press <Enter>.

Custom Configuration Available Options

```
Available Options

Set Operating System Options
Select Resource Sets
Select LAN Drivers
Select Disk Drivers
Select "Other" Drivers
Configure Drivers / Resources
Edit Resource List
Edit Resource Sets
Save Selections and Continue
```

The minimum required configuration for a NetWare file server is one LAN driver and one disk driver. You can, however, choose up to four LAN drivers, five disk drivers, one "other" driver (for a device such as Novell's internal tape backup) and six Resource Sets.

Once you have selected resource sets, LAN Drivers, Disk Drivers, and/or "Other" Drivers, the Configure Drivers/Resources option appears on the Available Option menu, allowing you to choose driver and resource configurations from the available options.

From this menu you set operating system options and LAN addresses. You can also edit the resource lists and sets (see Appendix A of the Novell Advanced NetWare 286 Installation manual for details).

You can either make all selection choices first and then configure all of them together, or you can select each and configure it before moving to the next selection. Which method you use doesn't matter unless there are conflicts among the devices you want to install. In that case, you will probably move between the options, making changes until you achieve compatibility.

As a general rule, choose the options that you are already constrained by first. For example, if you will be using a particular type of disk drive and controller, choose your Disk Driver first. On the other hand, if you are committed to a particular NIC from a particular manufacturer, then choose that first.

Setting the Operating System Options

Your Operating System Options depend on the version of NetWare you are installing. They are:

Advanced NetWare 286
 Advanced NetWare 286 / Dedicated
 Advanced NetWare 286 / Nondedicated

SFT NetWare 286
 SFT NetWare 286 with TTS (Transaction Tracking System)
 SFT NetWare 286 (without TTS)

For Advanced NetWare 286, dedicated file servers are almost always preferable to nondedicated file servers.

For SFT NetWare 286, Novell recommends choosing the TTS system even if you do not have applications that currently use it, since does not detract from performance of applications that are not tracked.

Selecting Disk Drivers

```
                    Selected Disk Drivers
0| IBM AT hard disk controller or compatible  (881012)
1|
2|
3|
4|
```

When you select a Disk Driver, NetGen will ask for the channel number. Channel 0 is used for AT and PS/2-type drives and controllers, while channels 1 through 4 are used by Novell's Disk Coprocessor, VADDs, etc.

The Disk Driver Options window (not shown) will show one or more of the following options:

Select Loaded Item—Allows you to select drivers from a list that is already loaded into the NetGen utility.

Load and Select Item—Allows you to load disk drivers from one or more disk files and then select the newly loaded driver(s). Drivers not supplied by Novell (VADDs) would generally be loaded in this manner.

Deselect an Item—Allows you to remove a previously selected disk driver.

The Selected Disk Drivers window contains a list of all previously selected disk drivers. You can add or delete drivers from this list. Disk drivers may be selected from a list already loaded into NetGen or from one or more lists that may be loaded from disk.

The Select Disk Driver Type window (not shown) will display available drivers for the selected channel. Only drivers that are compatible with previously selected hardware will be displayed on the "Select Disk Driver Type" list.

Selecting Resource Sets

```
                    Selected Resource Sets
---------------------------------------------------------
AT Compatible File Server
COM1
LPT1
Novell SS Keycard/UPS Monitor
Monochrome Adapter
LPT2
```

The Selected Resource Sets window contains a list of all previously defined resource sets. You may can add or delete resource sets, modify resource set names, or list the resources that make up a resource set.

Resources may be selected from a list already loaded into NetGen or from one or more lists that may be loaded from disk. Only resource sets that are compatible with previously selected hardware will be displayed on the "Available Resource" list (not shown).

Selecting LAN Drivers

```
                    Selected LAN Drivers
---------------------------------------------------------
A: WD Star/EtherCard PLUS V2.11.3 (111188)
B: Standard Microsystems ARCNET/Pure Data  V1.00 (881010)
C: NetWare NL1000 & NL/2 (AppleTalk)
```

Advanced NetWare 286 and SFT NetWare 286 allow you to install up to four LAN drivers and corresponding NICs of various types in a file server. The number of a particular type of NIC that can be installed varies from one to four, depending on the particular NIC.

Be careful to select exactly the right driver for your hardware. For example, two boards of different models made by the same manufacturer may require different drivers.

Each time you select drivers, conflicting drivers will be removed from the "Available LAN Drivers" list. When no non-conflicting drivers remain, your options are to accept your selected drivers or deselect one or more drivers and try other combinations.

If you cannot select the LAN drivers that you need, you can do a number of things:

- **Select a similar NIC from another manufacturer**. For example, you cannot install four SMC ARCNET boards in one file server, but you can install three SMC boards and one LANMASTER ARCNET board.

- **Release the LAN and Resource Configurations**. If you have already selected and configured LAN drivers or resources, releasing the configuration will sometimes free up options for other LAN drivers.

- **Deselect resources**. You may have to sacrifice a particular video card or printer port to accommodate your LAN drivers.

When you are satisfied with your selections, press ESCAPE to return to the Available Options screen.

Configuring LAN Drivers and Resources

```
Configure Drivers / Resources

Choose LAN Configuration
Choose Resource Set Configuration
Enter Server Information
```

The Configure Drivers/Resources window allows you to select configurations for the drivers and resources being used in the file server. The window will list all the hardware that needs to be configured. Once drivers and/or resources have been configured, you can also review the selected configurations.

If there is only one configuration option available for a driver or resource, then it will automatically be selected. Selecting a particular configuration for any item may limit available configurations for other items, so you may need to try a number of configurations.

```
Configure Drivers / Resources

Choose LAN Configuration
Choose Resource Set Configuration
Choose Disk Driver Configuration
Choose "Other" Driver Configuration
Enter Server Information
Review Selected Configurations
Release Resource Set Configuration
Release LAN Configuration
Release Disk Drive Configuration
Release "Other" Configuration
```

Configuring LAN Drivers

```
Unconfigured LAN Drivers

A: WD Star/EtherCard PLUS V2.11.3 (111188)
B: Standard Microsystems ARCNET/Pure Data  V1.00 (881010)
```

The Unconfigured LAN Drivers window shows the LAN drivers that have been selected but not yet configured. To configure a driver, highlight the selected driver and press <Enter> to display the Available LAN Configurations screen.

```
Unconfigured LAN Drivers

Available LAN Configurations

 0: IRQ = 2, I/O Base = 2E0h, RAM Buffer at D000:0
 1: IRQ = 2, I/O Base = 2F0h, RAM Buffer at D000:0
 6: IRQ = 5, I/O Base = 2E0h, RAM Buffer at D000:0
 7: IRQ = 5, I/O Base = 2F0h, RAM Buffer at D000:0
10: IRQ = 2, I/O Base = 300h, RAM Buffer at C000:0
13: IRQ = 5, I/O Base = 2E0h, RAM Buffer at C000:0
```

The Available LAN Configurations window shows the possible configurations for the selected driver. Only configurations that are compatible with other selected drivers and resources are displayed. Configuration Option 0 usually corresponds to the manufacturer's default switch and jumper settings. In general, this option should be selected if it is available.

To select a configuration, highlight it and then press the <Enter> key.

Configuring Resources

```
0: LPT1
1: LPT2
```

The Unconfigured Resource Sets window shows the resource sets that contain at least one unconfigured resource. To configure a resource set, you must configure all of its unconfigured resources. To select a resource set to configure, highlight that resource set, then press <Enter>.

```
LPT1
```

The Unconfigured Resources window shows resources that have not yet been configured in the selected resource set. To configure the resource, highlight it and press <Enter>.

```
0: IRQ=7, I/O Base=378h
1: IRQ=7, I/O Base=3BCh
```

The Available Resource Configurations window shows configuration options available for the selected resource. Only options that are compatible with the other selected resources and drivers are displayed. Option 0 is usually the default option for the resource, and generally reflects the standard switch and jumper settings. It should be selected if available. Highlight your selection, then press <Enter>.

Releasing Configurations

If you decide to change a configuration, choose the "Release Configuration" option. A list of configured resources will appear. Highlight the configuration you wish to release and press <Enter>. Because NetGen keeps as much configuration information in memory as possible, releasing all of the configured drivers and resource sets at once can use up all of your available PC memory. It is usually better to release and reconfigure as few drivers or resource sets as possible. If you do use up all available memory, you may receive a message warning that a particular resource or driver has been deselected due to insufficient memory. To free up memory, reconfigure some selected drivers or deselect some devices until further reconfigurations can be made.

Entering File Server Information

```
                    File Server Information

A: WD Star/EtherCard PLUS V2.11.3 (111188)
     Network Address: 2
B: Standard Microsystems ARCNET/Pure Data  V1.00 (881010)
     Network Address: 1
Communication Buffers: 40
```

Network Address

Each network in a NetWare internetwork must have a unique address. This address is assigned at each file server to the NIC attached to that physical network.

This is different from the physical hardware address that every NIC on a network must have, otherwise known as the Node address.
This address must be:

- A hexadecimal number between 1 and FFFFFFFF.

- Different from the address assigned to any other NIC installed in this file server.

- If a NIC is attached to a network that has another file server on it, both servers must assign the same address to the NICs attached to that network.

- This address must be different from the address of any other physical network connected to any file server in an internetwork, and it must be different than the addresses of any remote NetWare bridges and/or remote networks in the internetwork.

For example, if you are connecting a second file server to an existing network the LAN Driver in the second server must be assigned the same address as the LAN driver in the first server. If the LAN driver in the first server has been assigned the address 1, the LAN driver in the second server must also be assigned the address 1. In addition, LAN drivers for any other network attached to any connected servers must not be 1.

Communication Buffers

The Communication Buffers are file server memory set aside to hold data packets arriving from the network until the file server is able to process them. NetWare assigns a default value to Communications Buffers of 40. You can increase this to as much as 150 (as of 286 SFT NetWare 2.15), or decrease as low as 10. Novell recommends the following formula:

> Determine the maximum number of workstation shells that can be connected at one time. Multiply by 2. Add 10 for each LAN driver installed in the file server.

Say that 20 workstations will connect directly to the file server in our example. Multiply by 2 and get 40. We have three LAN drivers in the file server, so that's 10 x 3 = 30. 40 + 20 = 60.

After you server is up and running, you can monitor daily buffer usage using the FConsole utility and then make adjustments accordingly.

Reviewing the Configuration

```
                         Selected Configurations

LAN A: WD Star/EtherCard PLUS V2.11.3 (111188)
       Option 4: IRQ=2, I/O Base=340h, RAM at C000:0 for 32k, no DMA
       Network Address: 2
LAN B: Standard Microsystems ARCNET/Pure Data  V1.00 (881010)
       Option 2: IRQ = 3, I/O Base = 2E0h, RAM Buffer at D000:0
       Network Address: 1

OS Type: SFT NetWare 286 with TTS

Communication Buffers: 40
```

```
                         Selected Configurations

Disk Chan. 0: IBM AT hard disk controller or compatible  (881012)
              Option 0: AT controller  I/O base = 1F0h, Interrupt = 14

Resource Set  1: AT Compatible File Server
   Resource  1: AT Auxiliary ROM
             Option  0: Mem E000h-EFFFh
   Resource  2: Western Digital Floppy Controller
             Option  0: IRQ=6, I/O Base=3F0h, DMA=2

Resource Set  2: COM1
```

```
                         Selected Configurations

Resource Set  3: LPT1
              Option  0: IRQ=7, I/O Base=378h

Resource Set  4: Novell SS Keycard/UPS Monitor
              Option  0: Base I/O = 230h

Resource Set  5: Monochrome Adapter
              Option  0: I/O 3B0h-3BFh; Mem B000h-B0FFh

Resource Set  6: LPT2
              Option  0: IRQ=5, I/O Base=278h
```

After you have selected and configured the LAN Drivers, Disk Drivers, Resource Sets, and "Other" Resources, you are ready to generate the operating system. The "Choose LAN Driver Configuration" option is replaced with the option "Review Selected Configurations."

You should record the information on the configuration review screens for future reference. If you have a printer attached to your PC you can do this with the <PrtSc> key.

If you are satisfied with your selections, highlight "Save Selections and Continue," then press the <Enter> key.

```
Continue Network Generation Using Selected Configuration?

No
Yes
```

If you have properly completed your configuration, the screen prompts:

```
Continue Network Generation Using Selected Configuration?
```

If you would like to generate the operating system, highlight "Yes" and press the <Enter> key.

If you have modified any resource definitions you will be asked if you want to save your changes. Highlight "Yes" or "No" and press the <Enter> key.

The Network Generation Options menu will be displayed.

If NetGen prompts you to "Abandon Network Configuration and Exit?", then you have NOT completed selecting and configuring drivers and resources. Select "No" unless you really do want to abandon the choices you have made, and finish configuring the system.

```
            Network Generation Options
 Select Network Configuration
 Link/Configure NetWare Operating System
 Configure NetWare Operating System
 Link/Configure File Server Utilities
 Exit NETGEN
```

Generating the System

Select "Link/Configure NetWare Operating System" from the menu.

The generation process takes several minutes. A series of messages will display and you will be prompted to put the GENDATA disk in any drive. Use the working copy of GENDATA, not the original.

> Novell Linker, Version 2.0
> Linking OSEXE-1:NET$OS.EX1.
> Insert Disk GENDATA in any drive
> Strike a key when ready...
>
> Configuring OSEXE-1:NET$OS.EXE

After the operating system is generated, select "Link/Configure File Server Utilities" from the Network Generation Options menu. A series of messages will display while the utilities are being generated.

> Novell Linker, Version 2.0
> Linking UTILEXE-1:COMPSURF.EXE.
>
> Novell Linker, Version 2.0
> Linking UTILEXE-1:DISKED.EXE.
>
> Novell Linker, Version 2.0
> Linking UTILEXE-2:VREPAIR.EXE.

Novell Linker, Version 2.0
Linking NETGEN:INSTOVL.EXE.

Novell Linker, Version 2.0
Linking NETGEN:INSTOVL.EXE.

Configuring NETGEN:INSTOVL.EXE

```
Download Needed Files To Floppy Disk?

Yes
No
```

NetGen will first ask if you want to "Exit NetGen?", then ask if you want to copy the generated files to your working copies of NetWare disks. Highlight "Yes" and press <Enter>.

NetGen will prompt you to insert each disk as it needs it. When the copying is complete you will be returned to the DOS prompt.

Preparing the Server Hardware

When you have completed generating the operating system, make sure that the hardware configurations you declared match the actual settings. Switches and jumpers on NICS, disk controllers, and other resources must be set according to your installation parameters.

Enter the configuration information on the NetWare Hard Disk/Volumes Worksheet, the NetWare Installation Parameters Worksheet, the NetWare File Server LAN Worksheet, and the NetWare File Server Configuration Worksheet. These can be found in the back of the Advanced NetWare 286 Installation manual.

9

Generating Workstation Shells

The NetWare shell is the software that allows a DOS workstation to communicate with other devices on a network, including NetWare file servers.

The shell consists of two programs, IPX.COM and NETx.COM.

IPX.COM is the network communications software that communicates directly with the NIC in the PC workstation. It implements the low-level protocols (IPX/SPX) that allow the PC workstation to communicate through the NIC to other stations and devices on the network. The IPX.COM program is customized to enable it to communicate with the particular NIC that is installed.

NETx.COM is the software that establishes communication with a NetWare file server. This program is specific to an MS/PC-DOS version. NET2.COM is for DOS version 2.xx, NET3.COM is for DOS version 3.xx and NET4.COM is for DOS version 4.xx. NetWare is supplied with fully configured NETx.COM programs.

The IPX.COM program(s) is created using the ShGen program.

About ShGen

ShGen provides three modes for shell generation: *Default*, *Intermediate*, and *Custom*.

The default mode can be used in situations where workstation hardware conflicts are unlikely. The default mode does not give you a choice about the switch and jumper settings (interrupts, DMA channels, etc.) on your workstation NICs. Instead, ShGen defaults them, usually to the switch and jumper settings on the NIC as it is shipped from the factory. When you use the default mode, the only decision you need to make is the particular NIC you will be using.

In the default mode you cannot change the resource configurations of the NIC, nor can you change or add to the workstation's resource configurations.

The intermediate mode allows you to select alternate LAN Driver configurations. This allows you to select from among specific sets of interrupts, DMA channels, base I/O addresses, etc.

If you have other devices in your PC workstation(s) that will conflict with the default LAN Driver for your particular NIC, and you know what those conflicts are, use the intermediate mode to select an alternate NIC configuration.

The custom mode allows you to select alternate LAN Driver configurations. It also allows you to avoid conflicts with other workstation "resources" (printer and COM ports, video boards, clock cards, etc.) by using a *Resource List*. ShGen will not allow resource and LAN driver configurations that conflict.

Using ShGen

ShGen, like NetGen, lets you work from floppies, a hard disk, or a network drive. The most efficient way to use ShGen during NetWare installation is the hard disk method, where you can take advantage of the NetGen directories you have already installed when you generated the operating system.

The procedure for starting ShGen (hard disk method) is different the first time than it is for all subsequent times. Follow the instructions below for the first time. After that go to the \GENERATE\NETWARE subdirectory on your hard disk and type "SHGEN" <Enter> to run the program. If you choose the hard disk option and enter the correct drive letter, the program will run normally and you will not be prompted to upload any floppy diskettes.

Using ShGen For The First Time (Hard Disk Method)

Move to the GENERATE directory you created on your hard disk during network generation. If your drive is C, type:

```
C: <Enter>
CD \GENERATE <Enter>
```

Put the disk labeled ShGen-1 in drive A. If you have two floppy drives put the disk labeled ShGen-2 in drive B. Type:

```
A:
SHGEN <Enter>
```

The following screen will be displayed:

```
Shell Generation  V4.00

Shell Configuration Level

Default Configuration
Intermediate Configuration
Custom Configuration

Use the arrow keys to highlight an option, then press the SELECT key.
```

Choose the Default Configuration.

```
SHGEN Run Options

Standard (floppy disks)
Hard Disk
Network Drive                    Drive: C
```

Highlight "Hard Disk," then press <Enter>. At the Drive prompt, enter the letter of your hard disk, then press <Enter>.

The screen will display the message:

Uploading files from floppy disk.

If you have not put ShGen-2 in drive B, you will be prompted:

Insert disk SHGEN-2 in any drive.
<Press ESCAPE to Continue>

After ShGen-2 has loaded, you should see the following screen:

```
Upload Additional Diskettes?

Yes
No
```

If you have other shell driver disks that were not loaded when you ran the NetGen program then you may need load them here.

The software drivers for may LAN NICs are provided by Novell with the NetWare disks. Some NIC manufacturers, however, provide the drivers for their boards separately. For these drivers, follow the instructions included with the drivers. They may instruct you to answer "Yes" when ShGen asks if additional diskettes should be uploaded, or may provide other instructions for copying the drivers and returning to the ShGen process. If you need to upload additional diskettes, select "Yes," otherwise select "No."

ShGen will automatically read all of the LAN driver files it finds. When ShGen finishes with the diskette, it repeats the question, "Upload Additional Diskettes."

If you are prompted to load any other specific diskettes at this time, then you may not have started your installation from the correct directory, or the files loaded with NetGen are missing. Type <Ctrl><Break> at the load prompt, exit out of ShGen, and check your files and directories.

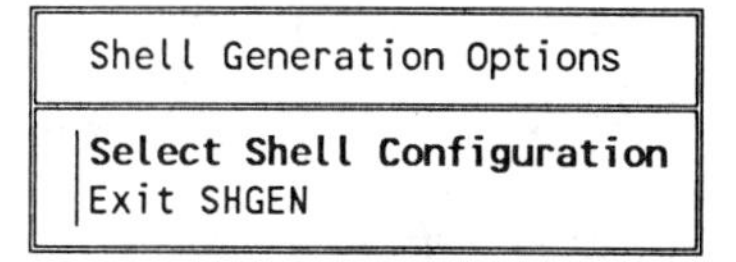

If you have installed the ShGen programs correctly, highlight "Select Shell Configuration" and press <Enter>.

Using the Default Configuration Level

After you choose the configuration method (in this case, the "Hard Disk" method), and after loading the appropriate diskettes, choose the LAN driver.

```
                    Available LAN Drivers

3Com 3C501 EtherLink  V2.50EC (881003)
3Com 3C503 EtherLink II  V2.30EC (880518)
3Com 3C505 EtherLink Plus  V2.41EC (880804)
3Com 3C523 EtherLink/MC  V2.30EC (881010)
Gateway Communications Inc. G/NET  V1.00 (880513)
```

The available LAN Drivers are displayed on a scrolling screen. Use the arrow keys to scroll through the list, then choose the driver you wish to select.

```
                    Selected Configurations

LAN Driver: Micom-Interlan NI5010  V2.30EC (880513)
       Option 0: IRQ = 3, IO Address = 300h, No DMA
```

```
Continue Shell Generation Using Selected Configurations?

No
Yes
```

The configuration of the selected driver is displayed, and you are prompted to confirm that you wish to use that driver for generating the shell. Select "Yes" to proceed, or press <escape> to select a different LAN Driver.

Note: If you know that the configuration for the selected driver will conflict with other hardware in your workstation, you should exit from ShGen and re-enter using the intermediate or custom method.

```
A valid shell has been placed on SHGEN-2
      <Press ESCAPE to Continue>
```

After the shell has been generated, NetGen will indicate that the files are located in the subdirectory SHGEN-2. This is a subdirectory of the NetWare subdirectory. Press <Esc> to continue.

```
Download Shell Files To Floppy Disk?

Yes
No
```

ShGen will now ask if you would like to download the shell files to a floppy disk. If you wish to do so, place a bootable diskette in drive A, highlight "Yes," then press <Enter>. ShGen will download IPX.COM, NET3.COM, NET4.COM, NETBIOS.EXE, and INT2F.COM (the last two files comprise the NetBIOS emulator).

ShGen creates a new IPX.COM file in the SHGEN-2 directory every time you generate a shell. If you want to create shells with different LAN Drivers, you should put a copy of each shell on diskette just after you generate it, so that the next ShGen procedure doesn't overwrite it.

If all of your workstations are using the same network hardware and configuration, you don't have to run ShGen again. You can make copies of your master diskette for each workstation by using the DOS DISKCOPY command. See the section "Setting Up Workstation Boot Disks" at the end of this chapter.

If you are using multiple types of network hardware and/or different configurations, you will need to run ShGen for each configuration.

To help ensure that each workstation uses the right version of IPX.COM, you might want to rename the file to a name that better identifies it. For example, you might rename the file 3COM3.COM for a 3Com board using interrupt 3, or MICOM5.COM for a Micom- Interlan card using interrupt 5. If you want to retain the name IPX.COM, label the diskettes clearly.

Using the Intermediate Configuration Level

The steps for beginning the intermediate level of ShGen are the same as for the default level. The difference is that you can choose a configuration for the driver. If you are unsure of how this works, read the next section on custom configuration, but ignore all information about resources.

Using the Custom Configuration Level

The purpose of the Custom Configuration mode of ShGen is much the same as the Custom Configuration mode of NetGen.

The Custom Configuration option allows you to:

- Select the configuration(s) of your workstation LAN driver. You can select the interrupts, DMA channels, I/O addresses, etc.

- Account for possible conflicts with other workstation devices through the use of "Resource Lists."

The Custom Configuration option can be used before you install the workstation hardware so that if you need to make any changes to switch or jumper settings, you can avoid removing boards from the workstation.

You can even use the Custom Configuration method to help choose the hardware you will purchase, allowing you to predict and avoid conflicts from the beginning.

Starting ShGen

If you are starting ShGen for the first time, see "Starting ShGen for the First Time" above.

If you are not starting ShGen for the first time, go to the hard disk with your ShGen programs, move to the \GENERATE\NETWARE subdirectory and type:

```
SHGEN <Enter>
```

```
Shell Configuration Level
-------------------------
Default Configuration
Intermediate Configuration
Custom Configuration
```

Select the "Custom Configuration" option from the Shell Configuration Level menu.

```
ShGen Run Options
-------------------------
Standard (floppy disks)
Hard Disk
Network Drive

Drive: C
```

Choose the Hard Disk Run Option and enter the letter of your hard disk.

ShGen will inform you if a previously defined shell file exists in the SHGEN-2 directory. If you elect to continue, any changes you make will over-write the existing shell configuration.

```
Available Options

Select Resource Sets (optional)
Select LAN Driver
Edit Resource List
Edit Resource Sets
Save Selections and Continue
```

The "Available Options" menu allows you to select LAN drivers and resources and edit resource lists and sets. If you have previously selected any drivers or resources, the "Configure Drivers/Resources" option will also appear on the menu.

Resource Lists and Resource Sets

One of the most valuable, and most misunderstood, features of the Custom Configuration option is the ability to use resource lists and resource sets. Resource Lists and Resource Sets are simply a means of avoiding hardware conflicts before they happen. By using them, ShGen becomes an evaluation and decision assistance tool.

For ShGen, a resource is any hardware device that could potentially conflict with the NIC, such as a video board.

A selected resource does not have to be installed in the workstation. You can select resources that are not installed to see how they would fit with other workstation devices if you did install them. (This is not true of the NIC, however. You must select a LAN Driver and it must match what is or will be physically installed). You can use the resource lists and sets to help you plan for future workstation expansion.

ShGen comes with a list of predefined resources, which you can add to and/or modify (See Appendix A of the Advanced NetWare 286 Installation manual for details on creating and modifying resources). Here is a partial resource list:

```
Resources

AT Auxiliary ROM
COM1
COM1 (No Interrupts)
Enhanced Graphics Adapter (No Interrupts)
Hercules Mono Adapter
LPT1
LPT1 (No Interrupts)
LPT2
```

Each resource has a definition file that lists the interrupts, DMA channels, etc., used for each possible configuration of that resource. For example, here are the configurations for printer port LPT1:

```
Resources
Resource Configurations

0: IRQ=7, I/O Base=378h
1: IRQ=7, I/O Base=3BCh
```

Actually, this screen only displays a descriptive summary of the configurations. Each configuration can be entered or displayed on a configuration screen that looks like this:

```
Configuration Information                          (Mode: Hex)

Number of I/O Address Ranges:     1   Bus: Standard
  Starting Address #1:   378         Range (bytes):           3
  Starting Address #2:               Range (bytes):
Number of Memory Address Ranges: 0
  Starting Segment #1:               Range (Paragraphs):
  Starting Segment #2:               Range (Paragraphs):
Number of Interrupt Lines:         1
  Interrupt Line #1:       7         Interrupt Line #2:
Number of DMA Lines:               0
  DMA Line #1:                       DMA Line #2:
```

ShGen can track all of the information about a particular resource and its configurations. In order for ShGen to use a resource, it must be put into a resource set. A resource set can consist of one or more individual resources. For example, the resource set for printer port LPT1 consists of a single resource:

```
LPT1
```

Using Resource Sets

When you select resource sets, ShGen reads the configuration file for each resource selected. Once a resource is selected, ShGen will not allow you to select another resource, LAN driver or disk driver that will conflict with that resource. In fact, ShGen will not allow you to select any driver or resource that will conflict with any other driver or resource. ShGen will also not allow you to select any configuration option that will create a conflict.

Selecting Drivers and Resources

The order in which you select drivers and resources depends on which resources and drivers are most critical to you.

If a particular LAN driver is critical, choose that first. For example, if company policy says that you will use IBM brand Token Ring boards, you may want to choose your LAN driver first.

If particular resources are most critical, choose them first. If, for example, you absolutely need an EGA monitor and three serial ports, you should select those first and your LAN driver and other resources after.

You can either make all of your selections first and then configure all of them together, or you can select each and configure it before moving to the next selection. Which method you use doesn't matter unless there are conflicts among the devices you want to install. In that case, you will probably move between the options, making changes until you achieve compatibility.

Selecting the LAN Driver

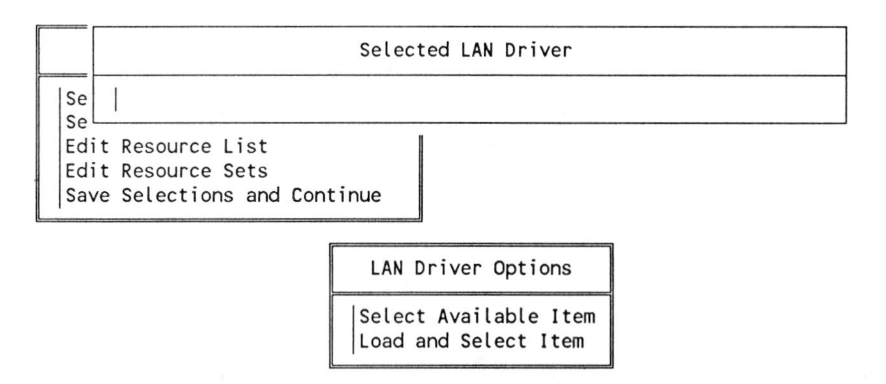

You can only select a single LAN driver for a workstation. When selecting a LAN driver, be careful to select exactly the right driver for your hardware. For example, two boards of different models made by the same manufacturer may require different drivers.

When you select a LAN driver, the "Load and Select Item" is replaced with the "Deselect" option. To select a different LAN driver, you must first deselect the current driver.

The LAN driver that you want may not be available if you have selected Resource Sets that conflict with it. If this occurs you can do a number of things:

- Select a similar NIC from another manufacturer.
- Release the Resource Configurations. If you have already selected and configured resources, releasing the configuration will sometimes free up options for other LAN drivers.
- Deselect resources. You may have to sacrifice a particular video card or printer port to accommodate your LAN drivers.

When you are satisfied with your selections, press ESCAPE to return to the Available Options Screen.

Selecting Resource Sets

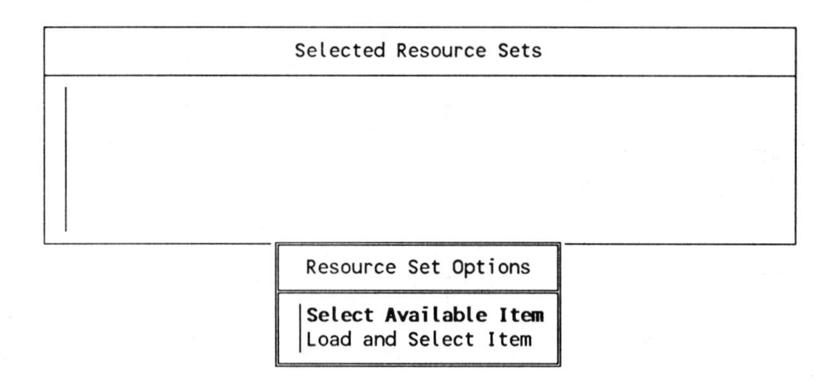

To select resource sets, highlight "Select Available Item" and press <Enter>. (For information on Loading resource sets see Appendix A in the Advanced NetWare 286 Installation manual.)

```
Selected Resource Sets

COM1
Enhanced Graphics Adapter (No Interrupts)

Available Resource Sets

Color Graphics Adapter
COM2
COM2 (No Interrupts)
IBM SDLC Adapter
LPT1
```

A scrolling list of available resource sets will be displayed. As you select a resource set, it will be transferred to the Selected Resource Sets window. As you select resource sets, conflicting sets will no longer display in the Available Resource Sets window.

Configuring the LAN Driver and Resource Sets

Configure Driver / Resources

Choose LAN Configuration
Choose Resource Configuration

After you have selected a LAN Driver and/or Resource Sets, you must configure those drivers and resources. If there is only one configuration option available for a driver or resource, then it will automatically be selected. Selecting a particular configuration for any item may limit available configurations for other items. Highlight Configure LAN Driver / Resource Sets, then press <Enter>.

To configure the LAN driver, highlight "Choose LAN Configuration." When the LAN driver description is displayed, press <Enter> to display the "Available LAN Driver Configurations" screen.

```
Unconfigured Driver

3Com 3C505 EtherLink II  V2.30EC (880518)
```

```
Available LAN Driver Configurations

0: I/O = 300h, INT = 3, DMA = 1, BNC
1: I/O = 310h, INT = 2, DMA = 3, BNC
2: I/O = 330h, INT = 4, RAM = C800, BNC
3: I/O = 350h, INT = 5, RAM = CC00, BNC
4: I/O = 250h, INT = 3, RAM = D800, BNC
5: I/O = 280h, INT = 2, RAM = DC00, BNC
6: I/O = 2A0h, INT = 4, DMA = 1, BNC
7: I/O = 2E0h, INT = 5, DMA = 3, BNC
```

Choose a configuration for the LAN Driver. If the default (0) configuration is available, you will usually want to select it since there is less likelihood that you will have to change switch settings or jumpers on the hardware if you choose the default configuration.

```
Resource Sets With Unconfigured Resources

1: Enhanced Graphics Adapter (No Interrupts)
2: LPT1
```

To configure resource sets, select Choose Resource Configuration from the menu. A list of unconfigured resource sets will be displayed. Highlight a resource set, then press <Enter>.

```
Resource Sets With Unconfigured Resources
  Unconfigured Resources

  0: Enhanced Graphics Adapter (No Interrupts
```

Each resource set is made up of one or more resources. When you select a resource set to configure, a list of its unconfigured resources will be displayed. Select an unconfigured resource, then press <Enter>.

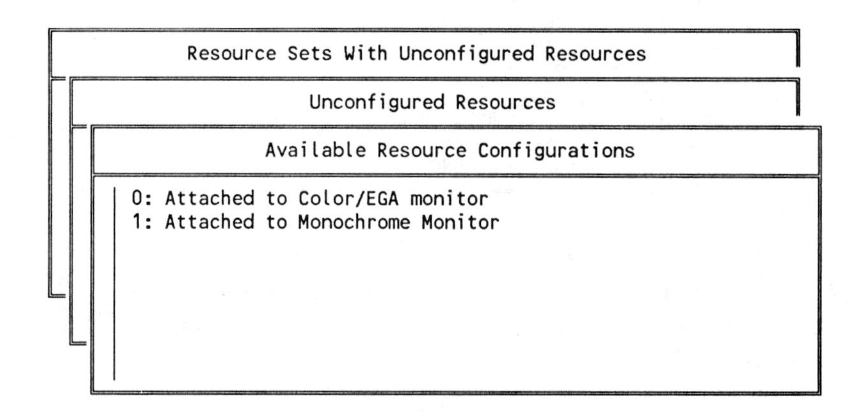

A list of possible configurations for the resource will be displayed. Select a configuration, then press <Enter>.

When configuration option 0 is available, it is usually best to choose it. Option 0 is usually the default configuration for the resource, and choosing it means that you will have fewer switches and jumpers to reset.

Reviewing the Selected Configuration

```
                          Selected Configurations

 LAN Driver: 3Com 3C501 EtherLink  V2.50EC (881003)
       Option 0: IRQ = 3, IO Address = 300h, No DMA, No ROM used (check
                 decode)

Resource Set  1: COM1
              Option  0: Int 4; I/O 3F8h - 3FFh

Resource Set  2: Enhanced Graphics Adapter (No Interrupts)
              Option  0: Attached to Color/EGA monitor

Resource Set  3: LPT1
              Option  0: IRQ=7, I/O Base=378h
```

Choose Review Selected Configuration from the Configure LAN Driver/Resources menu. Press <escape> to exit the review screen.

To reconfigure the LAN Driver, choose Release LAN Driver Configuration. Then you can either reconfigure the LAN Driver, or Deselect the LAN Driver and select another.

When you are satisfied with your selections, record this information on a NetWare Workstation Configuration Sheet (found in the back of the Advanced NetWare 286 Installation manual), and continue with the shell generation.

To complete the shell configuration, press <escape> to exit the Configure Driver/Resources option. Then choose Save Selections and Continue.

Generating the Workstation Shell

```
Continue Shell Generation Using Selected Configurations?

No
Yes
```

When you choose Save Selections and Continue, ShGen prompts you to confirm continuing shell generation with the selected configuration. Select "Yes" to continue, "No" to abandon, and press <escape> to continue configuring.

Linking the Shell

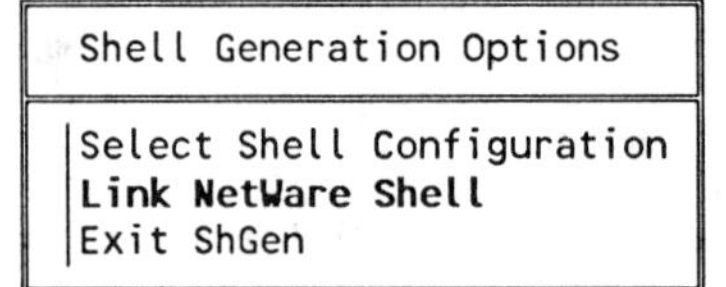

Shell Generation Options
Select Shell Configuration
Link NetWare Shell
Exit ShGen

Unlike the default and intermediate ShGen, custom ShGen does not automatically generate the shell when you confirm continuing with the selected configuration.

Instead, ShGen displays the "Shell Generation Options" menu. Choose "Link NetWare Shell" to generate the shell. ShGen displays a message indicating that it is linking the shell.

```
Exit SHGEN

Yes
No
```

When you have finished generating the shell, select "Exit Shgen" from the menu, then select "Yes" at the "Exit SHGEN" prompt. You will be prompted:

```
Download Shell Files To Floppy Disk?

Yes
No
```

If you select "Yes," the files IPX, COM, NET3.COM, and NET4.COM will be downloaded to a diskette in drive A. If you are going to need NET2.COM (for DOS 2.xx) or the NETBIOS.EXE and INT2F.COM files (only if you have applications that requrie NetBIOS.), they must be copied from the \GENERATE\NETWARE\SHGEN-2 directory manually.

Setting Up Workstation Boot Disks

The workstation boot disk is usually a diskette, but sometimes it is a hard disk formatted as a system (boot) disk with the DOS FORMAT command.

The boot disk should have the following files:

COMMAND.COM
IPX.COM
NET3.COM (or NET4.COM if you are using DOS 4.xx)
NETBIOS.COM (if required by your applications)
INT2F.COM (required with NETBIOS.COM)
CONFIG.SYS (optional)
AUTOEXEC.BAT (optional)
SHELL.CFG (optional)

The IPX.COM file is created with the ShGen program. IPX.COM is the hardware-specific portion of the NetWare Shell. It establishes communication between the workstation and the specific network interface you are using.

NET3.COM (or NET2.COM for DOS 2.xx) is the redirector portion of the NetWare Shell. This is the program that intercepts DOS calls and reroutes them to the NetWare servers. These files are identical for all DOS workstations regardless of the specific LAN hardware being used.

NETBIOS.COM and INT2F.COM comprise the NetWare "NetBIOS Emulator." These files must be loaded when using applications that specifically require NetBIOS.

The CONFIG.SYS file allows you to install DOS device drivers and change certain parameters in DOS.

AUTOEXEC.BAT is a batch file that is immediately processed by DOS upon booting a PC. The autoexec.bat is often used to run IPX.COM, NETx.COM, INT2F.COM, or NetBIOS.COM.

Setting up an autoexec.bat is discussed in the next section.

In the SHELL.CFG file, you can set options and change parameters about the IPX, NET3/NET4, and NETBIOS program files. In addition to changing specific parameters, SHELL.CFG allows you to patch any address in these programs. Some of the commonly used options for SHELL.CFG are:

> CACHE BUFFERS = <number> sets the number of 512 byte cache buffers used by the shell for caching of nonshared files. The default is five buffers.
>
> FILE HANDLES = <number> sets the number of files the workstation can open concurrently on the network. The default is forty files.
>
> LONG MACHINE TYPE = <name> sets the Long Machine Name in the shell. This parameter is used by the login script (usually with the %MACHINE variable or a conditional statement using the MACHINE parameter) usually to set a search path for the correct DOS version for a particular workstation. The long machine name is a text string with a maximum length of eight characters. When using this function, it is important to put the command "PC COMPATIBLE" or "COMPATIBLE" in the login script if the EXIT function is going to be used. In most cases long ma-

chine names (other than "IBM_PC") will be created by the system supervisor. The default long machine name is "IBM_PC."

SHORT MACHINE TYPE = <name> sets the Short Machine Name in the shell. This parameter is used to provide the correct screen displays for the NetWare utilities. Some computers, including some Compaqs and laptops, cannot display the utility screens properly. Using the parameter SHORT MACHINE TYPE = CMPQ in the SHELL.CFG file solves this problem by making the utilities load an alternate screen driver.

The default short machine name is "IBM," and the maximum length is four characters.

LOCAL PRINTERS = <number> sets the number of local printers on a workstation, over-riding the information that the shell reads from the BIOS. Setting the number of local printers to 0 prevents a workstation without a local printer from hanging if output is accidentally sent to a local printer port.

CONFIG.SYS is an ASCII text file used to load DOS device drivers and change parameters used by DOS. A typical CONFIG.SYS file could look like this:

DEVICE=ANSI.SYS	Loads the ANSI screen driver.
FILES=90	Sets the number of files that DOS can open at the same time. Number determined by application requirements.
BUFFERS=48	Sets the number of 512-byte buffers DOS uses for storing data read from disk. Number determined by application requirements.
^Z	End-of-file marker. Should always be on the line following the last text line.

Creating the AUTOEXEC.BAT File

If the workstation will use network resources frequently, you may want to automate connection to the network by invoking the shell programs in the workstation's AUTOEXEC.BAT file. The AUTOEXEC.BAT file executes a series of commands each time a PC is booted. A typical AUTOEXEC.BAT file might contain the following commands:

IPX	Load hardware-specific portion of the NetWare shell.
NET3	Load the shell redirector.
PROMPT $P $G	Make the directory name part of the prompt
NETBIOS	Load the NetBIOS emulator (if required)
INT2F	Load the NetBIOS emulator (second part)
F:	Go to the first network drive
LOGIN^Z	Run the LOGIN program.

Please note that the end-of-file marker (^Z) is on the last line of text, not following it. This is to prevent DOS from trying to execute another command from the AUTOEXEC.BAT file on the boot disk after you have logged into a server.

Creating the SHELL.CFG File

The SHELL.CFG file sets parameters in the NET3 (or NET4), IPX and/or NETBIOS files. A typical SHELL.CFG file for an ITT computer with no local printers might look like this:

LONG MACHINE TYPE = ITT_XTRA	Sets the long machine name so the login script can locate the correct DOS version.
LOCAL PRINTERS = 0	Prevents system lockup if output is accidentally sent to a local printer port.
FILE HANDLES = 90	Increases the number of files that the workstation can open on the server (the default is 40). This parameter should be based on application requirements.
^Z	End-of-file marker.

A typical SHELL.CFG file for a Compaq computer with a local printer might look like this:

LONG MACHINE TYPE = COMPAQ	Sets the long machine name so the login script can locate the correct DOS version.
SHORT MACHINE TYPE = CMPQ	Sets the short machine name so that the correct overlays (CMPQ$RUN.OVL) for the NetWare utilities will be found.

^Z End-of-file marker.

10

Installing File Server and Workstation Components

Installing components in PC-type file servers and workstations is really no different than installing components in stand-alone PCs. Included here are some tricks of the trade that might make your job easier.

1. **Document your work**. When you are dealing with multiple PCs it is easy to forget what went where. Always document the components installed in each file server and workstation. Novell's NetWare Installation manuals provide some very good worksheets for documenting the configurations of file servers and workstations. Use them (or something similar) to record the configurations of your LAN components. It is also a good idea to keep some documentation about the PC with the PC, preferably on a label. The documentation should list the components in the PC, their configurations, serial numbers, and purchase date.

2. **When possible, use similar components**. Using three or four different brands or models of Ethernet boards, for example, can make life difficult when you are attempting to diagnose problems.

3. **Standardize on configurations**. Don't generate five shell configurations, for example, if one or two will do.

4. **When making changes, change one thing at a time**. When a problem arises, the temptation to make five changes to your system at the same time is often overwhelming. By changing one thing at a time you can see what the effect of that change is. If you are making changes to diagnose a problem, and if changing a component does not solve the problem, put it back the way it was.

5. **Test your file server(s) under DOS**. Before you install your network operating system, boot your file server machine(s) with DOS to perform diagnostic testing. If you have DOS-compatible drives and controllers, initialize and format the drives for DOS. Many problems that are assumed to be network related are actually server hardware problems. Because of the extensive number of DOS-based diagnostic utilities available, pre-testing the server under DOS can eliminate problems later.

Cabling

Cabling is one of the major causes of LAN malfunctions, especially on new and improperly expanded LANs. The following tips can help make your cabling job easier:

1. **Hire a qualified cabling installation contractor**. If you are actually installing cabling in the walls or ceiling, you should hire a qualified cabling contractor. Local building codes, fire regulations and licensing issues may be involved in any cabling installation, and most cities require that cable installers be licensed contractors.

   If you do hire a contractor, be selective. Get references from your contractor candidates for companies with installations similar to yours.

2. **Use the correct cable**. If you are installing cable, make sure it meets your network's requirements. There are many different grades and types of cable. Coaxial cable, for example, varies in type and quality. The RG-58 coax used for Ethernet will not replace the RG-62 cable used for ARCNET.

   Make sure any cable installed meets any requirements or specifications prescribed by building management and local building codes. For example, teflon-coated "plenum" cable is required in many locations for cable routed above drop ceilings and through walls.

3. **Use the correct connectors and adapters**. Using incorrect connectors can result in poor connections and lost data packets. If you are using coaxial cable, avoid the screw-on coax connectors. Use crimp connectors instead.

4. **Be consistent**. If you are expanding or modifying an existing cabling system, use connectors and components that are similar to those already in use. This makes it easier for others who may have to work on the same system.

5. **Follow accepted color codes**. Twisted-pair wiring systems use standard sets of color codes for cables. It is important to learn them and use them. (See "Working with Unshielded Twisted-Pair Cable" and "Working with Shielded Twisted-Pair Cable" below.)

6. **Label everything clearly**. Label both ends of each cable so you or someone else can follow it later.

7. **Neatness counts**. Keep all wiring as neat as possible.

8. **Even if you hire a cabling contractor, you will eventually have to put connectors on cables**. As a LAN installer or system manager, the job of making things work after the cabling contractor leaves

will probably fall on your shoulders. This means that you should have the ability to make or repair cables.

9. **Use the proper tools**. You are less likely to damage equipment if you use the proper tools.

10. **Learn to use unfamiliar tools before attempting an installation**. You may waste a couple of connectors and a few feet of cable by doing this, but that is a minor cost compared to repairing damaged equipment.

The Right Tools

If you are going to install, manage, or maintain a LAN, you should have at least the following in your tool kit:

Basic PC tool kit. These usually sell for $20 to $30 and contain an assortment of screwdrivers, nut drivers, chip pullers, etc.

Connector crimper. For coaxial cable, a decent one will be $80 or more; for modular connectors used with unshielded twisted-pair cable they range in price from $8 to $125. If you are going to make your own cables, invest in a good crimper. The more expensive ones usually last longer, work better, and can often be used for different types of connectors.

Cable stripper. These can cost from a few dollars for UTP cable up to thirty or forty dollars or more for coaxial and shielded twisted-pair cable.

Volt Ohm Meter (VOM). An adequate VOM can be purchased for $20 to $30. For cable testing, an inexpensive unit that gives clear ohm readings in the 50 to 150 ohm range is usually sufficient. If you plan to use your VOM for critical voltage measurements, then buy a more expensive digital model. Some VOMs have a continuity function that beeps on a closed circuit. This can be very handy when you are working without an assistant.

Working with Unshielded Twisted-Pair Cable

Although the term unshielded twisted-pair (UTP) can apply to many types of cable, in the LAN industry it generally means telephone cabling. Most commonly, cable that conforms to AT&T's specification for D-Inside Wire (DIW), which is not as susceptible to noise and crosstalk as other unshielded cables. IBM's Type 3 cable specification corresponds to DIW.

DIW is easy to identify: it has a grey or beige vinyl jacket, and each pair has a characteristic color code. The first four pairs are colored as follows:

Pair 1: White with blue band, blue with white band
Pair 2: White with orange band, orange with white band
Pair 3: White with Green band, green with white band
Pair 4: White with brown band, brown with white band

Se Figure 10.1 for a complete 25-pair color code listing.

Figure 10.1: Common DIW Cable Pinouts with 25-Pair Color Codes

Table 1. Common DIW cable pinouts with 25-pair color codes

25 Pr Conn.#	50 Pin Conn.#	Wire Color (Wire/Stripe)	2-pair Pin #	3-pair Pin #	4-pair Pin #
			____	____	____
1	26	White/Blue	4	4	5
	1	Blue/White	3 Group	3	4
2	27	White/Orange	2 1	2 Group	1
	2	Orange/White	5 ____	5 1	2 Group
3	28	White/Green	4	1	3 1
	3	Green/White	3 Group	6 ____	6
4	29	White/Brown	2 2	4	7
	4	Brown/White	5 ____	3	8 ____
5	30	White/Slate	4	2 Group	5
	5	Slate/White	3 Group	5 2	4
6	31	Red/Blue	2 3	1	1
	6	Blue/Red	5 ____	6 ____	2 Group
7	32	Red/Orange	4	4	3 2
	7	Orange/Red	3 Group	3	6
8	33	Red/Green	2 4	2 Group	7
	8	Green/Red	5 ____	5 3	8 ____
9	34	Red/Brown	4	1	5
	9	Brown/Red	3 Group	6 ____	4
10	35	Red/Slate	2 5	4	1
	10	Slate/Red	5 ____	3	2 Group
11	36	Black/Blue	4	2 Group	3 3
	11	Blue/Black	3 Group	5 4	6
12	37	Black/Orange	2 6	1	7
	12	Orange/Black	5 ____	6 ____	8 ____
13	38	Black/Green	4	4	5
	13	Green/Black	3 Group	3	4
14	39	Black/Brown	2 7	2 Group	1
	14	Brown/Black	5 ____	5 5	2 Group
15	40	Black/Slate	4	1	3 4
	15	Slate/Black	3 Group	6 ____	6
16	41	Yellow/Black	2 8	4	7
	16	Black/Yellow	5 ____	3	8 ____
17	42	Yellow/Orange	4	2 Group	5
	17	Orange/Yellow	3 Group	5 6	4
18	43	Yellow/Green	2 9	1	1
	18	Green/Yellow	5 ____	6 ____	2 Group
19	44	Yellow/Brown	4	4	3 5
	19	Brown/Yellow	3 Group	3	6
20	45	Yellow/Slate	2 10	2 Group	7
	20	Slate/Yellow	5 ____	5 7	8 ____
21	46	Violet/Blue	4	1	5
	21	Blue/Violet	3 Group	6 ____	4
22	47	Violet/Orange	2 11	4	1
	22	Orange/Violet	5 ____	3	2 Group
23	48	Violet/Green	4	2 Group	3 6
	23	Green/Violet	3 Group	5 8	6
24	49	Violet/Brown	2 12	1	7
	24	Brown/Violet	5 ____	6 ____	8 ____
25	50	Violet/Slate	-	-	-
	25	Slate/Violet	-	-	-

Note: 2 and 3 pair pinouts refer to RJ-11 type modular jacks and plugs. 4 pair pinouts refer to RJ-45 type jacks and plugs.

Three types of connectors are commonly used when connecting UTP LANs: six position modular connectors, usually referred to as RJ-11 connectors; eight position modular connectors, usually referred to as RJ-45; and 50 pin connectors for 25-pair cable (Figure 10.2A).

Figure 10.2A: A 50-Pin to Six 8-Pin RJ-45 Adapter

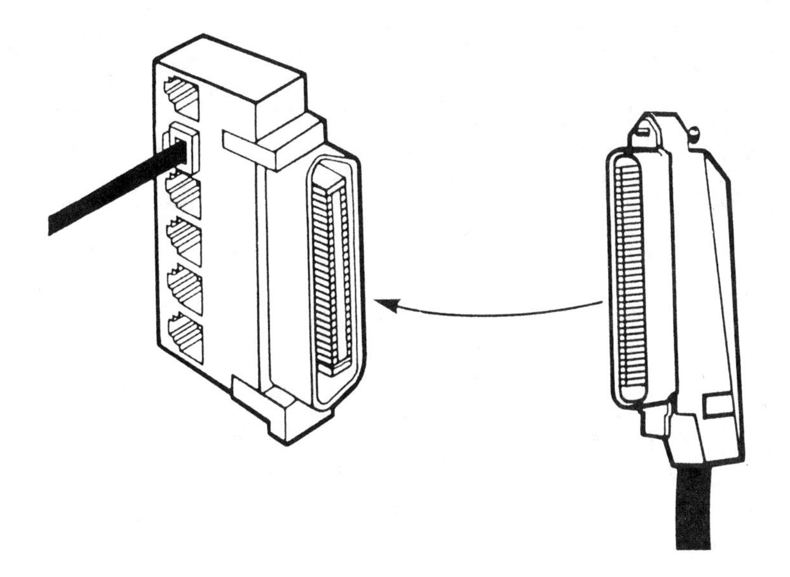

UTP is almost universally cabled in a star configuration from one or more central wiring closets. Almost all connections in the wiring closet are made through connecting devices called "S66 type Quick-Connect Blocks" or "punch-down blocks." Although available in several configurations, these usually have two double rows of 50 "punch-down" connectors (Figure 10.2B).

Figure 10.2B: "Punch-Down Connectors"

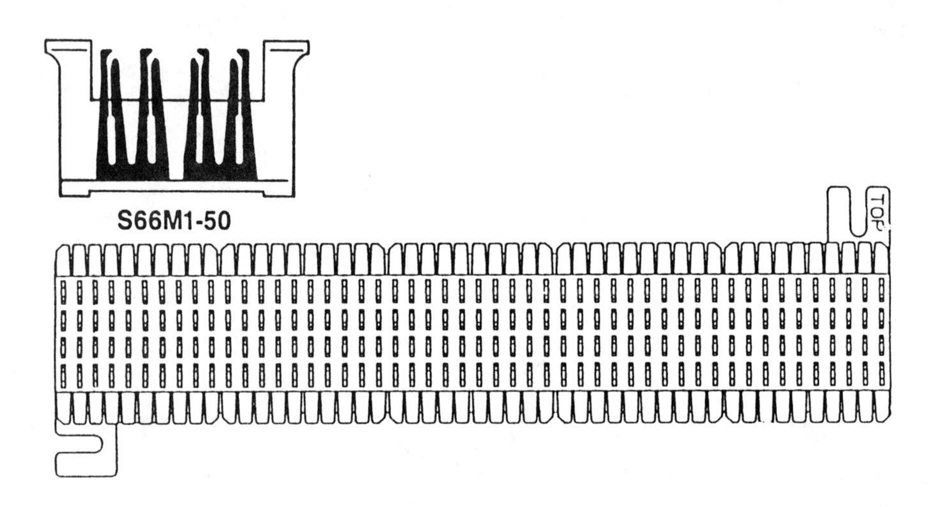

With the use of a special punch-down tool (Figure 10.3) solid copper DIW wires can be quickly and easily connected without stripping off the insulation (Figure 10.4). The blocks can be purchased with 50 pin connectors pre-installed for easy attachment of 25-pair cables.

Figure 10.3: Punch-Down Tool

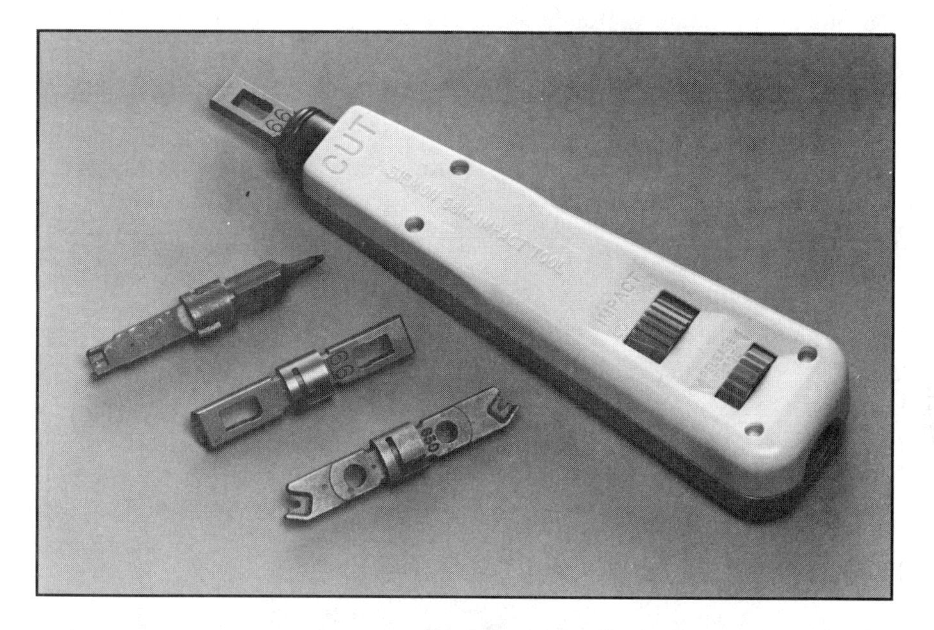

Figure 10.4: Terminating Wire on a 66 Block

(Figures 10.3 and 10.4 courtesy of The Siemon Company*)*

S66 blocks are usually attached to a backboard or distribution frame using special stand-off brackets. Cables can be routed behind the blocks, which snap onto the stand-off brackets (Figure 10.5A).

Figure 10.5A: Attaching a 66 Block to a Stand-Off Bracket

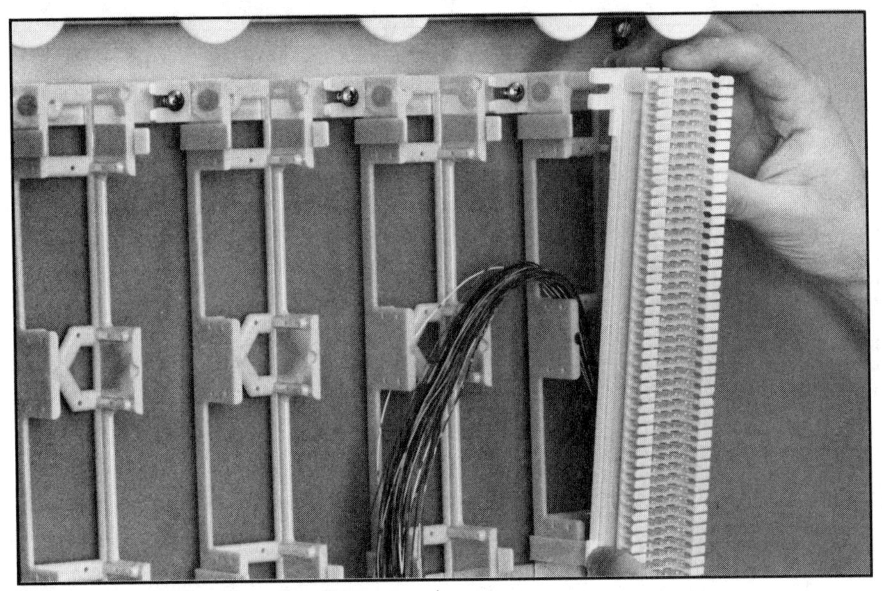

(Courtesy of The Siemon Company*)*

Cables should be attached to S66 blocks in a standard fashion. With 25-pair cable, for example, pair #1 should be at the top and pair #25 should be at the bottom. Two, three, and four pair cables are generally cabled in groups, with the first group starting at the top and the last group at the bottom of the block (see Figure 10.1). Connections between circuits can be made by cabling two circuits together on the same side of the S66 block, or by cabling circuits to either side of the block, and then using jumper wires or bridging clips to cross-connect the two circuits.

UTP station wiring is usually done with flexible cable using modular connectors. While telephone connections can be made with flat, parallel cable, modular connector cables should use twisted pairs. For Ethernet over unshielded twisted-pair and StarLAN, AT&T D8W or DW8A-DE cables or equivalent are usually recommended.

Modular connections can easily be made to S66 blocks by using adapters or patch panels, which usually attach to the block with a 50 pin connector. In addition, several companies supply blocks with adapters pre-installed.

Installing Modular Connectors

To install a modular connector:

- Trim the end of the cable so it is square.

- Strip the outer jacket 1/4" back for 2, 4, and 6 line connectors (RJ-11), and 1/2" for 8 line connectors (RJ-45) (Figure 10.5B). Do not strip the insulation from the wires.

Figure 10.5B: Cables Stripped for Modular Connection

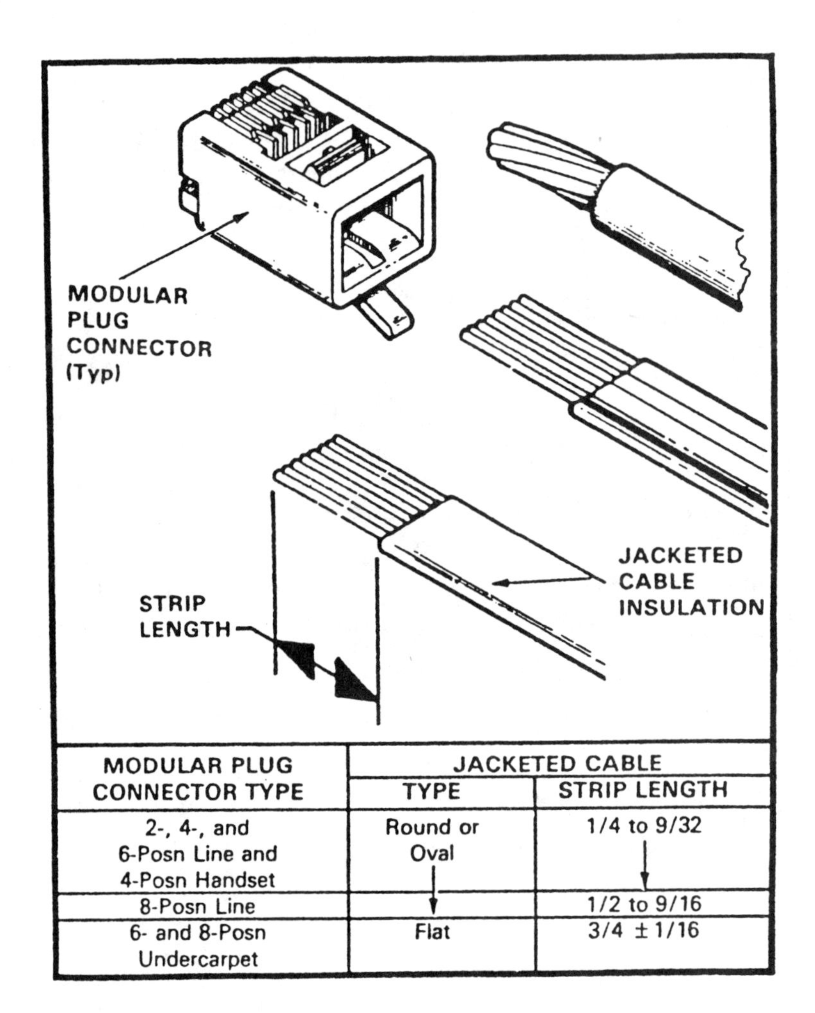

MODULAR PLUG CONNECTOR TYPE	JACKETED CABLE	
	TYPE	STRIP LENGTH
2-, 4-, and 6-Posn Line and 4-Posn Handset	Round or Oval	1/4 to 9/32
8-Posn Line		1/2 to 9/16
6- and 8-Posn Undercarpet	Flat	3/4 ±1/16

- Insert the cable into the plug until the wires bottom (Figure 10.6). Be sure to maintain polarity. Voice applications usually use reversed pinouts while data applications usually use straight-through pinouts (Figure 10.7A).

Figure 10.6: Inserting Cable in a Modular Connector

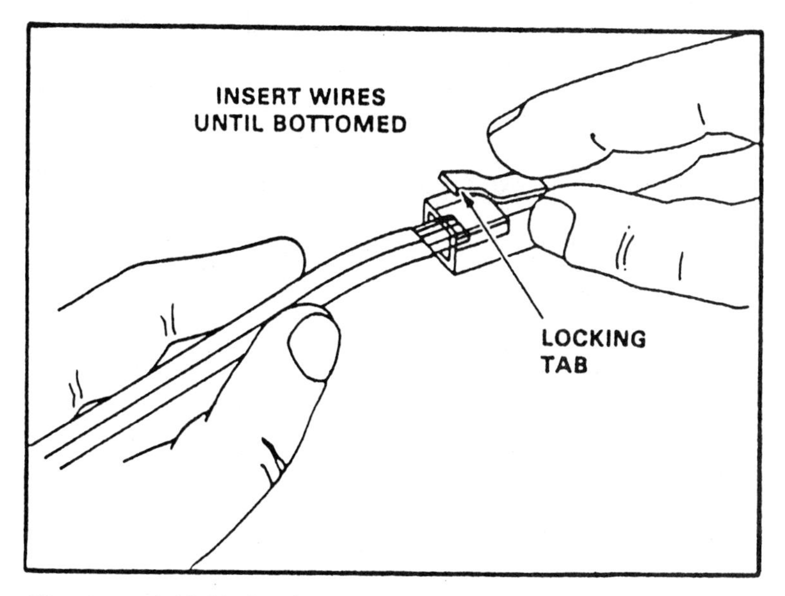

(Courtesy of AMP, Inc.*)*

Figure 10.7A: Cable Pinouts

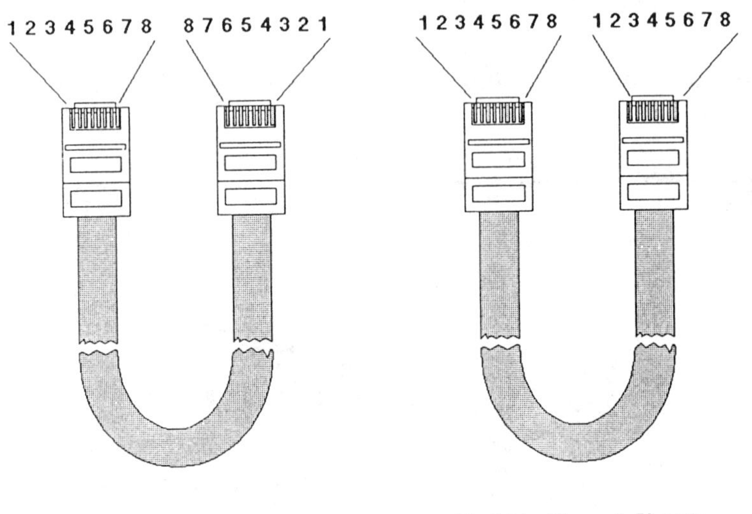

Reversed Pinouts

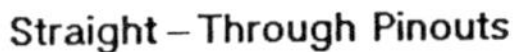
Straight – Through Pinouts

- Fully insert the connector into your crimper, holding the wires fully into the connector (Figure 10.7B).

Figure 10.7B: Crimping a Modular Connector

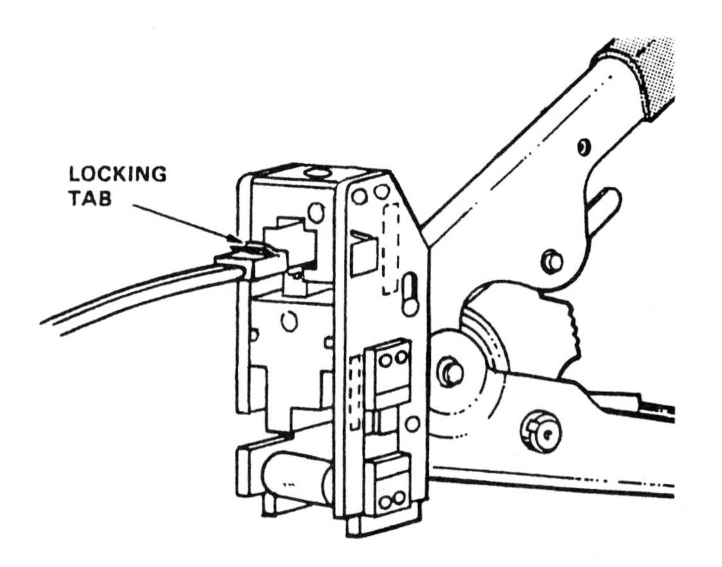

- Squeeze the crimper handles until the connector is properly crimped. More expensive crimpers sometimes use a ratchet mechanism that releases when the crimp is complete.

- Open crimper handles fully and remove the connector. With some crimpers you will have to depress the connector's lock tab to remove it.

- Inspect your connector to determine that the pins have been fully depressed, that crimped portion of the plastic body is retaining the outer jacket, and that the polarity is correct.

Working with Shielded Twisted-Pair

As LAN cable, Shielded Twisted-Pair cable is most commonly used in token ring networks. See "Cabling the 802.5 Token Ring" below for more information.

Working with Coaxial Cable

Unlike UTP, which is generally the same for all LAN types, different LANS that use coax require different types of coax. The coax cable used for Ethernet is not compatible with ARCNET and vice versa.

Coaxial cable is most commonly referred to by a military specification number that starts with the letters "RG," such as RG-58A/U, RG-62/U, etc. Cables with different RG numbers have different physical and electrical characteristics.

If you are planning to use coaxial cable, make sure you select the proper cable for your LAN hardware. ARCNET uses RG-62/U cable. Ethernet uses either RG-58A/U (called Thin Ethernet or Cheapernet) or thick Ethernet Cable. Thick Ethernet cable is a special version of RG-8/U. Thick Ethernet, sometimes referred to as "the yellow cable," is usually yellow or orange.

The most common type of connector used on light-weight coax (such as RG-58A/U or RG-62/U) is the BNC connector. These are designed for quick connect and disconnect. Three types of BNC cable connectors are available: crimp-on, bolt-on, and screw-on. Of the three, the crimp-on provides the most positive connection and is the most trouble-free.

The advantage of the bolt-on and screw-on connectors is that they do not require a crimper or other special tools to install, just one or more wrenches. The cost of troubleshooting the problems that they can cause, however, can more than offset the cost of the crimper.

If you plan on making or repairing coax cables, invest in a good crimper and a good wire stripper. Your crimper should be designed for the type of coax you will be using, and should be able to crimp the center connector pin as well as the outer ferrule.

Installing a BNC Connector on a Cable

Figure 10.8: BNC Connector Assembly

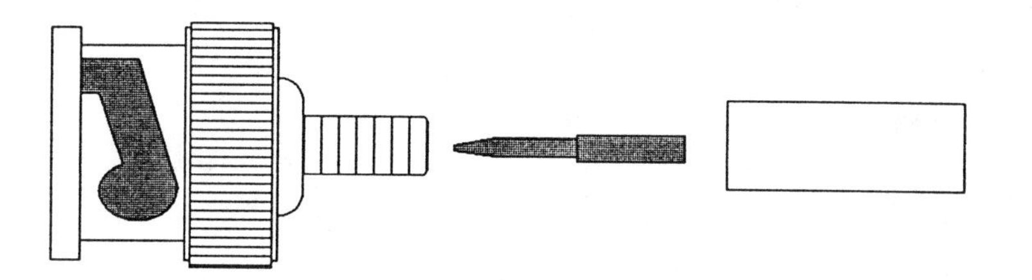

A BNC crimp connector has three parts: a body, a center contact, and a ferrule. These components are not necessarily interchangeable between different makes and models of connectors, so unless you are very experienced, don't try to mix and match. Also, make sure you are using the correct connector for the type of coax you are using.

To install the cable connector, follow these steps:

Figure 10.9: Coax Cable with Ferrule

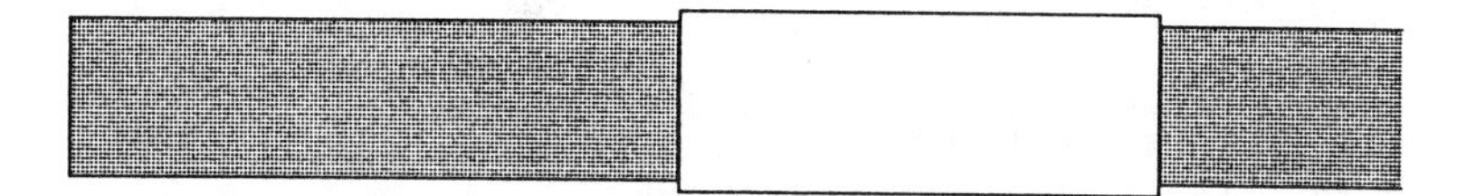

1. Slide the ferrule over the end of the cable.

Figure 10.10: Stripped Coax Cable

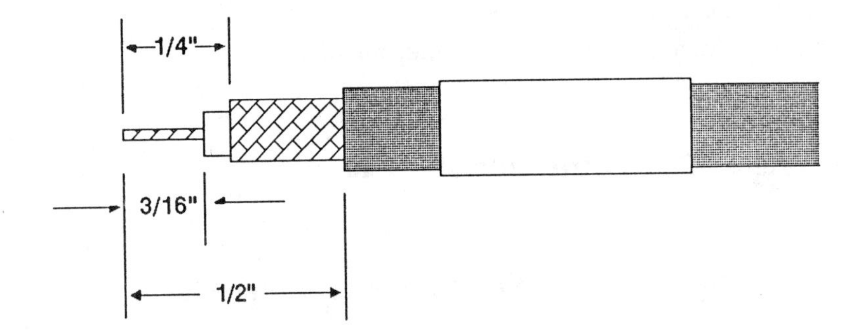

2. Strip the outer jacket back 1/2" from the end.

3. Strip the braided or foil shield back 1/4" from the end.

4. Strip the inner insulator back 3/16" from the end.

Figure 10.11: Center Conductor Installed on Cable

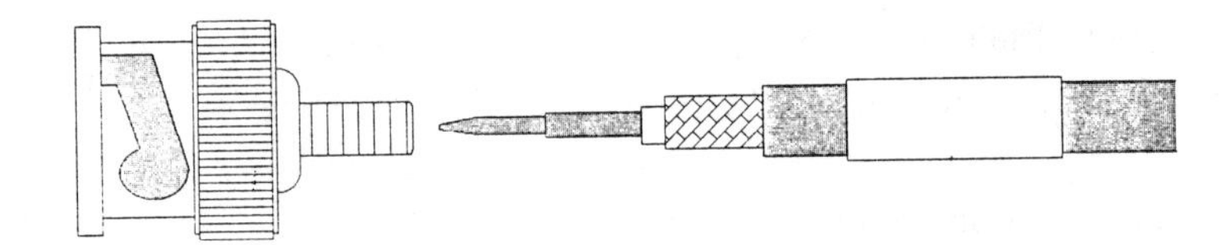

5. Make sure that the strands of the center conductor are tightly and smoothly twisted together and not frayed. Slip the center contact over the center conductor. Make sure all the strands of the center conductor are inserted into the center connector.

Figure 10.12: Connector Body Installed

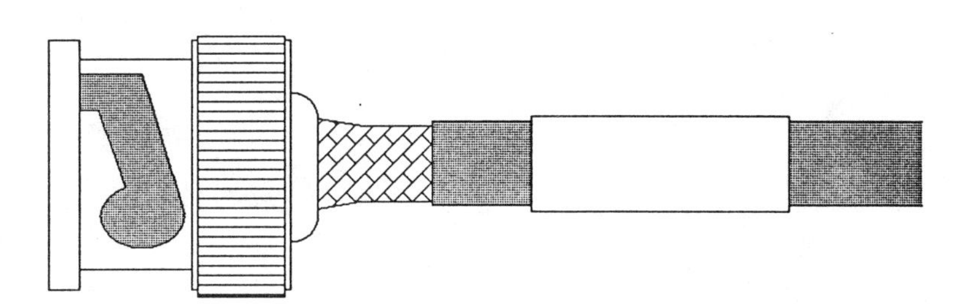

6. Crimp the center pin onto the center conductor with your crimper. Make sure no strands of wire are sticking out.

Figure 10.13: Ferrule Properly Positioned

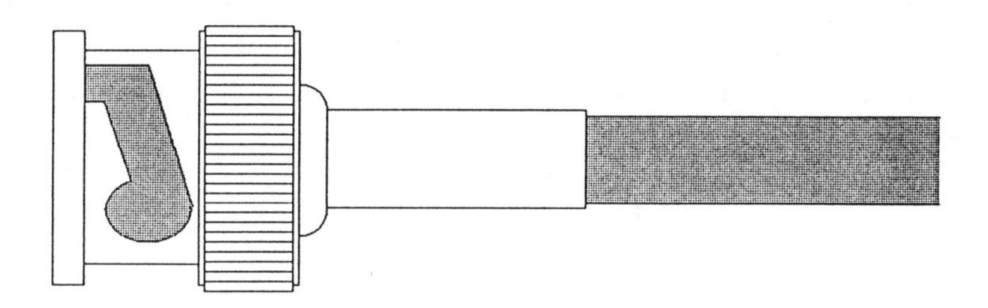

7. Install the connector body so that the sleeve slides over the inner insulator and under the foil or mesh shield. Slide the body back until the tip of the center contact is flush with the face of the connector body.

8. Slide the ferrule all the way up the cable until it makes contact with the connector body, then crimp the ferrule onto the cable.

Figure 10.14: Ferrule Properly Crimped

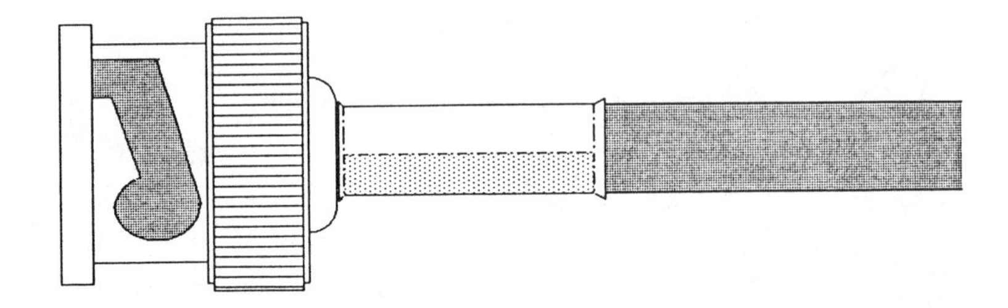

Cabling ARCNET

Standard ARCNET cable is RG-62 coaxial cable with an impedance of 93 ohms. UTP and fiber optics can also be used with ARCNET. The standard topology for ARCNET is a star-cluster, with ARCNET stations attached to distribution devices called hubs.

Figure 10.15A: ARCNET Topology

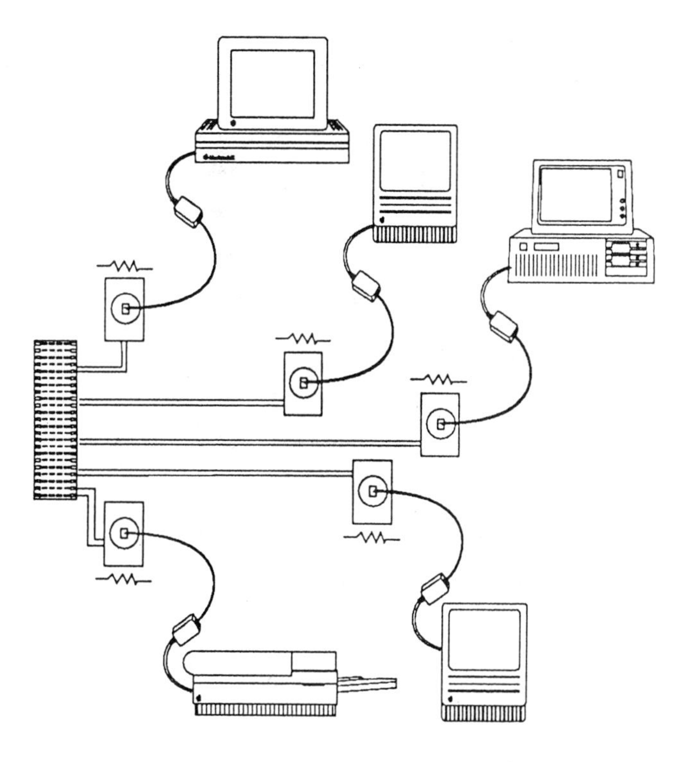

There are two types of ARCNET hubs: active and passive. An active hub is a powered unit that acts as a distribution device and signal amplifier. Active hubs may have between four and 64 ports. By using multiple hubs, an ARCNET can have a diameter as large as 20,000 feet, meaning a maximum cabling distance of 20,000 feet from any node on the network to any other node. In addition to coax hubs, UTP hubs are also available (see 'ARCNET on UTP" below).

Figure 10.15B: Stackable Active ARCNET Hubs

(Courtesy of Standard Microsystems Corporation*)*

Many newer active hubs have a special connector for connecting adjacent hubs. This not only saves one of the regular ports on a hub, but allows for easy interconnection between coax and twisted-pair hubs.

Passive hubs have four ports, and only distribute signals over short distances.

Linear Bus ARCNET

Linear Bus ARCNET, originally developed by Standard Microsystems Corporation (SMC) and now produced by many manufacturers, uses special circuitry to allow up to 8 to share the same linear cable. This cable can have a length of up to 1,000 feet. Attachment is made using the same type of BNC "T" connector used with thin Ethernet cable. The cable must be terminated at both ends with a 93 ohm terminating resistor, or one end may be terminated at an active hub, allowing interconnection with the star-cluster topology. Multiple linear buses may be connected using an active hub or 2 port "active links."

ARCNET on UTP

ARCNET boards and hubs designed to use UTP phone wire were initially developed by SMC and are now manufactured by several companies. Twisted-pair boards can be cabled up to 400 feet to special twisted-pair active hubs; and up to 10 boards can be daisy-chained within that 400 feet distance. Unlike other UTP LAN implementations, such as Ethernet and Token-Ring, only a single wire pair is required.

Standard coax ARCNET boards and hubs may also be connected over twisted pair using baluns designed for IBM 3270 terminals (Figure 10.16). A balun is a transformer for matching impedance between coax and UTP cable. Although there is no "official" specification for cabling in this manner, you can usually expect trouble-free operation at distances of up to at least 400 feet.

Figure 10.16: Coax to UTP Baluns

(Courtesy of The Siemon Company*)*

Fiber Optics

Longer distance point-to-point connections can be made with fiber optic cable. A fiber optic Active Link connects the fiber to coax. Fiber optic network interface cards are also available.

Two types of fiber optic connections are available for ARCNET: single-fiber links will connect at distances up to 4,000 feet, while dual fiber links connect at up to 11,500 feet.

Guidelines for Cabling ARCNET

- The maximum number of stations on an ARCNET is 255.
- The maximum cabling distance between active devices, including active hubs, network interface cards, active links, and fiber optic links is 2,000 ft.
- The maximum distance to a passive hub is 100 ft.
- The maximum length of a coax bus (using special high-impedance linear bus NICs) is 1,000 ft.
- The maximum number of stations on a coax bus is eight.
- The maximum length of a UTP cable or daisy-chain is 400 ft.
- The maximum number of stations on a UTP daisy-chain is ten.
- The maximum length of a single fiber-optic link is 4,000 ft.
- The maximum length of a dual fiber-optic link is 11,500 ft.
- The unused ports on a passive hub should be terminated with 93 ohm terminators.
- A passive may only be used between stations, or between stations and an active hub.
- A coax bus must be terminated at both ends, either with two 93 ohm terminators, or one terminator and an active hub.
- A twisted-pair daisy-chain or cable must be terminated at both ends, either with two 100 ohm terminators, or one terminator and an active hub.

- If you are using baluns, they should only be connected to standard ARCNET coax boards and coax active hubs. Baluns should not be used with high impedance linear-bus boards, or with UTP boards or hubs, or with passive hubs.

Cabling 802.3 Ethernet

Four types of cable are primarily used with Ethernet: (1) standard, thick Ethernet, a heavy coaxial cable roughly equivalent to RG-8; (2) thin Ethernet equivalent to RG-58; (3) UTP cable; and (4) fiber optics.

Thick Ethernet is most commonly used in large networks of terminals and other devices, attaching them to minicomputers or mainframes. Thin Ethernet cable is used in both large and small LANs.

UTP is gaining wide acceptance as Ethernet cabling. The 10BaseT Subcommittee of the IEEE 802.3 Committee is currently finalizing a standard for Ethernet over twisted-pair.

Due to its ability to electrically isolate segments of a LAN, and its ability to serve more efficiently over greater distances than coax, fiber optics are often used when networking between buildings. Also, because fiber optic cables do not radiate EMI emissions, they can be used in high-security environments. However, the cost of fiber and associated attachment devices is relatively high compared to coax. In PC Ethernet LANs, almost all coax used is thin Ethernet cable. There are two reasons for this:

- The cost of "Cheapernet" is more in line with microcomputer system costs.

- Most Ethernet interfaces for PCs have built-in transceivers for thin Ethernet cable. (A transceiver is the connector between a device and an Ethernet cable.)

Ethernet and 802.3 specifications call for specific cable segment lengths, where a segment is one or more cables attached in a linear fashion. The specifications also limit the maximum number of devices that can attach to a single segment.

Some vendors, however, have published nonstandard specifications that provide for longer cabling distances and a greater number of attached devices per cable segment when their own products are exclusively used. For example, the 802.3 standard calls for a maximum length of 185 meters and a maximum of 30 attachments for a thin Ethernet segment, however, 3Com specifies 300 meters and 100 attachments when its products are used exclusively.

Even if your Ethernet components provide for extensions, it is a good practice to stay within the standard Ethernet rules to assure compatibility with components that you may wish to add later.

Ethernet Connections

Every attachment to an Ethernet cable is made through a transceiver. In addition to providing attachment points, transceivers perform collision-detection functions. Transceivers can be built into Ethernet cards and other devices, such as repeaters, or they can be separate external units. Internal transceivers are usually designed to attach directly to thin Ethernet cable, although built-in transceivers for UTP are becoming more common.

External transceivers can be used with thick, thin and fiber optic cable. A four-pair cable, called an Attached Unit Interface (AUI) cable is used to connect a device to an external transceiver.

Guidelines for cabling Ethernet:

- No (coax) segment should be longer than 500 meters (185 meters for thin Ethernet, 1 kilometer for fiber.)
- There should be no more than 100 connections (transceivers) per segment (30 for thin Ethernet).
- There should be no more than three copper segments in series.
- The maximum length of any single series path must not exceed three active copper segments and two inter-repeater links.
- Both ends of each copper segment must be terminated with a 50 ohm terminator.
- Transceivers must be placed at a minimum interval of 2.5 meters along a copper segment (0.5 meters for thin Ethernet.)
- Each copper segment must be grounded at only one point.
- Thin Ethernet segments can be mixed with standard Ethernet and fiber optic segments using repeaters.

Every attachment to an Ethernet cable is through a transceiver. In addition to providing attachment points, transceivers perform collision-detection functions. Most Ethernet interfaces for PCs provide both an AUI port and a built-in transceiver designed to attach directly to thin Ethernet cable.

An AUI cable is used to connect a device to an external transceiver. AUI cables have a maximum length of 50 meters.

Figure 10.17: Three Copper Segments Linked by Repeaters

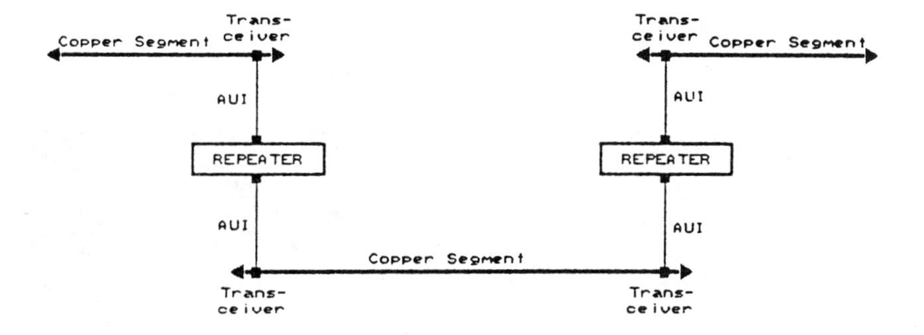

Figure 10.18: Three copper segments with repeaters and inter-repeater links (maximum linear Ethernet topology)

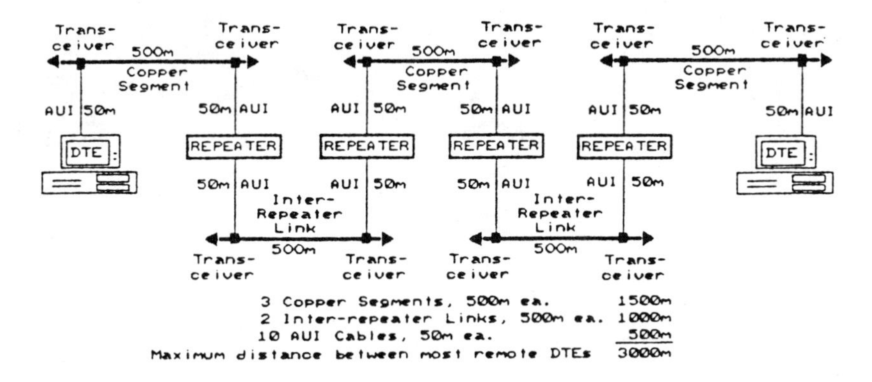

Multiple Ethernet segments can be connected using repeaters (Figure 10.19). Repeaters amplify signals from one cable segment, passing signals to another segment without changing the data. By using repeaters you can greatly increase your overall cable length. Up to three Ethernet segments can be daisy-chained using repeaters. In addition you can add to the overall length of the Ethernet by using up to two passive inter-repeater links (Figure 10.20). Inter-repeater links are coax segments that only have repeaters attached to them.

Figure 10.19: Ethernet Repeater

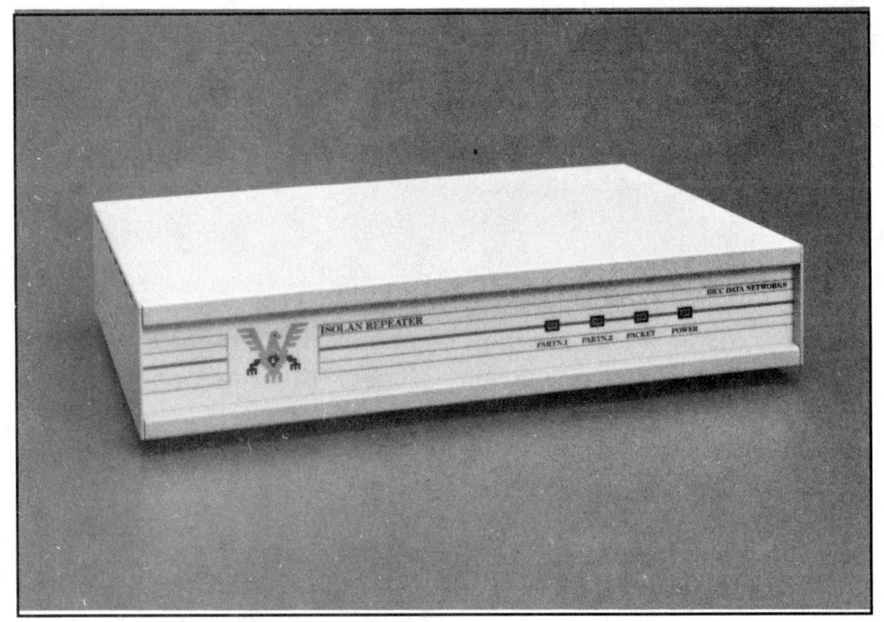

(Courtesy of BICC Data Networks, Inc.*)*

Figure 10.20: Ethernet Multiport Repeater

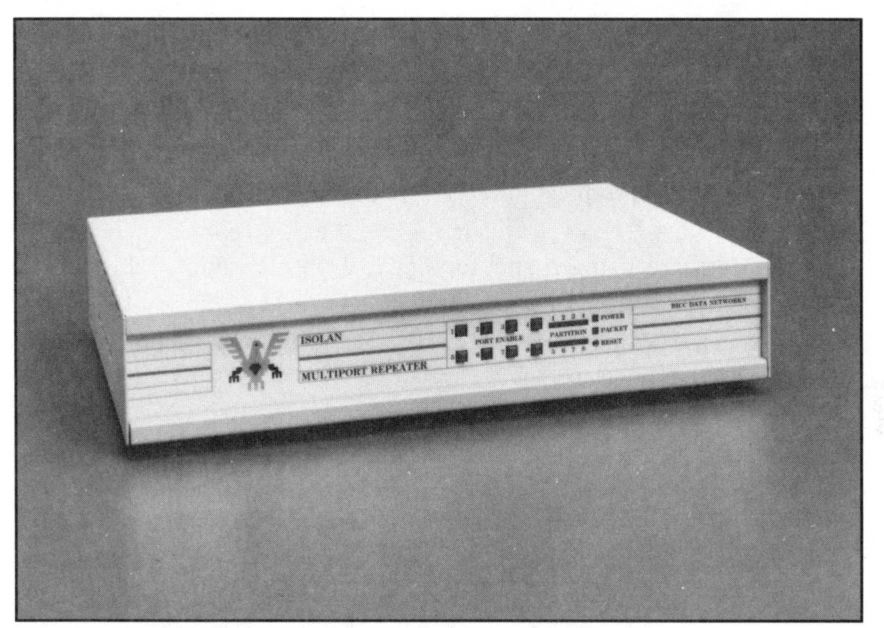

(Courtesy of BICC Data Networks, Inc.*)*

You can create parallel paths to extend your Ethernet cabling. As long as any single path does not exceed the maximum cable length, you stay within the specification.

You can create multiple parallel paths by attaching multiple repeaters to an Ethernet cable. Any number of repeaters can be attached to a cable segment, up to the maximum number of allowable transceivers. You can also use multi-port repeaters. Multiport repeaters allow the attachment of multiple cable segments in parallel. Repeaters and multiport repeaters usually provide for automatic partitioning of faulty segments, thus simplifying troubleshooting and problem resolution.

Novell's installation supplements for Novell, Micom Interlan, and 3Com Ethernet provide specific information on board switch and jumper settings, as well as basic cabling information.

Cabling Ethernet with UTP

Although the IEEE standard for Ethernet over UTP has yet to be set (as of this writing), a number of vendors, including SynOptics Communications, AT&T, David Systems, Hewlett Packard, DEC, and 3Com, are manufacturing products for UTP Ethernet.

Most vendors are using a star topology, with all station cables connecting to a central hub or concentrator. DEC and 3Com, on the other hand, are using a linear bus for UTP. The proposed standard is for the star-wired approach.

The star topologies generally provide for a hierarchical configuration, where two or more levels of concentrators are arranged into subnets (Figure 10.21), with the central concentrators usually attaching to a coax or fiber optic backbone. The star topologies require transceivers at the station end. UTP transceivers can be internal or external devices.

Figure 10.21: Hierarchial Star Topology

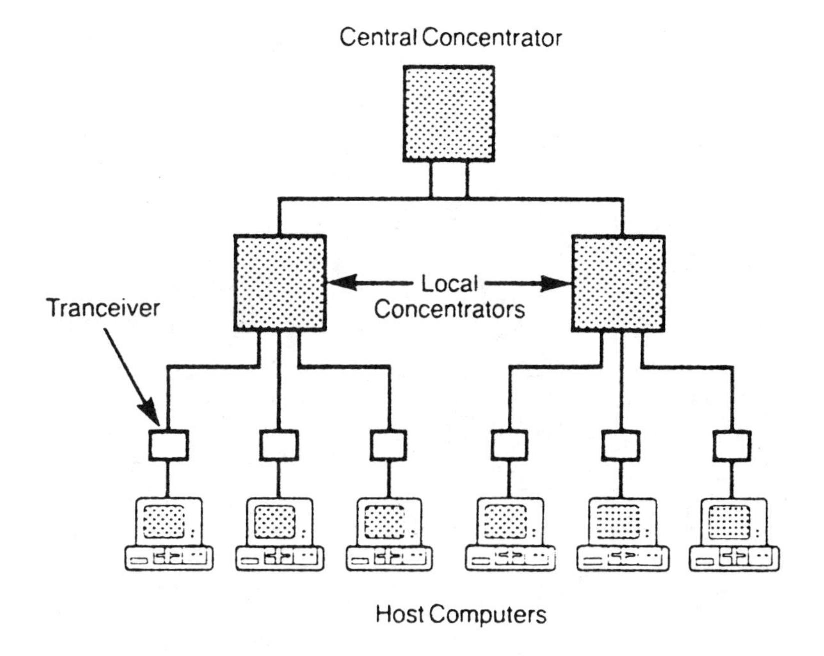

Because of the lack of standardization, it is difficult to discuss the specifics of cable lengths, but most vendors are quoting UTP cabling distances of about 100 meters.

Cabling the 802.5 Token Ring

Token Ring networks are usually cabled in a star configuration, with all station cables running to one or more central wiring closets.

Figure 10.22: Single-Wiring—Closet Installation

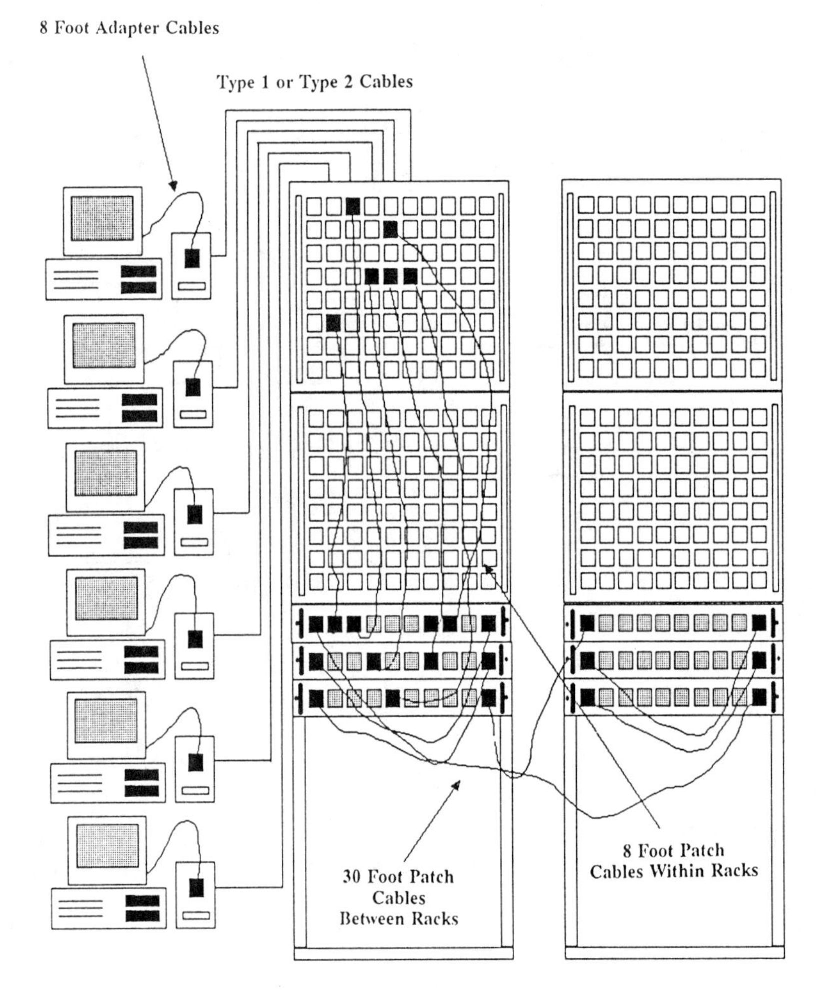

Figure 10.23: Token Ring MAU

(Courtesy of RAD Data Communications*)*

IBM's specifications call for all cables to terminate at patch panels on equipment racks in the wiring closet. Eight foot patch cables are used to connect from the patch panel to a hub called a Multi-station Access Unit (MAU), or between MAUs. The connections are made with and IBM Data Connector. These are often called "sexless" connectors, because any two connectors can be connected together. (Figure 10.24)

Figure 10.24: IBM Data Connectors

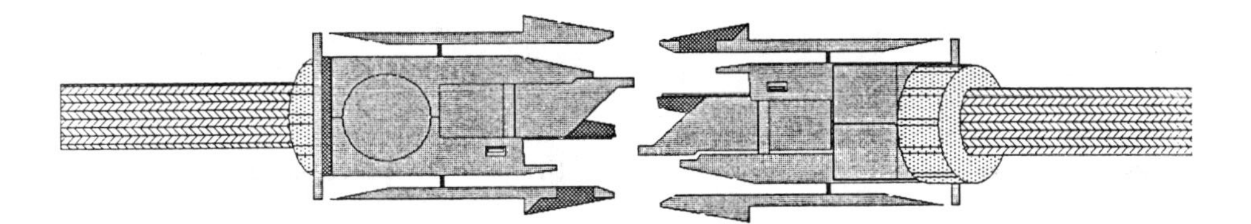

At the station side, a Token Ring Network Adapter Cable is used to connect between the IBM data connector at a wall plate and the DB-9 nine pin connector on the Token Ring card.

The primary cable used for the Token Ring is designated IBM Type one or IBM Type II. Type 1 consists of two twisted pairs of 22 gauge solid wire inside a copper braid shield covered with an outside insulating sheath. Type 2 is identical to type one, except that it has four additional twisted pairs outside the shield. These extra pairs are supplied for voice communications. For a standard installation, all drops (cables running from the wiring closet to the wall plate) must be Type 1 or 2.

Patch cables and adapter cables generally use Type 6. Type 6 consists of two twisted pairs of stranded 26 gauge wire inside a copper mesh shield with an outer insulating sheath.

Allowable cabling distances vary with the size and design of your ring, but the following applies to a ring using a single wiring closet:

Maximum number of stations:	260
Maximum number of MAUs:	33
Maximum cabling distance, distribution panel to wall plate:	100 meters (330 ft.)
Maximum length of a patch cable within a rack:	8 ft.
Maximum length of a patch cable between racks:	30 ft.
Maximum length of an adapter cable:	8 ft.

For detailed information about Token Ring planning and design, see IBM publication GA27-3677-1 "Token Ring Network Introduction and Planning Guide." Novell's "IBM Token-Ring Network Supplement" also provides excellent detailed information about board setup, etc.

Because improper cabling in a token ring can actually damage equipment, unless you are an experienced installer, you should not attempt to make your own cables.

Token Ring on Twisted Pair

A Token Ring can be cabled over UTP wire that corresponds to the specifications for IBM Type 3 or AT&T D-Inside Wire. Adapters are used at the equipment rack to convert from the IBM data connector to an RJ-11 modular connector. At the station end, a media filter is used to limit EMI radiation and to connect to the Token Ring network interface.

Several vendors currently supply MAUs designed specifically for UTP, and one vendor, Gateway communications, supplies a network interface card with a built-in media filter.

Allowable cabling distances vary with the size and design of your ring, but the following applies to a ring using a single wiring closet:

Maximum number of stations:	72
Maximum cabling distance, MAU to station:	100 meters (330 ft.)

11

Installing NetWare

Scheduling the Installation

Many people attempt to undertake LAN installations on weekends or during evening hours. This has the advantage of lessening the impact on users, if everything goes right. However, it usually has the severe disadvantage of limiting access to technical support.

Consider the following schedule:

- Choose equipment locations, meet power requirements, and install all cabling in advance.

- Prepare the file server and install the operating system in advance. These tasks are best done in a quiet location where you are not being constantly interrupted and where you will be free to make mistakes (if this is your first installation, you will probably make some). This could be a private office, a back room, or even somewhere off-site.

- When you have finished the operating system installation, connect at least one workstation to the file server and log in. Ideally, this would be the time to create users and directories, install applications, etc.

- Perform all of the above during times when technical support is available.

- Give yourself plenty of time. Many LAN installation disasters are the result of rushing.

- After these tasks have been completed, install the server on- site and begin attaching and testing workstations.

Installing NetWare

To install NetWare on your server, you will need the following:

- The file server PC. The required hardware (NICs, hard disk(s), RAM expansion, printer ports, etc.) should already be installed and configured in accordance with the parameters you specified when you generated the operating system.

  If you are using AT-type or PS/2-type drives and controllers, they should be installed and identified with the SETUP utility (AT-type systems) or the Reference Diskette (PS/2 systems).

  If you are using external disk drive subsystems, they should be attached and turned on. (Novell's DISKSET utility for installing drives with the DCB will be discussed shortly.) If you are using drives that require third-party value-added disk drivers (VADDs), you must refer to the VADD vendor's instructions before proceeding.

- The floppies containing the operating system you generated.

- A bootable DOS 3.x or DOS 4.x disk with the files parameter set to at least 10 in the CONFIG.SYS file.

- The file server's hard disk "Bad Block" list, which reports the physical location of any bad blocks the manufacturer found during their tests, by head number and cylinder. This list is supplied by the hard disk manufacturer, and is usually on a label or piece of paper attached to the drive.

  Unfortunately, getting to the list usually requires opening up the file server. If the disk is formatted for DOS many utilities, including most low-level format utilities (such as IBM's Advanced diagnostics), can scan the disk and read the bad block table.

  If you cannot locate the bad block list, you can usually contact the hard disk manufacturer (not the computer manufacturer) and obtain a copy. You will need to supply the manufacturer with the model number and serial numbers of your hard disk.

- The printouts (or other documentation) that specify the file server configuration parameters you selected when you generated the operating system with NetGen. Make sure you have the channel number, drive number and controller address for each internal and external hard drive and disk subsystem.

- The NetWare installation manual.

- You may want to have on hand the phone numbers of your Novell dealer and/or Novell's LANswer help line (If you don't have a Novell support contract, have your credit card handy.)

Preparing the File Server for Installation

To begin installing NetWare, first boot the file server with DOS 3.1 or above. Make sure your boot disk has a CONFIG.SYS file and that the files parameter is ten or greater.

Insert the NetGen diskette in the file server drive A. If the file server has a drive B, insert the SUPPORT diskette in drive B. (If the server doesn't have a B drive, NetGen will occasionally prompt you to switch between the two diskettes.)

NetGen gives you two installation options: *custom* and *default*. The default option automatically assigns configuration values, such as the number of files that can be opened concurrently, volume names, etc. These default parameters can change depending on you particular system configuration (NetWare version, drive size(s), etc.).

Selecting the Configuration Level

```
NetWare Generation And Installation  V4.00

System Configuration Level

Default Configuration
Custom Configuration

Use the arrow keys to highlight an option, then press the SELECT key.
```

If you select the default configuration level, you will *only* be able to select the Default Installation method.

If you select the custom configuration level, you will be able to select *either* the Default or Custom Installation methods, as well as the Analyze Disk Surface (CompSurf) utility.

Novell recommends that the first time installer choose the default method, but if your system requires parameters other than the default, that may not be possible.

Selecting the Run Option

```
NETGEN Run Options

Standard (floppy disks)
RAM Disk
Hard Disk
Network Drive
```

If you generated the network operating system using the hard disk or floppy disk methods, you should choose the Standard (Floppy Disk) run method here. If you are using the file server method (the NetGen programs and files are on another NetWare file server, and your new server is logged into it as a workstation), then choose the NetWork Drive method. This chapter will illustrate the floppy disk method.

Note: If you have selected the default installation option, proceed to the default installation section of this chapter.

Preparing the File Server Disk(s)

The first step in installing NetWare on a new file server is preparing the hard disk. There are two utilities supplied by Novell: Diskset and CompSurf.

> If you are using a Novell Disk Coprocessor Board (DCB), you will need to run the Diskset utility. This programs the EEPROMS on the DCB to recognize your particular disk drive(s).
>
> If you are using an internal PC, AT, or PS/2-type drive, you will need to run the CompSurf utility.
>
> If you are installing a non-Novell disk subsystem with a DCB, and the disks have not been "pre-Compsurfed," you will need to run the CompSurf utility.

Note: If you are using a drive that requires a Value Added Disk Driver (VADD), you should read the VADD vendor's instructions before proceeding.

Running Diskset (DCB Only)

```
Network Generation Options

Select Network Configuration
Link/Configure NetWare Operating System
Configure NetWare Operating System
Link/Configure File Server Utilities
Configure File Server Utilities
Configuration Util
Analyze Disk Surfa   Configuration Utilities
NetWare Installati
Exit NETGEN           DISKSET
                      Return to Previous Menu
```

To run Diskset, select Configuration Utilities from the menu, then select Diskset.

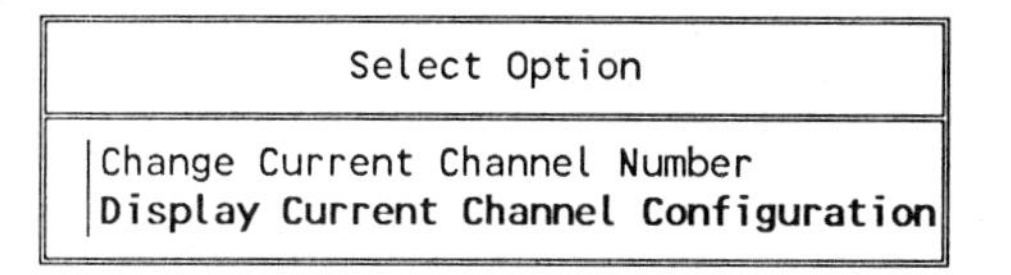

If you have multiple DCBs you can change to another disk channel from this menu. If you want to configure the drive(s) attached to the current channel, highlight "Display Current Channel Configuration."

```
Select a Disk/Controller

CDC WrenIII Half-Height
CDC WrenIII Embedded SCSI
FJ-M2243/A4000
FJ-M2243/A4000 , FJ-M2243/A4000
Fujitsu M2246AS/Embedded SCSI
Generic SCSI
Generic SCSI , Generic SCSI
Maxtor-1140/A4000
Maxtor-1140/A4000 ,  Maxtor-1140/A4000
Maxtor-1140/A4070 ,
Maxtor-1140/A4070 ,  Maxtor-1140/A4070
Maxtor-3280/Embedded SCSI
MiniScribe 4020
MiniScribe 4020 , MiniScribe 4020
Pyxis 27/A4000
Pyxis 27/A4000 , Pyxis 27/A4000
```

A window labeled *Controller Addr* and *Disk Types* will display. If this is a first-time installation, this window will be empty. Press <Ins> to display a list of supported drive/controller combinations. To add a drive/controller combination to the current channel, highlight your selected drive controller and press <Enter>.

```
Choose Controller Address

0
1
2
3
4
5
6
7
```

You will be prompted to select a controller address. This must correspond to the setting on your controller (you must refer to the controller or disk subsystem documentation for this information). Each controller attached to a DCB must have a unique address. Highlight the correct controller address and press <Enter>.

Repeat these steps if you are setting up more than one disk/controller combination. When you are finished, press the <Esc> key. When your configuration is correct, highlight "Yes" in the "Save this information?" window and return to the main menu.

Running CompSurf

```
Network Generation Options

Select Network Configuration
Link/Configure NetWare Operating System
Configure NetWare Operating System
Link/Configure File Server Utilities
Configure File Server Utilities
Analyze Disk Surface
NetWare Installation
Exit NETGEN
```

CompSurf provides several functions. It performs a low-level format on the selected drive; it performs a media analysis test on the selected drive; it places the bad block table in the location required by NetWare; and it updates the table with any bad blocks it finds during testing.

When to Use CompSurf

If your file server drives are not Novell drives or "pre-CompSurfed" drives, you must use CompSurf on the drives before installing NetWare.

> *Important Note*: If you choose to use the default installation method, and your file server disk drive is already partitioned for DOS, run CompSurf before proceeding with your installation. The default installation method does not usually CompSurf DOS-partitioned drives. When NetGen partitions the drive for NetWare, however, the DOS bad block table is not retained unless it is hand-entered through CompSurf. NetWare's HotFix is designed to fix any bad blocks that it encounters, but it is much better to enter known ones beforehand.
>
> If you would like to CompSurf a DOS-partitioned drive before the Default Installation, Select Custom Configuration when you initially enter NetGen. Follow the instructions for running CompSurf, below, then select NetWare Installation, followed by Default Installation.

To run CompSurf, do the following:

If you are using the Default Installation method, and your drive is partitioned for DOS, follow the instructions in the "Important note" above. If you are using the Default Installation method, and your drive is not partitioned for DOS, then follow the instructions in "Selecting Network Generation Options" below.

CompSurf may display one or more warning messages, and will then ask you to select the drive to be tested. It then asks if you want to format the drive. If you answer "Yes," it will ask you for the interleave factor (see below). If you elect to format the drive, you will be asked if you wish to maintain the current media defect (bad block) list. You will then be asked for the number of passes for the sequential I/O test and the number of I/Os in the Random test.

You will then be asked to verify that the parameters are correct. If you answer "No," you will be asked to re-enter the information. If you answer "Yes," the CompSurf process will begin.

CompSurf displays a warning similar to the following:

```
                         Error Report
DESCRIPTION
   Compsurf destroys all data on a disk when it is tested.  By
   repeatedly pressing ESCAPE you may back out of the test at any
   time before you have confirmed that the parameters you have
   entered are correct.

SEVERITY
   Program execution should continue normally.

                     <Press ESCAPE to continue>
```

If a printer is not attached to the server, you may receive the following message as well:

```
                        Error Report
DESCRIPTION
   Compsurf could not initialize the printer.  This is not a
   problem now and Compsurf will function correctly without a
   printer.  However, if the printer is not working, Compsurf may
    hang up if you try to print the test results.

SEVERITY
   Program execution should continue normally.

                 <Press ESCAPE to continue>
```

If you receive this message, you will not be able to print CompSurf's report of the bad blocks it finds (unless you connect a parallel printer). The CompSurf utility may hang if you ask it to print the bad block report while no printer is attached. If CompSurf hangs, you will have to re-boot to a DOS disk and begin the installation instructions again.

CompSurf lists the drives that are available to be analyzed. Select the drive you want to analyze.

```
                  Select the drive to be tested
| 1)  Chan. 0  Cont. 0  Drive 0   IBM AT Hard Disk  "C"    type  002
```

CompSurf will ask you a series of questions about the way in which it should operate. It adds each answer to its Program Operation Parameters window.

If the selected disk has never been properly formatted, CompSurf will do so automatically. If the disk has been formatted before, it asks if you want to reformat the disk.

```
Format the disk?
-----------------
No
Yes
```

```
Select the interleave
---------------------
1 - one
2 - two
3 - three
4 - four
5 - five
6 - six
7 - seven
8 - eight
```

The file server writes to the hard disk by sector in a fixed rotation. It writes to a specified point, then moves on. The actual data transfer can (and does) lag behind, missing the starting point on the next sector. When that happens, the disk has to make an entire revolution back to the sector to be in the correct position again.

To give the data transfer process enough time to accomplish the writes for which it is responsible, the disk can be designed to skip sectors in a specified way. The skip pattern is called an *interleave*. For example, if the disk writes every other sector, the interleave is 2. If it writes every third sector, the interleave is 3, and so on.

The interleave default for each disk type is specified as the most efficient for that disk. In general, Novell recommends that interleaves be left at the following default values:

Interleave 1 for IBM PS/2 file servers.

Interleave 2 for NetWare and IBM AT compatible file servers that use the IBM or Western Digital controllers.

Some disk/controller combinations are optimized for different interleave factors. If you are in doubt, consult the documentation for your disk controller or disk subsystem.

```
Maintain the current media defect list?
---------------------------------------
No
Yes
```

If you are running CompSurf during installation for the first time, you should answer "No" to maintaining the current media defect list, unless it is a Novell drive (Novell CompSurfs all drives at the factory.) Any existing Bad Block table on a non-Novell drive that hasn't been CompSurfed may not be NetWare compatible. If you are re-running CompSurf after it has completed successfully at least once before on the disk, then you can answer "Yes."

```
Enter media defects?
--------------------
No
Yes
```

If you answered "No" to "Maintain Current bad block table," you can elect to enter the bad block report supplied by the hard disk manufacturer. Novell recommends that you enter the manufacturer's specified bad blocks if you have them. If you answer "Yes" here, you will be prompted for the bad block information after you finish specifying the program operation parameters.

Number of Sequential Passes
0 - zero 1 - one 2 - two 3 - three 4 - four 5 - five

CompSurf tests the disk by writing patterns to it sequentially. Each sequential pass takes 30–45 minutes on a 20MB disk, and proportionally longer on larger disks. Novell recommends three sequential passes on the disk.

number of I/O's in Random Test
16000

Random I/O testing exercises the read/write heads and tests the head positioning mechanism. If any bad blocks that are not entered in the bad block table are encountered, CompSurf will update the table.

The default number of I/Os will appear in the window, and you can change this value. Novell recommends that you perform at least the default number of I/Os. The test will take about three minutes to do 1000 I/Os.

To change the number, use the arrow and backspace keys, then press <enter>. If the number is less than the recommended default, you will receive a warning message; press <escape> to continue.

```
Program Operation Parameters

The disk WILL be formatted.
The interleave is  2
The media defect list is cleared.
Media defects will be hand entered.
3 passes of Sequential Test
16000 I/O's in Random Test
```

```
Are these parameters correct?

No
Yes
```

The program will ask you to confirm that the parameters are correct. If they are, choose "Yes." If they are not, choose "No" and you will be returned to the point in the program where you selected the disk drive to CompSurf.

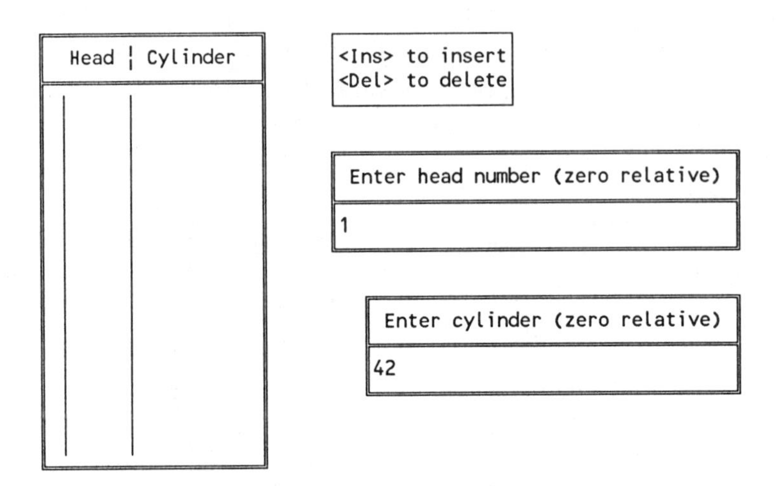

If you specified that the bad block table would be hand-entered, a screen will now appear where you can enter that information.

To add a bad block to the list, press <insert>. Enter the head number and press <Enter>. Then enter the cylinder number and press <Enter>.

To delete a bad block entry, highlight it and press <Del>. To delete multiple entries at once, mark each entry to be deleted with the <F5> key. Marked entries will appear in bold. Press <Del> when all entries to be deleted have been marked. In either case, after you press <Del> CompSurf will ask you to confirm deleting the marked item(s). Answer "Yes" to delete the blocks. Answer "No" or press <Esc> to return to the list. Press <F7> to unmark the marked entries.

When the bad block list is complete, press <Esc>. CompSurf will ask you to confirm that the entries are correct. Select "Yes" to begin the CompSurf process. Select "No" to continue editing the bad block list.

If you selected formatting, CompSurf will perform a low-level disk format, then perform its tests according to the parameters you set.

```
Surface Testing Finished - disk passed.

Display Bad Block Table
Print Bad Block Table
```

If the tests were successful, CompSurf will prompt you to display or print the bad block table. If you do not have a printer attached, do not attempt to print the bad block table. CompSurf may hang if you do.

Head	Cylinder
0	42
0	42
1	222
1	42
1	42
1	222
2	500
2	222
2	222
2	500
3	500
3	500

The CompSurf bad block table consists of the bad blocks it found, plus the bad blocks you entered. Do not be concerned if there are duplicate entries.

You should record the bad block table, keeping one copy with the hard disk and one copy with your other system documentation.

When you exit CompSurf you will return to the Network Generation Options menu. If there are more disks to CompSurf, select Analyze Disk Surface from the menu again, otherwise, select NetWare Installation.

Selecting Network Generation Options

```
        Drive Name       Channel  Controller  Drive    Status
|IBM AT Hard Disk  "C"  0          0           0
```

Choose NetWare Installation from the options menu. (*Note*: Depending on previous actions you have taken in the NetGen program, the Network Generation Options menu may not display all of the options listed here.)

NetGen may prompt you to insert your configured NETGEN and SUPPORT disks several times.

At this point you will see a message indicating that NetWare is analyzing the system to determine the kinds of disk drives that are connected. This may take several minutes, depending on what kind and how many disk drives are connected to the file server.

```
        Drive Name       Channel  Controller  Drive    Status
|IBM AT Hard D  Confirm Attached Drives    0
                |Drive List is Correct
                |Re-examine Drive List
                |Drive List Is Not Correct
```

NetGen reports the kind of disk drive(s) you selected earlier. If this information is not correct, NetWare may not function, or function incorrectly, and under certain circumstances can cause disk damage.

The information should be checked against the printout or other documentation you made while generating the operating system and should also be checked against the actual equipment installed in the file server.

This example reports the selection of an IBM AT hard disk installed as drive C using Channel 0.

```
Installation Options

Select Default Installation Options
Select Custom Installation Options
Continue Installation
```

If the drive list is Correct, choose that.

If the drive list is incorrect or incomplete, you should choose Incorrect Drive List. You will be prompted to exit, which you should do. Then go back to Chapter 8—Configuring the NetWare Operating System. Re-run NetGen, modify the disk drive selections as necessary, and regenerate the operating system. Then begin this chapter again.

After you verify the drive list, the menu for choosing default or custom installation will appear.

Note: If the drive has not been CompSurfed, a message will appear informing you to that effect. If this happens, you must run the CompSurf utility as outlined above.

Choosing Default or Custom Installation

```
Installation Options

Select Default Installation Options
Continue Installation
```

The NetGen Installation program allows you to choose a default or custom installation. The default installation makes certain assumptions and decisions based on your hardware configuration, and sets the installation parameters automatically. The custom installation allows you to control the parameters.

Novell recommends that first-time installers choose the default installation unless there is a particular parameter that needs to be changed. In that case, they say, choose the Custom Installation Option.

The Default Installation menu will display fewer options than the Custom Installation menu. In most cases the custom installation order and screens are similar to the default installation, except that the default mode displays defaults only, where the custom mode displays defaults and then allows you to change them.

If you choose the default installation, NetGen will assign default parameters where possible and prompt you for decisions it still needs from you.

Performing a Default Installation

Replace Current Partition Table with New NetWare Partition?
No Yes

At the installation options menu choose Select Default Installation Options. Depending on the Configuration option you chose earlier, this screen may have other options.

Drives/Volumes	Volume	Chnl	Ctrlr	Drv	Status
IBM AT Hard Disk "C"	SYS	0	0	0	

If the hard disk has previously been partitioned by another operating system (such as MS DOS), you will be asked to confirm replacing it with the new NetWare partition. Any files existing under the old partition will be lost. In order to install NetWare the old partition needs to be replaced. If you want to save any files on the disk select "No," exit out of NetGen, backup your files, then re-enter NetGen.

If you are using an AT or PS/2 internal drive, NetGen automatically partitions the whole disk for NetWare. If the disk is less than 255MB in size, NetGen then creates a single volume devoted to NetWare. (A volume is the largest physical division that can be made on a NetWare disk.) If the disk is larger than NetWare's maximum volume size of 255MB, NetWare will create one or more additional volumes.

It is possible to create more than one partition and to vary the size of partitions, but you will have to exit the Default Installation and select Custom Installation instead.

Select "Yes" to continue the Default Installation.

```
Fix the Master System Table?

No
Yes
```

NetGen displays the driver controller you selected in the generation program. Press <Esc>.

Fixing the Master System Drive Table

```
File Server Name:  ROSE1
```

If the "Fix System Drive Table" option appears, you must select this option before proceeding further. The Master System Drive Table stores information about all file server drives. Any changes made to drives and/or controllers can require the table to be updated.

Naming the File Server

```
System Configuration

File Server Name:              ROSE1
Number of Open Files:          240
Number of Indexed Files:       0
Transaction Backout Volume:    SYS
Number of Transactions:        100
Limit Disk Space:              No
Number of Bindery Objects:
```

NetGen supplies a window where you can enter a name for the file server.

The file server name:

- must be unique within your internetwork
- can be between 2 and 15 characters long
- cannot start with a period (.)
- cannot contain certain punctuation: ' "*+,/\:;=<>?[]

Press <Escape> when you are satisfied with the file server name.

Reviewing System Configuration

```
Use COM1 for a Network Printer?

No
Yes
```

NetGen automatically assigns defaults for the following parameters:

Number of Open Files — This is the maximum number of files that can be open on the file server at any one time. Managing open files takes server memory; the more open files permitted, the more memory required. The range for the variable is 20 to 1,000.

Number of Indexed Files — This is the number of files whose location can be indexed and held in server memory at any one time.

Transaction Backout Volume (TTS only) — This is the volumen onto which the TTS will keep transaction files. The default

	is SYS since that is the only volume created in a Default Installation.
Number of Transactions	This is the maximum number of transactions that TTS will track at any one time.
Limit Disk Space	This is whether to enable limiting the amount of disk space each user can occupy.
Number of Bindery Objects	This is defined only if "Limit Disk Space" is enabled. It limits the number of "objects" (users, groups, and other network entities) that can be defined on the file server.

Defining File Server Printers

Device	Spooled Printer #	Baud	Size	Stop	Parity	Xon/Xoff
COM1	0	9600	8	1	None	No
COM2	1	9600	8	1	None	No
LPT1	2					

NetWare will ask whether to assign various COM and LPT ports for printers.

In most cases, all ports should be selected for network printers during installation so that they don't have to be enabled later.

For serial printers, default communication parameters are assigned automatically.

```
Install Networking Software on File Server?

No
Yes
```

Press <Escape> to continue.

Continuing the Installation with the Selected Configuration

```
Fix the Master System Table?

No
Yes
```

To review and/or change any of the default configuration parameters, choose Select Default Installation Options again.

Press <Escape> to exit the installation procedure. You will be asked to confirm that you want to abandon the configuration you have selected.

Choose Continue Installation to proceed.

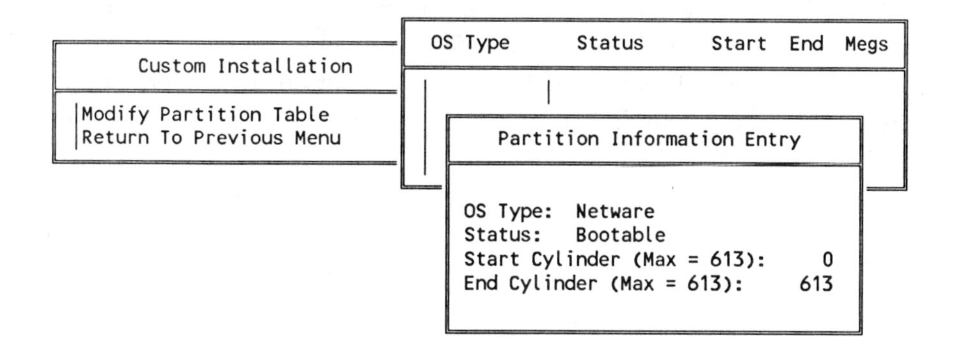

NetGen prompts you to confirm installing NetWare on the file server. If you select "No" you can go back to the configuration procedure or abandon the configuration and exit.

To continue, choose "Yes." NetGen will begin loading the operating system onto the server. This requires it to execute some programs, and to copy files from your customized NetWare disks and other NetWare diskettes. NetGen will prompt you to insert diskettes as it needs them, and will keep you informed of what it is doing. When the procedure is finished, NetGen will inform you that the installation is complete.

Performing a Custom Installation

Fixing the Master System Drive Table

```
Operating System Type

DOS 12-Bit FATs
DOS 16-Bit FATs
Extended DOS
Netware
Other
```

If the "Fix System Drive Table" option appears in the installation menu, you must select this option before proceeding further. The Master System Drive Table stores information about all file server drives. Any changes made to drives and/or controllers can require the table to be updated.

Partitioning the Disk

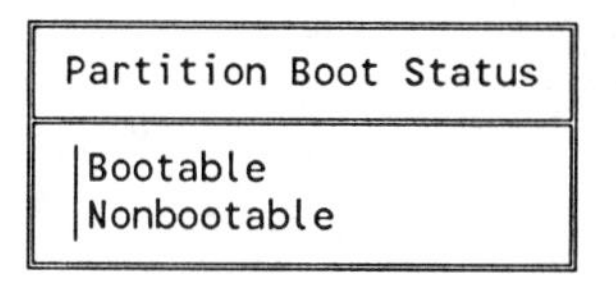

If you are using a PC, AT, or PS/2-type internal drive, you must partition the disk for NetWare. Although a disk may be partitioned for multiple operating systems, there is usually no point in doing so. In any case, the first partition must a bootable NetWare partition, and start at cylinder zero.

The MODIFY PARTITION TABLE window is the initial option available from the Custom Installation menu when IBM-type drives are present in the file server. A partition is an area on the disk assigned exclusively to one operating system. Partitions are referenced in the table by starting and ending cylinder numbers. You may have up to four partitions.

The table shows the type of operating system, its status, the beginning and ending cylinders of the partition, and its size in megabytes.

When you choose Modify the Partition Table, a blank window appears. Press <Ins> to add a partition entry.

When you press <Ins> to add a partition entry, a window appears that displays the default partition options. In general, NetGen defaults to one bootable NetWare partition, comprising the entire disk.

At this point you can accept the defaults or make changes by highlighting the entry you wish to change.

```
Custom Installation

Hot Fix Drives To Default
Modify Hot Fix Redirection Tables
Modify Partition Table
Return To Previous Menu
```

NetWare must be the first partition and must start at cylinder zero. For other partitions, see the NetWare Maintenance Guide and your DOS or other operating system reference manual for further discussion.

```
Custom Installation

Initialize a Disk
Modify Hot Fix Redirection Tables
Modify Partition Table
Return To Previous Menu
```

Only one partition can be bootable; all others must be nonbootable. To boot NetWare from the file server's hard disk, it must be the bootable partition.

When you have defined your partition(s), press <Esc> at the partition list. Highlight "Yes" at the save prompt to save the table and continue with the installation. If you do not wish to save your changes, highlight "No" to abandon your changes and return to the previous menu. Pressing <Esc> will allow you to re-edit your work.

Creating the Hot Fix Redirection Tables

```
Initialization        Channel  Controller  Drive   Status
IBM AT Hard Disk "C"  0        0           0

                    System Configuration
File Server Name:
Number of Open Files:          240
Number of Indexed Files:       5
Transaction Backout Volume:    SYS
Number of Transactions:        100
Limit Disk Space:              No
Number of Bindery Objects:
```

Every time NetWare writes data to the server disk(s), it re-reads that data to verify that it is correct. If it discovers that the data read from a particular disk block is not the same as the data that was written, NetWare redirects the data intended for that block to another area of the disk, called the Hot Fix Redirection Area, set aside for this purpose. The default size of this area is approximately 2 percent of the disk size. The size of the remaining area is called the "logical" disk size.

Novell recommends that unless you are pairing two drives for mirroring or duplexing that have slightly different sizes, you should use the default table size. See the NetWare installation manual for further instructions on mirrored drives.

To set the logical drive size to the default, choose Hot Fix Drives to Default. When Hot Fix has been installed on all server drives, this option will disappear from the menu.

Choose Modify Hot Fix Redirection Tables if you want to review a list of the drives, their configurations, and their logical sizes.

Press <escape> to return to the Custom Installation menu.

Initializing the Disk

```
System Configuration

File Server Name:              LARKSPUR
Number of Open Files:          400
Number of Indexed Files:       20
Transaction Backout Volume:    SYS
Number of Transactions:        100
Limit Disk Space:              Yes
Number of Bindery Objects:     500
```

On an initial installation, this option only appears after Hot Fix redirection tables have been created. On an existing system, it will also appear if there are disks connected to the file server that have not been initialized for NetWare.

```
      Volume          Megs  Directory Size  Cached

 |SYS               |  120       10752        Yes

            Volume Definition

 Volume Name:  SYS2
 Volume Size in Megs:   20
 Number of Directory Entries:   1792
 Cache the Directory:  Yes
```

NetGen lists the available disks. The first disk you select will become the "system" disk. Highlight the disk you want to initialize and press <Enter>. When you initialize the system disk, a list of default system configuration options will be displayed.

Setting the System Configuration Options

```
Custom Installation

Miscellaneous Maintenance
Modify Hot Fix Redirection Tables
Modify Partition Table
Reinitialize a Disk
Return To Previous Menu
```

To change a configuration value, highlight the item to be changed and press <Enter>. Delete the old entry with the backspace key, then enter the new value.

File Server Name. Each file server must have a name. If you have more than one file server on a network or internetwork, each file server name must be unique. The name can be between 2 and 45 characters long and should not contain most punctuation marks. Underlines and dashes, however, are permitted.

Number of Open Files. The maximum number of files that can be opened on the server at one time by all users. Although the default is usually sufficient for most situations, some applications, especially database applications, may require more. Any number between 20 and 1000 is acceptable. Every allotment for an open file requires approximately 100 bytes of file server memory.

Number of Indexed Files. The maximum number of indexed files that can be open concurrently on the file server. When indexed files are opened, the file server builds an index of their location(s) on disk, which can speed up disk access to large database files.

Transaction Backout Volume. This option only appears for SFT NetWare with the TTS. The TTS volume is where information necessary to back out a transaction is stored until a transaction is completed. The volume selected for this should always have enough space for the maximum number of simultaneous transactions that will occur; Novell recommends at least one megabyte.

If you have multiple DCBs, Novell also recommends selecting a volume on a disk using a different channel, since in that case writes to the transaction files and to the database files can be simultaneous; otherwise, they are one after the other.

The default volume is SYS, since it is the only volume defined at this point. To assign a different volume, come back to this point after defining another volume.

Number of Transactions. The maximum number of transactions the TTS system will track. The number must be between 20 and 200, and should be approximately twice the maximum number of concurrent users on the network.

Limit Disk Space. You can limit the amount of hard disk storage space users defined on the file server can use. If you select "Yes," you will be able to select space limitations for users as they are defined.

Number of Bindery Objects. If the Limit Disk Space option is set to "Yes," you must also specify the number of bindery objects that can be defined on the file server. Bindery objects include groups, users, print queues and other network resources. The number of bindery objects can be between 500 and 5,000.

When you are satisfied with the system configuration parameters, press <Esc>. NetGen presents the screen in which volumes will be listed as they are defined. Press <Ins> to define a volume, and the volume definition screen will be displayed.

Defining Volumes

```
Set Flag for Operating System Load?

No
Yes
```

For each volume, you must specify a name, a volume size, the maximum number of directory entries the volume can contain, and if the directory will be cached.

The system volume, SYS, is the first volume presented. Unless the disk is larger than 255MB, the default size for SYS will be the size of the disk (less the Hot Fix redirection area). The name of the system volume SYS cannot be changed.

If you have more than one physical disk drive, a drive larger than 255MB, or you decide to create volumes smaller than disk size, additional volumes will have to be defined.

Volume Names. Names of additional volumes can be from 2 to 15 characters, must be unique, cannot start with a period (.), and should not contain most punctuation marks. Underlines and dashes are permitted.

Number of Directory Entries. Directory entries are directory names, subdirectory names, and file names. Each available directory entry uses file server RAM. NetGen uses a formula to calculate an "average" for the default number of directory entries. If you plan to have a large number of small files in the volume, you should increase this value. If, however, you plan to have a small number of large files, decrease this value. The number of available directory entries can always be changed at a later time.

Directory Caching. Cached directories are kept in memory and can be searched much faster than directories on disk. Unless you are suffering severe file server memory limitations, always cache your directories.

```
Set Flag for System & Public Files Load?

No
Yes
```

When you have defined your volume(s), press <Esc>. Select "Yes" in the Create Volume window to create the volumes, select "No" to abandon your volume definitions, or press <Esc> to edit them. Repeat the volume definition procedure for each disk. Press <Esc> to return to the Custom Installation menu.

The option "Reinitialize a Disk" now appears on the Custom Installation window. This will allow you to make changes to your disk/volume definitions above.

Note: Once you have created volumes, you will not be able to reinitialize them without losing data in those volumes. You will, however, be able to change the volume name (other than SYS), the number of allowed directory entries and the caching parameter through the "Volume Information" option on the "Miscellaneous Maintenance" menu (see below).

If you have initialized two or more disks, the following options will appear on the menu:

> "Remove A Disk" allows you to logically remove a disk from the file server. Once a disk has been removed it can be restored with the "Restore a Disk" option.

"Modify Mirror Tables" allows you to establish, view, and unmirror mirrored disk pairs. When two drives become a mirrored pair, the secondary drive will maintain a mirror copy of information contained on the primary drive.

To proceed with the installation, choose "Miscellaneous Maintenance" from the Custom Installation Menu.

Miscellaneous Maintenance

```
                System Configuration

File Server Name:               LARKSPUR
Number of Open Files:           400
Number of Indexed Files:        20
Transaction Backout Volume:     SYS
Number of Transactions:         100
Limit Disk Space:               Yes
Number of Bindery Objects:      500
```

The "Miscellaneous Maintenance" option should now appear on the main menu. Miscellaneous Maintenance is used to load the operating system and the system and public files, change the file server name, modify the system configuration, view volume information, and modifying the spooled printers list.

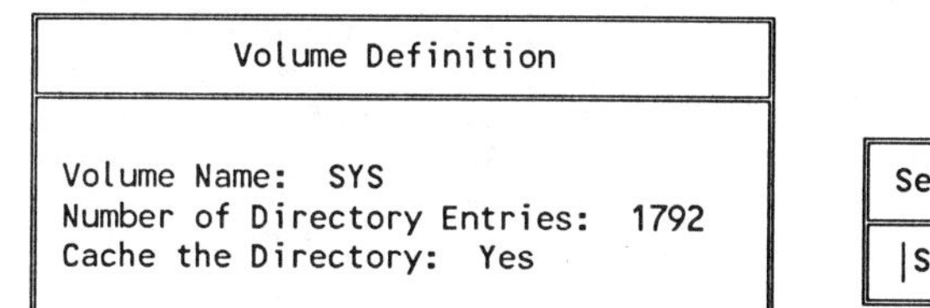


```
Select Volume

SYS
```

The "Load Operating System" option sets the "flag" to load the operating system onto the file server's hard disk from floppy diskettes.

The operating system will not be copied until the installation session is completed, at which time you will be prompted to insert the proper diskettes. If you are performing an initial installation, or upgrading from a previous version of NetWare, select "Yes" in the confirmation window.

Device	Spooled Printer #	Baud	Size	Stop	Parity	Xon/Xoff
COM1	Not Spooled					
COM2	Not Spooled					
LPT1	Not Spooled					

The "Load System and Public Files" option sets the "flag" to load the system and public files onto the file server's hard disk from floppy diskettes. The files will not be copied until the installation session is completed, at which time you will be prompted to insert the proper diskettes. If you are performing an initial installation, or upgrading from a previous version of NetWare, select "Yes" in the confirmation window.

Device	Spooled Printer #	Baud S
COM1	**Not Spooled**	
COM2	Not Spooled	
LPT1	Not Spooled	

Spooled Serial Printer

Device: COM1

Spooled Printer #:	0
Baud Rate:	9600
Word Length:	8 bits
Stop Bits:	1 bit
Parity:	None
Xon/Xoff Protocol:	No

System Configuration lets you change the file server name, number of open and indexed files, the Transaction Backout Volume, Maximum number of transactions to be tracked, the Limit Disk Space option, and the number of allowed Bindery objects.

Device	Spooled Printer #	Baud S
COM1	0	9600
COM2	1	9600
LPT1	Not Spooled	

Spooled Parallel Printer
Device: LPT1
Spooled Printer #: 2

The Volume Information menu lets you review and edit the volume(s) you have created. You can change the volume name (other than SYS), the number of allowed directory entries, and the caching parameter.

Defining File Server Printers

Device	Spooled Printer #	Baud	Size	Stop	Parity	Xon/Xoff
COM1	0	9600	8	1	None	Yes
COM2	1	9600	8	1	None	Yes
LPT1	2					

Printer Maintenance allows you to define file server LPT and COM ports as network printer ports. On a PC or AT-type file server, NetWare can recognize up to five printers attached to LPT1 through LPT3 and COM1 and COM2. This table shows which devices are currently being used and what their printer numbers are. The printers are numbered from 0 to 4. If you have only one printer, it must be assigned to printer number 0.

Each printer you define will either be parallel or serial, depending on the port to which it is connected.

For parallel printers you may select or edit the printer number. For serial printers you can select or edit the printer number, baud rate, word length, stop bits and parity, and specify whether the printer uses the Xon/Xoff protocol. The serial printer parameters should correspond to the configuration of the printer.

Parallel printers don't use communication parameters (baud rate, stop bit, word length, parity, and protocol.) To spool a parallel printer, simply select it and assign it a number.

When you have defined all printers, press <Esc> at the printer list, then select "Yes" to accept the printer definitions. You may also select "No" to abandon the definitions or press <Esc> to edit them.

Printer Definition is the last parameter on the Miscellaneous Maintenance menu. Press <Esc> to return to the Custom Installation menu, then press <Esc> again to return to the Installation Options menu.

Continuing the Installation

When you are satisfied with the installation parameters you have selected, highlight "Continue Installation" on the Installation Options menu, then select "Yes" in the confirmation window.

NetGen will now begin the installation. You will be prompted for the required diskettes.

Warning: Never attempt to abort the installation process while files are being transferred from a diskette. If you must abort the process, you may safely do so after a diskette has finished transferring files by pressing <Ctrl><Break>.

When the installation process is finished, select "Exit NetGen" from the main menu and return to DOS.

Booting the File Server

If your server has a bootable hard disk, you can boot from it as you would boot any PC with a hard disk. Bootable servers include Novell file servers, with or without a DCB, and PC, AT, or PS/2-type computers with standard drive/controller combinations.

Non-bootable drives include many drives using third-party Value Added Disk Drivers (VADDs), drives using the Novell DCB in non-Novell servers, and others.

If you do not have a bootable hard disk, first boot the server with a DOS 3.x or DOS 4.x diskette. Then insert a working copy of your NetWare OSEXE-1 diskette in the A: drive.

At the A> prompt, type

```
NET$OS
```

If you are using 5-1/4" disks, insert the OSEXE-2 diskette when you are prompted to do so.

The file server will display messages as it mounts volumes and checks system files.

After these checks have completed, NetWare displays the date and time. If you have created a "System Autoexec" file (you would not yet have one on a brand new server), other "Console Commands" may also be automatically executed.

The console will also display a colon (:) prompt where you can enter other Console Commands (see Chapter 16).

Logging In as Supervisor

After you have installed NetWare on the file server, you should move to a workstation connected to the file server. Insert the boot disk that you created in ShGen (see Chapter 9) and reboot the workstation by turning it off and then on, or by pressing the <Ctrl><Alt><Del> keys together.

The boot disk must be formatted with DOS as a bootable diskette, and should contain the following files:

```
IPX.COM
NET3.COM (or NET4.COM for DOS 4.x)
```

You must enter the following commands:

```
IPX<Enter>
      and
NET3<Enter>
```

These commands can be typed manually, or entered in an autoexec.bat file that will execute whenever you boot the disk. You will see messages similar to the following:

```
   Novell IPX/SPX V2.15
   (C) Copyright 1985, 1988 Novell, Inc.  All Rights Reserved.

   LAN Option: Standard Microsystems ARCNET/Pure Data V1.00
(881010)
   Hardware Configuration IRQ=2, I/O Base=2E0h, RAM Buffer at
D000:0

   NetWare V2.15 rev. A - Workstation Shell for PC DOS V3.x
   (C) Copyright 1983, 1988 Novell, Inc.  All Rights Reserved.
```

```
Attached to Server LARKSPUR
Sunday, April 16, 1989      9:03:47 am
```

If you will be running applications that require the NetBIOS emulator, you may need to type:

```
NETBIOS <Enter>
      and
INT2F <Enter>
```

The first network drive (shown as F: in the examples in this chapter) will vary depending on the version of DOS you are using, the type of workstation you are using, the hardware configuration of your workstation, and options specified in the CONFIG.SYS file.

Change to the first network drive, (usually F:) and execute the login program by typing :.

```
LOGIN
```

A note on DOS versions: Although NetWare supports DOS versions 2.0 and above, many current applications require the features of DOS 3.1 or greater when used on a network.

On any IBM PC, PC XT, PC AT, or PS/2 running DOS 3.x, the first network drive will usually be F.

If you are using DOS 2.x on an IBM PC with one or two floppy disk drives, the first network drive may be C. If you are using an IBM PC XT that has one hard drive, the first network drive may be D. Again, we recommend you upgrade to DOS 3.1 or greater.

If F:\LOGIN> appears on the screen, you have successfully changed to the first network drive. If the message "Invalid drive specification" appears, try typing other drive letters (e.g., D or E) until you find the correct network drive for your workstation.

When the F:\LOGIN prompt appears, you have connected to the network successfully, but you have no rights to do anything.

To log in to a single file server network, type

```
LOGIN SUPERVISOR <Enter>
```

Depending on the design of your network, the shell may find a different file server from one login to another.

To login to a particular file server on such a network, type:

```
LOGIN FileServer_Name/SUPERVISOR
```

Substitute the name of the file server you want to connect to for "FileServer_Name."

If you are including the login command in an autoexec.bat file, you can enter

```
LOGIN FileServer_Name/
```

LOGIN finds your user profile in the Bindery (the database of information about users, groups, and security), prompts you to enter your password, if you have one, then uses your user profile to set your access rights to volumes and directories on the file server. LOGIN then runs a Login Script, which contains instructions to assign drive letters and search paths to selected directories (called Mapping) and set other parameters for your own network environment.

When you first login in as Supervisor (which is the only user defined on a brand new file server) NetWare runs a default login script to set drive maps to certain directories that you will need to set up the system.

The screen will respond with a display similar to the following. (This is the "default Login Script" that executes for any user when there is neither a System Login Script nor a User Login Script.)

```
Good morning, SUPERVISOR.

Drive A maps to a local disk.
Drive B maps to a local disk.
Drive C maps to a local disk.
Drive D maps to a local disk.
Drive E maps to a local disk.
Drive F := file server/SYS:SYSTEM
Drive G := file server/SYS:LOGIN
Drive Y := file server/SYS:PUBLIC

SEARCH1 := Z:.[file server/SYS:PUBLIC]

F:\SYSTEM>
```

Shortly after the Supervisor logs in for the first time the Supervisor will modify the system defaults with a Netware utility called Syscon. Most of these defaults involve security matters, for instance whether to require a password, how often it should be changed, times of day the user can log in, and the like.

Attaching to Other File Servers

The ATTACH command logs a user into another file server without logging out of the current server. The ATTACH command prompts for a valid user name on the server to which the user is seeking attachment.

Syntax:

```
ATTACH <file server>/<username>
```

Examples:

```
ATTACH SERVER1
```

Attaches to SERVER1 then prompts for a username.

```
ATTACH SERVER1/JSMITH
```

Attaches to SERVER1 as user JSMITH. If user JSMITH has a password on SERVER1, the system will prompt him to enter one.

The LOGIN command will not allow you to attach to a second file server because it performs an automatic logout to all attached file servers. You would lose connection to the first file server if this were allowed to happen.

The ATTACH utility will not execute a login script. This takes place only when LOGIN is executed. Likewise, you must LOGIN to a file server before you can attach to another server. However, it is possible to re-LOGIN or re-ATTACH at any time without first using the LOGOUT command.

An automatic ATTACH is performed when you use the MAP command to map a drive to a network file server to which you are not already attached, if you have the same user name and password on both file servers. If you do not have the same login name or password, you will be prompted to enter them.

Logging Out From a File Server

The command

```
LOGOUT
```

logs you out of all attached file servers. If you specify a file server name, as in

```
LOGOUT LARKSPUR
```

you will be logged out from only that file server.

When you log out, all network drive mappings that are not saved in your login script are removed; the default drive is mapped to SYS:LOGIN of the default server. You may then login again without rebooting the workstation.

If your prompt is for a network drive, you will be pointed to the login directory of that server. If your prompt is for a local drive, the first network drive letter will be pointed to the login directory of that server. In either case, you will have (R)ead-only access to the programs in that directory.

Note that if you attach to another file server and move to a directory on that file server, LOGOUT will leave you pointing to the second, attached server, not to your default server.

For more information about System Login Script mapping and attachment, see Chapter 13—Setting Up System Defaults. For more about User Login Script mapping and attachment, see Chapter 14, Setting Up Groups and Users.

12

Setting Up File Server Directories

Setting up directories on a network file server is a little different from setting up directories on a stand-alone PC. Logical organization for use by a single user is usually the primary concern on a stand-alone PC. On a file server, however, you must be concerned with logical organization for use by multiple users, as well as security and access control.

NetWare System-Generated Directories

When you first load NetWare on a file server, the following directories are automatically created:

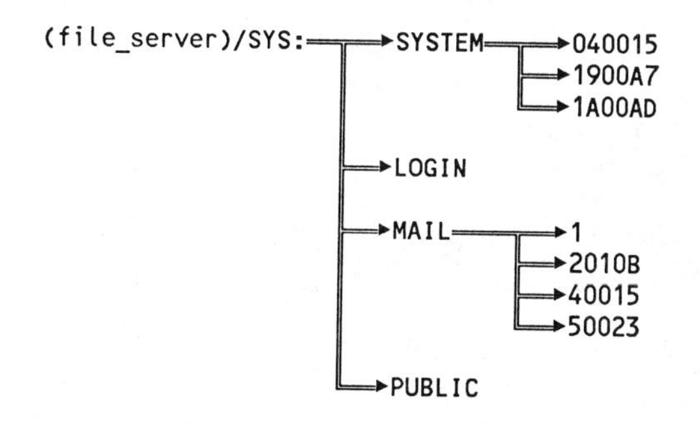

The SYSTEM directory contains the NetWare operating system, the Bindery (which is the NetWare database of information about users, groups, security, etc.) and supervisor utility programs. Subdirectories for print queues are also created under the SYSTEM directory.

The LOGIN directory is the only directory that a user can access after loading the NetWare shell and before logging in. The LOGIN directory contains the login program and the program Slist, which will display a list of available file servers.

The MAIL directory contains system-created subdirectories for each user. The name of each subdirectory corresponds to the user ID number that the system creates for each user. These subdirectories contain the user login scripts and printer definition files (see Chapter 16—Managing Network Printers).

The PUBLIC directory contains the NetWare utilities programs. These include utilities for queueing and printing, copying files on the server, removing directories, etc.

DOS Subdirectories

One component of PC-DOS/MS-DOS is the command processor Command.Com. Command.Com stays in your PC's memory until the space it uses is required by an application. Command.Com is then removed from memory, and reloaded when the application terminates. DOS uses an environment variable called COMSPEC to relocate Command.Com. (The environment is a memory space set aside to keep track of various types of information, including COMSPEC, DOS paths, etc.)

NetWare requires that at least one copy of Command.Com resides on a file server directory that is mapped as a search path. If you are using multiple versions of DOS, either different numbered releases

(3.20, 3.21, 3.30, etc.) or versions from different vendors (for example, IBM and Compaq) you must have a copy of each version's Command.Com available to that version's user(s).

A good approach is to create a directory for each version of DOS used that contains Command.Com as well as DOS utilities. This directory can be created as a subdirectory of the PUBLIC directory. Because the rights of the PUBLIC directory already match the rights you would want for the DOS directory, and since NetWare rights default down the directory tree, you do not have to grant any new rights to users or groups.

If you are creating multiple DOS directories, the directory structure for the DOS directories could be something like this:

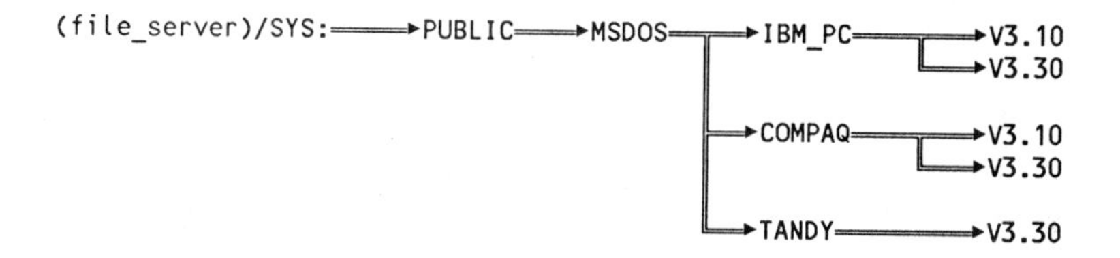

In this example, the directory names used correspond to the text values of identifiers used by the NetWare login scripts. This will allow you to make use of the login script identifiers OS, MACHINE, and OS_VERSION. These identifiers can be placed in a login script MAP command as variables in place of the actual operating system name, machine name, and operating system version numbers:

```
MAP SEARCH2:=SYS:PUBLIC/%OS/%MACHINE/%OS_VERSION
```

NetWare will read the appropriate information from the NetWare shell, the operating system, and the Shell.Cfg file on the workstation, then conditionally set a path to the correct DOS directory (see "Setting Up Workstation Boot Disks" in Chapter 9).

For example, If your workstation was using Compaq's version of MS-DOS 3.30, and your Shell.Cfg file contained the line "LONG MACHINE TYPE = COMPAQ", Your DOS path would be:

```
SEARCH2:=(file_server)/SYS:PUBLIC/MSDOS/COMPAQ/V3.30
```

Once a search path has been set to the proper directory, the login script command:

```
COMSPEC = S2:COMMAND.COM
```

will tell DOS were to find the command processor.

Application and Data Directories

The organization of application program directories on a file server can be similar to the organization you might use on a stand-alone PC. The organization of data directories, however, will vary based on the type of application used.

A common approach to creating program directories is as follows:

- Create a directory called APPS or PROGRAMS or something similar.
- Create a subdirectory under this directory for each application.
- Create any required subdirectories for each application's supplemental and utility files under that application's directory.

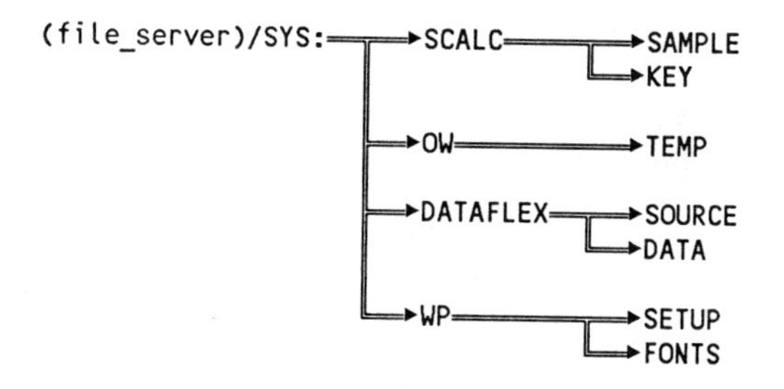

Data files fall under three main categories:

- Nonshared files. Any data file that is primarily used or edited by one person. This category could include spreadsheet files, graphics files, word processing files, etc.

- Non-concurrently-shared files. This includes any file that is going to be accessed or edited by a number of users, but only by one user at a time. This category could include spreadsheet files, graphics files, word processing files, etc.

- Concurrently-shared files, including database files, accounting files, etc.

Nonshared files can be placed in private directories created for each user called "home" directories. (See "Creating Users' Home Directories" below.)

Shared files, both concurrently-shared and nonconcurrently-shared, can be handled two ways:

- If the files are to be made available to all users of an application, they can be placed in a subdirectory under the application's directory.

- If the files are to be made available to specific groups of users, they can be placed in a directory created for that group. If only a particular application's data files will be in the directory, it could be a subdirectory under the application's directory. If files from more than one application will be in the directory, it could be a subdirectory under a USERS or GROUPS or HOME directory.

Users' Home Directories

It is a good practice to give each user a "home" directory. This gives each user space for his or her own files. One way to do this is to create a directory called USERS, HOME, or something similar, and then create subdirectories that correspond to each user's login name (if you keep each user's login name to eight characters or less this is easy to do). Usually a user's first network drive path will be the home directory.

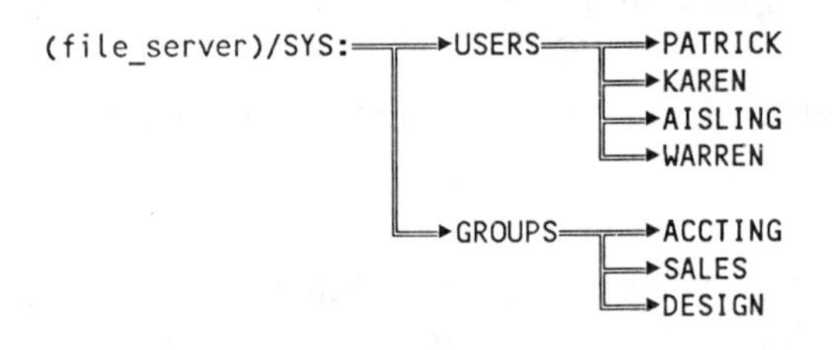

You may what to create directories for one or more groups. These can be subdirectories under the USERS or HOME directory, or you could create a directory called GROUPS for these subdirectories.

Planning the Directory Structure

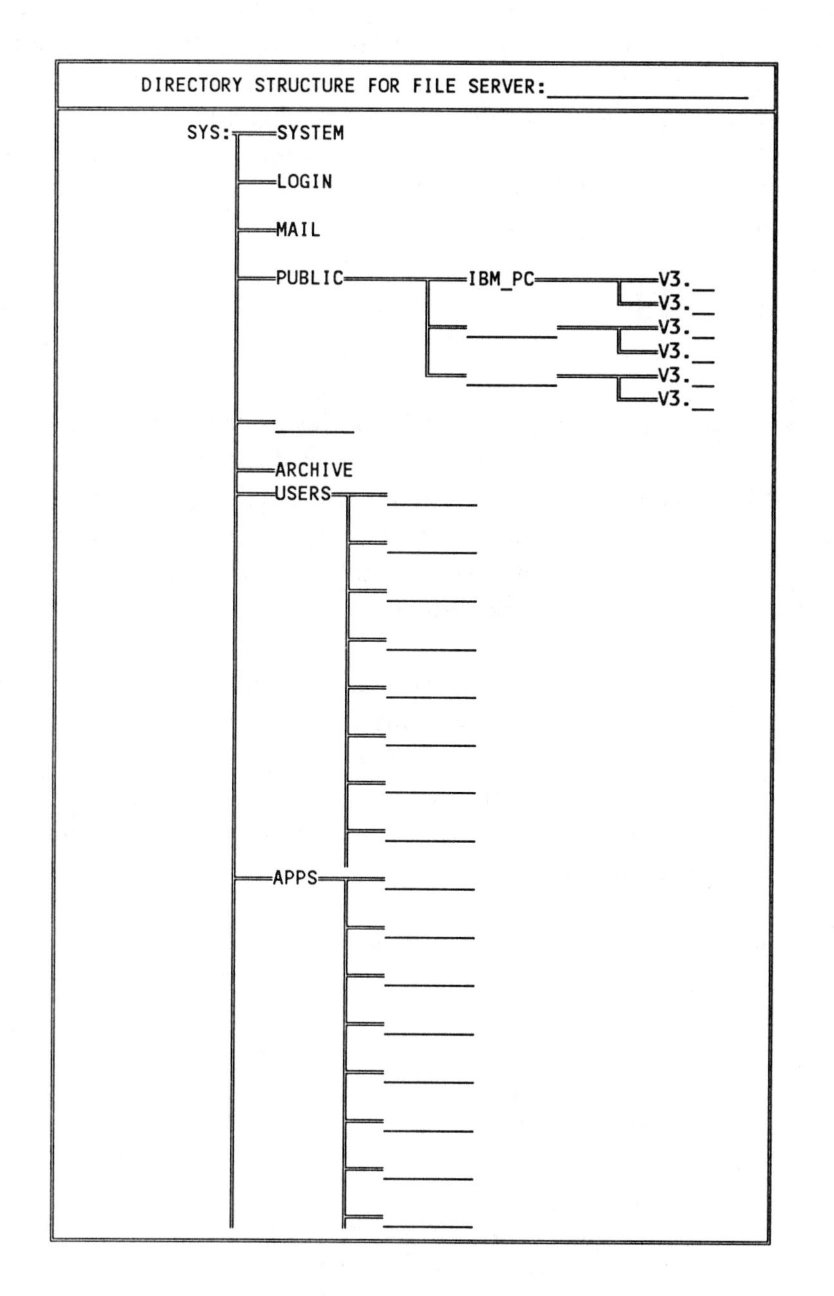

One of the easiest ways to plan the directory structure is by drawing a "tree" similar to the example above and filling in each of the directories you will need. When you are satisfied with the directory design, use this directory worksheet to plan the contents of the directories, the groups/users who will have access, and their access levels. You will then have at hand much of the information you need to create GROUPS and USERS.

NetWare Rights

NetWare allows you to grant up to eight levels of rights to a user or group of users. In addition, each file server directory has an Overall Rights Mask consisting of one or more of the eight rights. The Overall Rights Mask sets maximum available rights for a user to a directory. In effect, a user can have no rights to a directory that are not included in the Overall Rights Mask.

The overall rights mask can be set using the Filer utility, while user and group rights can be set with the SysCon utility, both of which are described in this and the following chapters. NetWare also provides the Grant, Remove, and Revoke utilities for setting user and group rights. These utilities are discussed in the NetWare Command Line Utilities manual.

A brief description of each right follows:

R	Read From Files
W	Write To Files
O	Open Existing Files
C	Create New Files
D	Delete Files
P	Parental Rights
S	Search For Files
M	Modify File Names/Flags

CREATE allows you to create new files in the selected directory. In order to write to a newly created file you must also have WRITE privileges. You can also create new subdirectories under the selected directory (version 2.15 or later).

DELETE allows you to delete files in the selected directory.

MODIFY allows you to modify the attributes associated with a file, to rename a file, and to modify the files creation, last accessed, and last modified dates. The MODIFY right also allows you to rename subdirectories and to change a subdirectory's creation date. If you have PARENTAL rights then you can also change the directory attributes with FLAGDIR (see "Directory Attributes" below).

OPEN allows you to open a file that already exists. You will also need the READ right to read from the file and the WRITE right to write to the file.

PARENTAL allows you to specify trustees in the selected directory and the rights that each trustee has. It also allows you to change the maximum rights mask of the selected directory. With NetWare versions prior to 2.15, PARENTAL is required to create subdirectories.

Note: If a user has PARENTAL rights to a directory, that user can grant any user, including herself or himself, all rights to that directory and its subdirectories.

READ allows you to read from an open file.

SEARCH allows you to view the name of the files in this directory. Without this right you can not see what files are in the directory. If a directory is flagged PRIVATE, then you must have SEARCH privileges to see subdirectory names in that directory.

WRITE allows you to write to an open file.

File Attributes

The following attributes can be placed on files on a NetWare file server:

HIDDEN—sets the DOS HIDDEN attribute so that the file will not appear in a directory.

INDEXED—indexes the file allocation table for this file. Used to speed access of large database files.

MODIFIED SINCE LAST BACKUP—sets the DOS flag indicating that the file has been changed since it was last backed up.

SYSTEM—sets the DOS SYSTEM attribute.

TRANSACTIONAL—used on data files that are protected by SFT NetWare's Transaction Tracking System.

READ ONLY—allows the file to be read or executed, but not modified or deleted.

READ/WRITE files can be read by users with read rights to the directory and can be written to by users with write rights to the directory.

SHAREABLE files can be accessed by multiple users concurrently, as long as they have appropriate rights. Only files being managed by multiuser application programs should be made shareable. These applications programs provide within them schemes for record or file locking so that two users don't write to the same data at the same time. Outside of these applications, concurrent file writes could collide and cause damage.

NONSHAREABLE files can only be accessed by one user at a time. If multiuser application data files are set to nonshareable, then they may not function correctly or at all.

Files flagged EXECUTE ONLY cannot be erased, read, modified, renamed, or copied. A file that is flagged EXECUTE ONLY can only be run. This prevents unauthorized copies of programs being removed from the network. This flag can only be set with the Filer utility (see "Using Filer," below).

Warning! Once a file is set to EXECUTE ONLY, it can only be executed or deleted and cannot be reflagged. If you want to modify the file you must delete it and then recopy the original file from its source diskette.

Flags can be set with the Filer utility (see below) or at the command line with the Flag command. For example:

```
FLAG SYS:DF/DAT/*.* SRW
```

would flag all files in the SYS:DF/DAT directory as shareable, read/write. For more information on the Flag command, see the NetWare Command Line Utilities manual.

Directory Attributes

As of version 2.15, NetWare allows you to set four attributes on directories: Normal, Hidden, System, and Private. These attributes, as well as the FLAGDIR command used to set them, are discussed in detail in Appendix C—NetWare for Macintosh.

Creating Directories

There are several ways to set up the directory structure. You can use the DOS MD (MKDIR) command, or one of the many file/directory utilities that work on PC's. Another way is to use the NetWare utility Filer. Filer has the advantage of allowing you to review and modify all eight directory/file attributes.

Using Filer

Filer is a utility for creating, and managing directories. Filer can be very useful when you are initially setting up a file server.

```
NetWare File Maintenance  V1.33c          Saturday  May 13, 1989  10:28 am
                          LARKSPUR/SYS:USERS/PATRICK

                    Available Topics

              Current Directory Information
              File Information
              Select Current Directory
              Set Filer Options
              Subdirectory Information
              Volume Information
```

Filer gives you the following options:

Current Directory Information will allow you to get information about the currently selected directory. The currently selected directory is the directory whose name appears in the header at the top of the screen. The information that you can get about the current directory includes the directory's creation date, owner, and maximum rights mask, the users who are granted trustee rights in the directory, and your effective rights in the directory.

File Information will show you a list of the files in the current directory. The options that you have will depend on your effective rights in the current directory. If you have the appropriate rights you can view and modify the files' attributes, date and time information, and owner. You can also delete, rename, and copy files.

Select Current Directory will allow you to change the directory that you are currently examining. You can type in a new directory path or get a list of all available file servers, volumes, and directories and select from that list.

Set Filer Options will allow you to change the defaults that are used by the File Information and Subdirectory Information options. These defaults include confirmation during file copying and deletion. They also allow you to specify that only files or directories that match certain patterns should be displayed.

Subdirectory Information will show you all of the subdirectories of the current directory. Depending on your rights in the current directory, you will be able to view and change the information associated with the subdirectories. This information includes the subdirectories' creation date, maximum rights mask, owner, and the users who are granted trustee rights in the subdirectory. You can also rename, delete, and insert subdirectories.

Volume Information will allow you to view information about the volume on which the currently selected directory is located. You will be able to see the volume's total size, the remaining free space on the volume, the maximum number of allowed directory entries, and the remaining unused directory entries.

Current Directory Information

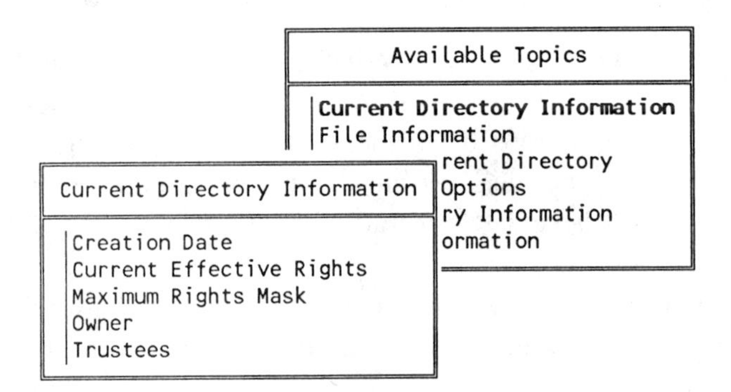

Current Directory Information allows you to view and/or modify the following:

Creation Date—Shows you the date on which the directory was created. If you have supervisor rights on the current file server, you will also be able to modify the creation date.

Current Effective Rights—Shows you what rights you have in the current directory.

Maximum Rights Mask—Shows you the maximum allowed rights in the current directory. If you have personal ownership rights in the current directory or in its parent directory, you will be able to modify the maximum rights mask.

Owner—Allows you to see the owner of the currently selected directory. If you have supervisor rights on the current file server, you will also be able to change the owner.

Trustees—This option will only appear if you have personal ownership rights in the current directory or in the current directories parent directory. It will allow you to see all the users that have trustee rights in the current directory and modify their rights. You will also be able to add or delete users from this list.

File Information

```
Files            Available Topics                 File Information

▲ ARCPLUS.ARC    Current Directory Information    Attributes
  BASICS.OVR     File Information                 Copy File
  BASICS3.FIL    Select Current Directory         Creation Date
  CH10.CAP       Set Filer Options                Last Accessed Date
  CONFIG.SH      Subdirectory Information         Last Archived Date
  CONSOLE.PR1    Volume Information               Last Modified Date
  CONSOLE.PR2                                     Owner
  CUSTLIST.FIL                                    Size
  CUSTOM.EXE                                      View File
  CYBER1
  DEADTAPE
  DIR.FRM
  DOSCOM.PRN
  DOWNLOAD
▼ FCONS2.CAP
```

If you have appropriate privileges, File Information will allow you to:

- View files on the current directory.

- Delete files from the current directory.
- Modify file names.
- View a file.
- View or modify file attributes.
- Copy files.
- View file creation and last accessed dates and last modified date and time. If you are a supervisor you may change these dates.
- View a file's owner. If you are a supervisor you may change the file's owner.
- View a file's size

File Information—Attributes

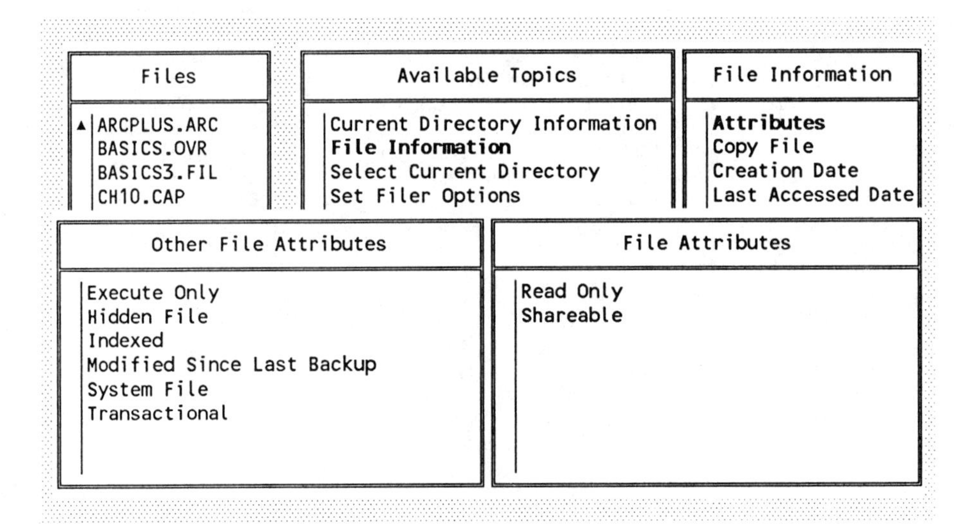

The Attributes screen allows you to view and modify the attribute flags set on the selected file. See the beginning of this section for a description of file Attributes.

Set Filer Options

```
Filer Options Settings

Confirm Deletions
Confirm File Copies
Confirm File Overwrites
Directories Exclude Pattern
Directories Include Pattern
File Exclude Pattern
File Include Pattern
File Search Attributes
```

Set Filer Options will allow you to change the defaults that are used by the Filer Information and Subdirectory Information options.

- CONFIRM DELETIONS allows you to confirm the deletion of each file individually when deleting multiple files. If it is not set to YES, you will be asked to confirm that you intended to delete the files once, then they will all be deleted.

- CONFIRM FILE COPIES has no effect since this version of filer does not support copying multiple files.

- CONFIRM FILE OVERWRITES—If this option is set to YES, when you copy a file to a directory where a file by the same name already exists you will be asked if you intended to overwrite the existing file before it gets copied over. If it is set to NO, the file will be overwritten without asking.

- DIRECTORIES EXCLUDE PATTERN lets you specify a pattern of directory names that you do not want to see while viewing Subdirectory Information. If you enter a pattern of A*, you would not see any subdirectories that begin with the letter A. Exclude patterns override include patterns.

- DIRECTORIES INCLUDE PATTERN determines what directories will be listed when you pick the Subdirectory Information option.

  Normally this default is set to *, which lists all of the directories. If you changed it to S* you would only see subdirectories that begin with the letter S. The directories exclude pattern will override the directories include pattern. So, if you enter a directory include pattern of S* and a directory exclude pattern of SE*, you will see all subdirectories that begin with S except those that begin with SE.

- FILE EXCLUDE PATTERN determines what files will be displayed when the File Information option is selected. If you specify a pattern of *.OBJ, none of the .OBJ files in the directory will appear in the list of files shown. The file exclude patterns override the file include patterns.

- FILE INCLUDE PATTERN determines what files will be displayed when the File Information option is selected. Normally it is set to * which displays all of the files. If you set it to *.exe and *.com, you would only see files with a .exe or a .com extension.

- FILE SEARCH ATTRIBUTES determines what files will be displayed when the File Information option is selected. Normally hidden and system files are not displayed. This default allows you to specify whether hidden and/or system files should be shown.

Subdirectory Information

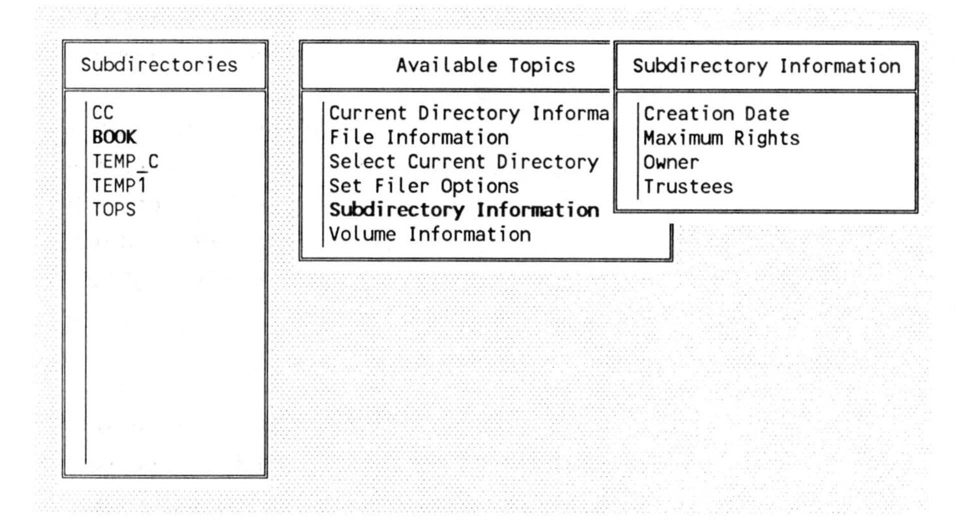

Subdirectory Information will show you all of the subdirectories of the current directory. Depending on your rights in the current directory, you will be able to view and change the information associated with the subdirectories. This information includes the following.

Creation Date displays the date and time that the subdirectory was created. If you have supervisor rights, you can change the creation date.

Maximum Rights will display the maximum right allowed in the subdirectory. If you have Parental Rights in the subdirectory, you can change the maximum allowed rights. OWNER will display the subdirectories owner. If you have supervisor rights, you can change the subdirectories owner.

Trustees will display the trustees that are specifically granted or revoked rights in the subdirectory. This option will not appear if you do not have Parental Rights. If it does appear, you can change the trustees of the directory.

You can also rename, delete and insert subdirectories from this screen.

Volume Information

Volume Information	
Server Name:	LARKSPUR
Volume Name:	SYS
Volume Type:	Fixed
Total Bytes:	60,817,408
Bytes Available:	5,341,184
Maximum Directory Entries:	4,224
Directory Entries Available:	1,997

Volume Information will allow you to view information about the volume on which the currently selected directory is located. You will be able to see the file server name, volume name, volume type (fixed or removable), the volume's total size, the remaining free space on the volume, the maximum number of allowed directory entries, and the remaining unused directory entries. The number of maximum directory entries can be adjusted by running the SYSED program from the File Server's console.

Setting Up Directory Structures

Using Filer commands to create directories and to assign rights and flags is not difficult. As in every aspect of the network, the trick is to strike the right balance among security, access, and manageability.

If you give the user too little access, you may find yourself inundated with requests to do things for users that they could do for themselves. If you give them too much access, or access with inadequate training, you may find yourself restoring mangled files or programs.

For example, some programs not designed for a network environment have to be reinstalled to change printer types. Say that your network has a laser printer and a high speed dot matrix printer. Your users want to be able to switch between them. The network spool commands can redirect print requests, but printing properly will require a change in the program configuration files.

If you give users the right to modify the program, you take two chances: first, that the users will perform the reconfiguration incorrectly; and second, that the users will not put the configuration back to normal when they are finished.

If you don't give the users the right to modify the program, then you have to do it for them.

You can often work around problems like this. For example, you could keep the configuration files in a separate directory and have a batch file copy requested printer configurations to the program directory, then have it copy the normal configuration file back when the user exits the application.

13

Setting Up System Defaults

When you log in for the first time, you will usually set up some system defaults. System defaults set parameters for the network and for network users, including setting default security parameters for new users and creating a system login script.

The system defaults are set with the SysCon utility. You can run SysCon from any directory by typing:

```
SysCon <Enter>
```

About SysCon

SysCon is NetWare's primary system configuration tool. It gives you the following options:

• The Accounting option allows you to track usage of file server resources, install accounting on a file server, view and modify what file server services are being charged for and the amount that is being charged, and view and modify who is allowed to charge for file services. For more information about accounting, see the NetWare Supervisor Reference Manual.

• The File Server Information option allows you to list the file servers that are attached to your network, view information about the configuration of a file server, view the number of users currently attached to a file server, and see what version of NetWare a file server is running.

- The Group Information option allows you to list the groups that are defined on a file server, and view and modify group information. More about this in the next chapter.

- Supervisor Options are available ONLY if you have supervisor privileges. The options include setting security and access defaults, and editing the system login script. You will be using this option to set the system defaults.

- The User Information option allows you to list all users on a file server, and view and change user information. More about this in the next chapter.

Using SysCon to Set System Defaults.

```
NetWare System Configuration  V2.12        Saturday  May 13, 1989  10:31 am
                    User PATRICK On File Server LARKSPUR

                        Available Topics

                      Accounting
                      Change Current Server
                      File Server Information
                      Group Information
                      Supervisor Options
                      User Information
```

From the SysCon main menu, select "Supervisor Options."

```
Supervisor Options

Default Account Balance/Restrictions
Default Time Restrictions
Edit System AUTOEXEC File
File Server Console Operators
Intruder Detection/Lockout
System Login Script
View File Server Error Log
```

Only users with supervisor rights on the currently selected file server can select this option. The Supervisor Options are:

DEFAULT ACCOUNT BALANCE/RESTRICTIONS—allows you to view and change the security restriction defaults for newly-created users.

Note: Changing the security restrictions defaults does not affect existing users.

If accounting has been installed on the file server, you can also view and change the default account balance for new users.

DEFAULT TIME RESTRICTIONS—allows you to view and change the default times that a new user will be able to log in when his account is first created.

Note: Changing the default login time restrictions will not change the login time restrictions of any user account that has already been created.

EDIT SYSTEM AUTOEXEC FILE—The system AUTOEXEC file is a file which contains console commands that the file server should "automatically execute" when it is first brought up. This option will allow you to view and modify the system AUTOEXEC file. This option is discussed in Chapter 15, "Managing File Server Resources."

FILE SERVER CONSOLE OPERATORS—allows you to view and change which users and groups have been authorized to run the file server console from a workstation.

INTRUDER DETECTION/LOCKOUT—allows you to see if the file server is tracking attempts to break into user accounts, specify the criteria for the file server to determine how many incorrect login attempts constitute an intruder, and specify if the file server should lock an account if it detects an intruder attempting to break into it.

SYSTEM LOGIN SCRIPT—allows you to view and modify the system login script. The system login script is a script that is run for all users when they log in to the file server before the user's individual login script is run. The system login script is an ideal place to enter login script commands that every user should execute when logging in.

VIEW FILE SERVER ERROR LOG allows you to view the errors that are recorded in the error log and clear the error log. The file server error log is a file where all serious errors that occur while the file server is running are recorded.

Select Default Account Balance Restrictions.

Setting Default Account Balance Restrictions

```
              Default Account Balance/Restrictions

Account Has Expiration Date:         No
   Date Account Expires:
Limit Concurrent Connections:        Yes
   Maximum Connections:              1
Require Password:                    Yes
   Minimum Password Length:          5
Force Periodic Password Changes:     Yes
   Days Between Forced Changes:      10
   Limit Grace Logins:               Yes
      Grace Logins Allowed:          3
Require Unique Passwords:            Yes
Account Balance:                     0
Allow Unlimited Credit:              Yes
   Low Balance Limit:
Limit Disk Space:                    Yes
Maximum Disk Space (in KB):          10000
```

You can set the following defaults, which will apply to users created after this point:

ACCOUNT HAS EXPIRATION DATE—If this default is set to "Yes," the account will be automatically disabled at a specified date and cannot be used after that date unless the Supervisor renews the account.

DATE ACCOUNT EXPIRES—If "Account Has Expiration Date" is set to "Yes," then this field contains the account expiration date.

LIMIT CONCURRENT CONNECTIONS—If this is set to "Yes," it indicates that the user is limited as to the number of workstations that he or she can log in from at the same time.

MAXIMUM CONNECTIONS—If "Limit Concurrent Connections" is set to "Yes," then this field specifies the maximum number of stations a user can be logged in on at the same time.

REQUIRE PASSWORD—If this is set to "Yes," then the user is required to have a password.

MINIMUM PASSWORD LENGTH—If "Require Password" is set to "Yes," then this field contains the minimum length of the required password. This length can be between one and twenty characters. Generally, the longer the password, the more secure it is.

FORCE PERIODIC PASSWORD CHANGES—If "Require Password" is set to "Yes," then this field indicates if the user is required to change his or her password at regular intervals. If this is set to "Yes," the password will expire periodically and the user will be asked to change it.

DAYS BETWEEN FORCED CHANGES—If "Force Periodic Password Changes" is set to "Yes," then this field contains the number of days the user can use a password before it expires.

How often passwords should be changed depends on many factors, including the need for security, the physical opportunities for unauthorized network access, and the sensitivity of the particular files to which an intruder could gain access using this account. Against these factors, you should balance the trouble it will be for users to memorize new passwords on a regular basis, and the additional time and effort that will be required for system management.

DATE PASSWORD EXPIRES—If "Force Periodic Password Changes" is set to "Yes," then this field indicates the next date on which a user's password expires. After this date is past, the file server will inform the user that his or her password has expired each time the user logs in to the file server. In addition, if "Limit Grace Logins" is set to "Yes," then the file server will not allow a user to log in if the expired password has not been changed within the specified number of grace logins.

Each time a user changes his or her password, the file server will set the next password expiration date automatically. If the Supervisor changes a user's password, then the file server will mark the password as expired, forcing the user to select a new one.

LIMIT GRACE LOGINS—If "Force Periodic Password Changes" is set to "Yes," then this field indicates whether the user is forced to change the password, or if an expired password is simply a reminder to change to a new password. If this field is set to "Yes," then the user has a limited number of chances to change the password. If the user does not change the password within the specified limit he or she will no longer be able to log in.

GRACE LOGINS ALLOWED—If "Limit Grace Logins" is set to "Yes," then this field indicates the number of chances the user gets to change an expired password. If the user does not change the password within the specified number of logins, then he or she will not be allowed to login.

REMAINING GRACE LOGINS—If "Limit Grace Logins" is set to "Yes," then this field shows the remaining number of time that the user can log in using an expired password. When this number reaches zero the user will not be allowed to log in again until the Supervisor gives the user more grace logins, or changes the password expiration date so that the password is not expired. This field is automatically reset to the value in "Grace Logins Allowed" each time the password is changed.

REQUIRE UNIQUE PASSWORDS—If "Require Password" is set to "Yes," then this field indicates whether the user should be forced to use a different password each time the password is changed. If this is set to "Yes," the user will not be allowed to change the password to a password that was previously used.

DEFAULT ACCOUNT BALANCE RESTRICTIONS—If accounting has been installed on the file server, you can view and change the default account balance for new users.

LIMIT DISK SPACE—This option will only appear if the option to track the amount of disk space a user is using was selected during the NetWare operating system installation. If this is set to "Yes," then the "Maximum Disk Space" field specifies the default maximum amount of disk space that the user can use on the file server.

MAXIMUM DISK SPACE—If "Limit Disk Space" is set to "Yes," then this field specifies the default maximum amount of disk space a user can use. Since disk space is allocated in blocks of 4K this field is used to specify how many blocks can be allocated to a user. Note that a file's size must be rounded up to the next 4K boundary when determining the amount of disk space it is using.

These default values can be changed for each user (see Chapter 14, "Setting Up Users and Groups").

Setting Default Time Restrictions

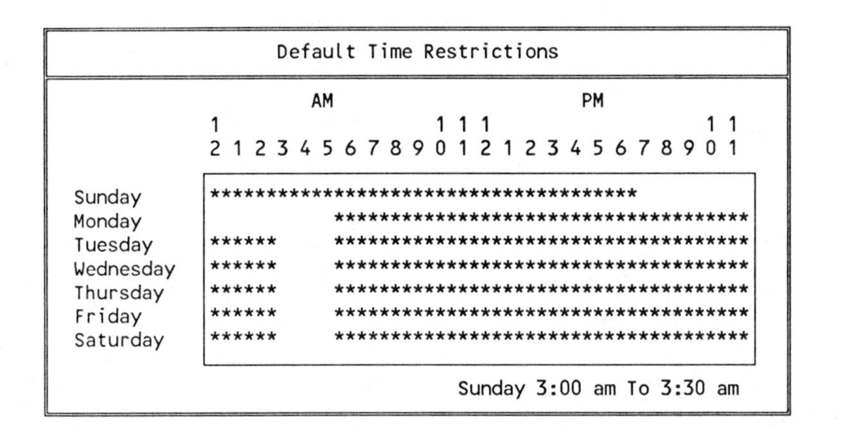

This option allows you to view and change the default time restrictions that will be in effect when a new user is created.

Each day of the week is divided into half-hour time blocks, with an asterisk (*) indicating a time period when the user can be logged in, and a space ( ) indicating when he or she cannot be logged in. The bottom right-hand corner of the screen displays the day and time period represented by your current cursor position.

To change the default for a particular time period, move your cursor the the selected location and press the space bar or the asterisk key.

Note: Changing the default login time restrictions will not change the login time restrictions of any user account that has already been created.

Assigning File Server Console Operators

File Server Console Operators	
NET$$MAN	(User)
PATRICK	(User)
SUPERVISOR	(User)

This option allows you to view and modify the list of users and groups that have been authorized to operate the file server console from their workstations with the FConsole utility.

The file server console commands include utilities for monitoring the status of technical parameters of the Network. They are discussed in detail in Chapter 16, "Managing File Server Resources."

Before you can use this option, you will need to create users and/or groups.

By pressing the <Ins> key, you will display a list of users and groups who are not file server console operators. To select a console operator, highlight the user's or group's name in this list and press <Enter>.

Setting up Intruder Detection

```
                     Intruder Detection/Lockout

Detect Intruders:                 Yes

Intruder Detection Threshold
Incorrect Login Attempts:         3
Bad Login Count Retention Time: 1  Days    0  Hours    0  Minutes

Lock Account After Detection:     Yes
   Length Of Account Lockout:     0 Days    0  Hours    15 Minutes
```

INTRUDER DETECTION LOCKOUT—allows you to decide what constitutes an intruder, and what to do about it.

The operational definition of an intruder is someone trying to log in to the network with the wrong password more than a given number of attempts in a given period of time. The person may really be unauthorized. It could also be that a legitimate user has forgotten his or her password or is a terrible typist.

The Supervisor determines how many attempts in how much time constitutes intrusion, then specifies if the file server should lock an account after an attempted break-in, and for how long the account should remain locked.

It is possible for someone with a list of system users (that means any user on your system) to force all accounts, including the Supervisor's, to be locked. This should be considered when setting the time an account should remain locked. You may also wish to create a second user who is granted Supervisor Equivalence. Then you can only be locked out if both the Supervisor and the second user are intruded upon.

Creating the System Login Script

```
                    System Login Script
MAP DISPLAY OFF
PC COMPATIBLE
DOS BREAK OFF
MAP S1:=SYS:PUBLIC
MAP S2:=SYS:PUBLIC/%OS/%MACHINE/%OS_VERSION
MAP S3:=SYS:PCAPPS/FLEX/DATA
MAP S4:=SYS:PCAPPS/FLEX
MAP S5:=SYS:PCAPPS/WP
MAP S6:=SYS:PCAPPS/SCALC
MAP S7:=SYS:PCAPPS/OW
COMSPEC=S2:COMMAND.COM
IF P_STATION = "0000C0BF8811" BEGIN
  MAP INSERT S1:=SYS:PUBLIC/EGACFG
  MAP S16:=C:\
END
IF MEMBER OF "ACCOUNTING" MAP H:=SYS:PCAPPS/NV
MAP N:=SYS:DOCUMENT\SHARWARE
DOS SET LOGIN_NAME="%LOGIN_NAME"
DOS SET PROMPT="$P$G"
```

The system login script specifies actions that will occur for all users when they log in. The commands in the system login script are executed before the commands in an individual user's login script.

Login scripts are made up primarily of login script commands and login script identifiers. Commands tell the LOGIN program to perform specific actions, such as, set a drive path, or display some text to the screen. Identifiers are predefined symbols that can be used within the LOGIN commands above. Identifiers are variables, they represent information that can change. For example, the identifier

DAY_OF_WEEK represents the literal string "Monday," "Tuesday," or whatever the current day is. Identifiers may be displayed (see WRITE command), or may be used in comparisons (see IF...THEN command).

Login scripts, like batch files, can get complicated. It is good practice to document all of the login scripts so that they can be recreated quickly. (See Appendix E, "Network Utility Software" for information on tools to document login scripts.)

Login Script Identifiers

Login script identifiers may be placed anywhere in a login script. Identifiers preceded by a percent (%) sign will be replaced by their corresponding text value. When used with the % sign, identifiers MUST be in ALL CAPITALS.

LOGIN SCRIPT IDENTIFIERS	
Identifier	Text Value
HOUR	1 to 12
HOUR24	00 to 23
MINUTE	00 to 59
SECOND	00 TO 59
AM_PM	am or pm
MONTH	01 to 12
MONTH_NAME	June, May, etc.
DAY	01 TO 31
YEAR	1983, 2016, etc.
SHORT_YEAR	83, 16, etc.
DAY_OF_WEEK	Monday, Tuesday, etc.
NDAY_OF_WEEK	1 to 7 (1=Monday)
LOGIN_NAME	User's login name
FULL_NAME	User's full name
STATION	Station number
GREETING_TIME	Morning, Afternoon, or Evening
NEW_MAIL	Yes or No
OS	MSDOS
OS_VERSION	V2.11 or V3.00
MACHINE	IBM_PC, COMPAQ, etc.
SHELL_TYPE	Shell type number
P_STATION	Physical station number
SMACHINE	Short machine name
MEMBER OF	No text value

Login Script Commands

Each login script command must be written on its own line. Blank lines will be ignored by LOGIN. The following commands are available for use in a login script:

MAP
WRITE
EXIT
DRIVE
IF...THEN
BREAK
DOS BREAK
(EXEC)
REMARK
COMSPEC=
INCLUDE
DISPLAY
FDISPLAY
PAUSE
MACHINE NAME=
DOS SET
ATTACH
PC COMPATIBLE

The login script commands are discussed alphabetically below.

ATTACH

After a user logs into one file server, ATTACH logs the user into a second server (if there is more than one server, of course).

For example, if a user has logged in to file server FS1, the login script command:

```
ATTACH FS2
```

will log that user into file server FS2. If users have the same login name and password on the second file server, they will be automatically attached; otherwise, they will be required to enter valid FS2 user names and passwords. ATTACH does not run a login script on the server to which the user is ATTACHing. Therefore, any drive mapping, etc., to the second server should be done in the current login script. For example, to map drive letter L: to the directory DOCS, of volume SYS:, on file server FS2, you would put the following command in the current login script:

```
ATTACH FS2
MAP L:=FS2/SYS:DOCS
```

BREAK (See also DOS BREAK below)

The command is either BREAK ON or BREAK OFF. The default is BREAK OFF, which means that the user cannot use the BREAK key to cancel or interrupt execution of the login script.

Generally, the Supervisor will leave the default BREAK equal to OFF.

COMSPEC

COMSPEC is a DOS environment variable that tells DOS the command processor's name and where it can be found. The default location is the root directory of the boot disk and the default name is COMMAND.COM. NetWare requires that the command processor from which the workstation boots also be loaded on a network drive. A search drive must also be mapped to the directory containing the command processor.

For example, if you boot a PC from Drive A, the COMSPEC is A:\COMMAND.COM. You can verify what the current COMSPEC is by typing SET <Enter>.

The login script COMSPEC command tells DOS where to find the command processor after a user logs in to a file server. Usually, the command processor is called COMMAND.COM, but there are some third-party command processors available that have different names. To set the COMSPEC, you must map to the directory containing the appropriate command processor, and set your COMSPEC to that drive and file. For example:

```
MAP S1:=SYS:PUBLIC MAP
S2:=SYS:PUBLIC/%MACHINE/%OS_VERSION
COMSPEC=S2:COMMAND.COM
```

specifies that COMMAND.COM be loaded from the second search directory, and that the second search directory is mapped to the appropriate DOS subdirectory containing the correct version of COMMAND.COM. If you typed the DOS command SET, you would now see:

```
COMSPEC=Y:COMMAND.COM
```

DOS BREAK

The command is either DOS BREAK ON or DOS BREAK OFF. The default is DOS BREAK ON, which enables CTRL/BREAK.

This setting determines whether the user can interrupt DOS commands with CTRL/BREAK during the login process. DOS BREAK OFF disables CTRL/BREAK for DOS commands during the login procedure.

DOS SET

Use the DOS SET command to set DOS environment variables. For example:

```
DOS SET PROMPT = "$P$G"
```

sets the system prompt to the current drive and directory with a "greater than" sign (>), as in

```
F:\USERS\JSMITH\>
```

DOS SET USERNAME = "%LOGIN_NAME"

Sets a variable called USERNAME that is equivalent to the user's login name. The value specified after the equals sign (=) must be in quotes. If the user's login name is JSMITH, when you entered a DOS SET command, you would see:

```
USERNAME=JSMITH
```

DOS VERIFY

The syntax for this command is DOS VERIFY OFF or DOS VERIFY ON. The NetWare command NCOPY automatically verifies that copied data was copied correctly. The DOS COPY command does not. If DOS VERIFY OFF is declared in the login script, then verify occurs only if you include the parameter /v. For example, copy filename a:/v

If DOS VERIFY ON is included in the login script, then all Copy commands will verify copied data.

DRIVE

The syntax for this command is

```
DRIVE n: (where n is a letter)
```

or

```
DRIVE *N: (where n is a number)
```

Use this command to fix the drive letter of the current drive. NetWare defaults to making the first network drive the current drive at login.

This command can be used in conjunction with the MAP command (below) to locate the user in a particular directory at login:

```
MAP F:=SYS:%LOGIN_NAME
MAP G:=SYS:APPS\ACCTING
DRIVE G:
```

The user's prompt would be:

```
G:\APPS\ACCTING\>
```

or

```
MAP *1:=SYS:%LOGIN_NAME MAP *2:=SYS:APPS\ACCTING
DRIVE *2:
```

If the first network drive (*1:) is F:, and the second network drive (*2:) is G:, the user's prompt would be

```
G:\APPS\ACCTING\>
```

or

```
DRIVE C:
```

which could be used to make a local hard disk current. In this case, the prompt would probably be C:\>

DISPLAY and FDISPLAY

The syntax for these commands is:

```
[F]DISPLAY [directory/]filename
```

These commands allow you to display a text file as a message at login. DISPLAY shows the exact characters in the file "as is," including control characters and special codes. FDISPLAY filters WordStar codes out of the message.

For example:

```
MAP *1=SYS:%LOGIN_NAME
MAP *S1=SYS:PUBLIC
MAP *S2=SYS:%MACHINE_NAME\%OS\%OS_VERSION
FDISPLAY S1:daily.msg
```

would display a file named DAILY.MSG from the directory PUBLIC. It could, for example, contain a message reminding users of the Saturday backup:

```
Remember, the LAN is being backed up from 8 am until noon on
Saturday.
```

If the file or directory does not exist when the user logs in, no error message will display.

EXIT

The syntax of this command is:

```
EXIT "command"
```

The EXIT command terminates execution of the login script and executes the specified command. The command may be a .COM, .EXE, or .BAT command, must be in quotes, and may not exceed fourteen characters in length. For example:

```
EXIT "menu"
```

would exit a user from the login script to a command named MENU.COM, MENU.EXE, or MENU.BAT

The most obvious use of EXIT is to exit to a menu or batch file, or within an IF...THEN construction that terminates execution in the presence of a specific condition. For example:

```
IF DAY_OF_WEEK = "Saturday" and LOGIN_NAME <> "SUPERVISOR" BEGIN
       FDISPLAY "enduser.msg"
       EXIT "logout"
END
```

If it is Saturday, and the username is not Supervisor, a message file called "enduser.msg" will be displayed, and the user will be automatically logged out.

If you wish to load RAM-resident programs from the login script, they should be loaded using an EXIT command, since EXIT actually functions after LOGIN is removed from memory.

Note: See the command PC_COMPATIBLE, below.

EXEC or EXTERNAL PROGRAM EXECUTION (#)

The syntax for this command is:

```
#[directory/]command parameter line
```

External program calls must appear on a line by themselves in the login script. Notice that you precede the program name with a # sign.

This command lets you execute a .COM or .EXE command or program that is external to the login script. It lets you specify any parameters that are valid for the program you are calling, just as if you were executing the program from the DOS command line. For example:

```
#CAPTURE
```

redirects printer output to the default network print queue.

The user must have appropriate rights to access and use the program you call, and the Login program must be able to find it. The workstation must have sufficient memory to run the program and log in at the same time. When RAM-resident programs are loaded with EXEC, they do not release the memory used by LOGIN; use the EXIT command to release LOGIN memory.

FIRE PHASERS

The syntax for this command is

```
FIRE PHASERS [n] TIMES
```

or

```
FIRE [n]
```

FIRE PHASERS causes a phaser sound (from the television series "Star Trek"). For example:

```
FIRE PHASERS 4 TIMES
```

Causes four phaser sounds when the user logs in.

IF...THEN

The IF...THEN command allows you to limit execution of login script commands to specific circumstances. You can make use of any of the identifiers described above in constructing an IF...THEN sequence. For example:

```
IF LOGIN_NAME IS EQUAL TO "SUPERVISOR" THEN MAP *1:=SYS:SYSTEM
```

would map the first network drive to SYS:SYSTEM

As another example:

```
        IF DAY_OF_WEEK = "Friday" THEN DISPLAY *3:fridays.msg
```

would display a file called "fridays.msg" from the third network drive if today is Friday.

Multiple conditions can be specified, separated by the word AND, or by commas:

```
IF DAY_OF_WEEK = "Friday" AND AM_PM = "pm" DISPLAY *3:fridays.msg
```

would display a file called "fridays.msg" from the third network drive if it is Friday afternoon or evening.

Finally, you can break the command onto more than one line by using BEGIN and END:

```
IF DAY_OF_WEEK = "Friday" AND AM_PM = "pm" BEGIN
        DISPLAY *3:backup.msg
        WRITE "Have a great weekend!"
END
```

The conditionals allowed in the IF...THEN command are:

```
        Equal   Not Equal
        IS      IS NOT
        =       !=
        ==      <>
        EQUALS  DOES NOT EQUAL
                NOT EQUAL TO
```

The other four relationships may be represented as follows:

```
        >       IS GREATER THAN
        <       IS LESS THAN
        >=      IS GREATER THAN OR EQUAL TO
        <=      IS LESS THAN OR EQUAL TO
```

Literal text must be enclosed in double quotes, like "Friday" or "Hello."

Double quotes that you want to display as literal text must be preceded by back slashes:

```
\"Hi!\"  for "Hi!"
```

INCLUDE

The syntax for the INCLUDE command is:

```
INCLUDE [directory\]filename
```

If you find yourself constructing complex IF...THEN commands to grant different rights to different users, you should consider reorganizing your login scripts by way of the INCLUDE command.

The INCLUDE command reads files created outside of SysCon and interprets them as continuations of the login script. You can use any text editor or word processor that can produce flat ASCII files. Place valid login script commands in the file. Then put the command:

```
INCLUDE directory\filename
```

in each user login script. The user must have Read and Open rights in the directory where you place the INCLUDE file. A good place to put INCLUDE files is in the user's mail subdirectory. (This is the directory created when the user was created in SysCon. The directory name is the same as the user's USER ID; you can find the USER ID in SysCon User Information.) Another approach is to create a directory for all INCLUDE files, and give users (R)ead and (O)pen rights there. This works well when you will share INCLUDE files among multiple users.

The INCLUDE script files you create can contain further INCLUDE commands. This "nesting" can be up to ten layers deep.

MACHINE NAME=

The syntax for this command is:

```
MACHINE NAME = "name"
```

You can use the MACHINE NAME command to set the NetBIOS machine name of the station to the specified name. The MACHINE NAME command is necessary for some programs written to run with NetBIOS.

If the installation instructions for your application program does not specifically say that you need to use a machine name or NetBIOS name, you probably do not need to use this command.

The machine name may contain up to fifteen characters, and can include such identifier variables as %P_STATION.

Note: This command should not be confused with the login script identifier MACHINE, which returns the LONG MACHINE TYPE from the NetWare shell.

MAP

The syntax of this command is:

```
MAP [drive_letter]:= <[file_server]/[volume_name]>:[directory]
```

For example:

```
MAP G:=FS2/SYS:USERS\JSMITH
```

MAP is used to assign drive letters to directories. The user must also have rights to the directories assigned to be able to actually use them.

Traditionally, the first network drive is assigned to the user's home directory. The first network drive default is usually F.

```
MAP F:= \JSMITH
```

This could be made universal:

```
MAP F:= \%LOGIN_NAME
```

If the login script does contain this command, it will be translated for user JSMITH into

```
MAP F:=\JSMITH
```

```
Drive  A:   maps to a local disk.
Drive  B:   maps to a local disk.
Drive  F: = LARKSPUR/SYS:USERS/JSMITH
Drive  I: = SERVER1/SYS1:/GROUPS/SALES/REPORTS
Drive  J: = LARKSPUR/SYS:DOCUMENT/SHARWARE
      -----
SEARCH1:  = Z:. [LARKSPUR/SYS:PUBLIC]
SEARCH2:  = Y:. [LARKSPUR/SYS:PUBLIC/ITT_XTRA/V3.20]
SEARCH3:  = X:. [LARKSPUR/SYS:PCAPPS/FLEX/DATA]
SEARCH4:  = W:. [LARKSPUR/SYS:PCAPPS/FLEX]
SEARCH6:  = U:. [LARKSPUR/SYS:PCAPPS/WP]
SEARCH7:  = T:. [LARKSPUR/SYS:PCAPPS/SCALC]
SEARCH9:  = R:. [LARKSPUR/SYS:PCAPPS/OW]
```

When the user logs in, the mapping is displayed. You can turn off the display with:

```
MAP DISPLAY OFF
```

and turn it back on with:

```
MAP DISPLAY ON
```

PAUSE or WAIT

The syntax for this command is simply:

```
PAUSE
```

or

```
WAIT
```

This command displays the message "Strike a key when ready..." before the login script continues. The LOGIN program suspends execution until the user presses a key.

This command is used to give a user as much time as he needs to read a message on the screen. The command can also be used to give the user an opportunity to cancel further execution of the login script.

For example, you could display the following message and then pause the script:

```
WRITE "Press the spacebar to enter Word Processing or"
WRITE "Press Control-C to reach the DOS prompt"
PAUSE
```

PC_COMPATIBLE

If the Machine_Name you specified in the shell.cfg file on the boot disk for this workstation is not IBM_PC, then you must specifically declare that your machine is PC_COMPATIBLE to enable the EXIT command in login scripts. To do so, simply precede the EXIT command with a line that declares compatibility:

```
PC_COMPATIBLE
```

or

```
COMPATIBLE
```

Some machines formerly supported by NetWare that did not have type-ahead keyboard buffers would lock up when the EXIT command, which does use the keyboard buffer, was invoked. NetWare requires that the default machine name in the shell be IBM_PC, or that there be an explicit declaration of compatibility before the EXIT command is enabled. The PC_COMPATIBLE command may be anywhere in the system or user login script as long as it precedes any EXIT command(s).

REMARK

Any line in the script that starts with REMARK is ignored. Use REMARK to document the script. Also use REMARK to disable a command that you want to consider reinvoking later.

WRITE

The syntax for this command is:

```
WRITE ["text strings"; ...identifier(s);...]
```

Use the WRITE command to create customized messages for users to see at login. These messages can be personalized for multiple users by using identifiers as part of the command(s). For example:

```
WRITE "HI,";%LOGIN_NAME;"!"
```

When user JSMITH logs in, she will see:

```
HI, JSMITH!
```

This example made use of the identifier %LOGIN_NAME. Any of the login script identifiers can be made part of the WRITE message.

To cause multiple WRITE commands to display on the same line, place a semi-colon at the end of each WRITE command except the last.

You can place what NetWare calls "super-characters" within WRITE command text strings. The super-characters available are:

`\r`	for a carriage return
`\n`	for a new line
`\"`	for an embedded double quote that will display as part of the WRITE message
`\7`	to sound a beep

LOGIN COMMAND LINE PARAMETERS

You can give the users the flexibility to vary aspects of their configurations from one login to another. The users type the variations they want on the same line as the login command. Each variation is numbered, and corresponds to a number in the login script.

The first variable is always the user's login name. It is numbered %1, and can be substituted in any login script command with the user's login name. For example:

```
MAP G:=%1
```

assigns drive G: to the directory that has the same name as the user's login name.

You could give the user the ability to choose which directory to assign a drive to at any given login. This is useful when a user works with many different data subdirectories.

```
MAP G:=%1
MAP H:=%2
```

At one login, the user would type:

```
login jsmith \lotus\ap\88
```

which would give her access to her accounts payable Lotus worksheets for 1988. On another login, she would type:

```
login jsmith \lotus\ar\89
```

which would give her access to her accounts receivable Lotus worksheets for 1989.

The supervisor should already have given the user TRUSTEE RIGHTS to use any directories which will be accessed in this way.

The Default Login Script

If you do not create a system login script or a user login script, a default login script will automatically be invoked. The default login script is:

```
WRITE "Good %GREETING_TIME,%LOGIN_NAME."
MAP DISPLAY OFF
MAP ERRORS OFF
Remark: Set 1st drive to most appropriate directory
MAP *1:=SYS:;*1:%LOGIN_NAME
IF"%1"=SUPERVISOR" THEN MAP*1:=SYS:SYSTEM
Remark: Set search drives (S2 machine-os dependent)
MAP S1:=SYS:PUBLIC;S2:=S1:%MACHINE/%OS/%OS_VERSION
Remark: Now display all the current drive settings
MAP DISPLAY ON
MAP
```

14

Setting Up Groups and Users

Introduction

When you create a user, you assign certain levels of access to network resources, including directories, print queues, etc. One way to do this is to grant to each user the appropriate access right to each resource on an individual level. Although there is nothing wrong with this, there is an easier way.

In addition to defining network users, you can also define groups of users. A group usually consists of one or more users who have similar access needs to certain resources.

For example, most users in the accounting department may need similar access levels to the accounting software and data. By creating a group for them, you can grant the appropriate access rights once, instead of over and over for each user.

Another group of users from various departments may need access to a CAD/CAM application and a shared plotter. By creating a group for these users you could can grant them access to the necessary software and the plotter all at once.

The main advantage of setting up groups is that you can change access rights for several users by changing the group rights once. There is no limit to the number of members a group may have, or the number of groups a user can belong to.

Group and user rights are additive. This means that adding a user to a particular group does not limit the access rights he or she has as an individual user or a member of another group.

A group, like an individual user, can be assigned rights to directories and print queues. Users become members of groups and by membership inherit group rights. The more users in the network, the more benefit you will gain from assigning users to groups instead of granting all their rights as individuals.

NetWare automatically creates a default group called EVERYONE and grants membership to all new users.

There is no specific order in which users or groups must be set up.

Usually, you will create groups whose users access the same or similar resources. This may mean that you will create departmental groups with each having access to several applications; and/or applications-oriented groups, with access to specific applications. Decide what is most appropriate for your situation.

Generally speaking, you will grant groups minimum access rights, and then grant exceptions to individual users. For example, the group ACCTING (for the accounting department) may have limited access to certain accounting directories. The department manager, however, who is also a member of the group ACCTING, may also have additional access rights as an individual.

For example, if you assign individual rights to sixteen users to Read, Open, and Search (ROS) a directory, and then decide you want to grant Write privileges as well, you have sixteen changes to make. If you had set up a group with the (ROS) rights and assigned the

NetWare™ Group Worksheet

FILE SERVER NAME: ______________________________

GROUP NAME: ______________________________

GROUP FULL NAME: ______________________________

GROUP MEMBERS:

FULL NAME	LOGIN NAME

DIRECTORY NAME	GROUP RIGHTS	DIR. RIGHTS	EFFECTIVE RIGHTS

NetWare™ User Worksheet

FILE SERVER NAME: ______________________________

USER'S NAME: ______________________________

USER'S LOGIN NAME: ______________________________

GROUPS BELONGED TO:	SECURITY EQUIVALENCES:

DIRECTORY NAME	USER RIGHTS	GRP/EQV RIGHTS	DIR. RIGHTS	EFFECTIVE RIGHTS

sixteen users to that group, adding the Write (RWOS) privilege would require only one change.

You can use the NetWare utility SysCon to create both groups and individual users. You can make your work in SysCon easier by preplanning the groups and users you will create using the planning sheets on the following pages. Also, refer to the DIRECTORY and APPLICATION structures that you developed in the last chapter.

Creating Groups

To access SysCon, type at a network prompt:

```
SYSCON <Enter>
```

Any user can run SysCon to obtain limited information about the file server and the groups and users that exist on it, and change his or her user login script.

Only the Supervisor or a user with Supervisor equivalence can create, modify, or delete users or groups. To create or modify groups, select "Group Information" from the SysCon main menu.

```
Group Names          vailable Topics

EVERYONE             ounting
                     nge Current Server
                     e Server Information
                     up Information
          New Group Name: SALES
```

GROUP INFORMATION displays a list of existing groups. To create a group, press the <Ins> key, type in the name of the new group, then press <Enter>. You may create as many groups as you need. To view or change information about a group, highlight the group's name and press <Enter>.

```
        Group Names          | vailable Topics | Group Information
                             |                 |
 ACCOUNTING                  | ounting         | Full Name
 BATCHGROUP                  | nge Current Serv| Member List
 EVERYONE                    | e Server Informa| Other Information
 SALES                       | up Information  | Trustee Assignments
 DESIGN                      | ervisor Options
 Q_OPS                       | r Information
 Q_USERS
```

Information about the selected group will be displayed. To view the information, highlight the desired option, then press <Enter>. A brief description of each option follows:

FULL NAME allows you to view or change the group's full name.

```
Group Names        vailable Topic       Group Members

ACCOUNTING         ounting              AISLING
BATCHGROUP         nge Current Se       KAREN
EVERYONE           e Server Infor       PATRICK
SALES              up Information       WARREN
DESIGN             ervisor Option
Q_OPS              r Information
Q_USERS
```

MEMBER LIST lists the users on the current file server that belong to this group. You can select MEMBER LIST to add or delete users from the group.

To add a user to the group, press the <Ins> key. SysCon will display a list of users that are not in the group. Press the first letter of the user name, or use the cursor control keys to move around on the list. Press <Enter> to select a user.

To delete a user from the group, highlight the user's name, then press the <Del> key.

OTHER INFORMATION shows the group ID number and tells you if the group is a console operator (allowed to use the FConsole utility).

```
Group Names          | vai | Trustee Assignments
ACCOUNTING           | oun | SYS:MAIL              [ W C      ]
BATCHGROUP           | nge | SYS:PCAPPS/FLEX       [RWO     S ]
EVERYONE             | e S | SYS:PCAPPS/OW         [RWOCD   S ]
SALES                | up  | SYS:PCAPPS/SCALC      [RWOC    S ]
DESIGN               | erv | SYS:PCAPPS/WP         [RWOC    S ]
Q_OPS                | r I | SYS:PUBLIC            [R O     S ]
Q_USERS              |     |
```

TRUSTEE ASSIGNMENTS lists the directories in which the group has trustee rights, along with the rights granted in each directory. To grant Trustee rights to a new directory, press the <Ins> key, then enter the directory name in the form:

```
VOLUME:DIRECTORY/SUBDIRECTORY
```

If the directory you name does not exist, SysCon will ask if you want to create it. Move the cursor to "Yes" or "No" and press <Enter>. SysCon will create the directory if you select "Yes."

When you make a group a Trustee of a directory, the default rights assigned are Read, Open and Search (all eight rights prior to version 2.15).

To modify a group's rights to a directory, highlight the directory name and press <Enter>. The list of granted rights appears.

To delete a right, move the cursor to that right and press <Del>. To grant a new right, press <Ins>. The list of Rights Not Granted will appear. Move the cursor to the right you want to grant and press <Enter>. Continue to grant and delete rights in this way until you are satisfied with the rights granted, then press <Esc>.

Creating Users

The process of creating users is similar to the process of creating groups. When you create users, you grant access rights to directories, place users into groups, set time and account restrictions, and create login scripts.

```
User Names          vailable Topic    User Information

AISLING             ounting           Account Balance
KAREN               nge Current Se    Account Restrictions
PATRICK             e Server Infor    Change Password
SUPERVISOR          up Information    Full Name
WARREN              ervisor Option    Groups Belonged To
                    r Information     Intruder Lockout Status
                                      Login Script
                                      Other Information
                                      Security Equivalences
                                      Station Restrictions
                                      Time Restrictions
                                      Trustee Assignments
```

From the SysCon main menu, select USER INFORMATION to Create, Modify, and Delete users.

USER INFORMATION lists users on the file server. The Supervisor can view, create, and modify user information. Users can view most information about themselves, but can only see limited information about other users.

Setting up a new user in SysCon usually involves:

- Declaring the user
- Assigning a password
- Assigning the user to groups
- Granting the user Trustee rights to directories
- Creating a user login script

To review an existing user, press the first letter of the user name, then the down arrow key until the user is highlighted, and finally press <Enter>.

To create a new user, press <Ins>, and enter a user name. Although the user name can be up to twenty-three characters, it is a good practice to limit user names to eight characters or less. This makes it easy to map the user to his or her "Home Directory" in the login script.

After you have created the user, highlight the user's name, then press <Enter>. The User Information menu will display, allowing you to view or change information about that user.

Setting the Account Balance

This option, which shows the user's current account balance and credit limit, only appears if you have implemented accounting on the file server. For more information about account see the NetWare Supervisor Reference Manual.

Setting or Changing Account Restrictions

```
            Account Restrictions For User KAREN

Account Disabled:                  No
Account Has Expiration Date:       No
   Date Account Expires:
Limit Concurrent Connections:      Yes
   Maximum Connections:            1
Allow User To Change Password:     Yes
Require Password:                  Yes
   Minimum Password Length:        5
Force Periodic Password Changes:   Yes
   Days Between Forced Changes:    10
   Date Password Expires:          May 23, 1989
   Limit Grace Logins:             Yes
      Grace Logins Allowed:        3
      Remaining Grace Logins:      3
Require Unique Passwords:          Yes
Limit Disk Space:                  Yes
Maximum Disk Space (in KB):        10000
```

The Supervisor can accept the default account restrictions (set up in SysCon's Supervisor Options) for a user, or the Supervisor can change them. Changes can be either more or less restrictive than the system defaults. Account Restrictions gives the Supervisor considerable power to control users' access to the network. Account Restrictions are described in Chapter 13, "Setting System Defaults."

Assigning a Password

You have the option of assigning passwords or letting each user create his or her own. You can assign an initial password, then let the user change it. Passwords are encrypted; the Supervisor can assign or change a user's password, but cannot view it.

One of the Supervisor Options in SysCon allows the Supervisor to declare whether passwords should be required and how often they should be changed.

For security reasons, a password should not contain:

- any portion of the user's name
- any portion of a family member's name
- the name of the user's pet or make or model of his or her car
- any keyword of the user's job or function, like "entry," or "finance"
- any known interest of the user, like "bicycles," or "49ers"

The longer and less meaningful the password, the harder it is to guess, but of course, don't make it so hard the user can't remember it.

Entering the User's Full Name

You can enter the user's full name here. This can be important in larger networks where several users have similar login names.

Assigning Users to Groups

```
Groups Not Belonged To  |vailable Topic|  Groups Belonged To

LANASSIST               |ounting       |  ACCOUNTING
PRINT_SERVERS           |nge Current Se|  BATCHGROUP
Q_OPS                   |e Server Infor|  EVERYONE
Q_USERS                 |up Information|
                        |ervisor Option|
                        |r Information |
```

The Supervisor can assign a user to any existing group(s). When a user is a member of a group, that user has all the rights granted to that group. If the group's rights are changed, the user's rights change also (unless, of course, the user also has the same rights as an individual or as a member of one or more other groups). NetWare automatically assigns new users to the group EVERYONE.

To assign a user to a group, highlight "Groups Belonged To" on the User Information menu, then press <Enter>. The "Groups Belonged To" screen will display. Press <Ins> and the "Groups Not Belonged To" screen will display. Highlight the group that you wish to add the user to, then press <Enter>. When you are through adding the user to groups, press <Esc> to return to the User Information menu.

To delete a user from a group, highlight "Groups Belonged To" on the User Information menu, then press <Enter>. The "Groups Belonged To" screen will display. Highlight the group from which you want to remove the user and press <Del>. Select "Yes" at the prompt, then press <Enter>. When you are through, press <Esc> to return to the User Information menu.

Viewing the Intruder Lockout Status

```
                    Intruder Lockout Status

Account Locked:          No
Incorrect Login Count:  0
Account Reset Time:
Time Until Reset:
Last Intruder Address:  00000001:00000000001F:4003
```

If you have enabled the Intruder Detection option, this option will display the user's intruder lockout status and allow you (the Supervisor) to unlock a locked account. For more information on intruder detection, see Chapter 13, "Setting System Defaults."

Creating User Login Scripts

```
                 Login Script For User KAREN

MAP *1:=SYS:USERS/%LOGIN_NAME
MAP *2:=SYS:GROUPS/SALES/REPORTS
FIRE 2
MAP DISPLAY ON
MAP
EXIT "MENU MAIN"
```

The Supervisor and/or the user can also create user login scripts. The user login script contains commands that execute only for that user. The commands in the user login script are executed after the commands in the system login script.

User login scripts use the same commands and identifiers used in the system login script. These are described fully in Chapter 13, "Setting System Defaults."

Other Information

```
Last Login:                      May 1, 1989  2:25:46 pm
File Server Console Operator:    No
Maximum Disk Usage:              10000K
Disk Space In Use:                1432K
User ID:                         00070031
```

This option displays the last time the user logged in, whether the user is a Console Operator (allowed to use the FConsole utility), the amount of disk space available and in use, and the user's system- assigned ID number.

Assigning Security Equivalences

Other Users and Groups	
AISLING	(User)
DESIGN	(Group)
PATRICK	(User)
SALES	(Group)
Q_OPS	(Group)
Q_USERS	(Group)
SUPERVISOR	(User)
WARREN	(User)

Security Equivalences	
ACCOUNTING	(Group)
BATCHGROUP	(Group)
EVERYONE	(Group)

You can declare a user to have the same access rights as another user. If a user is a member of a group, the user has security equivalence to that group. If the rights of the equivalent user are changed, the rights of any dependent user change as well.

To grant a user security equivalence to another user, highlight "Security Equivalences" on the User Information menu, then press <Enter>. The "Security Equivalences" screen will display. Press <Ins> and the "Other Users And Groups" screen will display. Highlight the user that you wish to grant security equivalence to, then press <Enter>. When you are through, press <Esc> to return to the User Information menu.

To delete a security equivalence, highlight "Security Equivalences" on the User Information menu, then press <Enter> to display the "Security Equivalences" screen. Highlight the user that you want to delete from the list and press <Del>. Select "Yes" at the prompt, then press <Enter>. When you are through, press <Esc> to return to the User Information menu.

SETTING STATION RESTRICTIONS allows you to limit the user to specific workstations. You can restrict a user to one or more physical networks, and/or limit the user to specific workstations on a physical network. In order to implement this option, you need to know the physical addresses of the networks and workstations to which you are going to restrict the user.

The NetWare command USERLIST with the /E option will display all currently logged-in users and the physical addresses of their networks and workstations. The asterisk (*) indicates you and your workstation.

```
F:\SYSTEM> USERLIST /E

User Information for Server LARKSPUR
Connection  User Name        Network     Node Address   Login Time
----------  --------------   --------    ------------   -------------------
     1        KAREN          [       2] [     C0290005]  5-19-1989  8:42 am
     2        WARREN         [       2] [     C0280001]  5-19-1989  8:42 am
     3      * SUPERVISOR     [       2] [     C0FC2100]  5-19-1989  9:43 am
     4        AISLING        [       2] [     C0E81400]  5-19-1989 12:19 pm
     5        PATRICK        [       2] [     C0BF8811]  5-19-1989  7:03 am
```

Setting Time Restrictions

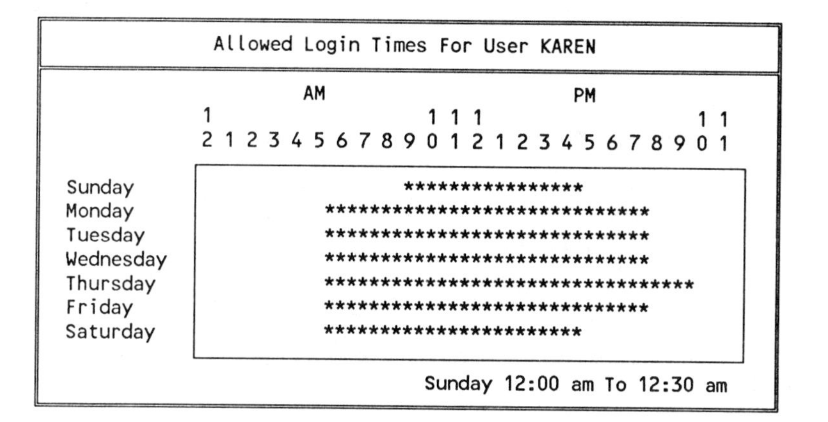

This option allows you to view or change the times during the week when a user is allowed to be logged into the file server. An asterisk (*) indicates that a user may be logged in during the indicated half-hour block of time.

Default time restrictions are set up through SysCon's Supervisor Options. You can accept the default restrictions or change them. Time restrictions are described in Chapter 13, "Setting System Defaults."

Adding Trustee Assignments

Trustee rights give users access to files in the directories assigned. You can grant a user up to eight different rights to a directory. When rights are granted to a directory, by default they are granted to any subdirectories also, unless rights to the subdirectory are specifically changed.

The eight rights are:

R	Read From Files
W	Write To Files
O	Open Existing Files
C	Create New Files
D	Delete Files
P	Parental Rights
S	Search For Files
M	Modify File Names/Flags

For a detailed discussion of effective rights, see Chapter 13, "Setting System Defaults."

To grant trustee rights, select TRUSTEE RIGHTS. NetWare automatically assigns rights to the user's MAIL subdirectory, which NetWare automatically creates for each user. The MAIL subdirectory name corresponds to the user's system-assigned user ID number. This is the directory in which login scripts and printer definition files are kept.

To add rights, press <Ins>. Type the volume name, a colon, and the directory to which you are granting rights. For example

```
SYS:USERS\JSMITH
```

to grant JSMITH rights in his or her home directory, or

```
SYS:APPS\ACCTING\DATA
```

to grant JSMITH rights to the subdirectory of ACCTING called DATA.

If the directory you name does not exist, SysCon will ask if you want to create it. Move the cursor to "Yes" or "No" and press <Enter>. SysCon will create the directory if you select "Yes."

When you make a user a Trustee of a directory, the default rights assigned are Read, Open, and Search (all eight rights prior to version 2.15). To modify rights, move the cursor to the directory whose rights you want to modify and press <Enter>. A window showing rights granted will appear. To delete rights, move the cursor to the right you want to delete and press <Del>. To add rights, press <Ins>. A list of rights not granted appears. Move the cursor to the right you want to add and press <Enter>. When you are finished modifying rights, press <Esc>.

Exiting SysCon

To exit SysCon, press <Esc>. You will go back up one screen per <Esc> until you reach the "Exit SYSCON" prompt. Selecting "Yes" at the prompt will exit you from SysCon.

15

Managing File Server Resources

The NetWare File Server Console

The file server console lets you control and monitor server functions and resources. From the console you can control network printers and print queues, monitor how the file server is being used, bring down the server, etc.

Console functions can be performed in three ways:

- By entering commands directly at the file server console.
- By putting commands in the AUTOEXEC.SYS file, to be automatically executed when the file server is booted.
- By using the FConsole utility from a workstation.

Console Commands

Console commands can be entered directly at the system console. Some of the commonly used commands are:

BROADCAST

BROADCAST allows you to send messages to all workstations that are logged in or attached to the file server.

Syntax:

```
BROADCAST [message]  <Enter>
```

Example:

```
BROADCAST System going down for maintenance in five
minutes!
<Enter>
```

BROADCAST is often used to signal users that the file server is being shut down, usually after a DISABLE LOGIN command is executed (see DISABLE LOGIN below).

CONFIG

CONFIG displays configuration of the network boards installed in the server.

Syntax:

```
CONFIG <Enter>
```

Information similar to the following will appear on the console screen:

```
Hardware Configuration Information for Server LARKSPUR

Number of Service Processes:   4
```

```
LAN A Configuration Information:
  Network   Address:  [      02] [  C0290005]
  Hardware     Type:  WD Star/EtherCard PLUS 2.11.3 (111188)
  Hardware Settings:  IRQ = 2, I/O Base = 340h, RAM Buffer
  at
  C000:0 for 32K, no DMA

LAN B Configuration Information:
  Network   Address:  [      01] [      86]
  Hardware     Type:  Standard Microsystems ARCNET/Pure Data
  V1.00 (881010)
  Hardware Settings:  IRQ = 3, I/O Base = 2E0h, RAM Buffer
  at
  D000:0
```

You can use this information when installing other file servers or bridges to ensure that the settings on the boards and the network names and addresses do not conflict.

CONSOLE

CONSOLE switches a nondedicated server from DOS mode to console mode. CONSOLE is a DOS command, not a console command. It is executed when a nondedicated file server is in DOS mode. CONSOLE can only be executed at the file server.

Syntax:

```
CONSOLE <Enter>
```

DISABLE LOGIN

DISABLE LOGIN prevents stations from logging in to the file server. You can use this command to prevent users from logging in to the file server when you need to shut it down. You can use BROADCAST after issuing a DISABLE LOGIN command to tell users that you are DOWNing the file server (see the DOWN command below).

Syntax:

```
DISABLE LOGIN <Enter>
```

DOS

DOS switches a nondedicated server into DOS mode. This command only works with nondedicated file servers. In order to receive messages directed to the console, or enter console commands, you must be in console mode (see the CONSOLE command above).

Syntax:

```
DOS <Enter>
```

DOWN

DOWN clears all network files and shuts down the file server.

DOWN should always be used before turning off the server. It insures that open files are closed, disk writes in cache are completed, and directory and FAT tables are updated. Even though DOWN warns of open files on the server, it is good practice to make sure all users are logged out before issuing a DOWN command (see DISABLE LOGIN and BROADCAST above). Remember, some applications do not hold files open, but may not allow a user to save work if the network drive becomes invalid (drives become invalid when the server goes down).

To ensure data integrity, always use the DOWN command before turning off the power to any file server.

Syntax:

```
DOWN <Enter>
```

ENABLE LOGIN

ENABLE LOGIN re-enables login capability after a DISABLE LOGIN command has been issued. If you DOWN a file server, and then restart it, login capability is automatically re-enabled.

Syntax:

```
ENABLE LOGIN <Enter>
```

MONITOR

MONITOR displays the console monitor screen, which displays logical station attachments six at a time. Since the monitor display adds slightly to the operating system overhead, Novell recommends that you turn it off with the OFF command when not needed (see the OFF command below). Turning the monitor display off can also help protect the file server console from "screen burn."

Syntax:

```
MONITOR [station number] <Enter>
```

Examples:

```
MONITOR <Enter>
```

Displays the first six stations.

```
MONITOR 22 <Enter>
```

Displays stations 19 through 24.

OFF clears the console screen and moves the cursor to the upper left-hand corner. This command is usually used to clear the monitor display (see the MONITOR command above).

Syntax:

```
OFF <Enter>
```

SEND

SEND will send a message to one or more specific stations. You can use this command to send message to stations using their logical station number. The logical station number for a particular user or workstation can vary depending on the order in which workstations logged on or attached to the file server. The logical number is the number displayed by the console monitor screen.

To use SEND, type the command SEND, followed by your message in quotes (up to forty characters), followed by the word "TO" (optional), finally followed by one or more station numbers separated by commas or spaces.

Syntax:

```
SEND "message" [TO] [STATION#] [stationlist] <Enter>
```

Example:

```
SEND "Will you PLEASE logout NOW!!!" to 4 12 18 <Enter>
```

SET TIME

SET TIME sets the date and time kept by the file server. SET TIME is used when the file server time needs to be corrected. After using SET TIME, it is good practice to have users issue a SYSTIME command from their workstations to synchronize their workstation clocks with the new file server time.

Although SET TIME resets the file server time, it will not reset the internal clock of a 286 or 386 server. That must be done with the server's setup utilities.

Syntax:

```
SET TIME [month/day/year] [hour:minute:second] <Enter>
```

You may set both the date and time in the same command, or you may set either one separately. Either the date or the time may be entered first. If you set only one parameter, the other parameter will remain unaffected. You can enter the time in either standard or military format, and you can also specify the AM or PM designation. If you do not specify an AM/PM designation, the file server will assume that you are entering the time during usual working hours.

The time can be entered in the following formats:

```
2:25:45
2:25:45 PM
14:25:45
```

All three examples would set the time to 2:25:45 p.m.

The date can be entered in the following formats:

```
15/21/89
May 21, 1989
21 May 1989
```

Examples:

```
SET TIME 2:25:45 15/21/89 <Enter>

SET TIME 2:25:89 PM <Enter>

SET TIME May 21, 1989 <Enter>
```

TIME displays the file server date and time in the following format:

```
MAY 21,  1989       2:25:45 pm
```

Syntax:

```
TIME <Enter>
```

Note: For a complete listing of console commands, see the NetWare Console Reference Manual.

Console Printer and Queue Commands

Printer and print queue commands are covered in Chapter 16, "Managing Network Printers."

The AUTOEXEC.SYS File

```
System AUTOEXEC File

Printer 0 ADD PRINTQ_0
Printer 1 ADD PRINTQ_1
Printer 2 ADD PRINTQ_1
Spool 0 to Queue PRINTQ_0
Spool 1 to Queue PRINTQ_1
Spool 2 to Queue PRINTQ_2
MONITOR
```

NetWare allows you to create a console batch file called the AUTOEXEC.SYS file. The console commands in this file execute every time you boot the file server. This file, which is kept in the SYS:SYSTEM directory, can be created with SysCon or with a text editor.

The most important console commands to include in the AUTOEXEC.SYS file are the printer mappings. Printer mappings indicate which printer will print or service the jobs in a given print queue.

If there is no AUTOEXEC.SYS file, the file server will create one default print queue for each network printer. (You defined the network printers during the NetWare installation with NetGen.)

If you do create an AUTOEXEC.SYS file, you must include at least the default printer mappings. If an AUTOEXEC.SYS file exists, the system will execute only those mappings listed in the file. It will not automatically map one print queue to each physically attached printer or spool old printer numbers into a queue as it does if there is not an AUTOEXEC.SYS file.

For more information on printer, queue, and spool mappings, see Chapter 16, "Managing Network Printers."

To create the AUTOEXEC.SYS file, load the SysCon utility by typing:

```
SYSCON <Enter>
```

```
Available Topics
Accounting
Change Cur
File Serve
Group Info
Supervisor
User Infor

Supervisor Options
Default Account Balance/Restrictions
Default Time Restrictions
Edit System AUTOEXEC File
File Server Console Operators
Intruder Detection/Lockout
System Login Script
View File Server Error Log
```

Select "Supervisor Options" from the main menu, then select "Edit System AUTOEXEC File." When you are through editing the file, press <Esc>, and select "Yes" on the Save changes screen. Use <Esc> to exit from SysCon.

Using FConsole

FConsole (File server Console) allows you to control console functions and access information that you can use to analyze the file server's operation and fine tune its performance.

You can execute FConsole from any network station. FConsole is available to the supervisor and users designated by the supervisor as console operators.

Although much of the information provided by FConsole is designed to be used by programmers, other information can be helpful in the day-to-day management of a network. With FConsole you can monitor file server parameters such as allowable open files, communications buffers, available file handles, etc., to avoid hitting the limits of your configuration. You can monitor the effectiveness of disk caching to see if or when you need additional file server memory. You can monitor the Hot Fix tables to track the quantity of detected bad blocks and the number of Hot Fix blocks remaining.

To run FConsole type:

```
FCONSOLE <Enter>
```

```
Available Options

Broadcast Console Message
Change Current File Server
Connection Information
Down File Server
File/Lock Activity
LAN Driver Information
Purge All Salvageable Files
Statistics
Status
Version Information
```

FConsole provides the following options:

BROADCAST CONSOLE MESSAGE

```
Available Options

Broadcast Console Message
Change Current File Server
Connection Information
Down File Server

Message: Put whatever 55 character message you want to send here

Statistics
Status
Version Information
```

BROADCAST CONSOLE MESSAGE allows you to send a message to all stations logged in or attached to the file server. The message will be sent as a system console message. The message can be up to fifty-five characters long.

CHANGE CURRENT FILE SERVER

CHANGE CURRENT FILE SERVER allows you to select another file server as the current file server. Your level of access to another file server through FConsole depends on the rights they have been granted on that server.

CONNECTION INFORMATION

```
Current Connections          | ble Options
                             |
PATRICK                  1   | Con   Connection Information
KAREN                    2   | ren
WARREN                   5   |  In  Broadcast Console Message
SUPERVISOR               6   | Ser  Clear Connection
AISLING                 10   | Act  Logical Record Locks
                        12   |  In  Open Files/Physical Records
                        13   | Sal  Other Information
                        18   |      Semaphores
                        19   |      Task Information
                             | for  Usage Statistics
```

CONNECTION INFORMATION displays a list of all logged in or attached users.

BROADCAST CONSOLE MESSAGE

BROADCAST CONSOLE MESSAGE on the CONNECTION INFORMATION menu allows you to send a console message to the connection you have selected.

CLEAR CONNECTION

CLEAR CONNECTION allows you to clear the selected connection. This is the equivalent of console command CLEAR STATION. Clearing a connection breaks the user's connection with the file server. Any program the user is running will be aborted and if the user's current directory is on the file server, the current drive will become invalid.

LOGICAL RECORD LOCKS

LOGICAL RECORD LOCKS will display all logical record locks in use by the selected connection. This option is primarily used by programmers.

OPEN FILES/PHYSICAL RECORDS

OPEN FILES/PHYSICAL RECORDS will display all files that are held open by the selected connection. This can be useful when diagnosing applications problems. It can also be useful in determining if you are exceeding the maximum number of open files allowed by a workstation shell (or CONFIG.SYS file), or why you are exceeding the maximum number of open files on the file server.

Files In Use By KAREN[5]	Task
SYS:PCAPPS/FLEX/DATA/DELFILE.DAT	3
SYS:PCAPPS/FLEX/DATA/SYSFILE.DAT	3
SYS:PCAPPS/FLEX/DATA/CUST2.DAT	3
SYS:PCAPPS/FLEX/DATA/CUST2.FLX	3
SYS:PCAPPS/FLEX/DATA/FLEXERRS.DAT	3
SYS:PCAPPS/FLEX/DATA/FILELIST.CFG	3

This option will also show the read/write and lock status of a file and any physical record locks that the connection has in a file.

```
SYS:PUBLIC/SYS$HELP.DAT

File is open in share mode.
Open for read only.
Allow reads, but deny writes from other stations.
```

OTHER INFORMATION

OTHER INFORMATION shows the object (user) name and type for the connection, as well as its connection date and network address. Object Type 1 is a user.

```
Object Name:      SUPERVISOR
Object Type:      1
Login Time:       April 15, 1989  3:50:53 pm
Network Address:  00000002:0000C0E81400
```

SEMAPHORES

SEMAPHORES shows the status of any semaphores being used by the selected connection. Semaphores are used for file protection and are also used to control the number of users concurrently accessing an application.

TASK INFORMATION

TASK INFORMATION deals primarily with information about record and file locks and transaction status. This is primarily for use by programmers.

USAGE STATISTICS

USAGE STATISTICS shows connection time, requests received by the file server from this connection, and the number of bytes read from and written to the file server.

Connection Usage Statistics	
Connection Time:	3 Hours 4 Minutes
Requests Received:	11,518
Disk Bytes Read:	2,229,544
Disk Bytes Written:	438,192

DOWN FILE SERVER

Down File Server LARKSPUR
No
Yes

DOWN FILE SERVER will allow you to down the file server. You will be warned if there are files currently open and asked if you want to force down the file server. You must have Supervisor privileges to select this option.

FILE/LOCK ACTIVITY

FILE/LOCK ACTIVITY allows you to examine information about open files, physical record locks, logical record locks, semaphores, and active transactions.

This option shows information about a single file, logical record name, or semaphore name. It shows all connections that are using the file, lock or semaphore and their current status. It will also show all stations that have transactions currently in progress.

LAN DRIVER INFORMATION

```
                        LAN B Configuration

Network Address: 00000001   Node Address: 000000000086
LAN Board Type:  Standard Microsystems ARCNET/Pure Data  V1.00 (881010)
Configuration:   2
Hardware Option: IRQ = 3, I/O Base = 2E0h, RAM Buffer at D000:0
```

LAN DRIVER INFORMATION will show the LAN configuration of the file server. This includes the number and type of LAN cards in the file server and the network address assigned to each one. This option can be selected by any LAN user. This option is equivalent to the console command CONFIG.

PURGE ALL SALVAGE FILES

PURGE ALL SALVAGE FILES allows you to purge all salvageable deleted files on the currently selected file server. When a file is deleted, it is temporarily kept by the file server as a salvage file so that it can be recovered by the user who deleted it. The disk space used by these files is not released until the salvage file is purged by the operating system. Salvage files are automatically purged if the user deletes another file or creates a new file. If you are very short on disk space, this option allows you to throw away all salvage files being kept by the operating system. To use this option you must be a file server console operator or have Supervisor privileges.

STATISTICS

```
File Server Statistics

Cache Statistics
Channel Statistics
Disk Mapping Information
Disk Statistics
File System Statistics
LAN I/O Statistics
Summary
Transaction Tracking Statistics
Volume Information
```

STATISTICS gives you detailed information about file server performance. While much of the information provided is overkill for most system managers, the statistics summary screen provides a wealth of information that should be monitored on a regular basis.

The statistics are updated once a second. This information is not kept in a disk file by NetWare, so when the file server is downed the statistics reporting starts at zero. If you plan to track any of these statistics, it is a good idea to check them just before you down the file server.

```
                     File Server Statistics Summary
File Server Up Time: 0 Days 10 Hours 36 Minutes 48 Seconds
Number Of File Service Processes:     4  Current Server Utilization:  16%
Disk Requests Serviced From Cache:  99%  Packets Routed:                0
Total Packets Received:         147,855  File Service Packets:          6
Total Number Of Cache Buffers:      704  Dirty Cache Buffers:           1
Total Server Memory:          4,849,664  Unused Server Memory:      4,096

                      Maximum      Peak Used   Currently In Use
Routing Buffers:           40              5                  0
Open Files:               246             33                 28
Indexed Files:             20              0                  0
Transactions:              90             13                  1
Bindery Objects:          500             47                 47
Connections:              100             19                 19
Dynamic Memory 1:      18,110          7,344              6,256
Dynamic Memory 2:      27,004          5,580              5,270
Dynamic Memory 3:      47,104            962                326
```

The statistics SUMMARY screen provides the following information:

FILE SERVER UP TIME—The elapsed time since the file server was last brought up.

NUMBER OF FILE SERVICE PROCESSES—The number of file service processes available. Multiple file service processes can service requests concurrently. The number of file service processes is dependant on the number and type of LAN and disk drivers in the OS and the features the OS supports, including Value-added processes.

CURRENT SERVER UTILIZATION—The percentage of time that the file server CPU is being used. This percentage is calculated by tracking the amount of time that the CPU is idle.

DISK REQUESTS SERVICED FROM CACHE—The percentage of read or write requests that were serviced from cache memory rather than from disk. This figure should be above 80-85%. If it falls below that, consider adding more file server RAM.

PACKETS ROUTED—The number of packets that the file server routed in the last second. Packets that are routed are received on one LAN and sent out on another LAN so that they can get to their destination address.

TOTAL PACKETS RECEIVED—The total number of packets that the file server has received since it was last brought up. This includes file service requests and packets to be routed.

FILE SERVICE PACKETS—The number of file service request packets that were received in the last second.

TOTAL NUMBER OF CACHE BUFFERS—The total number of cache buffers that this file server has. Each cache buffer is 4 K.

When the operating system is initialized, memory is allocated for all server functions except file caching. All the remaining memory is used for cache buffers. The number of cache buffers can be changed by adding or removing memory from the file server, or by changing other server parameters, such as the number of directory entries available, etc. NetWare 286 will use up to six megabytes for cache buffers.

DIRTY CACHE BUFFERS—The number of cache buffers with updated information that needs to be written to the disk. Because NetWare places a higher priority on disk reads, information can stay in cache buffers up to three seconds before it is written to disk.

TOTAL SERVER MEMORY—The amount of memory installed in the file server. The amount of memory is shown in bytes.

UNUSED SERVER MEMORY—The total amount of memory that is not in use. This is memory that is in fragments too small to be used.

There are three values displayed for the following statistics—Maximum, Peak Used, and Currently in Use. Maximum refers to the available quantity. This value is usually determined during operating system configuration. Some of the maximums are fixed values, and will be noted in the test. Peak Used refers to the quantity in use at any given time since the file server was brought up. Currently in use refers to the quantity in use at the present time.

The relationship between Maximum and Peak Used should be monitored. If any of the Peak Used values approach or meet the Maximum values, you should consider reconfiguring the operating system and/or adding more memory.

ROUTING BUFFERS—used to store incoming packets when no file service processes are available, and to store all packets being sent by the file server except replies to file service requests. If the server runs out of available routing buffers, packets can be lost. When packets are lost they must be re-sent, adding to LAN traffic and degrading overall performance.

OPEN FILES—The number of files held open by all attached workstations and processes. If you reach the open file limit, workstations can lock up, or may not be able to open applications or files. With NetWare 286 this value is configurable up to a maximum of 1000 open files per file server.

INDEXED FILES—Turbo-FAT indexing increases the performance of random reads and writes to large database files. These operations will speed up by a factor of two to four times for database files larger than one megabyte if the file is flagged as indexed. When the file server opens an indexed file, it builds an index in memory of where the file is located on the disk. This index allows rapid access to any position in the file without scanning through the FAT tables.

TRANSACTIONS—The transaction tracking system will track all changes made to files flagged as transactional files. The original data and the new data are remembered until the entire transaction has been completed and all changes have been successfully written to the disk.

If a workstation, network, or file server fails for any reason, before all changes made during the transaction have been written to disk, then the file server will back out the transaction. When a transaction is backed out, all the original data is restored. This prevents database files from becoming corrupted by updates that were only partially completed.

If transaction tracking is not implemented then N/A will be shown for these entries.

BINDERY OBJECTS—This is used to track and limit the amount of disk space that any object can use. This entry is configurable during network installation. If you choose not to use the ability to restrict the amount of disk space an object can use, then these entries will show N/A, and the number of bindery objects will not be limited. Bindery objects include users, groups, print queues, print servers, and file servers.

CONNECTIONS—The number of objects connected to the file server. This number is not configurable.

DYNAMIC MEMORY 1—For 8086 and 80286 versions of NetWare, this memory is used for mapping directories and for temporary buffers while a file service request is being processed. This is not configurable.

DYNAMIC MEMORY 2—For the 8086 and 80286 versions of NetWare this memory is used for keeping track of open files, file locks and record locks. The amount of memory in this pool is configurable during network installation by setting the maximum number of files that can be open at the same time.

DYNAMIC MEMORY 3—For the 8086 and 80286 versions of NetWare this memory is used to track server and routing information, and it is not configurable.

Other statistics reported include:

CACHE STATISTICS—shows detailed information about the file server's disk cache performance.

DISK CHANNEL STATISTICS—shows information about the disk channel(s) on the file server.

DISK MAPPING INFORMATION—displays information about the file servers disk drivers, including what channels are being used, how many drives the file server has, and, with SFT NetWare, which drives are mirrors of other drives.

DISK STATISTICS

```
                         Physical Disk  0

File Server Up Time:   0 Days 10 Hours 35 Minutes 33 Seconds
Disk Type:  0. IBM AT Hard Disk  "C"    type  045
Non-Removable Drive
Disk Channel:   0   Controller Number:   0   Drive Number: 0
Controller Type: 0.
Drive Size (less hot fix area): 78,643,200 bytes
Drive Cylinders:  1,023  Drive Heads:   9   Sectors Per Track:  17
IO Error Count:       0
Hot Fix Table Start: 19,200         Hot Fix Enabled
Hot Fix Table Size:  364 blocks     Hot Fix Remaining: 310 blocks
```

DISK STATISTICS shows information about the disk drive(s) on the file server. The information displayed includes information about the disk and controller hardware and information about the Hot Fix tables.

It is a good practice to monitor this screen regularly for changes in number of remaining Hot Fix blocks. If this value decreases it means that new bad blocks have been detected on your hard disk. If this value decreases rapidly it may mean that you are about to experience major hard disk problems.

FILE SYSTEM STATISTICS

FILE SYSTEM STATISTICS provides information about the file system, including the number of requests to open a file, read from a file, write to a file, etc. The information most useful to a system manager from this screen is also displayed on the summary screen.

LAN I/O STATISTICS

```
                        LAN I/O Statistics

File Server Up Time:    0 Days 10 Hours 36 Minutes 43 Seconds
Total Packets Received:          147,809  Packets Routed:             13,205
File Service Packets:            128,585  NetBIOS Broadcasts:              0
Packets With Invalid Slots:            0  Invalid Connections:             0
Invalid Sequence Numbers:              0  Invalid Request Types:           0
Detach With Invalid Slot:              0  Forged Detach Requests:          0
New Request During Processing:         0
New Attach During Processing:          0  Ignored Duplicate Attach:        0
Reply Canceled By New Attach:          0
Detach During Processing Ignored:      0
Reexecuted Requests:                   0  Duplicate Replies Sent:          0
Positive Acknowledges Sent:            4  File Service Used Route:         5
Packets Discarded Because They Crossed More Than 16 Bridges:         0
Packets Discarded Because Destination Network Is Unknown:            0
Incoming Packets Lost Because Of No Available Buffers:               0
Outgoing Packets Lost Because Of No Available Buffers:               0
```

LAN I/O STATISTICS is information about the number of packets being received and routed by the file server, and information about lost and invalid packets. If your LAN is large or very busy, or if you are experiencing performance problems, this screen should be monitored to detect lost or discarded packets.

Lost or discarded packets, re-executed requests, duplicate replies, etc., can indicate problems with LAN hardware or software. Packets lost because of no available buffers usually indicates that the file server needs to be reconfigured for a greater number of routing buffers.

TRANSACTION TRACKING STATISTICS

TRANSACTION TRACKING STATISTICS show the number of transactions, number of backed out transactions, the volume where backout information is being stored, the size of the transaction backout files, etc. This is only available if Transaction Tracking has been implemented.

VOLUME INFORMATION

```
                         Volume Information

File Server Up Time:    0 Days 10 Hours 37 Minutes  2 Seconds
Volume Name:       SYS                  Volume Number:         0
Volume Mounted:    Yes                  Volume Removable: No
Volume Hashed:     Yes                  Volume Cached:    Yes
Block Size:         4,096               Starting Block:        4
Total Blocks:      14,848               Free Blocks:         141
Maximum Directory Entries:        4,224
Peak Directory Entries Used:      2,487
Current Free Directory Entries:   1,859
Logical Drive Number:      0
Volume Mirrored:          No
Primary Disk Number:       0            Mirror Disk Number: N/A
```

VOLUME INFORMATION provides information about each volume on the file server, including whether the volume's directory is cached in memory, the size of blocks on the volume, if the volume is hashed, and maximum and peak directory entries.

This screen should be monitored regularly to track the number of available directory entries. If the number of free directory entries approaches zero, you may want to delete files from the volume or reconfigure the operating system to allow more directory entries.

VOLUME statistics are updated once a second. If the volume is dismounted then the only information that will be shown are the volume name, and that the volume is not mounted.

STATUS

```
                    File Server Status
Server Date:  April 15, 1989       Time:  4:10:51 pm
Allow New Users To Login:  Yes
Transaction Tracking:      Enabled
```

STATUS shows the server date and time and if logins and transaction tracking are enabled. The supervisor or a console operator can change the status of any of these items.

VERSION INFORMATION

```
                 Version Information
Novell  SFT NetWare 286 TTS V2.15  12/11/88
(C) Copyright 1983, 1988 Novell Inc.
All Rights Reserved.
```

VERSION INFORMATION shows the version of NetWare that is running on the file server. Anyone can select this option.

EXITing FConsole

```
Exit FConsole

No
Yes
```

To exit FConsole, press <Escape> until the "Exit FConsole" query appears. Select "Yes."

For more detailed information on FConsole and the FConsole statistics, see the NetWare Supervisor Reference Manual.

Supervisor Utilities

NetWare provides a number of utilities in the SYS:SYSTEM directory to assist you in managing the file server, including:

BINDFIX

BINDFIX, which repairs damaged bindery files, is intended to correct certain system security problems. Some of the problems that may be corrected using BINDIFX include:

- A user name cannot be deleted or modified.
- A user password cannot be changed.
- A user's rights cannot be modified.
- When spooling, the error "unknown server" occurs, even though you are spooling on the default server.
- Errors referring to the bindery are being displayed on the console.

To use BINDFIX, you must be logged into the network as the Supervisor, with your default drive mapped to the SYS:SYSTEM directory. BINDFIX will close the bindery files and then make backup copies of them, with the extension .OLD. BINDFIX will then scan the current bindery files for consistency and will attempt to correct any problems found. BINDFIX will ask you if you want to delete mail subdirectories of users that no longer exist and if you want to remove users that no longer exist from directory trustee lists.

BINDFIX will work on all versions of Advanced NetWare since 1.0. It is included with NetWare 2.1x and is available from the NetWare on-line database for use with earlier versions.

BINDREST

BINDREST restores the .OLD bindery files into operation, returning the system to the state it was in before the BINDFIX utility was run. BINDREST is useful particularly if BINDFIX was not able to run to completion.

SECURITY

SECURITY checks for possible security weaknesses, examining the bindery file for the following:

- Users with no assigned password.
- Users with easy-to-guess passwords.
- Users who are not required to change their passwords at least every sixty days.
- Users with unlimited grace logins after their passwords have expired.
- Users who are not required to have "unique" passwords.
- Users (or groups) with Supervisor equivalence.
- Users (or groups) with rights to the root directory of a volume.

- Users who do not have login scripts.
- Users or groups with excessive rights to certain standard directories.

MAKEUSER

Available Options
Create New USR File
Edit USR File
Process USR file

MAKEUSER creates and/or deletes multiple users. You have the following options:

- Create New USR File: To create a new USR file where you specify key words and their values concerning creating/deleting users.

- Edit USR File: To edit the existing USR files.

- Process USR File: To scan and process USR files. Errors will be reported to you as the file is scanned. If there is no error, the file will be processed and the results will be saved in the matching .RPT file.

Creating or Editing a USR File

```
                         Creating a new USR file
#HOME_DIRECTORY SYS:
#LOGIN SCRIPT SYS:SYSTEM/LOGIN.ALL
#MAX_DISK_SPACE 500
#ACCOUNT_EXPIRATION JUNE 15, 1989
#ACCOUNTING 1000, -100
#CONNECTIONS 1
#PASSWORD_LENGTH 6
#PASSWORD_PERIOD 30
#PASSWORD_REQUIRED
#UNIQUE_PASSWORD
#STATIONS 100, C0290005, D0380004
#RESTRICTED_TIME EVERYDAY 12:00 A.M.,7:00 A.M.; EVERYDAY 6:00 P.M.,12:00 A.M.
#CREATE BILL; William T. Smith; GOFORIT; ACCTING, SALES; SYS:SHARWARE [ALL]
#CREATE SUSAN; Susan R. Miller; YOUGOTIT; SALES
#REM This is a USR file for BILL and SUSAN
```

Creating or editing a USR file is similar to creating a login script. You may use any ASCII editor or the MAKEUSER editor.

MAKEUSER processes USR files for creating multiple users. MAKEUSER is both a command line utility and a menu utility. As a menu utility, MAKEUSER allows you to create USR files for batch creation and deletion of users, and allows you to process those files. As a command line utility, MAKEUSER allows you to process USR scripts created with the menu utility or a text editor. MAKEUSER resides in the SYS:PUBLIC directory.

The syntax is:

```
MAKEUSER filename <Enter>
```

MAKEUSER will process the named USR file. The file must be in the current directory.

For information on other supervisor utilities supplied with NetWare, see the NetWare Supervisor Reference Manual. For information on third-party utilities, see Appendix B, "Network Utility Software."

Managing Disk Space

One of the most important day-to-day responsibilities of the network manager is managing resources. This includes regular monitoring of server disk space usage, printer utilization, and network traffic.

Chief among these concerns in most networks is disk space management. Left unchecked, users tend to add files to network volumes without ever removing them. Files that are no longer required on-line (or required at all) are never deleted.

Disk storage is relatively inexpensive; the solution to chronic shortages of space is often to increase the amount of available space by installing a bigger disk on the file server or adding another server to the network. Increasing disk storage also means increasing the time and resources necessary for backing up files.

Since many programs run in cycles, they can use much more space in one phase than in another. The end-of-month closing of an accounting system is a good example of this. In this setting, running out of disk space becomes a crisis. The critical phases of programs have been disrupted, which can mean having to start a complex process over again, the loss of data, missed deadlines, and emergency backups so that other files can be removed from the server to create enough space for processes to complete.

The primary tools supplied with NetWare for monitoring disk space on the file server are the utilities CHKVOL, VOLINFO, and NDIR. (See Appendix B, "NetWork Utility Software" for third-party tools.)

CHKVOL

CHKVOL displays the size of the selected volume, the number of existing files, the amount of disk space used, the number of directory entries available, and the amount of disk space available.

Syntax:

```
CHKVOL <Enter>
```

or

```
CHKVOL F: <Enter>
```

or

```
CHKVOL SYS: <Enter>
```

or

```
CHKVOL FS1:\SYS: <Enter>
```

VOLINFO

Page 1/1	Total	Free	Total	Free	Total	Free	Total	Free
Volume name	SYS		SYS2					
KiloBytes	59392	5948	17392	5544				
Directories	4224	1999	1536	997				
Volume name								
KiloBytes								
Directories								

VOLINFO simply gives you a quick report of disk space available and used on each volume. The Network Manager can use it frequently to check space, and investigate further only when VOLINFO reports low space on a file server volume.

VOLINFO displays volume usage statistics for all volumes on the current default file server. The display is updated approximately every five seconds. (The update interval can be increased or decreased by the user.)

You must execute VOLINFO from a drive that is currently mapped to the desired server. Use VOLINFO rather than the DOS CHKDSK command; CHKDSK will not give proper statistics for a network volume.

Syntax:

```
VOLINFO <Enter>
```

NDIR

The NDIR command reports the disk space used by files on the file server. A sample NDIR report is listed below.

NDIR will search for files and subdirectories and display extended information about them. NDIR works on a single volume at a time.

Syntax:

```
NDIR [FilePath [Option ... Option]]
```

Options:

Basic File Information: [NOT] Operators Value, [FLAGS] [NOT] FileAttributes, [REVERSE] SORT [ON]

Basic File Information: FILES ONLY, DIRECTORIES ONLY, SHORT | BRIEF, SUBDIRECTORY, and HELP

Basic File Information: FILENAME, OWNER, ACCESS, UPDATE, CREATE, and SIZE

Operators: EQUAL, GREATER THAN, and LESS THAN, etc.

File Attributes: SYSTEM, HIDDEN, MODIFIED, EXECUTE ONLY, SHAREABLE, READ ONLY, READ WRITE, INDEX, and TRANSACTIONAL

Examples:

```
NDIR SYS:*.DAT SUBDIRECTORY SIZE GREATER
THAN 10000 UPDATE LATER THAN 01-01-86
FLAGS NOT READ ONLY REVERSE SORT ON
CREATE
```

NDIR will search for files and subdirectories and display extended information about them. In the example above, NDIR has been asked to display a list of files:

- on all accessible directories and subdirectories of the current volume SYS:,
- on the current server,
- with the extension .DAT,
- greater than 10,000 bytes in size,
- that have been updated since 1-1-86,
- that are not flagged READ ONLY.

The output is sorted by directory, then by date of creation in reverse order.

NDIR LARKSPUR/SYS:*.DAT MODIFIED SUBDIRECTORY REVERSE SORT ON SIZE

This NDIR request will display a list of files:

- on all accessible directories and subdirectories of volume SYS,
- on file server LARKSPUR,
- that have been modified since last backup.

The output is sorted by directory, then by size, larger to smaller.

NDIR Sample Output

NDIR SYS:*.DAT SUBDIRECTORY SIZE GREATER THAN 10000 UPDATE LATER THAN 01-01-86 FLAGS NOT READ ONLY REVERSE SORT ON CREATE

```
SYS:SYSTEM
File Name      Size     Last Update     Accessed Created  Flags      Owner
-------------- -------- --------------- -------- -------- ---------- ----------
NET$ACCT DAT      26250  6-22-88  9:10a  6-22-88  4-13-88 [W-M--S--] LARKSPUR
       1 file using 26250 bytes

SYS:SYSTEM/NUTIL
File Name      Size     Last Update     Accessed Created  Flags      Owner
-------------- -------- --------------- -------- -------- ---------- ----------
SYS$MSG  DAT      19201  12-1-86  2:00p  6-21-88  8-27-87 [W-------] Supervisor
       1 file using 19201 bytes

SYS:APPS/DATAFLEX/DATA
File Name      Size     Last Update     Accessed Created  Flags      Owner
-------------- -------- --------------- -------- -------- ---------- ----------
HD2      DAT      41300   4-9-88 12:03p  6-16-88   4-9-88 [W----S--] PATRICK
MENUTEMP DAT      19328   3-2-88 11:38a   6-3-88   3-2-88 [W----S--] PATRICK
MENU     DAT      19328  4-10-88 12:34p  6-16-88   3-2-88 [W----S--] PATRICK
DELFILE  DAT      63488  4-10-88  5:39p  6-16-88   3-2-88 [W----S--] PATRICK
       4 files using 143444 bytes

SYS:GENERATE/NETWARE/DSK_DRV_.001
File Name      Size     Last Update     Accessed Created  Flags      Owner
-------------- -------- --------------- -------- -------- ---------- ----------
SYS$MSG  DAT      22297  9-30-87  5:24p   6-3-88  5-30-88 [W-------] PATRICK
       1 file using 22297 bytes

SYS:GENERATE/NETWARE/SHGEN-1
File Name      Size     Last Update     Accessed Created  Flags      Owner
-------------- -------- --------------- -------- -------- ---------- ----------
SYS$MSG  DAT      22297  9-30-87  5:24p   6-3-88  5-22-88 [W-------] PATRICK
SYS$HELP DAT      17343  8-11-87 10:06a   6-3-88  5-22-88 [W-------] PATRICK
       2 files using 39640 bytes

SYS:GENERATE/NETWARE/SUPPORT
File Name      Size     Last Update     Accessed Created  Flags      Owner
-------------- -------- --------------- -------- -------- ---------- ----------
SYS$MSG  DAT      22297  9-30-87  5:24p   6-3-88  5-30-88 [W-------] PATRICK
       1 file using 22297 bytes

SYS:GENERATE/NETWARE/UTILEXE-.1
File Name      Size     Last Update     Accessed Created  Flags      Owner
-------------- -------- --------------- -------- -------- ---------- ----------
SYS$MSG  DAT      22297  9-30-87  5:24p  6-12-88  5-30-88 [W-------] PATRICK
       1 file using 22297 bytes

Total: 11 files using 295426 bytes
```

NDIR Sample Output

NDIR LARKSPUR/SYS:*.DAT MODIFIED SUBDIRECTORY REVERSE SORT ON SIZE

```
SYS:SYSTEM
File Name        Size     Last Update      Accessed Created  Flags       Owner
-------------- -------- --------------- -------- -------- ---------- -----------
NET$ACCT DAT       26250  6-22-88  9:10a  6-22-88  4-13-88 [W-M--S--] LARKSPUR
        1 file using 26250 bytes

SYS:MAIL/1
File Name        Size     Last Update      Accessed Created  Flags       Owner
-------------- -------- --------------- -------- -------- ---------- -----------
PRINTCON DAT        2454  6-16-88  1:57p  6-16-88  6-16-88 [W-M--S--] Supervisor
        1 file using 2454 bytes

SYS:MAIL/8001B
File Name        Size     Last Update      Accessed Created  Flags       Owner
-------------- -------- --------------- -------- -------- ---------- -----------
PRINTCON DAT        2940   6-8-88  2:11p  6-12-88   6-8-88 [W-M--S--] PATRICK
        1 file using 2940 bytes

SYS:MAIL/21005F
File Name        Size     Last Update      Accessed Created  Flags       Owner
-------------- -------- --------------- -------- -------- ---------- -----------
PRINTCON DAT        2697   6-6-88  2:23p   6-6-88   6-6-88 [W-M--S--] KAREN
        1 file using 2697 bytes

SYS:PUBLIC
File Name        Size     Last Update      Accessed Created  Flags       Owner
-------------- -------- --------------- -------- -------- ---------- -----------
NET$LOG  DAT         538   6-5-88  2:32p  6-22-88   6-5-88 [R-M--S--] Supervisor
        1 file using 538 bytes

SYS:APPS/FLEX/DATA
File Name        Size     Last Update      Accessed Created  Flags       Owner
-------------- -------- --------------- -------- -------- ---------- -----------
CUST2    DAT        3584   6-4-88  4:34p  6-16-88   3-2-88 [W-M--S--] PATRICK
        1 file using 3584 bytes

SYS:KAREN
File Name        Size     Last Update      Accessed Created  Flags       Owner
-------------- -------- --------------- -------- -------- ---------- -----------
SNIPEINI DAT          55  6-16-88  1:28p  6-16-88  6-16-88 [W-M--S--] KAREN
SNIPESYN DAT          50  6-16-88  1:28p  6-16-88  6-16-88 [W-M--S--] KAREN
        2 files using 105 bytes

SYS:GENERATE/NETWARE/SUPPORT
File Name        Size     Last Update      Accessed Created  Flags       Owner
-------------- -------- --------------- -------- -------- ---------- -----------
DRVRDATA DAT        7516  6-16-88  4:04p  6-16-88  6-16-88 [W-M-----] PATRICK
        1 file using 7516 bytes

Total: 9 files using 46084 bytes
```

Backup Procedures

Being able to standardize and control backups is one of the major advantages of moving to a LAN from stand-alone PCs. Stand-alone PC users are notorious for ignoring backup policies and procedures. On a LAN, the administrator can take care of backups on behalf of dozens of users at once.

The primary purpose of backup is to restore lost or damaged data. Many people assume that disk crashes, power problems, and hardware problems are primarily responsible for data losses. Most data losses, however, are cause by operator error.

The importance of the distinction lies in the difference in procedure implied by the two kinds of breakdowns. For example, some backup systems make restoring whole directories at a time relatively easy but individual file restores more difficult. Backup systems of this design are predicated on the assumption that hardware crashes affecting entire disks is the norm and individual file restores the exception. When the reverse is true, these systems are more difficult to use. (For a more complete discussion of the design and purchase of backup systems, see Chapter 7, "Choosing Lan Components.")

When a hard disk crashes or the power goes down, you usually know that it happened right away. Administrators who assume that such crashes are the main purpose for backups will tend to have very current backups on hand. You detect the problem and restore from the most recent backup. A common practice is to alternate between two sets of backup tapes, reusing each set every other day.

Unfortunately, accidentally damaged or erased files may go unnoticed for days or weeks, and in some cases even for months. For example, some programs only use certain data in cycles. Until the cycle needs the data, it may not notice damage to it. If you only have current backups on hand, you will not be able to restore these files.

For problems like this, historic and cyclical backups are crucial.

Backup Cycles

Establish a standard backup cycle. The rule of thumb is to backup as often as you are willing to lose data, given the overhead in time and materials, and to keep as many historical backups as possible.

There are several general schemes for backup:

1. Backup all files, programs and data every day. This will give you the greatest ability to restore files quickly because all files on the last tape are the most current. This approach also uses the greatest amount of backup media and time.

2. Backup changed files everyday, backup all files once a week. This is a workable solution, but usually requires going back to the last full backup, then restoring each partial backup in order, making restoring a slower process. One potential problem with this approach is that the more tapes you have to rely on to accomplish a restore, the more likely that one of them will be unreadable.

3. Backup all data files every day, and backup all program files on a separate cycle only when there are changes. This is a workable solution as long as menus, batch files, etc., are properly backed up as well as programs and data.

4. Backup changed data files every day, backup all data files once a week, and backup program files on a separate cycle only when there are changes. This uses the least amount of backup media and backup time, but could potentially make the restore process slower than the other approaches, and has the drawbacks of number 2 above.

The backup procedure you choose may depend on the organization of your server volumes, directories, and files. Whatever method you choose, you should also consider following this pattern:

- Backup files (all, changed, or data) every (work) day.
- Backup all files (or at least all data files) at least once a week. If you are backing up program files on a separate cycle, make sure your program backups are kept current.
- Keep your daily backups for at least a week.
- Keep your weekly backups for at least a month.
- Keep monthly backups for at least a year.
- Archive a tape at the end of the year.
- Do additional milestone backups before and after potentially dangerous or important events occur, like accounting year-end, software upgrades, or office moves.

If you are backing up program files on a separate cycle, make sure that program files are backed up after any reconfigurations or changes. Attempting to reinstall and reconfigure software from original disks can be difficult and time-consuming.

Scheduling Backups

Some backup systems, such as Novell's file server-based tape drives, require you to bring down the server to perform backups and restores. This means that someone must be available when the file server is not in use to perform backups.

Even if your system allows you to perform backups/restores while the server is running, it will not be able to backup open files, so it is usually best to schedule backups during off hours.

Most backup systems can be programmed to execute at predefined days and times; some can even exchange tapes (again, see Chapter 7.)

To prevent open files, you should make sure all users are logged off the network and then disable login. The time restriction capability of NetWare makes this easy for scheduled backups.

Off-Site Storage

Consider storing at least some backups off-site, to guard against possible disasters such as fire or theft. Backups of original software and weekly backups are good candidates for off-site storage. Smaller companies sometimes store their backup library in a safe deposit box. Another alternative is to contract an off-site storage company, which will pick up the backups regularly and store them in environments that are well-protected against disasters. You arrange a regular rotation of tape exchanges with the company, and they return the tapes immediately when you need to perform a restore.

16

Managing Network Printers

NetWare provides extensive capabilities for network printing, including:

- **Shared Printers.** NetWare allows up to five shared printers attached to a file server. In addition, NetWare supports the use of third-party print server software, allowing printers attached to workstations to be shared using the NetWare queuing facilities.

- **Queuing Facilities.** NetWare provides complete print queuing facilities. A printer can be served by a single queue or multiple queues and multiple printers can be served by a single queue.

- **Print Job Customizing Facilities.** NetWare allows you to create printer definition files that send control codes to printers to change fonts, margins, etc., then use those definition files, as well as other parameters, to create customized print job configurations.

- **Queue Management Facilities.** NetWare provides extensive control over printers and print queues.

- **Printing and Printer Redirection Facilities.** NetWare provides the capability to print disk files to network printers, redirect output destined for local printers to network printers, and allow applications to print to network printers.

These features and capabilities are described in this chapter.

Printers, Queues, and Queue Mapping

In order to allow effective shared access to network printers, NetWare never allows a user to access a printer directly. All printer access is handled by print queues. A print queue is a system that tracks print requests a passes them to a printer in a specific order, usually the order in which the requests were received.

When you print to a network printer, you are actually printing to a disk file. When you are through printing a particular job, the disk file containing your printer output is placed in a queue and will be printed in its turn.

NetWare print queues are created by the operating system or by the system supervisor. NetWare automatically creates one print queue for each printer that you defined during the operating system installation. NetWare then automatically "maps" each queue to a printer.

Figure 16.1—Printers Defined During NetWare Installation

Device	Spooled Printer #	Baud	Size	Stop	Parity	Xon/Xoff
COM1	0	9600	8	1	None	Yes
COM2	1	9600	8	1	None	Yes
LPT1	2					

The default print queues are named PRINTQ_1, PRINTQ_2, etc., and are mapped to the respectively numbered printers.

NetWare also automatically sets default "spool mappings." Spool mapping is used to provide compatibility with programs designed to work with the print spooler of NetWare versions prior to 2.1. These programs, such as the network version of WordPerfect, access network printers by printer number. The spool mapping maps a spool number to a print queue.

You can create additional print queues, either from the console with the console command QUEUE or from a workstation with the PConsole utility (both are described later).

If you do create additional queues, they need to be mapped to printers. This can be done at the system console with the QUEUE command each time the file server is brought up.

You can also set queue mappings (and spool mappings) in the AUTOEXEC.SYS file so that they are automatically mapped each time the server is brought up.

Figure 16.2—Sample AUTOEXEC.SYS File

```
System AUTOEXEC File

Printer 0 ADD PRINTQ_0
Printer 1 ADD PRINTQ_1
Printer 2 ADD PRINTQ_1
Spool 0 to Queue PRINTQ_0
Spool 1 to Queue PRINTQ_1
Spool 2 to Queue PRINTQ_2
MONITOR
```

If you do create an AUTOEXEC.SYS file, you must include at least the default printer mappings. If an AUTOEXEC.SYS file exists, the system will execute only those mappings listed in the file. It will not automatically map one print queue to each physically attached printer or spool old printer numbers into a queue as it does if there is not an AUTOEXEC.SYS file.

For more information on creating the AUTOEXEC.SYS file, see *Chapter 15—Managing File Server Resources.*

Printing and Print Management Tools

Most software, even most network or multiuser software, is not designed to take full advantage of the capabilities of NetWare's printers (The network version of WordPerfect is an exception). Because of this, NetWare has facilities to allow you to customize the way your software uses network printers.

The first tool is PrintDef. PrintDef allows you to create and modify a printer definition database that defines the available functions of network printers.

PrintCon allows you to use the printer definitions to create customized Print Jobs. A print job specifies printing parameters such as the print queue printer output will be directed to, if a banner will be printed, etc. A print job can also send control codes to the printer to specify fonts, pitch, spacing, etc.

PConsole allows you to create and manage print queues and print jobs within each queue.

NetWare also provides tools for redirecting printer output and printing existing disk files from the DOS command line, as well as printer and print queue management facilities at the system console.

These will be described on the following pages.

Defining Print Devices and Forms with PrintDef

PrintDef is a utility that allows you to define network print devices, such as printers and plotters, and it lets you define forms (the size or type of paper you will print on) to be used with those devices.

To use PrintDef, type:

```
PRINTDEF <Enter>
```

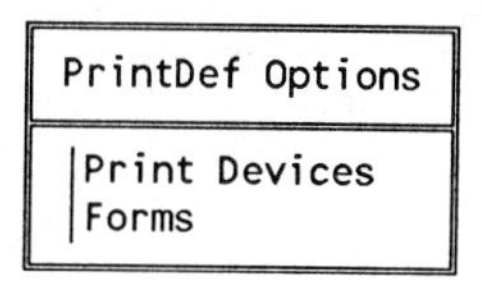
PrintDef Options

Print Devices
Forms

The PrintDef main menu has two options:

PRINT DEVICES—allows you to import, export, and edit printer names and definitions. It also allows users to view printer names and definitions.

A Print Device is any printing device used on the network that can be defined or controlled by PrintDef Functions. In PrintDef the term Printer has the same meaning as Device.

FORMS—Allows you to create, delete, or modify form names and definitions. Also allows users to view form names and definitions.

A Form may be single sheets of paper, continuous-feed paper, sales orders, labels, etc.

PrintDef creates a data base of Device and Form definitions. Although network users other than the supervisor (or users with supervisor equivalence) may not create or modify print devices, functions, modes or forms, they may view those that the supervisor has set up, and use this information when they create their own print jobs with PrintCon.

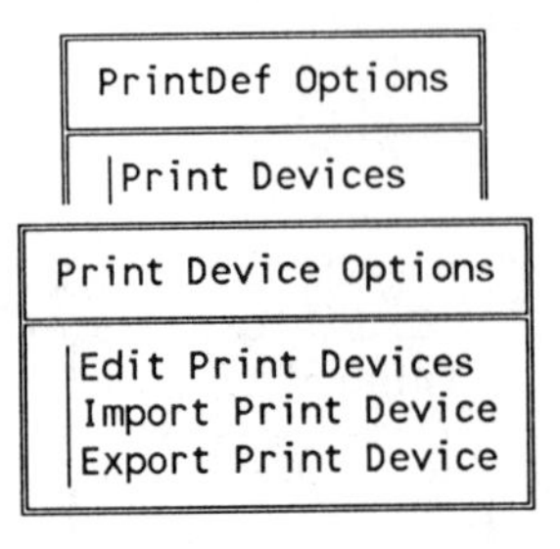

From the PRINT DEVICE OPTIONS screen you can create, delete, or modify printer names and definitions, save the selected printer name and definition to a special .PDF file, or insert a previously exported printer name and definition.

Importing and Exporting Print Device Definitions

NetWare comes with predefined .PDF files for many popular printers. These files, which are in the SYS:PUBLIC directory, can be imported into the PrintDef database with the Import Print Device function.

If you have created a printer definition for a particular printer, and you have a similar printer on another file server, you can export a definition from the first server and import it to the second to avoid re-creating a similar definition.

The Export feature in PRINTDEF copies the printer definition to a special .PDF file. To import a definition, PRINTDEF copies a .PDF File to the server's NET$PRN.DAT file in the SYS:PUBLIC directory.

```
Source Directory
LARKSPUR/SYS:PUBLIC

Print Device Options
  Edit Print Devices
  Import Print Device
  Export Print Device

Available .PDFs
  EPEX86.PDF
  EPLD2500.PDF
  EPLQ800.PDF
  EPLX80.PDF
  EPLX800.PDF
  HPLASER.PDF
  IBM4201.PDF
  IBMPRO2.PDF
  NEC2050.PDF
  NEC8810.PDF
```

To import a print device definition, highlight Import Print Device on the PRINT DEVICE OPTIONS screen. Enter the server, volume, and directory where the files are located, then press <Enter>. Highlight the file you wish to select, then press <Enter>.

```
Destination Directory
SERVER1/SYS:USERS/WARREN

ASCII FILE
Diablo 630
Hewlett Pa
IMAGEWRITE
LASERWRITE
LASERWRITER630

Export File Name (max 8 chars, no extension)
ASCII
```

Exporting a definition is just the opposite. Select Export Print Device on the PRINT DEVICE OPTIONS screen. Enter the server, volume and directory where the file is to be exported, then press <Enter>. Type the name you want for your export file, then press <Enter>.

Editing and Creating Print Devices

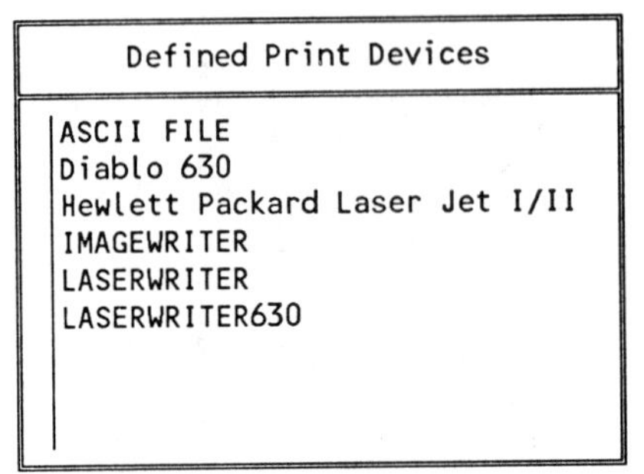

Defined Print Devices
ASCII FILE
Diablo 630
Hewlett Packard Laser Jet I/II
IMAGEWRITER
LASERWRITER
LASERWRITER630

DEFINED PRINT DEVICES is a list of the print devices currently defined on your file server. You can add, delete, and modify print device names and their definitions. To create a print device, place the cursor over Print Devices on the main menu screen and press <Enter>. Your cursor is in the Defined Print Devices screen. Press <Ins>. You will now be prompted to enter the name of your printer or print device. Enter the name that you want and then press <Enter>.

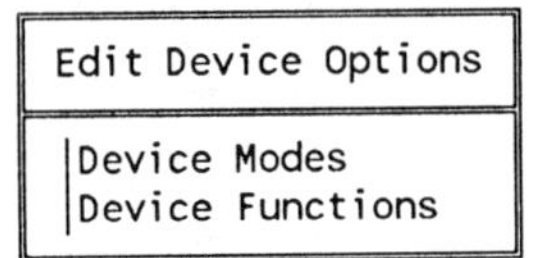

From the EDIT DEVICE OPTIONS screen you can edit or examine the current device's mode names and definitions, or edit or examine the current device's function names and function definitions.

To edit device options, place the cursor over the selected Print Device in the Defined Print Devices screen and press <Enter>.

Editing and Creating Device Functions

Hewlett Packard Laser Jet I/II Functions	
Big Font	<ESC>%$3g
Character Set - Line Draw	<ESC>(0B
Character Set - Roman Extension	<ESC>(0E
Character Set - Roman-8	<ESC>(8U
Character Set - USASCII	<ESC>(0U
End-of-Line Wrap - Disable	<ESC>&s1C
End-of-Line Wrap - Enable	<ESC>&s0C
Font - Courier	<ESC>(s3T
Font - Helv2	<ESC>(s4T
Font - Letter Gothic	<ESC>(s6T
Font - Linedraw	<ESC>(s0T
Font - Lineprinter	<ESC>(s0T
Font - Tms Rmn	<ESC>(s5T
Orientation - Landscape	<ESC>&l1O
Orientation - Portrait	<ESC>&l0O
Paper Source - Lower Tray	<ESC>&l4H
▾ Pitch - 6	<ESC>(s6H

Make sure that you have your printer manual and the NetWare Supervisor Reference Manual close at hand before you begin defining print device functions. For the specific syntax of entering function codes, see your Supervisor Reference Manual or the Help screens in PrintDef.

Note: If you are not familiar with printer escape sequences and how to use them, be prepared to spend a lot of time and to experience considerable frustration in setting up device functions. It may be worthwhile to find someone who already has experience in this to help you.

To edit or examine device functions, place the cursor over Device Functions in the Edit Device Options screen and press <Enter>. A list of functions that are already defined for this print device will display.

To enter a device function, put your cursor in the function list for the selected device and press <Ins>.

```
Function Definition Form

Name Left Margin = 20

Escape Sequence <ESC>&a20L
```

In the "Function Definition Form" entry box, enter a name for the printer command. Each function name must be unique for a given print device (two print devices could have functions with the same name, however). A function name should be a meaningful name that is understood by network users, such as the name used in the printer's manual.

For example, if you wanted to include the print function for setting the left margin to twenty spaces on a HP LaserJet II, you would type:

```
Left Margin = 20 <Enter>
```

The cursor will move to the "Escape Sequence" option.

Enter the escape sequence for the function and press <Enter>. (You will find escape sequences for various functions in your printer's manual.)

To enter the escape sequence for a left margin of 20 on the HP LaserJet II, for example, you would type:

```
<ESC>&a20L  <Enter>
```

Note: For this example you type the characters "<", "E", "S", "C," and ">", not the <Esc> key. See the PrintDef help screens or the Supervisor Reference Manual for details.

Press <Esc> and then <Enter> to save and insert the new escape sequence into the functions list.

If you are creating a new printer definition, define the printer's reset function. This will be used to create the "reinitialize" mode that resets the printer after each print job.

Repeat this process for each function that you want to enter.

To edit any of the device functions, move the cursor to the function you want to change and press <Enter>. Press <Esc> and then <Enter> to save the modified function.

When you are finished adding or editing device functions, press <Esc> to return to the Edit Device Options menu.

Defining Print Device Modes

```
Hewlett Packard Laser J... Modes   Def Options

Condensed                          t Devices
Letter Head
Letter Quality                     vice Options
Lotus 123 Spread Sheet
Memo                                Modes
P-CAD Drawings                      Functions
Sideways
Times
(Re-initialize)
```

A print device mode is a group of one or more printer functions that can be sent to a printer with a print job. A printer device mode could tell the printer to use a certain font, set the pitch, set the page orientation, etc. Modes can use print device functions in almost any combination to fit particular needs. Print device modes are used by the PrintCon utility to create customized print jobs.

To define a print device mode, move your cursor to Device Modes in the Edit Device Options menu and press <Enter>.

To edit an existing mode, highlight that mode and press <Enter>.

```
Condensed Functions

Reset
End-of-Line Wrap - Enable
Orientation - Landscape
Pitch - 16.66
Vertical Motion Index - 5.4
```

A list of the functions that make up the mode will display. To remove a function, highlight it and press <Del>. To add a function to the end of the list, press <Ins>, then select the function that you want from the Additional Functions list. If you wish to insert a function in a particular location in the list, move your cursor to the line that you want to insert the new function above and press <F5>, press <Ins>, then select the function that you want. Press <Esc> to return to the modes screen.

To create a new mode, press <Ins>.

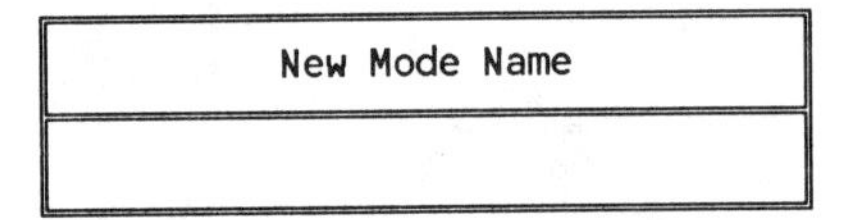

Enter the name of your new mode in the New Mode Name box, then follow the procedures outlined for editing modes, above.

If you are defining a new printer, the (reinitialize) mode name will appear in the modes screen. This mode must be defined in order to reset the printer after each print job. Most printers have a single escape sequence or control code for resetting. If yours does not, then you will need to enter all your printer's "Cancel" functions into the Reinitialize mode.

Defining Forms

In order to create print job configurations with the PrintCon utility, you need to define at least one form. Print Form definitions are descriptive only—the are used to identify the form and have no direct effect on printer operation. For example, defining a form with a length of 84 lines does not tell the printer that the paper size is fourteen inch (at six lines per inch, legal-size paper is eighty-four lines long), it only describes the form. (Form length commands would be sent to the printer as part of a print mode.)

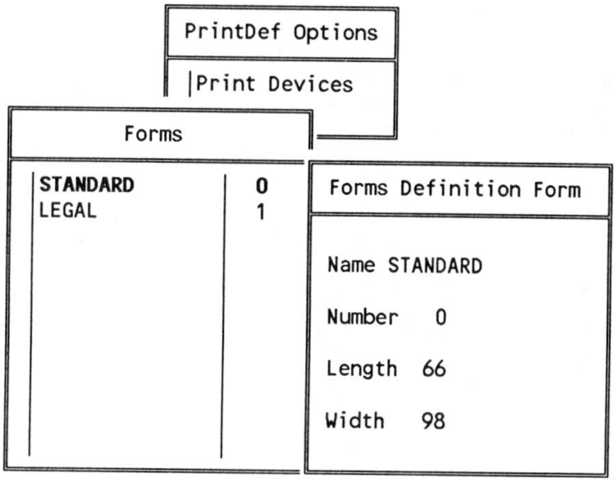

```
PrintDef Options
|Print Devices

Forms
STANDARD        0
LEGAL           1

Forms Definition Form
Name STANDARD
Number    0
Length   66
Width    98
```

To define a print form, move your cursor to Forms in the PrintDef Options screen, press <Enter>, then press <Insert>.

In the Forms Definition entry box, type the name of the new form you want to define and press <Enter>. The first character of the form name must be A through Z (or a through z), and the form name cannot exceed twelve characters or contain any spaces.

Type the number you want to assign to the form and press <Enter>. You should designate the most commonly used form for the selected printer as form 0, since 0 is the default form. This means that

NetWare assumes that this form is in the printer when you start up a file server. Allowable form numbers are 0 through 255.

Enter the page length in lines (1 to 255), press <Enter>. then enter the page width in characters per line (1 to 999), and press <Enter>.

To save your changes, press <Esc>, answer "Yes" to the "Save Changes" confirmation by pressing <Enter>. The new form will now be listed in the Forms list for the selected printer.

Repeat the above for each form you want to define.

To edit a form, move your cursor to that form name in the Forms list, then press the Modify key. <F3> is usually the Modify key on most machines. Make the appropriate changes and then save them as described above.

To delete a form, move your cursor to the form name, then press <Del>. Press <Enter> to confirm your deletion.

Exiting PrintDef

```
Exit PrintDef
-------------
No
Yes
```

To exit PrintDef, press <Esc> until you reach the Exit PrintDef screen, highlight "Yes" and press <Enter>. If you have made any changes, the Exit Options menu will display.

```
Exit Options
------------------------------
Save Data Base, then EXIT
EXIT without saving Data Base
Do Not EXIT
```

If you want to save your changes, move your cursor to "Save Data Base, then EXIT" and press <Enter>.

Creating Print Job Configurations with PrintCon

The PrintCon utility is used to set up a file of instructions that controls the way a print job is to be printed. You can use the forms and modes that have been set up in PrintDef, along with other parameters, to define a print job configuration. This means that instead of manually entering print job specifications (through the CAPTURE command or at the printer directly, a user can choose a print job configuration that controls those parameters.

You can create print job configurations for all users, using the forms, devices, and modes defined in PrintDef; select the default print job configuration; and copy print job configurations from one user to another. Users can set up their own print job configurations, or the supervisor can do it for them. Print job configurations automatically send a reset command to the printer, returning it to its default settings after the print job is completed.

You do not have to create print job configurations, but they can make network printing easier and more efficient. Print job configurations can be selected when printing with PConsole (discussed in the next section of this chapter), and when printing with NetWare command line utilities NPRINT and CAPTURE. You can also override the print job configurations with those three utilities.

To use PrintCon, type:

```
PRINTCON <Enter>
```

The PrintCon "Available Options" menu will display.

```
Available Options

Edit Print Job Configurations
Select Default Print Job Configuration
Supervisor - Copy Print Job Configurations
```

Move your cursor to Edit Print Job Configurations and press <Enter>. The Edit Print Job Configurations list will display.

```
Edit Print Job Configurations

COURIER_10_PITCH                  (default)
LASERWIDE
Line_Printer
TIMES_ROMAN_FIXED
```

Creating a Print Job Configuration

The first print job configuration you create becomes your default print job configuration. Once other configurations are created, however, you can select another default.

To create a print job configuration, press <Ins>. The Enter New Name screen will be displayed. Type the name of the print job configuration you want to create (thirty-one characters maximum), then press <Enter>. The Edit Print Job Configuration screen will display.

```
Edit Print Job Configuration "COURIER_10_PITCH"

Number of copies:      1           Form name:       STANDARD
Suppress form feed:    No          Print banner:    No
File contents:         Text        Banner name:
Tab size:              8           Banner file:

Local printer:         1           Enable timeout:  Yes
Auto endcap:           Yes         Timeout count:   2

File server:           LARKSPUR
Print queue:           PRINTQ_0
Device:                HP LaserJet II
Mode:                  Courier 10 Pitch Portrait
```

To define a new print job configuration, specify the following parameters:

NUMBER OF COPIES—Enter the number of copies you want printed (1 to 65,000).

SUPPRESS FORM—Enter "Y" if you want suppress the automatic form feed at the end of a print job. This would be important if you are using preprinted forms.

TAB SIZE—Changes the TAB size from the default (8) to any size between 1 and 18, if the File Contents field is set to TEXT. If File Contents is set to "Byte Stream," this field will be blank.

FORM NAME—Press the Enter key to see a menu of forms you can choose from. (These are forms previously defined with PrintDef.)

PRINT BANNER—If you choose the default setting of "Yes," a banner page identifying the file, user, etc., will be printed immediately before the file is printed.

BANNER NAME—The default banner name is the name that you logged in with. If you wish to change it, enter a new name here.

AUTO ENDCAP—This setting affects print jobs created with the CAPTURE command. If you choose "Yes," the file you are capturing will be printed when you exit a program, otherwise it will only be printed after you issue an ENDCAP command (the timeout function of PrintCon, below, and the timeout function of CAPTURE will also affect this).

ENABLE TIMEOUT—This setting affects print jobs created with the CAPTURE command. If you choose "Yes," you must enter a timeout value in seconds in the Timeout Count field. Once a print job stops sending data, the counter begins. If no more data is sent before the counter "times out," the print file will be closed and put into the print queue, and a new print file will be opened. If you choose "No," the captured file will be sent to the queue according to the "Auto Endcap" setting.

PRINT QUEUE--Press a key to list the available print queues. Move your cursor to the selected print queue, then press <Enter>.

DEVICE—Press the <Enter> key to list the available print devices. Move your cursor to the selected device, then press <Enter>.

Note: The device you choose must be mapped to the queue you chose above.

MODE—Press a key to list the available modes for the selected print device. Move your cursor to the mode that you want.

To exit this screen, press <Escape> once to exit a field, then press <Escape> again to exit the screen. The "Save Changes" confirmation box will appear. To save the specified parameters, move your cursor to "Yes" and press <Enter>.

Deleting a Print Job Configuration

You can delete any print job configuration except the current default configuration. To delete a print job configuration, list your present print job configurations, move your cursor to the print job configuration you want to delete and press <Delete>. The "Delete Current Print Job Configuration" confirmation box will be displayed. Move your cursor to "Yes" and press <Enter>. The specified print job configuration will be deleted and you will be returned to the "Edit Print Job Configurations" list.

Modifying a Print Job Configuration

To modifying an existing print job configuration, move your cursor to the name of the print job in the Edit Print Job Configurations screen that you want to edit, then press <Enter>. Follow the instructions in Creating a Print Job Configuration discussed earlier in this chapter.

Choosing the Default Print Job Configuration

The default print job configuration you choose is the default for files you print with PConsole, NPRINT, and CAPTURE. If you print a file with either NPRINT or CAPTURE, you can override the print job parameters with by specifying NPRINT or CAPTURE options.

To specify a default Print Job Configuration, do the following:

At the PrintCon Available Options screen, move your cursor to Select Default Print Job Configuration, then press <Enter>. Move your cursor to the print job configuration that you want to be the default in the Select Default Print Job Configuration list, then press <Enter>. "(Default)" will appear in the right column of the Edit Print Job Configurations list, indicating your new default print job configuration.

Copying Print Job Configuration

Each user has a unique print job configuration file that will store any print job configurations created by or for that user. This file, PRINT-CON.DAT, is stored in the user's mail directory.

As supervisor, you can copy print job configurations from one user to another. Unfortunately, you cannot copy a single job configuration at a time, you can only copy the whole file, including all job configurations. When you copy one user's print job configuration file to another user, the copied file overwrites the target user's existing file. Since users can create their own print job configurations, you will want to check with users before copying another user's file over the top of their existing files.

To copy a print job configuration, do the following:

> At the Available Options screen, move your cursor to Supervisor—Copy Print Job Configurations, then press <Enter>.
>
> Enter the name of the user whose print job configuration file you want to copy into the Source User entry box, then press <Enter>.
>
> Enter the name of the user whose print job configuration file you want to replace into the Target User entry box, then press <Enter>.
>
> This copies the file, and the target user can now use all the source user's job configurations.

Managing Network Printing with PConsole

PConsole is a utility to manage and control network printing. Network security provides various levels of access to PConsole. As a queue user, you can submit print jobs to print queues. If you entered a print job into the queue, you can change the printing configurations you defined at any time unless the print job is already being printed. Once the job is being printed, you can still delete it from the queue. You can also see information about print queues.

Users designated by the supervisor as print queue operators can edit other user's print queue entry information and delete any entry from a queue. Queue operators can also change the order of print jobs in a queue.

The supervisor (or a user with supervisor equivalence) can create and rename print queues, assign queue users, and assign queue operators.

Working with Print Queues

Before a print job can be printed on a network printer, it must first be in a disk file. This disk file can be on either a network or local drive if it is being printed with PConsole or NPRINT. If printer output is being captured with the CAPTURE command, a special temporary file is automatically created. Each file is sent to a print queue to wait until a printer is available to print it. Files created with the CAPTURE command must be closed before they can be put in a queue. A file can be closed several ways, including issuing a new CAPTURE command, issuing an ENDCAP command, or by using the CAPTURE timeout function.

When a file server is first installed, one default print queue for each printer attached is automatically created. The supervisor can use PConsole to create, rename, and delete print queues. The supervisor can define multiple print queues, and can attach more than one print queue to each printer, and/or multiple printers to each queue. When you print a file, you must choose the print queue to which the file will be sent (this is usually handled by the Print Job Definitions create with PrintCon).

Using PConsole

To use PConsole: type:

```
PCONSOLE<Enter>
```

The PConsole "Available Options" menu will be displayed.

```
Available Options

Change Current File Server
Print Queue Information
Print Server Information
```

The Main Menu options are:

CHANGE CURRENT FILE SERVER—Allows you to attach to other file servers so you can examine their print queues and servers, attach to or logout from a server or change the user name you are logged in under.

PRINT QUEUE INFORMATION—Allows you to examine the print queue and add, modify, or delete print jobs. Only supervisors or queue operators can modify or delete other users entries. Supervisors can also add, delete, or rename print queues.

PRINT SERVER INFORMATION— Allows you to examine the list of print servers. Supervisors can also add, delete, or rename print servers.

To work with queues, move the cursor to Print Queue Information and press <Enter>. A list of the defined print queues will be displayed. To examine a particular queue, place your cursor over the Queue name in the Print Queue list and press <Enter>, and the Print Queue Information screen will appear.

```
Print Queues                         Print Queue Information

PRINTQ_0        vailable Opt   Current Print Job Entries
PRINTQ_1                       Current Queue Status
DISKFILE        ge Current F   Currently Attached Servers
REMOTE          t Queue Info   Print Queue ID
                t Server Inf   Queue Operators
                               Queue Servers
                               Queue Users
```

PRINT QUEUE INFORMATION provides the following options:

CURRENT PRINT JOB ENTRIES—Shows the jobs currently in this queue and allows jobs to be submitted, modified, and deleted. This option is only available to supervisors, queue operators, and users of this queue.

CURRENT QUEUE STATUS—Shows the current status of this print queue. This option is only available to supervisors, queue operators, and users of this queue.

CURRENTLY ATTACHED SERVERS—Lists the print servers that are currently attached and servicing jobs from this queue.

This option is only available to supervisors, queue operators, and users of this queue.

PRINT QUEUE ID—The ID number (the NetWare "Object" ID) of the selected print queue.

QUEUE OPERATORS—Shows the current queue operators and allows addition or deletion of queue operators. This option is only available to Supervisors.

QUEUE SERVERS—The print servers that are allowed to service this queue. Queue operators may add or delete servers from this list.

QUEUE USERS—Users who may submit print jobs to this queue. Queue operators may add or delete servers from this list.

Creating Print Queues

To create a print queue, do the following:

At the Available Options screen, place your cursor over Print Queue Information and press <Enter> to display the Print Queues list. The current print queues will be displayed. To create a new queue, press <Ins>, and the New Print Queue Name entry box will be displayed. Enter the name of the queue you want to create, then press <Enter>. The new queue will now be listed in the Print Queues list. To use the queue, you must attach the queue to a printer at the file server console or with the AUTOEXEC.SYS file.

Use the console command:

```
P[RINTER] nn ADD queue name
```

For example, if you created a queue named FILE_QUE and wanted to attach it to PRINTER 0 (printer numbers are assigned during installation), you would type:

```
P 0 ADD FILE_QUE  <Enter>
```

Unless you enter this command into the AUTOEXEC.SYS file it must be entered at the console every time the file server is powered up.

Deleting Print Queues

To delete a print queue, go to Print Queues list, place your cursor over the queue that you want to delete, then press <Del>.

In the Delete Print Queue confirmation box, place your cursor over "Yes" and press <Enter>. The queue will then be deleted.

Any print job configurations that use the deleted queue should be edited.

Assigning and Deleting Queue Users and Operators

You can assign and delete Queue Users and Queue Operators by entering the appropriate list and <Ins>erting new users or operators or <Del>eting existing ones.

When a queue is created, the group EVERYONE is automatically assigned as a queue user. If you want to restrict access to a queue, <Del>ete EVERYONE and <Ins>ert the appropriate users or groups.

Listing the Jobs in a Queue

To display the jobs in a queue, move your cursor to Current Print Job Entries, then press <Enter>. A list of jobs waiting to be printed will be displayed.

```
Seq Banner Name  Description                          Form Status   Job

  1 KAREN        LPT1 Catch                             0 Ready     479
  2 SUPERVISOR   LPT1 Catch                             0 Ready     480
  3 PATRICK      CUST2.FR4                              0 Ready     489

                    Print Queue Entry Information

Print job:            489           File size:          13122
Client:               PATRICK[3]
Description:          CUST2.FR4
Status:               Ready To Be Serviced, Waiting For Print Server

User Hold:            No            Job Entry Date:     May 31, 1988
Operator Hold:        No            Job Entry Time:     11:21:46 am
Service Sequence:     3

Number of copies:     1             Form:               STANDARD
File contents:        Text          Print banner:       No
Tab size:             8             Banner name:
Suppress form feed:   No            Banner file:

Defer printing:       Yes           Target date:        June 1, 1988
                                    Target time:        2:00:00 am
Target server:        (Any Server)
```

CURRENT PRINT JOBS ENTRIES—lists the print jobs that are currently in the queue, and is updated every five seconds. You can add jobs to or delete jobs from the queue or display and edit the following print job information:

PRINT JOB displays the number assigned to the queue file.

FILE SIZE is the size of the queue file in bytes.

CLIENT is the name of the user that entered the file into the queue.

DESCRIPTION is usually the filename or, in the case of printer output rerouted with CAPTURE, an indicator of the local port output was rerouted from (as in "LPT1 Catch").

STATUS is changed automatically by USER HOLD and/or OPERATOR HOLD entries below. Messages are: "Ready To Be Serviced, Waiting For Print Server, User Hold, or Operator Hold.

USER HOLD allows a user may elect to put his or her job on hold. If this is done, the job will not be printed until it is released by the user, a queue operator or a supervisor.

OPERATOR HOLD allows a queue operator to put a job on hold. It will not be printed until a queue operator releases it.

JOB ENTRY DATE is the date the job was entered in the queue.

JOB ENTRY TIME is the time the job was entered in the queue.

SERVICE SEQUENCE is the position of this job in the queue. Queue operators and supervisors may move jobs forward or backward in the queue.

NUMBER OF COPIES is the number of copies of this job to be printed. This value may be changed by a user on her/his own files. Queue operators and supervisors may change this value for any file.

FORM is the form number that this job will be printed on. This value may be changed by a user on her/his own files. Queue operators and supervisors may change this value for any file.

FILE CONTENTS—"Text" will expand tab characters based on TAB SIZE below. "Byte stream" sends file contents "as is." This value may be changed by a user on her/his own files. Queue operators and supervisors may change this value for any file. "Byte stream" should be used for programs that do their own formatting, such as graphics programs, desktop publishers, word processors, etc. "Text" should be used for ASCII files, database and accounting reports, etc.

PRINT BANNER determines if a banner page is to be printed before the job. This value may be changed by a user on her/his own files. Queue operators and supervisors may change this value for any file.

TAB SIZE is the number of spaces the tabs in this file will be expanded to. This value may be changed by a user on her/his own files. Queue operators and supervisors may change this value for any file.

SUPPRESS FORM FEED suppresses NetWare generated Form Feed command after a print job. By default, the NetWare spooler will issue a form feed command to the printer at the end of a print job. This can cause problems when using pre-printed forms, etc. A "No" entry suppresses the NetWare generated form feed. This value may be changed by a user on her/his own files. Queue operators and supervisors may change this value for any file.

BANNER NAME is the text to be printed in the first large print area of the banner. This is usually the user login name, but can be changed by the user. Queue operators and supervisors may change this name for any file.

BANNER FILE is the text to be printed in the second large print area of the banner. This is usually the file name, but can be changed by the user. Queue operators and supervisors may change this name for any file.

DEFER PRINTING allows files to be printed at a later date and/or time. This can be used to group specific file types, or to print long reports at a more convenient time. This value may be changed by a user on her/his own files. Queue operators and supervisors may change this value for any file.

TARGET DATE is the date the print job will be printed, if printing is deferred. This value may be changed by a user on her/his own files. Queue operators and supervisors may change this value for any file.

TARGET TIME is the time the print job will be printed. This value may be changed by a user on her/his own files. Queue operators and supervisors may change this value for any file.

TARGET SERVER is the print server that this file is directed to. If a specific print server is not specified, the value "(Any Server)" will be specified. This value may be changed by a user on her/his own files. Queue operators and supervisors may change this value for any file.

Printing a File

To print a file with PConsole, go to the Current Print job Entries screen for the queue to which you want the file sent. Press the <Ins> key, enter the specifications for the directory in which the file is located, then press <Enter>. Select the desired file from the Available Files screen and press <Enter> again. Select a print job configuration from the Print Job Configurations screen, then press <Enter>. Now select any desired parameters from the New Print Job to be Submitted screen, then press <Esc>. The file to be printed will be placed at the bottom of the queue.

Canceling a Print Job

A print job is cancelled when it is deleted from a queue. To delete a print job from a queue, go to the Current Print job Entries screen for the queue from which you want to delete the print job.

Place the cursor over the name of the selected print job, and press the <Del> key. If you have sufficient rights to delete the print job, it will be deleted, otherwise you will get an error message.

You can delete an entry only if you are the owner of the job or a print queue operator.

Changing the Order of Print Jobs in the Print Queue

To move a print job to a higher or lower priority in a queue, go to the Current Print job Entries screen for the selected queue.

Place the cursor over the name of the selected print job, and press the <Enter> key. Move your cursor to the Service Sequence field in the Print Queue Entry Information screen and change the priority.

If you do not have sufficient rights to change priority, your cursor will not enter the Service Sequence field.

Viewing Print Queue Status

By selecting Current Queue Status, you can view the number of entries in the queue and view the number of print servers attached to the queue. If you are a print queue operator or supervisor, you can also change the operator flags.

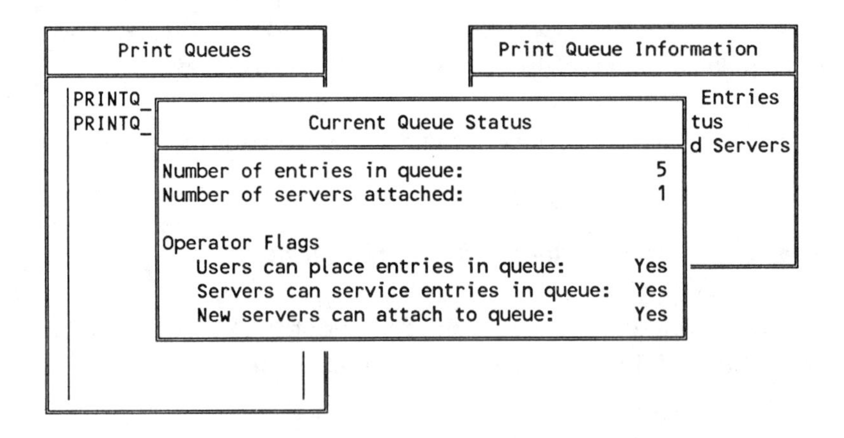

Current Queue Status shows the current status of the print queue, updated every five seconds. If you are a queue operator, you can change the settings of the operator flags.

NUMBER OF ENTRIES IN QUEUE—The number of pending print jobs in this queue.

NUMBER OF SERVERS ATTACHED—The number of print servers currently attached to this queue.

OPERATOR FLAGS—These control the following:

USERS CAN PLACE ENTRIES IN QUEUE—If this flag is set to No, then users will not be allowed to submit jobs to the queue (until the flag is reset to Yes).

SERVERS CAN SERVICE ENTRIES IN QUEUE—If this flag is set to No, then servers will not be allowed to service jobs in the queue (until the flag is reset to Yes).

NEW SERVERS CAN ATTACH TO QUEUE—If this flag is set to No, then servers will not be allowed to attach to the queue (until the flag is reset to Yes).

Supporting Print Servers

A print server takes the print jobs from the queue and sends them to the printer. The print server process is currently part of the file server. However, NetWare can support third-party VAPs or remote workstation print servers. See *Appendix B—Network Utilities* for information on third-party print server software.

Print Server Information in the Available Topics menu allows a supervisor to add, delete, or rename print servers. Queue Servers in the Print Queue Information menu lists the print servers that can to service a queue. A supervisor can add or delete servers from this list. The Currently Attached Servers option in the Print Queue Information menu displays the servers that are currently servicing a queue.

Viewing Currently Attached Servers

Only print servers that are attached to a queue can service that queue. To see which servers are currently attached to a queue, go to the Print Queue Information screen for the selected queue. Place your cursor over Currently Attached Servers and press <Enter>. The Currently Attached Servers list will be displayed.

Viewing the Print Queue Servers

The print queue servers that are allowed to service a selected queue will be listed in the Print Queue Servers list. For a print server to service a queue, the queue must be attached to the print server. (See

Creating Print Queues earlier in this chapter.) To see the queue to which a print server is attached, select Print Queue Information from the main menu to display the Print Queue list. Place your cursor over the print queue whose print servers you want to view, press <Enter>, and the Print Queue Information screen will be displayed. Place your cursor over Queue Servers and press <Enter> to display the Print Queue Servers list.

Command-Line Printing Commands

CAPTURE

CAPTURE redirects output from a local printer port to a network print queue. You can use CAPTURE with applications that do not send files directly to network printers. You can also use CAPTURE to print screen dumps or to save output to a disk file.

You can change parameters by adding "flags" to the CAPTURE command (see below).

To use CAPTURE, type:

```
CAPTURE <Enter>
```

or

```
CAPTURE (flags) <Enter>
```

Note: Although the entire flag name can be specified, only the letters printed below in uppercase need to be used.

Flags can specify the following:

Server specifies the file or print server the print job should be sent to. The default is your default server.

```
Syntax: /S=server_name
```

Example:

```
CAPTURE /S=SERVER1
```

would send printer output to a queue of file server SERVER1.

Queue specifies the queue the print job should be sent to.

```
Syntax: /Q=queue_name
```

Example:

```
CAPTURE /Q=PRINTQ_1
```

would send printer output to the queue PRINTQ_1.

Printer specifies the printer number (0 through 4) the job should be sent to. The default is Printer 0.

```
Syntax: /P=number.
```

Example:

```
CAPTURE /P=2
```

would send printer output to Printer 2.

Local specifies the local printer port designation (LPT1, 2, or 3) to reroute output from. You can CAPTURE from all three concurrently. The default is LPT1.

```
Syntax: /L=local_LPT_number   (1, 2 or 3)
```

Example:

```
CAPTURE /L=3
```

would reroute output from LPT3.

Copies specifies the number of copies to print (up to 256).

```
Syntax: /C=number_of_copies (0 to 255)
```

Example:

```
CAPTURE /C=5
```

would print 5 copies of the current print job.

Job specifies the print job configuration to use (you define print jobs using PrintCon).

```
Syntax: /J=print_job
```

Example:

```
CAPTURE /J=DISKFILE
```

would use the printing specifications from the print job configuration DISKFILE.

Form specifies the kind of form on which you print (you define forms using PrintDef). You can specify forms by name or number.

```
Syntax: /F=form_name
        /F=form_number (0 through 255)
```

Example:

```
CAPTURE /F=LEGAL
```

would stop the specified printer and signal the console operator to mount the form LEGAL in the printer.

CReate specifies the directory path and name of the file you want to create. This option allows you to direct output to permanent disk files. To save the file in your default directory, give the filename only.

```
Syntax: /CR=file_name
        /CR=server_name/volume:directory_path/file_name
```

Example:

```
CAPTURE /CR=SYS:USERS/KAREN/SCREENFIL.DAT
```

would send printer output to the file SCREENFIL.DAT in the SYS:USERS/KAREN directory of the current file server.

Banner specifies a word or phrase up to 12 characters long to appear on the lower half of your banner page. The default is LST:. An underline character represents a space (for example, PRINT_JOB).

```
Syntax: /B=file_name
```

Example:

```
CAPTURE /B=PRINT_JOB
```

would print the name PRINT_JOB on the lower half of the banner.

NAMe specifies the user name you want to appear on the upper half of your banner page. Use underlines for spaces. The default is the name you logged in with.

```
Syntax: /NAM=user_name
```

Example:

```
CAPTURE /NAM=KAREN
```

would print the name Karen on the upper half of the banner.

NoBanner specifies that no banner page will be printed. CAPTURE by default prints a banner.

```
Syntax: /NB
```

Example:

```
CAPTURE /NB
```

would disable banner printing.

FormFeed sends a form feed character to the printer after your job has printed.

```
Syntax: /FF
```

Example:

```
CAPTURE /FF
```

would send a form feed character to the printer at the end of the print job.

NoFormFeed tells CAPTURE not to send a form feed character to the printer at the end of a print job. CAPTURE by default sends a form feed.

```
Syntax: /NFF
```

Example:

```
CAPTURE /NFF
```

would eliminate the form feed character being sent at the end of a print job.

Keep ensures that the file server keeps all data it receives, in case your workstation hangs or loses power while you are capturing data. Fifteen minutes after your workstation hangs or loses power, the file server sends the data to a network printer.

If you do not include KEEP in your CAPTURE command and your workstation hangs or loses power in mid-capture, the file server discards the data it has received.

```
Syntax: /K
```

Example:

```
CAPTURE /K
```

would save a partially completed print file.

Autoendcap closes the print file and sends data to a network printer or file when you exit or enter an application, and then opens a new print file. The default is Autoendcap enabled.

```
Syntax: /A
```

Example:

```
CAPTURE /A
```

would close the print file, place it in the specified queue, and then open a new print file each time you enter or exit an application.

NoAutoendcap prevents data from being sent to a network printer or file when you enter or exit an application. The default is Autoendcap enabled.

```
Syntax: /NA
```

Example:

```
CAPTURE /NA
```

would disable Autoendcap.

Tabs sets the number of spaces between tabs (0 to 18). This is only used if your application does not have a print formatter (most do). The default is 8.

```
Syntax: /T=number (0 to 18)
```

Example:

```
CAPTURE /T=5
```

would set tab spacing to 5.

NoTabs tells the printer to ignore tab characters and other formatting characters, such as form feeds. This flag is rarely used.

```
Syntax: /NT
```

Example:

```
CAPTURE /NT
```

would disable tab characters.

TImeout sends data to the print queue a specified number of seconds after you press the print keys in an application, or after an application has finished sending data to a print file. The default is TI=0 (TImeout disabled).

```
Syntax: /TI=number (0 to 1000)
```

Example:

```
CAPTURE /TI=5
```

would close a print file 5 seconds after data has stopped being sent.

SHow displays the current CAPTURE parameters. Do not use this option with any other CAPTURE option.

Syntax:

```
/SH
```

Example:

```
CAPTURE /SH
```

would show the current CAPTURE parameters.

To use CAPTURE, issue the CAPTURE command (with the appropriate flags, if necessary), then call your application program.

For frequently used programs that cannot direct output to a network printer, it is recommended that you put your CAPTURE commands in batch files to be used to call those programs.

Examples:

```
CAPTURE /C=3/P=0/B=DATAFILE <Enter>
```

Reroutes output to printer 0 on the default file server, prints three copies, and prints the file name DATAFILE on the banner.

```
CAPTURE /J=DISK_FILE/CR=SYS:USERS/KAREN/TEMPFILE.CAP <Enter>
```

Reroutes output the file TEMPFILE.CAP in the SYS:USERS/PATRICK directory of the current file server using print job configuration DISK_FILE.

```
CAPTURE S=SERVER1/P=3/NFF/TI=10 <Enter>
```

Reroutes output to printer 3 on file server SERVER1, suppresses form feeds, and times out after 10 seconds. (The timer starts when output to the print file is stopped. If output is not restarted within the specified time, the current print file is closed and put in the print queue and a new print file is opened.

Batch File Examples:

```
CAPTURE/S=SERVER1/P=1/NB/TI=10/NA
WS
ENDCAP
```

This batch file reroutes output to printer 1 on file server SERVER1, does not print a banner, sets the time out function for ten seconds, disables Autoendcap, calls the program WS, and, upon exit from the program issues an ENDCAP command.

```
CAPTURE/P=3/B=DATAFLEX
FLEX
ENDCAP
```

This batch file reroutes output to printer 3 on the current default server, prints the file name DATAFLEX on the banner, and runs the program FLEX and upon exit from the program issues an ENDCAP command.

If a default print job configuration and form are defined for a user, CAPTURE uses the default job configuration. If not, CAPTURE uses the following defaults:

- Data is redirected from LPT1 to a print queue on your default file server (usually PRINTQ_0). Output to LPT2 and LPT3 is not redirected.

- One copy is printed.

- A banner page is printed before the copy is printed with your user name on the upper half and the word LST: on the bottom half.

- Autoendcap is enabled and TImeout is disabled.

- Tabs characters are converted to eight spaces.

- A form feed is issued at the end of the print job.

When sending output to a printer you can use all options except CReate and SHow. When sending output to a file you can use Autoendcap, NoAutoendcap, TImeout, Local, and CReate.

ENDCAP

ENDCAP will close the print file, place it in the print queue and redirect output back to a local printer port. Issuing a new CAPTURE command will also close the current print file, but will not redirect output back to a local printer. CAPTURE, LOGIN, LOGOUT, and NPRINT all execute an automatic ENDCAP when they are executed. (If you execute CAPTURE and a print command, but do not execute

ENDCAP—explicit, implicit or automatic—the capture file will remain on the file server's hard disk.)

Syntax:

```
ENDCAP flags <Enter>
```

Flags:

`ALL`	Ends CAPTURE and prints all data queued to LPT1, LPT2, and LPT3.
`C`	Cancels CAPTURE and deletes all data queued to LPT1.
`C ALL`	Cancels CAPTURE and deletes all data queued to LPT1, LPT2, and LPT3.
`L=n`	Stops queueing and prints all data queued to LPTn.
`CL=n`	Cancels queueing and deletes all data queued to LPTn.

Examples:

```
ENDCAP <Enter>
```

Closes capture file and places it in the print queue. Also redirects output to a local printer.

```
ENDCAP /C <Enter>
```

Deletes open capture file on LPTn. Also redirects output to a local printer.

NPRINT

Use NPRINT to print files that already exist in the form you wish to print them. NPRINT will queue the specified file for printing. Jobs are placed into and printed from the print queue in the order they are received.

Syntax:

```
NPRINT directory_path/filename /flags <Enter>
```

NPRINT uses the same flags as CAPTURE except TImeout, Keep, and SHow.

NPRINT has one additional flag, Delete, that will delete the file after it is printed. Use this flag only if you want the file to be printed PERMANENTLY DELETED.

Syntax:

```
/D
```

If there is no default print job configuration, and no flags are used, NPRINT defaults to Printer 0 on the current file server, prints one copy using form 0, and prints a banner with the user's login name and the name of the file being printed.

Examples:

```
NPRINT MYFILE.DAT,JUNK.LST /NO BANNER/COPIES=2/PRINTER=3 <Enter>

NPRINT MYFILE.DAT,JUNK.LST /NB/C2/P3 <Enter>
```

Console Printer Commands

NetWare provides a number of console commands to help you manage network printers and queues. These commands let you map print queues to printers, move queues from one printer to another, stop and start printers, etc. Some of the commands duplicate functions available in PConsole, but many others are only available at the console. This section provides an overview of some of the most commonly used console printer commands. The NetWare Console Commands Manual provides information on all of the console printer commands.

Note: In the command syntax examples below, lowercase text is to be replaced with its equivalent value, and text in square brackets ([ ]) is optional.

Adding Queues to Printers

You can map more that one print queue to a single printer, or map one queue to multiple printers. You can also set queue priority levels so that print jobs in a high-priority queue will be printed before print jobs in a low-priority queue.

To add a queue to a printer you would use the following command syntax:

```
P[RINTER] printer_number ADD [QUEUE] queue_name [[AT] [PRIORITY]
number] <Enter>
```

or

```
P[RINTER] printer_number = [QUEUE] queue_name [[AT] [PRIORITY]
number] <Enter>
```

Priority levels can be between 1 and 32,767.

Examples:

Mapping one queue to one printer:

To map PRINTQ_0 to Printer 0 you would type:

```
P 0 ADD PRINTQ_0 <Enter>
```

Mapping one queue to multiple printers:

To map PRINTQ_0 to Printer 0 and Printer 1, you would type:

```
P 0 ADD PRINTQ_0 <Enter>
P 1 ADD PRINTQ_0 <Enter>
```

Now PRINTQ_0 is servicing both printer 0 and Printer 1; send each job to the next available printer.

Mapping multiple queues to one printer:

To map PRINTQ_0 and PRINTQ_1 to Printer 0, you would type:

```
P 0 ADD PRINTQ_0 <Enter>
P 0 ADD PRINTQ_1 <Enter>
```

Printer 0 would alternately accept print jobs from PRINTQ_0 and PRINTQ_1.

To map PRINTQ_0 and PRINTQ_1 to Printer 0, giving PRINTQ_0 a higher priority, you would type:

```
P 0 ADD PRINTQ_0 <Enter>
P 0 ADD PRINTQ_1 AT PRIORITY 2 <Enter>
```

PRINTQ_0 would be added at the default priority, 1, and PRINTQ_1 would be added at a lower priority, 2. Jobs in PRINTQ_0 would be printed before jobs in PRINTQ_1.

If the above commands are typed at the console keyboard, they will temporarily change the queue mapping(s). To permanently change the queue mapping(s), add the commands to the AUTOEXEC.SYS file.

Removing Queues from Printers

To remove a queue from a printer you would use the following command syntax:

```
P[RINTER] printer_number DELETE [QUEUE] queue_name <Enter>
```

If the specified print queue is mapped to the printer in the AUTOEXEC.SYS file, this command would only remove the queue from the printer until the next the next time you bring up the file server. To permanently remove the queue from the printer, remove the corresponding queue mapping command from the AUTOEXEC.SYS file.

Changing the Form Type Mounted in the Printer

When you bring up the file server, NetWare assumes that Form 0 is mounted in each printer. If you have mounted a form other than Form 0 in a printer, you can tell NetWare by typing:

```
P[RINTER] printer_number FORM [MOUNT] form_number <Enter>
```

or

```
P[RINTER] printer_number MOUNT [FORM] form_number <Enter>
```

or

```
P[RINTER] printer_number FORM form_number [MOUNT[ED]] <Enter>
```

For example, if you wanted to indicate that Form 3 is mounted on Printer 2, you would type:

```
P 2 FORM 3 <Enter>
```

To permanently change the default form number, add this command to the AUTOEXEC.SYS file.

Mark Top of Form

This command is primarily used to align continuous-feed preprinted forms.

It prints a row of asterisks (*) across the first printable line of the page. The syntax is:

```
P[RINTER] printer_number MARK [[TOP OF] FORM] <Enter>
```

or

```
P[RINTER printer_number FORM MARK <Enter>
```

For example, to mark the top of the form in Printer 3, type:

```
P 3 MARK <Enter>
```

Issuing a Form Feed

This command can be used with the MARK TOP OF FORM command to advance to the next page after you have correctly aligned the form. The syntax is:

```
P[RINTER] printer_number FORM FEED <Enter>
```

or

```
P[RINTER] printer_number FF <Enter>
```

For example, to issue a form feed to printer 0, type:

```
P 0 FF <Enter>
```

Stopping a Printer

It is sometimes necessary to stop a printer to realign forms, reprint pages, etc. The command syntax to do this is:

```
P[RINTER] printer_number STOP <Enter>
```

For example, to stop Printer 2, type:

```
P 2 STOP <Enter>
```

Starting a Stopped Printer

The command syntax to restart a stopped printer is:

```
P[RINTER] printer_number START <Enter>
```

For example, to stop Printer 2, type:

```
P 2 START <Enter>
```

Rewinding A Printer

This command will stop a print job and rewind it either the specified number of pages (1 to 9) or rewind to the beginning of the print job. The syntax is:

```
P[RINTER] printer_number REWIND [number] [PAGES] <Enter>
```

For example, to rewind Printer 2 five pages, type:

```
P 2 REWIND 5 <Enter>
```

To rewind Printer 1 to the beginning of the current print job, type:

```
P 1 REWIND <Enter>
```

Listing a Printer's Print Queues

This command will list the print queues mapped to a printer. It will also specify the priority level of each queue. The syntax is:

```
P[RINTER] printer_number [Q[UEUE[S]]] <Enter>
```

For example, to list the queues mapped to Printer 0, type:

```
P 0 <Enter>
```

You should see a display similar to the following:

```
Printer 2:  Running  On-Line  Form 0 mounted  Servicing 3 queues

Servicing PRINTQ_0        at priority  1
Servicing REMOTE          at priority  2
```

Listing the Printer Status

This command will give you the status of each printer attached to the file server.

It will tell you if the printer is on-line or off-line, which form is mounted, and the number of queues the printer is servicing. The syntax is:

```
P[RINTER[S]] <Enter>
```

To list the status of the file server's printers, type:

```
P <Enter>
```

You should see a display similar to the following:

```
Printer 0:  Running  On-Line  Form 0 mounted  Servicing 2 queues
Printer 1:  Running  On-Line  Form 0 mounted  Servicing 1 queues
Printer 2:  Running  Off-Line  Form 2 mounted  Servicing 0 queues
```

Listing Spool Mappings

Spool mappings are used to maintain compatibility with NetWare 0a and below. The syntax for listing Spool mappings is:

```
S[POOL] <Enter>
```

To list the current spool mappings, type:

```
S <Enter>
```

You should see a display similar to the following:

```
Spooler 0 is directed into queue PRINTQ_0
Spooler 1 is directed into queue PRINTQ_1
Spooler 2 is directed into queue PRINTQ_2
```

```
Spooler 3 is directed into queue SCRIPTEN
```

Changing Spool Mappings

The syntax for changing a spool mapping is:

```
S[POOL] spooler_number [TO] [QUEUE] queue_name <Enter>
```

or

```
S[POOL] spooler_number [=] queue_name
```

For example to map Spooler 4 to print queue PRINTQ_0, type:

```
S 4 PRINTQ_0
```

Appendixes

Appendix A

Glossary

The following glossary presents terms as they are used in NetWare PC LANs. Some are Novell's own definitions. In other environments they may have different meanings, as vendors adapt industry jargon to fit their technical realities and perspective.

Active hub A device used to amplify transmission signals in ARCNET LANs. An active hub can be used either to add additional workstations to a network or to lengthen the cabling distance between LAN stations. See also **Passive hub**.

Address, memory A number that identifies each location in computer memory.

Address, network A unique number that identifies a particular network or network station.

ANSI American National Standards Institute. ANSI develops and publishes technical standards.

Application A software program or program package that allows a user to perform a specific job (such as accounting or word processing).

API Application Program Interface. A method of allowing an application to interact directly with certain functions of an operating system or another application.

APPC Advanced Program-to-Program Communications, a component of IBM's System's Network Architecture. APPC is designed to allow communications between programs running on different systems on a more or less peer-to-peer basis.

Architecture A system's architecture typically describes the type of components, interfaces, and protocols it uses and how they fit together.

Archive A backup made for the purpose of preserving the system as of a particular event. See **Backup**.

ARCNET A widely used LAN architecture developed by Datapoint Corp. that uses a logical token-passing access method at 2.5 Mbps.

ARPANET A wide area network developed by the Defense Advanced Research Projects Agency that primarily connects universities and government agencies.

ASCII American Standard Code for Information Interchange. A standard for encoding characters (including the upper- and lowercase alphabet, numerals, punctuation, and control characters) using 7 bits. The standard is 128 characters; IBM expanded the set to 256 by adding an eighth bit to each existing character. The expanded set provides graphics characters, greek, scientific, financial, and foreign language characters.

Asynchronous Transmission — A transmission method which allows characters to be sent at irregular intervals by adding start and stop bits to identify the beginning and ending of each character, where synchronous communications uses synchronized time intervals. Asynchronous communications have a 20% overhead (the 2 stop/start bits) added to each 8-bit byte. See also **Synchronous transmission**.

Attach — With NetWare, to access additional file servers after having logged in to one file server.

Attributes — See **File attributes**.

AUI Cable — Attached Unit Interface Cable. A four-twisted-pair cable that connects an Ethernet device to an Ethernet external transceiver.

Backbone network — A network that interconnects other networks.

Backing Out — The abandoning of an incomplete transaction because of system failure. NetWare's Transaction Tracking System (TTS) views a sequence of database changes as a single transaction that must be wholly completed or wholly "backed out" (no changes made at all). TTS stores all the information necessary to back out of a transaction and return the

	database to its previous state. See also **Transaction rollback**; **TTS**.
Backup	A copy of a file, directory, or volume on another storage device for the purpose of retrieval in case the original is accidentally erased, damaged, or destroyed.
Bad Block Table	A list of blocks on a disk that are unusable.
Baud Rate	The rate at which data is transferred over a serial interface.
Base I/O Address	The beginning address of an I/O port.
Baseband	A transmission system in which the signal is broadcast at its original frequency (that is, not modulated), one signal at a time.
Base Memory Address	The beginning address of a block of memory.
Bindery	NetWare's database of network objects (users, groups, printers, etc.) and their characteristics (passwords, addresses, etc). Located in the SYS:SYSTEM directory.
BIOS	Basic Input Output System. The programs with which the CPU communicates with other PC devices (such as printer ports, keyboards, the console, etc.)
Bit	A binary digit; must be either a 0 ("off") or a 1 ("on").

Block A unit of disk storage. DOS disks usually store data in 2K blocks, and Novell NetWare stores data in 4K blocks.

Boot To start up a computer and load it's operating system into RAM.

Bridge A device used to connect LANs by forwarding packets addressed to other similar networks across connections at the Media Access Control data link level. Routers, which operate at the protocol level, are often called bridges also.

Bridge, NetWare Technically a router, a NetWare Bridge allows the interconnection of networks using Novell's IPX/SPX protocols. A NetWare Bridge can be a file server (internal bridge) or another PC (external bridge). NetWare bridges each support up to four network interface cards of similar or dissimilar types.

Broadband A transmission system in which signals are encoded and modulated into different frequencies and then transmitted simultaneously with other signals.

Broadcast A LAN data transmission scheme in which data packets are heard by all stations on the network.

Buffer A temporary storage area for data. Buffers are used to store data being transferred from two systems that process it at different rates. Examples are communication buffers and printer buffers.

Bus — A common connection. Networks that broadcast signals to all stations, such as Ethernet or ARCNET, are considered bus networks.

Bus (PC) — The connectors on a PC motherboard that expansion boards plug into.

Byte — Usually the eight bits that represent a character.

Cache — To read data into a memory buffer so that the data is available the next time it is needed and does not have to be read from the disk again. See also **Directory caching; Disk caching**.

Cache buffer — An area in RAM used for caching. See also **Cache**.

CCITT — Comité Consultatif Internationale de Télégraphique et Téléphonique. A international communications standards-setting body.

Channel — A data communication path. See also **Disk channel**.

Character set — The group of characters a computer can recognize and process (e.g., ASCII).

Cheapernet — A slang name for Ethernet thin coaxial cable (RG-58A/U), so-called because it is less expensive than the thick coaxial cable that is also used for Ethernet.

Client — In a client/server database system, the computer (usually a workstation) that makes service requests.

Client/Server — A network system design in which a processor or computer designated as a server (file server, database server, etc.) provides services to other client processors or computers.

CMOS RAM — In a PC, random access memory for storing system configuration data (number of drives, type of drives, amount of memory, etc.). The CMOS RAM is battery maintained and is not available to the computer's operating system.

Coaxial cable — A commonly used cable type that is relatively insensitive to noise interference, consisting of one or two insulating layers and two conductors. A central conductor wire is surrounded by the first layer of insulation. An outer shielding conductor is laid over the first layer of insulation and then usually covered with the second layer of insulation.

Cold boot loader — A program written onto the file server system hard disk during installation that automatically loads the NetWare operating system after a cold boot.

Collision detection — The detecting of simultaneous transmissions on the communication medium. See **CSMA/CD**.

COM1, COM2 — See **Serial port**.

Communication buffers RAM on a NetWare file server or bridge that is set aside to temporarily hold packets arriving from the various network stations until the file server or bridge is ready to process them and send them to their destination. Also called *routing buffers.*

Communication medium The physical connection medium over which data travels. The medium is usually cable (coaxial, twisted-pair, or fiber optic), but it can also be other media, such as infrared, radio, or microwave.

CompSurf Comprehensive Surface Analysis. A utility used during NetWare installation that tests and formats the file server hard disk.

Connection A number assigned to any station that attaches number to a NetWare file server; it may be a different number each time a station attaches. The file server's operating system uses connection numbers to control each station's communication with other stations. Current connection numbers can be ascertained with the WHOAMI or USERLIST command-line utilities.

Console The monitor and keyboard from which you view and control NetWare file server activity. At the console, you can type in commands to control printers and disk drives, send messages, set the file server clock, shut down the file server, and view file server information.

Controller address The number that is physically set on a hard disk controller board, and which is used by the operating system to locate the controller on a disk channel.

Controller board A device that enables a computer to communicate with a particular device (disk, network interface board, tape drive, etc.). The controller board manages input/output and regulates the operation of its associated device.

Copper Segment An Ethernet coaxial bus.

Coprocessor An additional CPU in a computer usually used for a specific task. See **Disk Coprocessor Board**.

CSMA/CD Carrier Sense Multiple Access with Collision Detection. CSMA/CD is Ethernet's cable access method.

Cylinder Distinct, concentric storage areas on a hard disk (roughly corresponding to tracks on a floppy diskette).

DARPA Defense Advanced Research Projects Agency—the developer of the government/university ARPANET network.

Data Link Layer The OSI level that performs the assembly and transmission of data packets, including error control.

Database server A database server is the "back end" processor that manages the database and fulfills database requests in a client/server database system.

DCB See Disk Coprocessor Board.

Dedicated file server A file server that cannot be used as a user's server workstation. See file server.

DECnet Digital Equipment Corp's. proprietary network protocols used on 802.3 Ethernet.

De facto standard A standard based on broad usage and support.

Default A value or option that is chosen automatically when no other value is specified.

De jure standard An "official" standard developed or approved by one of the industry standard committees (IEEE, ANSI, etc.)

Device driver A program that translates operating system requests into a format that is recognizable by specific hardware (for example, a hard disk). Each device is normally linked with the operating system via its device driver.

Direct memory access (DMA) A method of transferring data to and from a computer's memory.

Directory A logical subdivision of a disk in which files are stored, like a file folder. Directories are usually created in a tree hierarchy, branching from the main root directory into subdirectories. See **Directory rights**.

Directory caching

A method of decreasing the time it takes to determine a file's location on a disk. The file allocation table and directory entry are written into a computer's memory. A file's location can then be read from memory, which is much faster than reading from the disk.

Directory entries

On a NetWare volume, directory entries include file names, directory names and a directory's Trustee list. The maximum number of directory entries that can be created on a volume is specified during installation.

Directory hashing

A method of indexing file locations on a disk so that the time needed to locate a file is significantly reduced. By indexing directories in each volume and then indexing files by volume and subdirectory, hashing reduces the number of references made in search of a specific file. Rather than searching sequentially through all entries, a computer using directory hashing only has to look at a few.

Directory rights

Restrictions specific to a directory that regulate trustee activity within it. See also **Rights**.

Directory structure

The specific levels of directories (parent directories, subdirectories, etc.) organized to form a hierarchy on a disk. See also **Directory name**.

Disk cache block

A block of data written into a cache buffer during a disk read. See also **Cache buffer**; **Disk caching**.

Disk caching Reading portions of requested files into a computer's memory (into a cache buffer). This decreases the number of times the disk is read and thus increases the speed of access. Data placed in memory can be accessed up to 100 times faster than data on disk.

Disk channel A data transmission route. In a NetWare file server, a disk channel can be an internal disk drive or any data bus added by a Disk Coprocessor Board or third-party disk interface. NetWare file servers can accommodate up to five disk channels. See also **Disk Coprocessor Board**; **Disk duplexing**.

Disk controller A hardware device associated with a disk drive that controls how data is written to and retrieved from the disk.

Disk Coprocessor Board (DCB) A board that acts as an interface between a computer microprocessor and the disk con troller. The Disk Coprocessor board relieves the microprocessor of data storage and re trieval tasks, thus increasing the computer's performance time. A Disk Coprocessor board and its disk subsystems make up a disk channel.

Disk duplexing An SFT NetWare method of safeguarding data in which the same data is copied simultaneously to two hard disks on separate channels. If one channel fails, the data on the other channel remains unharmed. When data is duplexed, read requests are sent to whichever disk in the pair can respond faster, thus increasing the file server's efficiency. When two or more read requests occur together, the requests are split and can be processed at once. See also disk mirroring.

Disk mirroring — An SFT NetWare method of safeguarding data in which the same data is copied to two hard disks on the same channel. If one of the disks fails, the data on the other disk is safe. Because the two disks are on the same channel, mirroring provides only limited data protection—a failure anywhere along the channel could shut down both disks and data would be lost. See also Disk duplexing.

Disk subsystem — An external unit that attaches to a computer that contains hard disk drives.

DMA — See **Direct Memory Access**.

Drive mapping — See **Map**.

Driver — See **Device driver**.

DTE — Data Terminal Equipment. A terminal, PC, or other device attached to the LAN.

Duplexing — See **Disk duplexing**.

Effective rights — On a NetWare file server, the rights a user may actually exercise in a given directory. There are two factors that determine effective rights: Trustee rights granted to a particular user and/or group of users, and Directory rights specified in the directory's maximum rights mask. Effective rights are the intersection of Trustee and Directory rights:

right has to be specified for both the trustee and the directory.

Embedded SCSI A hard disk controller board built into the hard disk unit that uses a SCSI interface. See **SCSI**.

Ethernet, 802.3 The IEEE 802.3 official standard. A popular LAN architecture that uses a bus topology and CSMA/CD at 10 Mbps. Although 802.3 is technically not Ethernet, the name is commonly used because of the roots of 802.3. See **Ethernet, E.SPEC VER.1, E.SPEC VER.2**.

Ethernet, E.SPEC VER.1, E.SPEC VER>2 A proprietary LAN developed by DEC, Intel and Xerox that was the basis for the IEEE 802.3 specification. The VER.1 spec was released in September 1980, VER.2 in November 1982, and 802.3 in January 1985.

Expanded memory Additional memory (beyond 640 KB) that conforms to the Lotus-Intel-Microsoft (LIM) specification for expanded memory. This memory is only available to DOS applications that support it, and cannot be used by NetWare, UNIX, or most other operating systems.

Extended memory In an 80286 personal computer, extended memory is memory above the 1MB address range. For MS-DOS, this memory is normally only available as a virtual disk (memory that is treated as though it were a disk drive). Novell's NetWare uses this memory as working memory.

External bridge	See **Bridge, NetWare**.
Fan-out Unit	A device that attaches to an Ethernet transceiver to allow multiple devices to attach to the transceiver in a star-cluster fashion.
FAT	See **File allocation table**.
Fault tolerance	See **SFT**.
File allocation table (FAT)	A table on a disk that records the disk location of all the parts of a file.
File attributes	Designations that regulate how a file may be accessed on a NetWare file server. For example, a file can be assigned the attributes *Shareable* and *Read/Only*. Shareable means that more than one user may access the file at the same time; Read/Only means that users can read the file, but they cannot alter it. The *Normal* attribute is defined as shareable and read/write.
File server	A computer that provides network stations with controlled access to shareable resources. The NetWare Operating System is loaded on the file server, and most shareable devices (disk subsystems, printers, etc.) are attached to it. The file server controls system security; it also monitors station-to-station communications. A dedicated file server can be used only as a file server while it is on the network. A nondedicated file server can be used simultaneously as a file server and a workstation.

File Server Console — See **Console.**

File sharing — Provisions in the network operating system that allow more than one user to access the same file.

Form — In a printer command, the design or shape of the printing surface, such as letter-size paper, labels, continuous-feed paper, etc.

FTP — The File Transfer Protocol of TCP/IP.

Gateway — A device that provides routing and protocol conversion among physically dissimilar networks and/or computers (e.g., LAN to HOST, LAN to LAN, X.25, SNA gateways).

Hashing — See **Directory hashing.**

Hexadecimal — A numeric notation system frequently used to specify addresses in computer memory. In hexadecimal notation, the decimal numbers 0 through 15 are represented by the decimal digits 0 through 9 and the alphabetic "digits" A through F (A = decimal 10, B = decimal 11, etc.).

Home directory — A network directory that the network supervisor creates specifically for each user. The supervisor usually includes a drive mapping to the home directory in the user login script so that the user is located in the home directory after login.

Host — A computer attached to a network that provides services to another computer beyond simply storing and forwarding information. Mainframes, minicomputers, and file servers are sometimes called hosts, but the term is often used more broadly. For example, the network station that a remote caller takes over and controls is referred to as the host.

Hot Fix

A feature of NetWare that, along with read-after-write verification, protects data from hard disk defects. If data cannot be written and then read back reliably from a particular block on the hard disk, Hot Fix stores the data in the redirection area (a small portion of the hard disk reserved for this purpose during installation). The location of the defective block is added to the bad block table, and the operating system will not try to store data in that block again. See also **Bad block table**; **Read-after-write verification**.

Hub

1) A device used on certain network topologies that modifies transmission signals, allowing the network to be lengthened or expanded with additional workstations. The hub is the central device in a star topology. See also **Active hub; Passive hub**.

2) A computer that receives messages from other computers, stores them, and routes them to other computer destinations.

IBM Token Ring

IBM's version of the 802.5 token-passing ring network.

IEEE

The Institute of Electrical and Electronic Engineers. A group that develops and publishes many of the official LAN-related standards (including 802.3 Ethernet and 802.5 Token Ring).

Impedance The opposition that circuit elements present to the flow of alternating current, including resistance and reactance.

Internal bridge See **Bridge, NetWare**.

Internetwork Two or more networks connected by bridges and/or routers; a network of networks.

Internetwork Packet Exchange See **IPX.**

Interrupt A signal that temporarily suspends a program, permitting the program eventually to proceed from where it left off. During the suspension, another task may appropriate the computer's resources. Interrupts can be divided into two general types, hardware and software. A hardware interrupt is caused by a signal from a hardware device, such as a printer. A software interrupt is created by instructions from within a software program.

Interrupt line A circuit used by an I/O device to send interrupt signals to the microprocessor. Sometimes abbreviated as IRQ for hardware interrupt lines.

I/O Input/output. The process of moving data, as in the transmitting of data from memory to disk.

IPX	Internetwork Packet Exchange. The NetWare protocol for the exchange of message packets on an internetwork. IPX passes application requests for network services to the network drivers and on to other workstations, servers, or devices on the internetwork. IPX is based on Xerox Corporation's Internetwork Packet Protocol.
IPX.COM	The program that runs on a NetWare workstation that loads the IPX/SPX protocols, providing communication to the network interface. See **IPX; SPX**.
IRL	Inter-Repeater Link. This is a passive copper (or fiber) Ethernet segment with no active devices attached.
ISO	The International Standards Organization. ISO developed the milestone Open Systems Interconnection (OSI) model.
KB	Kilobyte. A unit of measure for memory or disk storage capacity; two to the tenth power (1024) bytes.
LAN	Local Area Network. See **Network**.
Liner Bus Topology	A cabling topology in which devices link to different points along a single length of cable.
LocalTalk	The network hardware built into Macintosh computers.
Logical Record	A collection of information items that can be geographically distributed among different

physical records in the same or in multiple physical databases.

LAN driver Software that allows a network station to communicate with its network interface card. With Novell NetWare, the LAN driver is linked into the operating system and workstation shells when the are generated with NetGen and ShGen.

LAN Manager 1) One who manages a LAN.

2) Microsoft's file server operating system based on OS/2.

LAN Server 1) A file server, database server, or other server on a LAN.

2) IBM's file server operating system based on Microsoft's LAN Manager.

Login (noun) The process of accessing a NetWare file server after physical connection has been established with IPX.COM and NET3.COM.

Login script A set of instructions that execute at login on a NetWare file server. The network supervisor can create a system-wide login script that instructs all workstations to perform the same actions upon login. The individual user login scripts execute after the system-wide login script; specifying individual drive mappings.

LPT1 The primary printer port of a PC. See also parallel port.

Map or mapping

To assign a drive letter to a particular directory path on a particular volume of a particular NetWare file server. This is done with the MAP command line utility and in login scripts. For example, if you map (assign) drive F: to the directory SYS:ACCOUNT/RECEIVE, you will access that directory every time you type F: at the DOS prompt.

Maximum rights mask

A feature of NetWare directory security that controls the rights that all trustees may exercise in one directory. If a particular right is removed from a directory's rights mask, no user (other than SUPERVISOR) will be able to exercise that right in that directory or its subdirectories, even if the user has that trustee right. See also **Directory rights**; **Effective rights**; **Trustee rights**.

MB

Megabyte. A unit of measure for memory or disk storage capacity. Two to the twentieth power (1,048,576) bytes.

Mbps

Megabits per second (one million bits per second).

Message packet

The unit of information by which the network communicates. Each packet contains a request for services, information on how to handle the request, and the data to be transferred.

MHS Message Handling Service. Novell's electronic mail platform protocol for LAN message handling and routing. See also **X.400**

MHz Megahertz. One million cycles per second. See also **Hz**.

Mirroring See **Disk mirroring**.

Monitor display A formatted screen that can be displayed on a NetWare console screen by entering the MONITOR console command. The Monitor Display shows file server activity and accepts console commands.

Multiport repeater A repeater that attaches multiple Ethernet segments in parallel.

Multiserver network A network that has two or more file servers operating on it.

NetBIOS The low-level, station-to-station communications protocol developed by IBM for its PC LAN systems. Most network operating system vendors supply software to emulate this protocol to support applications that require it.

NetWare The family of Networking operating systems from Novell, Inc.

NetWare bridge See **Bridge, NetWare**.

NetWare shell The RAM-resident communication software that allows a DOS workstation to communicate with file servers and other devices on a NetWare- based LAN.

Network address A unique identifying number assigned to each separate attached network during installation of each NetWare file server. If a file server contains more than one network interface board (and therefore is operating on more than one network), each additional network must have its own network address. The network address assigned to a physical network will be the same in every file server attached to that physical network.

Network Interface Card (NIC) A circuit board installed in each network station to allow communication with other stations.

Network station Any PC (or other device) connected to a network by means of a network interface board and some communication medium. A network station can be a workstation, bridge, or server.

NFS Network File System. A networking protocol suite developed by Sun Microsystems and used widely in the UNIX world.

NIC See **Network Interface Card.**

Node Any network station.

Node address See **Station address**.

Nondedicated file server See **File server**.

Object A NetWare entity that has access to file server resources. Objects include users, groups, and print queues. Objects are recorded in NetWare's bindery database, located in the SYS:SYSTEM directory of the file server.

Packet See **Data packet**.

Parallel port A printer interface that allows data to be transmitted a byte at a time, with eight bits moving in parallel. See also **Serial port**.

Parity A method of checking for errors in transmitted data. The transmitting end adds the bits being transmitted. If parity is set to odd, then the transmitter attaches a bit if the total is even, making it odd. If parity is set to even, the transmitter attaches a bit if the total is odd. The receiving end adds all the bits, which should always be odd for odd parity and even for even parity because of the adjustments made by the transmitter to ensure the result. If the total is of the wrong type, the communications software on the receiving end detects that an error has occurred during transmission and requests that the data be retransmitted.

Partition A portion of a hard disk's physical storage space that is allocated to an operating system (NetWare, DOS, etc.). Once created, a partition belongs exclusively to the specified operating system; no other operating system can access that area.

Passive hub — A device used in ARCNET networks to split a transmission signal, allowing additional workstations to be added. A passive hub cannot amplify the signal, and so it must connect directly to a workstation or an active hub. See also **Active hub**.

Peripheral — A physical device (such as a printer or disk subsystem) that is externally attached to a workstation or to directly to the network.

Port (verb) — To move an operating system or application from one processor environment to another. For applications, it also means to move from one operating system to another.

Port, hardware — A connecting component that allows a microprocessor to communicate with a compatible peripheral. See also **Parallel port**; **Serial port**.

Print job configuration — The characteristics that determine how a job is printed to a NetWare printer. Some of the factors may include printer control codes, forms, and the particular printer that will be used.

Print server — A device and/or program that manages shared printers. Print service is often provided by the file server but can also be provided from a separate LAN PC.

Protocol — Rules for communicating, particularly for the format and transmission of data.

Queue A method for managing separate requests to process data (usually, to be printed).

Random access memory See **RAM**.

RAM Random Access Memory. A dynamic data storage location in which data can be accessed in any order.

Read-after-write verification A data safeguard that reads back data written to a hard disk and compares it to the original data that is still in memory. See also **Bad block table; Hot fix; Redirection area**.

Read-only A type of data security that protects files. If a file is flagged Read-Only, a user can access the data in the file but cannot change it. See also **File attributes**.

Read-only memory See **ROM**.

Repeater A device used to extend cabling distances by amplifying or regenerating signals.

Record A collection of related information that is treated as one unit within a file.

Record locking A data-protection scheme that prevents different users from performing simultaneous writes to the same record in a shared file, thus preventing overlapping disk writes and ensuring data integrity.

Redirection area A small portion of space on a NetWare file server hard disk set aside during installation. The redirection area is set up as a table to hold data blocks that are "redirected" from bad block locations on the disk.

Repeater

A device that amplifies and regenerates signals, thus allowing multiple Ethernet segments to be attached together.

Resource

In NetWare installation programs, any device, circuit board, or built-in circuitry that uses one or more of the following to communicate with the file server's microprocessor: interrupt lines, DMA lines, I/O addresses, or memory addresses (RAM or ROM).

Resource set

In NetWare installation programs, a collection of related resources.

Ring Topology

A closed loop topology in which data passes in one direction from station to station on the LAN. Each workstation on the ring acts as a repeater, passing data to the next workstation on the ring.

Rights

With NetWare, privileges (assigned by the network supervisor) that control how users may work with files in a given directory (for example, controlling whether a user may read a file, change a file, or delete a file). Trustee rights are assigned to individual users, and control each user's rights within directories. A Maximum Rights Mask is assigned to each individual directory and restricts the rights of all users (except SUPERVISOR) in that directory, overriding the individual trustee rights of a user.

ROM — Read-Only Memory. Permanent memory built into a device. The data in ROM cannot be erased or changed. See also **RAM**.

Root directory — The highest level in a hierarchical tree directory structure. It is the main directory on a volume; all other directories are subdirectories of the root directory.

Router — Hardware and software that routes data between similar or dissimilar networks on the protocol level. NetWare bridges, for example, route data using the IPX/SPX protocols. Technically a NetWare bridge is a router. Routers can support one or more protocols.

Routing — The path a message must follow to reach its destination, or the procedure used to decide the best path data should take to reach that destination.

Routing buffers — On a NetWare file server or bridge, portions of memory reserved to temporarily store and queue the message packets sent between communicating stations when the network bus is busy. See also **Buffer**.

SCSI — Small Computer System Interface. Usually pronounced "scuzzy." An industry standard that sets guidelines for connecting peripheral devices and their controllers to a microprocessor. The SCSI defines both hardware and software standards for communication between a host computer and a peripheral.

Security equivalence — A feature of NetWare security that allows the supervisor to quickly and easily assign one user or group the same trustee rights as another user or group.

Serial port — A port that allows data to be transmitted one bit at a time. On PC-compatible computers, COM1 and COM2 are serial ports.

Server — A network device that provides services to client stations. Servers include file servers, disk servers, print servers, etc.

SFT — System Fault Tolerance. A NetWare scheme for protecting data by duplicating it on multiple storage devices so that if one storage device fails, the data is available from another device. There are several levels of hardware and software system fault tolerance; each level of redundancy (duplication) decreases the possibility of data loss. See also **Disk duplexing; Disk mirroring; Hot fix**.

Shielded Twisted-Pair — Twisted-Pair wire surrounded by a foil or mesh shield to reduce susceptibility to outside interference and noise.

Spool — To transfer data that was intended for a peripheral device (usually a printer) into temporary storage. From there the data can be transferred to the peripheral at a later time, without affecting or delaying the system as it performs other operations.

SPX — Sequenced Packet Exchange. A NetWare protocol by which two workstations or applications communicate across the network. SPX uses IPX to deliver the messages, but SPX guarantees delivery of the messages and maintains the order of messages on the packet stream.

Star Topology A LAN topology in which each workstation connects to a central device.

Star-Wired Topology A ring network (such as a token-passing ring) cabled through centralized hubs or connection devices to create a physical star topology. By using a star topology, individual stations and whole sections of the network can easily be removed or added.

Station See **Network station**.

Station address A unique number assigned to each station on a network. It may be specified in either decimal or hexadecimal format. Also called *physical node address* or *node address*.

Station number See **Connection number**.

Stop bit A control bit used to indicate the end of a group of data bits being sent in asynchronous transmission.

Supervisor The network supervisor is the person responsible for the operation of the network. The network supervisor maintains the network, reconfiguring and updating it as the need arises.

With NetWare, the user SUPERVISOR is a special username that is automatically created when a file server is initialized. This user is permanent and cannot be deleted or renamed. The user SUPERVISOR has all rights in all file server volumes and directories, and these rights cannot be revoked. Other users or groups may be granted a security equivalence to the SUPERVISOR. In NetWare manuals, SUPERVISOR may mean either the SUPERVISOR or any user with a security equivalence to the SUPERVISOR.

Synchronous transmission Transmission in which receiver and trans mitter are regulated by a clock signal. In synchronous transmission, events take place at fixed times and do not need to acknowl edge the completion of preceding events. See also **Asynchronous transmission**.

System console See **Console**.

System Fault Tolerance See **SFT**.

Terminating resistor A load-balancing resistor placed at the end of a bus, line, or cable to prevent signals from being reflected or echoed. Sometimes shortened to "terminator."

Terminator See **Terminating resistor**.

Token A unique combination of bits transmitted on a physical token-passing network whose possession is permission to transmit across the network.

Token bus A network that uses a logical token-passing access method. Unlike a token-passing ring, permission to transmit is usually based on node address rather than position in the network. A token bus network uses a common cable set, with all signals are broadcast across the entire LAN.

Token-passing ring A LAN design in which each station is connected to an upstream station and a down stream station. An electronic signal, called the token, is passed from station to station around the ring. A station may not send a transmission to another station unless it has possession of a "free" token, or a token that is not currently in use. Since only one token is allowed on the network, only one station may broadcast at a time. See **Star-wired ring**.

Topology The physical layout of network cabling.

Tracks Physical locations on a disk. Tracks are divided into sectors which form the fundamental units of disk storage.

Transaction A set of operations that completes a unified task. See **TTS**.

Transaction Rollback A scheme for avoiding data corruption when the network fails by abandoning a current incomplete transaction and returning the database to its original state. See **TTS**.

Transaction See **TTS**. Tracking System

Transceiver

A device that converts digital information to a signal that can be transmitted over the main network communication medium. The transceiver attaches a device to the network cable. Usually transceivers are built-in on PC Ethernet boards.

Trustee

On a NetWare file server, a user who has been given specific rights to work in a particular directory or subdirectory.

Trustee rights

On a NetWare file server, the rights granted to an individual user allowing that user to work in a particular directory or subdirectory. See **Rights**.

TTS

Transaction Tracking System. A NetWare system that protects databases from being corrupted if the computer fails in the middle of a transaction. Each database change is viewed as one transaction, which must be either completed successfully or entirely aborted. If the workstation fails in the middle of a transaction, the transaction is "backed out" and the database is restored to its last completed state. See also **Backing out**.

Twisted pair wire

Two wires that are wrapped around each other to reduce induction between them. Commonly used for telephone and LAN wiring.

Uninterruptible power supply

See **UPS**.

UPS — Uninterruptible Power Supply. A backup power unit that provides continuous power when the normal power supply is interrupted. UPS systems can be stand-by, only supplying power when the regular supply is interrupted, or full-time, relying on regular power and/or batteries to supply it while it supplies power to the protected device.

Utility — An operating system or third party program that performs one or more basic operating system tasks, such as copying files or monitoring system resources.

UTP — Unshielded Twisted Pair wire. See **Twisted-pair wire**.

VADD — Value-Added Disk Drivers. On NetWare file servers, drivers for disk drives provided by third party vendors.

VAP — Value-Added Process. An application that runs "on top" of the NetWare network operating system (in much the same way a word processing or spreadsheet application runs on top of DOS). VAPs tie in with the network operating system so that applications such as print servers, archive servers, and database servers can provide services without interfering with the network's normal operation.

Volume — A portion of hard disk storage space of predetermined size. A volume is the highest level in the hierarchical directory structure (the same level as a DOS root directory). A

	hard disk is divided into one or more volumes by the network installer.
WAN	Wide Area Network. A network linking computers, terminals and other equipment over a large geographic area.
WNIM	Wide Area Network Interface Module. Often used for X.25 and asynchronous gateways.
Word length	The number of significant data bits in each word or byte. When data is accessed, it is moved in a word across an interface cable; also called *transmission word size* or *character length.*
Workstation	A desktop computer that performs local processing and accesses LAN services.
Workstation number	See **Connection number**.
X.25	A CCITT standard protocol for communication over wide area networks.
X.400	A CCITT standard for message exchange in electronic mail.
XON/XOFF protocol	A software handshaking protocol used to establish communication (such as that between a host microprocessor and a printer) so that data is not sent faster than it can be received.

Appendix B

Network Utilities

Many utility packages are available for LANs. The utilities listed here have helped LAN managers and LAN users solve problems. This is not an exhaustive list, and there are many other fine products that are not included here.

Electronic Mail Packages

The time is rapidly approaching when virtually any computer user with a modem or LAN connection can have the capability to communicate with any other user. Electronic mail and the ability to interconnect different mail systems is becoming increasingly important.

cc:Mail

cc:Mail is one of the most popular third-party LAN electronic mail packages in large companies. cc:Mail uses a friendly interface and paper mail vocabulary that makes it readily intelligible to novices. It operates at each workstation using a 320K workstation RAM to run the full program, and 70K to run the memory resident "pop-up" program. Although messages and routing tables reside at the file server, all mail processing takes place at user workstations.

cc:Mail provides all the electronic mail tools you would expect for composing, answering, and managing mail. One nice feature is that you can include up to twenty items in one message, whereas in some other mail systems you are limited to one file attachment per message. An item can be text, program files, snapshots—almost anything. cc:Mail messages are encrypted and compressed for resource management and security reasons.

cc:Mail provides tools with which (sophisticated) users can build gateways of their own to other systems like CompuServe or MCI Mail. cc:Mail provides gateways to MHS and Telenet's Telemail, either of which can be used as an intermediary for connecting to X.400 systems. cc:Mail does not, at present, provide a direct X.400 gateway.

cc:Mail Remote enables users on stand-alone PCs with modems to check their LAN mail.

cc:Mail Gateway allows you to create Wide Area Networks (WANs) over bridges to other LANs' file servers, or by modem and telephone line to remote LANs, WANs, minis, mainframes, and public access mail systems.

cc:Mail for Macintosh enables Mac users and DOS or OS/2 users to communicate, and it can be used to provide transparent file transference between the two environments. For example, a DOS user and a Mac user can share Excel spreadsheets in this way.

cc:Mail PROFSlink provides a gateway to the IBM PROFS mail system. Links to DEC VAX and Facsimile are promised by mid-1989.

cc:Mail contains a full-featured word processor, including an import utility for translating documents from other word processing packages, and a graphics package with predefined and user-defined symbols.

The cc:Mail TSR allows you to use some cc:Mail features while working in other packages. For example, cc:Mail lets you take "snapshots" of screens in other programs for inclusion in cc:Mail messages. This feature can be used, for example, to forward copies of sales orders or inventories to users on other LANs.

cc:Mail runs on most PC LANs.

cc:Mail is a product of cc:Mail, Inc., 385 Sherman Avenue, Palo Alto, CA 94306, telephone (800) 448-2500.

Da Vinci eMail

Da Vinci Systems' eMail is an easy-to-use electronic mail system that is available in a Microsoft Windows or standard DOS version. The standard version can be run in background mode, using about 100K RAM in a workstation. When running in background, users running DOS applications are notified when mail arrives, and can use all of eMail's features within the other application.

Users can password-encrypt mail, and can send blind cc's (where the TO: recipient does not see that the message is being cc'd to someone else.) Multiple files can be attached to a single message. Messages and file attachments can be sent to other MHS-based programs after the usual administration (adding user names, routings and hub telephone numbers). eMail can exchange mail with other systems via its X.400 and MHS dispatchers.

When installed on a NetWare file server, eMail automatically creates eMail users by reading the user information from the NetWare bindery files.

eMail runs on most PC LANs.

eMail is a product of Da Vinci Systems Corporation, P.O. Box 5427, Raleigh, NC 27650, telephone (919) 839-2000.

Network Courier

Network Courier is available in either a standard DOS or Microsoft Windows version. The DOS version includes a program called Monitor. Monitor runs in background and notifies the user of incoming mail. Monitor also includes an abbreviated version of Network Courier that a user can call up while in an application to read and respond to mail. Network Courier has a friendly, Lotus 1-2-3-like interface and good documentation.

A useful feature is that the sending user is notified when receivers opens their mail, which silences some of the "lost in the mail" excuses that have carried over from paper to electronic mail.

Besides providing alias addressing, so that users don't have to use formal address routings, Network Courier has address search features that can check through file server post offices to locate an address, even based on partial information. Network Courier also provides easy exchange of address lists with other networks.

Network Courier consists of a family of e-mail products. Inter-network Courier, for example, provides gateways from Network Courier to X.400, DEC's All-in-1, IBM's PROFS, and MCI Mail. Using the MCI link, users can connect to any NetBIOS LAN, and using REMS accounts, to CompuServe, HP 3000s, Wang Office, and 3Com 3+ Mail. Users can exchange mail with MCI users to any telex address, and even use MCI's Print Mail hard copy delivery service to get a paper copy of a message to practically anyone.

Because of its X.400 compatibility, Telenet (the data communications division of U.S. Sprint) has certified Network Courier, which means that users can communicate not only with Telenet's public Telemail user base, but can use Telenet to connect with other X.400 systems.

Network Courier runs on most PC LANs.

Network Courier is a product of Consumers Software, 73 Water Street, #603, Vancouver, B.C. V6B 1A1, telephone (604) 688-4548.

RetixMail

RetixMail provides translation services that allow LAN users to transfer messages and files to other LAN users, to other LANs via X.25 to public networks like Telenet, and to mini and mainframe host systems that use the X.400 standard.

RetixMail has also been certified by Telenet, enabling RetixMail users to communicate with Telemail also, and to connect via Telenet to other X.400 systems.

Through Retix's Openserver 400, message and file forwarding can be conducted through a LAN workstation running server software. Up to 100 users are supported, but the software that must run at each workstation requires Microsoft Windows.

RetixMail runs on most PC LANs.

RetixMail is a product of Retix, 2644 30th Street, Santa Monica, CA 90405-3009, telephone (213) 399-2200.

Groupware

Although definitions vary, essentially groupware is software that enables individuals to work together as a group, or software that facilitates meeting group goals.

The Coordinator

The Coordinator, from Action Technologies, is an electronic mail/calendaring package based on the Message Handling System

(MHS) also created by Action Technologies, and widely promoted by Novell.

The Coordinator structures message exchanges by offering context-sensitive response options, depending on the stage of a conversation being conducted via the program. The structure attempts to provide the same flow of conversation that occurs in "live" conversations. If, for example, someone announces completing a project, "thank you" appears as a reply option for the receiving user. If the message makes a request, the reply options are the same as those in a verbal conversation: to accept, decline, make a counteroffer, delegate, defer answering, ask questions, etc. Some users find this structure unnecessarily complex; others find it a useful management tool. Messages can be looked up by calendar (date made and date due), status, and user assigned multiple categories.

Coordinator users can receive and send messages, and attached files of any kind, either transparently to other MHS packages, or by gateway to other e-mail systems.

Users can be assigned workgroup aliases that simplify address and routing administration. When a user is added, the Coordinator automatically creates a corresponding LAN user with appropriate directories and rights.

The Coordinator stores messages unencrypted at the file server, so the administrator has to rely on NetWare directory rights to prevent unauthorized users from looking at other users' mail.

The built-in ASCII word processor makes good use of disk swapping for editing files too big to keep in memory, and for managing the sixteen user files that can be open at one time. The Coordinator is not shy about using resources. It takes 640K RAM to load, about 2 megabytes of disk storage for program files, and about 1 megabyte per user mailbox. There is no TSR pop-up menu, but it allows other programs (like Lotus 1-2-3) to run as program calls from within it.

The Coordinator runs on most PC LANs.

The Coordinator is a product of Action Technologies, 220 Powell Street, Eleventh Floor, Emeryville, CA 94608, telephone (800) 624-2162, Dept. H11.

Higgins

Higgins provides a family of LAN products intended to function as a workgroup's central application. An underlying relational database allows users to organize information across other applications. For example, a user can relate customer spreadsheets, memos, graphics, e-mail messages, invoices, and the like, regardless of which user and application produces each piece.

Modules of the Higgins workgroup software include e-mail, group scheduling, calendaring, telephone messages, expense reports, and to-do lists. Accessories provide tools like calendars, a telephone dialer, and a reminder alarm. The scheduling feature polls users' schedules to find an open time for the meeting, and then proposes that time to users. When the users accept, the meeting is entered in their calendars.

Higgins provides for remote access, and for gateways to FAX, MHS, IBM's PROFS, IBM's SNADS for DISOSS, and 3COM's 3+ Mail. Higgins also provides a Mail API with which a sophisticated developer can build a customized gateway, or an application that uses Higgins as its communications and transportation platform.

Higgins runs on most PC LANs.

Higgins is a product of Enable Software/Higgins Group, 1470 Doolittle Drive, San Leandro, CA 94577, telephone (415) 430-8875.

WordPerfect Office

WordPerfect Office is designed to support a group working on a LAN by providing file, scheduling, and communication tools. For example, a user can query other users' schedules to find mutual free time for a meeting. When a time is scheduled, each user confirms acceptance before the appointment is entered. Then the user can use Office to book resources, like conference rooms or video cameras. Besides the scheduler and basic e-mail, Office provides a calculator, file manager, macro and program editor, and a straightforward notebook database. The database can be used for managing names, addresses, phone numbers, and personal information, like birthdates and family information.

WordPerfect Office runs on most PC LANs.

WordPerfect Office is a product of WordPerfect Corporation, 1555 North Technology Way, Orem, UT 84057, telephone (801) 225-5000.

Office Works

Office Works provides electronic mail, telephone messaging, calendaring and scheduling, a name and address database, and document control. Office Works mail system, which the vendor says will be enhanced to provide X.400 connectivity, currently supports remote mail transmission by Telex, FAX, and the postal system.

Office Works has the ability to swap itself out to disk, leaving only a 7K kernel in RAM. This allows a user to run another program and return to the same place in Office Works.

When installed on a NetWare LAN, Office Works utilizes the NetWare login names and the SEND function for messaging.

Office Works is written in Data Access' DataFlex DBMS, and source code is available to holders of DataFlex development licenses for $15,000.

Office Works runs on most PC LANs.

Office Works is a product of Data Access Corporation, 14000 South West 119th Terrace, Miami, FL 33186, telephone (305) 238-0012.

Menus

Although LAN OS vendors often include menu systems with their software, they are usually lacking in features and flexibility. Novell's menu program is a good example. Two menu systems that are feature-rich are Saber Menu System from Saber Software, and Automenu from Magee Enterprises.

Saber Menu System

Saber Menu System is a very flexible menu system that includes utilities for metering software usage and enhancing security. Saber is designed as a network menu system, and allows conditional branching and execution based on user ID and/or physical station number. When used with Novell NetWare LANs, Saber Menu automatically reads user and station IDs, and with other LANs it uses environment variables. Although Saber uses about 32K of RAM while programs are executing, it provides a batch mode which completely removes it from memory while an application is running.

Saber Menu System is somewhat complex to set up, and the documentation is difficult to follow the first time through. The power of the product, however, easily offsets these flaws.

Saber Menu System is compatible with most PC networks.

Saber Menu System is product of Saber Software, P.O. Box 9088, Dallas, TX 75209, telephone (800) 338-8754.

Automenu

Automenu has been widely distributed as shareware and is also being commercially distributed through dealers. Version 4.5 has added features that make it much easier to use on a network than previous versions.

Although Automenu does not provide all of the capabilities of Saber, it is a very flexible menu system that provides for multiple sub-menus with conditional branching. Automenu uses about 27K of RAM while programs are executing, but like Saber it also provides a batch mode to completely remove itself from memory. Initially, configuring Automenu for effective use on a LAN requires some effort, but the documentation is very clear and concise. Automenu is priced at $50 per server. The shareware version (which you can try before you buy) can be found on CompuServe and most bulletin boards, and the commercial version is available from dealers.

Automenu is compatible with most PC networks.

Automenu is a product of Magee Enterprises Inc., P.O. Box 1587, Norcross, GA 30091, telephone (404) 446-6611.

Print Server and Printer Control Software

There are a number of third-party software packages available to enhance the print service capabilities of NetWare LANs. These packages allow sharing of local printers attached to LAN workstations and/or background printer control.

Printer Assist

Printer Assist (formerly known as Hot Server) allows local printers to be shared. Printer Assist uses the NetWare print queues with all versions of NetWare 2.0 and above.

Because NetWare versions prior to 2.1 did not provide programming "hooks" into the NetWare print queues, Printer Assist uses one of the available NetWare print queues when installed with NetWare version 2.0x. Printer Assist's print servers monitor that queue for print jobs with specific forms numbers. If a print job is placed in the queue with a form number that is recognized by a print server, that server then "grabs" the print job from the queue and prints it. By using multiple form numbers, multiple printers can effectively use the same print queue. When used with NetWare 2.0x, Printer Assist requires that the operating system be patched to allow all users to delete files from print queues.

With NetWare versions 2.1x, Printer Assist uses the NetWare print queues in the standard fashion.

Printer Assist assigns users as print servers, and more than one user can be assigned as a print server for a particular queue. A user defined as a print server must log in to his or her assigned print server workstation and load the print server software. If a user logs off a print server PC while a job is being printed, the job is stopped, rewound, and kept in the queue. When any user designated as a print server logs in to the station running Printer Assist, the job starts printing again from the beginning.

Printer Assist uses about 5K RAM on a print server PC for each shared printer. Since it uses the NetWare queues, it uses no additional RAM on workstations accessing the print server.

Printer Assist is a product of Fresh Technology Group, 55 Hoover Avenue, Suite 9, Mesa, AZ 85210, telephone (602) 827-9971.

PS-Print

PS-Print provides print service on local printers in a non-dedicated (background) mode. PS-Print uses the NetWare 2.1 queueing facilities, and therefore shared local printers function like standard NetWare server-attached printers, retaining all of the 2.1 print queue functionality. In addition, PS-Print includes TSR, or "memory resident," software that allows users to change printers or print job configurations while in an application.

The print server console program, which can optionally be loaded optionally as a TSR, is provided for use on print server PCs. One disadvantage of PS-Print is that since local print queues are logically connected to users instead of physical workstations, users must be logged in to print server workstations in order for the printer server to function for them. This arrangement requires more attention to security, where security is a concern.

PS-Print works with NetWare versions 2.1 and above.

PS-Print is a product of Brightwork Development, P.O. Box 8728, Red Bank, NJ 07701, telephone (800) 552-9876.

LAN Spool

LAN Spool, when implemented in background mode for nondedicated print service, is currently the only print server package that is implemented as a NetWare Value Added Process (VAP). In this mode, LAN Spool runs entirely on a NetWare file server or external bridge, and uses no memory on the print server PC other than that required for the NetWare shell.

LAN Spool uses the NetWare 2.1 print queueing facilities, and local printers function as standard NetWare server-attached printers, retaining all the 2.1 print queue functionality. Users can log in and out of the print server PC without affecting print service. For high-volume printing, or in situations where server resources need to be conserved, LAN Spool can be installed in dedicated mode, running entirely in a dedicated print server PC instead of as a filer server VAP. LAN Spool does not include TSR printer control software for users, nor does it include a print server console program for use in background mode. In addition, the background version ignores the Forms switch of the NetWare PConsole and Capture utilities.

LAN Spool works with NetWare versions 2.1 and above.

LAN Spool is a product of LAN Systems, Inc., 599 Broadway, New York, NY 10012, telephone (212) 431-1255.

File Server Management

File server management utilities provide tools for managing server resources, including monitoring security and disk space, file and directory manipulation, user management, and archiving.

XTreeNet

XTreeNet is the LAN version of the popular XTreePro file manager for PCs. XTreeNet provides menu-driven file and directory management, including the ability to mark multiple files (in multiple directories) for file operations. XTreeNet performs file operations, including DOS commands, but also some commands not available in DOS such as Move, which can only be accomplished in DOS by a two-step copy/delete operation. Other non-DOS commands in XTreeNet include renaming directories, and copying directory and subdirectories with a single command. XTreeNet conforms to NetWare security defined in SYSCON and FILER, but lets a system supervisor restrict access even further. XTreeNet includes a WordStar-like file editor with onscreen; control-key help and pull-down menus.

XTreeNet is compatible with NetWare 2.0a or later.

XTreeNet is a product of XTree Company, a division of Executive Systems, Inc., 4330 Santa Fe Road, San Luis Obispo, CA 93401, telephone (805) 541-0604.

NetBack

Netback is a flexible server information and file archive utility that backs up both DOS and Macintosh files on a NetWare file server. Netback features include:

Creating Vaultfiles. NetBack allows you to archive file server bindery information so that the file server's directory and group/user structure can be reconstructed quickly. This feature can also be used to construct a duplicate of the file server structure on a second server, which can save you from entering group, user, and other server information on the second server by hand.

Archiving and Packing Files and Directories. NetBack allows you to copy or backup complete directory structures, including all files and subdirectories. In addition, NetBack allows you to pack a directory structure into compressed file. NetBack will archive and restore and/or pack and unpack both DOS and Macintosh files.

Netback provides reports about file server users, groups, security equivalences, trustee assignments, and disk usage.

Netback is compatible with NetWare 2.0 or later (2.15 or later for Macintosh file compatibility).

NetBack is a product of Cheyenne Software, Inc., 55 Bryant Avenue, Roslyn, NY 11576, telephone (800) 243-9462.

Network Management Report Utilities

Network Management Report Utilities provide information about NetWare file server usage, especially with respect to user and group usage of files, directories, and disk space. Although much of the information is available from NetWare utilities such as FConsole and Syscon, NetWare makes no provision for creating a database of statistics for historical reporting.

Most of these reports can be run for all of a given resource (such as a directory or user), or for a portion of the resource. The program prints reports to files using its own naming convention. Generated reports can also be viewed on the screen at the user's discretion.

The reports include:

- NDISK, which reports disk space usage by subdirectory.
- NFILE, which reports detailed information about files in one or more subdirectories including file size, attributes, owner, last access, last update, and creation date.
- NUSER, which reports about selected users, including trustee rights, security equivalences, and group membership.
- NDIR, which reports about users and their rights in subdirectories of the selected volume.
- NSET, which prints user login scripts.
- NSECU, which reports the security parameters set for each user, including account and password expiration, password expiration interval, grace logins, and the like.
- NAUDIT, which reports on user usage of server resources during specified periods.

Network Management Report Utilities is compatible with NetWare 2.0a and above.

Network Management Report Utilities is a product of J.A. Lomax Associates, 695 DeLong Avenue, Suite 130, Novato, CA 94945, telephone (415) 892-9606.

ANET NetWork Utilities

Like the Lomax utilities (above), ANET also reports about file server disk space, and user and group statistics. ANET supports NetWare's security provisions; if you are not the SUPERVISOR you will not be allowed to run certain restricted reports. The reports include:

- NETRPT, which reports disk usage by user, and security information about users and groups.

- USAGE, which reports disk space usage across volumes for a given user. USAGE can be run by each user to monitor his own disk usage, or by the Supervisor to monitor all users' disk usage.

- PRTCHK, which reports about network printers, including status, forms mounted, rerouting, jobs waiting, and the like.

- SCRIPT, which produces a listing of user login scripts.

- LASTACS, which reports on the last date each directory was accessed (when a file was actually opened).

- OLDFILES, which reports, by subdirectory, a count and detail about all files that have not been accessed since a given date, their location, disk usage, and owner. This is particularly useful when disk space becomes critical and files must be archived and deleted from the server.

Two additional utilities can be used to overcome the shortcomings of many archive programs.

DATESAVE records the access dates of all files. This is usually used before an archive and saved with the archive. Should a restore be necessary, DATEREST will restore the access dates that most archive/restore programs overwrite.

ANET is compatible with Advanced or SFT NetWare.

ANET NetWork Utilities is a product of Brightwork Development, P.O. Box 8728, Red Bank, NJ 07701, telephone (201) 530-0440.

Document Managers

Document managers provide tools for keeping track of all shared files in one structure, regardless of the applications in which they are created. Document managers help organize files so that they can be located by different criteria (such as by author, date created, keyword, etc.)

Workgroup

Workgroup (called LANscape in previous versions) is primarily a tool for managing files (called documents) so that they are easy to locate. When you want to create or retrieve a document, you enter the required information into Workgroup and it will create/retrieve the document and call your application program (word processor, spreadsheet, etc.). Workgroup can assign descriptive titles, keywords, and other identifying information to a file. You can locate documents by scrolling descriptive titles, by full or partial keywords, and by other search criteria. Other search criteria includes Author ID, document type, disk location, DOS file name, application program, department, recipient, and date created, archived, and last updated. Workgroup contains an import facility for adding documents to its catalogues that were either created before Workgroup was installed or that are being brought in from other systems.

Workgroup is compatible with Novell Advanced or SFT NetWare, 3Com 3+ 1.1 or greater, 10NET 3.1 or greater, or AT&T Starlan Network Program 1.1 or greater.

Workgroup is a product of Ncompass Software Inc., 270 Lafayette Street, Suite 702, New York, NY 10012, telephone (212) 431-9572

Document Manager

Document Manager is a menu-driven document management utility that indexes the entire document for retrieval by almost any criteria.

Document Manager tracks by author, date range, title, subject, document class, as well as by free-text search criteria defined by the user. Text searches will find all files containing a word, but can also find files in which a given word does not occur. For example, "*communication* NOT *data* NOT *voice*" would find documents in which the word communication occurs, but in which neither the word data nor voice occur. Wildcard searches are permitted and the boolean evaluators AND, NOT, and OR are supported. Document Manager will also search for documents in which words occur in a certain proximity to one another. For example, you could ask for "*data w/4 communication*," which will create a list of documents in which the word "communication" occurs within 4 words of the word "data."

Document Manager provides various tools to aid in file housekeeping. For example, it lets you assign expiration dates to files. When documents expire they are marked for deletion and appear in a different graphic on the screen. They appear on a list of files marked for deletion, but are not actually deleted until a delete instruction is issued. When files are being deleted, the system offers to archive them first. Archived file profiles are maintained in the search indexes, so that archived files can still be located during searches. Up to four billion documents can be managed on one server.

Document Manager is compatible with most major PC LANs.

Document Manager is a product of Persona, Unit 1, Silverglade Business Park, Leatherhead Road, Chessington, Surrey, England KT9 2NQ, telephone 44 1 272 9611

Reference Point

Reference Point uses library concepts and terminology in providing document management services to users. Reference Point provides a main menu that is the user's interface to the network. From its Main Library, the user can search for and select ("check out") documents. Documents checked out by one user are unavailable to other users. Users can be required to check all documents back in before they exit Reference Point. When a document is checked out by a user, Reference Point automatically runs the application program with which the document was written. Reference Point can load the document into the application automatically. The application can be word processing, spreadsheet, database, or any other LAN application.

Reference Point organizes documents into "projects" and "subprojects," which correspond to directories and subdirectories on the file server hard disk. Existing documents can quickly be organized into the Reference Point library catalogues by using the Create Project command to create appropriate directories, then copying existing files into the Projects (directories), and running a Reference Point option called "synchronize." Basic file information will be recorded, and catalogue cards generated.

Reference Point provides a strong structure for file organization, but with less search flexibility than the other document managers profiled here.

Reference Point is compatible with NetWare, 3Com 3+, 3Com 3+ Open, IBM PC Network, Banyan's VINES, and Microsoft LAN Manager, and will work across multiple file servers.

Reference Point is a product of LAN Systems, Inc., 599 Broadway, New York, NY 10012, telephone (212) 431-1255.

Remote Access Utilities

One of the easiest, least complicated, and often least expensive ways to access a LAN from a remote site is to use a remote control software package designed for remote support of PC users.

Carbon Copy Plus

Carbon Copy Plus is a PC-to-PC remote control package that includes the terminal emulation, file transfer, and other capabilities found in standard communications packages.

Carbon Copy Plus provides remote access, where one PC can "take over" the other, so that keystrokes at the "remote" PC are translated into keystrokes at the "host" PC. The remote PC monitor mirrors the host monitor, so that the remote user can run programs and use the local resources of the host PC.

If the host PC is a LAN workstation, a remote user can log in to that workstation and function as a LAN user. Carbon Copy Plus can be loaded onto dedicated workstations, set aside for remote communications, or loaded on users' workstations when they leave the office, allowing evening and weekend access to the LAN.

Carbon Copy Plus provides an auto reboot option that automatically reboots the host computer after a disconnection. This can be used to prevent unauthorized users from accessing the network if a remote user forgets to log out.

In addition to its remote access capabilities, Carbon Copy Plus can function as a standard communications package for accessing bulletin boards, on-line databases, etc.

Two copies of Carbon Copy Plus are required for each remote connection, one at the host end and one at the remote end. Carbon Copy Plus requires about 50K RAM at the host computer.

Carbon Copy Plus is a product of Microcom Software Division, 41 Kenosia Avenue, Danbury, CT 06810, telephone (203) 798-3800.

Close-Up

Close-Up, like Carbon Copy, is a PC-to-PC remote control package that includes the terminal emulation, file transfer, and other capabilities found in standard communications packages.

Close-Up is comprised of two packages: Close-Up Customer/Terminal, and Close-Up Support/ACS (Automated Communications System). Customer/Terminal runs on the machine where the applications programs are run (a LAN workstation, for example), while Support/ACS runs on the remote PC.

The Customer side of Customer/Terminal allows the remote user to control the PC keyboard and see the PC screen, while the Terminal side allows access to bulletin boards, on-line databases, etc. Both functions run in background.

The Support side of Support/ACS allows you to access a PC running the Customer side of Customer/Terminal, while the ACS side allows you to automate communications tasks, such as operating a remote computer, transferring files, etc., in an unattended mode. ACS runs as a background task.

The features of Close-Up include:

- The ability to disable the screen and keyboard of the Customer station from the Support station.
- The ability to record and playback support sessions and create a support library.
- The ability to keep a transaction log for time and billing purposes.

Close-Up is a product of Norton-Lambert Corp., P.O. Box 4085, Santa Barbara, CA 93140, telephone (805) 964-6767.

LAN User Support

LAN user support programs allow one LAN user to assist another user across the LAN.

Close-Up/LAN

Close-Up/LAN enables LAN users to monitor and control other users' stations on the network. Close-Up/LAN can be used for providing instant support to other workstations (in the next room or on the next floor) without having to leave the support desk. Close-Up/LAN is also used to train users, either one at a time, or in a class setting. In a Close-Up/LAN support session, the keystrokes you make at your workstation execute at the remote workstation as if you were typing there. Your screen display mirrors the display at the remote. You can converse with the remote user you are supporting in windows that do not interfere with whatever application is running on the remote workstation. LAN users can use Close-Up/LAN to run a communication program on another workstation (where a modem is installed), turning the workstation into a communication server for the entire LAN.

Close-Up/LAN runs as a TSR on your workstation, requiring about 50K RAM on the host station, and about 80K on the viewer station. You can connect to another workstation to provide support, and then toggle between the remote workstation and your own workstation. This lets you check in with the remote station intermittently with a minimum of keystrokes. Close-Up/LAN is compatible with NetWare 2.0a and above, and most NetBIOS-based LANs.

Close-Up/LAN is a product of Norton-Lambert Corp., P.O. Box 4085, Santa Barbara, CA 93140, telephone (805) 964-6767.

LAN Assist Plus

Like Close-Up/LAN, LAN Assist Plus enables LAN users to monitor and control other stations on the network. With LAN Assist Plus you can view any station on the LAN (and across bridged servers to other LANs). You can support stations on remote networks by using LAN Assist Plus in conjunction with one of the available remote access software packages and appropriate dial-up equipment.

Keystrokes you make at your keyboard are acted upon as if you were typing on the remote workstation's keyboard. Your monitor mirrors the remote monitor. You see what is happening there and can take action to diagnose and correct problems. While you are working, the remote user is seeing what you do, so that your actions become a training session. LAN Assist Plus provides a two-way "chatter box" in which you and the remote user can ask and answer questions. You can disable the remote workstation's keyboard to prevent the local user from taking action, and you can prevent the local user from rebooting during a LAN Assist Plus session.

In order for a remote station to be accessed, it must have resident a small kernel of software that enables it to communicate with other workstations. This kernel varies from 3K to about 7K, depending on which LAN Assist Plus features are being used. Security parameters (such as requiring a password for the calling workstation) are set at the local workstation. LAN Assist Plus is compatible with NetWare 2.0a and above.

LAN Assist Plus is a product of Fresh Technology Group, 55 West Hoover Avenue, Suite 9, Mesa, AZ 85210, telephone (602) 827-9971.

NETmanager

NETmanager is a utility for controlling PC workstations remotely. The remote workstation must run a kernel called NRLISTEN, which takes from 9K to 31K of workstation RAM. The workstation that takes over remote workstations (called the Help Desk) must run a program called NETMAN, which requires 250K RAM.

The remote workstation can be configured to require a password of the Help Desk, but a second system password can also be set that overrides the local password requirement. When you run NETMAN, the user workstations that display (for you to take over) are those on the primary server you are logged in to. On a multiple server network, you can select to browse through other servers and select a workstation from one of them.

One of NETmanager's strongest features is its dBASE III-compatible database for logging support calls for later diagnosis or billing. NETmanager records much of the log information automatically, including the user name, user address, date, time, and call duration. Detail and summary log reports are provided, and you can develop additional reports if you have a copy of dBASE III.

NETmanager is compatible with Novell NetWare and most NetBIOS-based LANs.

NETmanager is a product of Brightwork Development, P.O. Box 8728, Red Bank, New Jersey 07701, telephone (800) 552-9876.

Application Usage Metering and Control

Application metering programs allow a LAN administrator to control the number of concurrent users who have access to a given program or file for the sake of ensuring compliance with licensing agreements

Sitelock

Sitelock provides tools for limiting the number of users that can access a particular application simultaneously. The user limit can be set anywhere between zero and 255 for each application, and up to sixty application limits can be set. Sitelock contains various tools for viewing, modifying, and printing application access statistics.

Sitelock is compatible with SFT and Advanced NetWare 1.0 and later.

Sitelock is produced by Brightwork Development, P.O. Box 8728, Red Bank, New Jersey 07701, telephone (800) 552-9876.

Saber Meter

Saber Meter monitors and lets you set limits to user access to applications. Users who attempt to access a metered application or file after the limit has been reached can obtain a list of current users so that they can make arrangements with them to access the application. Saber Meter creates and maintains a dBASE III database of user access to applications, including date/time in and out, and minutes used. The database can be viewed with the dBASE Browse command, and usage statistics reports and graphs are available.

Saber Meter works with Novell NetWare, Banyan Vines, 3Com 3+, CBIS Network OS, POWERlan, IBM LAN Program, and MS-Net compatible LANs.

Saber Meter is a product of Saber Software, PO Box 9088, Dallas, TX 75209, telephone (800) 338-8754.

Resource Sharing

These utilities enable and help manage the sharing of non-file server resources.

Map Assist

Map Assist lets a user workstation make its local drives available to other workstations on the LAN. A 6K kernel running in the workstation's memory designates which local drives, volumes, or directories to share, and which users or groups should be allowed access. The workstation sharing its resources is the host workstation. Other workstations on the LAN load a program from the file server which "maps" the host's local drive as a drive letter on the user's NetWare map. The degree of access other users have to the local drive can be limited by file attributes such as read/write or read/only, and access can be unlimited or limited to one outside user at a time.

Map Assist requires NetWare 2.0a or later.

Map Assist is a product of Fresh Technology Group, 55 West Hoover Avenue, Suite 9, Mesa, AZ 85210, telephone (602) 827-9971.

PS-Batch

PS-Batch enables you to send batch processes off to other LAN stations to be processed, freeing up your workstation for other tasks. One of the uses for a batch file is to automate certain kinds of tasks so that user intervention is not required. (Although DOS batch files do let you automate tasks, you still lose the use of your workstation while the batched tasks are being processed.) Since PS-Batch sends the batched tasks to another PC's processor, your workstation is freed up to do other things. Batch processing can be used for:

- Off-loading time-consuming tasks, such as database reports and program compiles to other stations.

- Creating specialized servers, such as plotter servers and backup servers.

PS-Batch offers a number of options, including named batch-server types, priority queueing, log files, and jobs repeated on a daily basis. Jobs can be "tagged" to wait for the completion of other jobs before executing. PS-Batch also provides queue management facilities.

PS-Batch uses about 42K of RAM in the batch server, and there is no RAM-resident software required at the user workstation. PS-Batch requires NetWare version 2.0a or later, and is licensed for a single file server. There is no limitation on the number of users or batch servers (within the limitations of NetWare, of course).

PS-Batch is a product of Brightwork Development, P.O. Box 8728, Red Bank, NJ 07701, telephone (800) 552-9876.

Network Statistics Monitoring Utilities

Network technical statistics utilities monitor and report on various network events and processes. For the most part, the utilities profiled here report the same statistics, varying in the level of detail, the degree of history available, and the availability and ease of reporting.

NetWare Care

NetWare Care is Novell's utility for managing and diagnosing network operations. When NetWare Care is invoked it displays a map of the network which distinguishes workstations, dedicated and nondedicated file servers and bridges, file servers with VAPs, and S-Net file servers (among other devices). The map can be updated with current users logged in at workstations and file server names at file servers. Among the reports available are:

Show Network Traffic. Provides statistics about network traffic in terms of the number of packets transmitted and received by each current node.

Node Information: Provides statistics and other information about particular nodes, including:

- IPX version, maximum number of IPX sockets allowed open simultaneously, SPX version, and the maximum number of SPX connections supported simultaneously.

- The NetWare shell version, OS name (e.g., MS-DOS), OS version (e.g., v3.10), hardware type (e.g., IBM_PC), and the server name to which the workstation is attached.

- The LAN driver version, description (e.g., NetWare Ethernet NE-1000), the IRQ, I/O base, DMA, ROM addresses, and other driver configuration parameters.

- A graph display of submitted malformed packets, transmit route failures, and IPX Socket Utilization.

- Graphs of shell-related errors, such as server response timeout, server write errors, and corrupt packets received.

- A graph of shell driver-related errors, such as receive packet overflows, receive checksum errors, transmit packets too big, transmit packets too small, and transmit collisions.

NetWare Care will perform a point-to-point test between any two network nodes, including across file servers and bridges. The test will send a given number of packets, and will graph transmission errors and the percent packets not received by the destination point.

File server statistics include reports and graphs about physical write requests and cache buffer hits and misses. Included in this report, for example, is the percent of Disk Requests Serviced from Cache. If this number falls below 70%, Novell recommends increasing file server RAM.

LAN I/O statistics monitor packet traffic and packets lost for various reasons.

Many of the file server statistics are the same as those maintained by NetWare's FCONSOLE utility. Unlike FCONSOLE, however, NetWare Care statistics can be recorded in a history file. To maintain a complete history of the network, the history file can be updated before each downing of the server.

The NetWare Care manual is one of the few LAN tools that provide specific ballpark recommendations for managing network resources from the statistics provided, including possible causes of trouble and possible solutions. This alone makes it an invaluable tool for the network manager looking for a place to start in managing and diagnosing network errors. NetWare Care is compatible with NetWare 2.1 or later.

NetWare Care is a product of Novell, Inc., 122 East, 1700 South, Provo, UT 84601, telephone (800) 453-1267.

NWRANGER

NWRANGER reports many of the same workstation, file server, and bridge statistics as NetWare Care, except that NWRANGER monitors LAN traffic at an even greater level of detail than NetWare Care does. For example, NWRANGER reports on IPX SPX socket failures, ECB requests and failures, and AES events. It includes batch files that define limits of normal operation. It will scan the network, reporting statistics that overstep the boundaries. Boundaries can be adjusted by the user arbitrarily according to actual scanned traffic behavior.

NWRANGER does not provide reporting or graphs, nor does it provide for a historical database. NWRANGER is designed for the more technical users and support personnel. The documentation is minimal, and no recommendations are provided, since the intended audience is assumed to be familiar with the nature and meaning of the statistics provided. NWRANGER is compatible with NetWare 2.1 or later.

NWRANGER is a product of SARBEC, 12326 Deerbrook Trail, Austin, TX 78750, telephone (512) 331-0966.

Monitrix

Monitrix is unique among network statistics packages in that it runs as a Value Added Process (VAP) on the file server or bridge, which allows it to monitor the network constantly, as opposed to the current snapshots to which NetWare Care and NWRANGER are limited. Monitrix maintains a historical database on which reports can be run, and exports files in dBASE format for customized reporting.

The statistics that Monitrix monitors are much the same as those monitored by NetWare Care. The level of detail lies between NetWare Care and NWRANGER.

Besides its VAP mode, Monitrix can be run in real-time mode, like NetWare Care and NWRANGER, where it scans and reports on current network activities. Monitrix is compatible with NetWare 2.1 or later.

Monitrix is a product of Cheyenne Software, Inc., 55 Bryant Avenue, Roslyn, NY 11576, telephone (800) 243-9462.

Appendix C

NetWare for Macintosh

Novell's NetWare for Macintosh allows Apple Macintosh users to access a NetWare file server on an AppleTalk network using Appleshare, Apple's networking software for the Mac. This means that the NetWare file server looks like an AppleShare server to Macintosh users.

AppleTalk is the term used for the hardware and software that make up the Apple network. AppleShare refers to the software used by a Mac workstation to communicate on an AppleTalk network. File servers on an AppleTalk network are called AppleShare servers.

NetWare provides additional functions to Mac users that an AppleTalk file server does not provide, including:

- NetWare's high-level security.
- File sharing between PCs and Macs (with applications that allow it).
- Print spooling for AppleTalk printers. Mac users and PC users can access Apple LaserWriter and other Postscript printers attached to a LocalTalk LAN through the NetWare print queues. (See LocalTalk below.)

Currently NetWare for Macintosh supports two LAN transports (NICs) in a NetWare file server: a Novell-supplied LocalTalk card and a 3Com 3C505 (Ver. 2012) Ethernet board.

LocalTalk

LocalTalk is the Macintosh's native LAN hardware. The Mac printer port is used as the LocalTalk connector, and its data transfer rate is a relatively slow .234 Mbits/sec. Although LocalTalk was designed to use Shielded, Twisted-Pair cable, the use of Unshielded Twisted-Pair (UTP) phone cable is common. UTP requires adapters, such as the PhoneNET adapters from Farallon Computing, Inc. UTP adapters allow LocalTalk to be cabled in a daisy-chain, trunk, or star topology.

Farallon's PhoneNET Connector User's Guide provides excellent instructions for cabling LocalTalk with UTP.

Ethernet

The .234 Mbits/sec. transfer rate of LocalTalk is adequate for occasional file transfers and printer sharing, but can often prove inadequate for remote program loading and transaction-oriented LAN applications. The 10 Mbits/sec. transfer rate of Ethernet usually proves to be a more effective, if more costly, solution.

Macs can be connected to an Ethernet network in several ways:

- Internal Ethernet NICS for the Mac II and Mac SE. These are available from Apple, 3Com, and Kinetics.

- Ethernet Adapters that attach to the SCSI disk drive port on the Mac. SCSI/Ethernet adapters are currently supplied by Kinetics and Adaptec. This method is generally used when no expansion slot is available for an internal Ethernet NIC in the file server.

- Bridging LocalTalk to Ethernet using a bridge such as the Kinetics FastPath bridge. This method limits the data transfer rate to LocalTalk's .234 Mbits/sec.

Both PCs and Macs can reside on the same Ethernet cable and can communicate with the NetWare file server through the same Ethernet NIC.

Print spooling to an Apple printer is currently supported only on LocalTalk, not on Ethernet.

Value-Added Processes (VAPs)

A Value-Added Process is an application that runs in a NetWare file server or external NetWare bridge. A VAP runs on top of NetWare much like a word processor or spreadsheet runs on top of DOS. A VAP will allow a non-NetWare function to be linked into the operating system.

NetWare for Macintosh is a group of VAPs that connect the AppleTalk network to NetWare:

- The LAN Driver VAP implements the drivers that support the AppleTalk media (LocalTalk or EtherTalk).

- The File Services VAP translates the Apple File Protocols (AFP) to NetWare's native NetWare Core Protocols (NCP). Novell calls this translation function a Service Protocol Gateway (SPG).

- The Print Service VAP allows a file server or bridge to become a gateway to an Apple printer, giving PC users, as well as Mac users, access.

- The Queue Service VAP allows PCs and Macs to use the NetWare print queues with an Apple printer. The Queue Service VAP creates a an AppleTalk queue server that emulates an Apple printer. Print jobs are sent to the queue server, then sent to a NetWare print queue. The print jobs are then spooled to the Apple printer on the AppleTalk network. Currently, NetWare for Macintosh requires that Apple printers be connected to a NetWare file server or external bridge using LocalTalk hardware.

Clients, Targets, and Hosts

The NetWare for Macintosh VAPS, and in particular the Service Protocol Gateway (SPG), use Clients, Targets, and Hosts:

- Clients are any workstations or printers on a non-NetWare network that access NetWare services through an SPG. In NetWare for Macintosh AppleTalk workstations (Macs) and Apple printers are clients, even when the Macs are on the same physical network as PCs.

- A Host is a NetWare file server or bridge on which some or all of the NetWare for Macintosh VAPs are running.

- A Target is a NetWare file server that provides services to an SPG even if the SPG is not directly attached to that file server. For example, the NetWare for Macintosh VAPs could be installed on a NetWare Bridge (Host), but use the file and print services of a NetWare file server (Target).

Requirements

Note: NetWare for Macintosh can be installed on either a NetWare file server or on an external bridge. For clarity, the instructions here will refer to file server installations. Please refer to Novell's documentation for bridge installation instructions.

To install NetWare for Macintosh on a file server you will need:

- A NetWare-compatible 286 or 386 file server PC
- One or more PC workstations
- One or more Macintosh workstations. The following are supported:

  Macintosh II
  Macintosh SE
  Macintosh Plus
  Macintosh 512K Enhanced (not supported on Ethernet)

- LocalTalk or Ethernet network. If you plan to use Ethernet, you will also need appropriate network interfaces for the Mac workstations.
- AppleTalk NIC for the file server. If you are using LocalTalk, you need a Novell NL-1000 card. If you are using Ethernet, you need a 3Com 3C505 card, version 2012.
- NetWare version 2.15 or above.
- NetWare for Macintosh software, including VAPs, installation and support software, and Mac workstation software.

File Server Installation Overview

The NetWare for Macintosh software and hardware can be installed as part of an initial NetWare file server installation, or can be installed on an existing file server.

Listed below is a summary of the steps you will take to install NetWare for Macintosh. Each step is discussed in detail in the sections that follow.

- Use NetGen to install the AppleTalk LAN driver into NetWare.
- Use NetGen to install the (re)configured NetWare OS on your file server.
- Use MACINST and MACSETUP to install and configure the VAP files.
- Create a startup disk for each Macintosh workstation. This includes installing or updating the following files:

  System
  Finder
  Chooser
  AppleShare

  If your Mac has only 512KB RAM, you may not want to use the latest system files. NetWare works with System V4.2 and above.
- Install the NetWare Desk Accessory on each startup disk.
- Create Macintosh users and groups
- Create folders for Mac applications and files.
- Install the NetWare Control Center on the file server.

Installing the AppleTalk LAN Driver on an Existing File Server

In order to install the AppleTalk LAN driver on an existing file server, you will have to reconfigure and reinstall the NetWare operating system.

If you used the Hard Disk run option when you originally configured your NetWare OS, and you have retained your NetGen directories and files, your job is easy. Do the following:

Review *Chapter 8—Configuring the NetWare Operating System.*

Locate your working copies of NetGen diskettes (GENDATA, SUPPORT, NETGEN, UTILEXE-1 and -2, and OSEXE-1 and -2). Also, locate the disk labeled LAN_DRV_180 that came with NetWare for Macintosh.

Go to your hard disk. Type:

MD \GENERATE\NETWARE\LAN_DRV_.180

to create a subdirectory for your AppleTalk LAN drivers. Copy the contents of the LAN_DRV_180 diskette into this subdirectory.

Go to the \GENERATE\NETWARE directory on your hard disk and type NETGEN. Select the Hard Disk run option, then select the "Custom Configuration" option. To make your changes, follow the instructions in the "Using the Custom Configuration Method" section of Chapter 8. To load the AppleTalk drivers, select the "Load and Select Item" option in the LAN Driver Options

The following message should display:

```
The "NetWare NL1000 & NL/2 (AppleTalk)" file was read
successfully.
Press ESCAPE to continue.

The "3Com 3C505 EtherLink Plus With AppleTalk" file was
read successfully.
Press ESCAPE to continue.
```

Then follow the instructions to "Select Loaded Item."

Note: If you are using the 3Com 3C505 board, make sure that you select the driver "3Com 3C505 EtherLink Plus With AppleTalk."

When you are through with the NetWare Configuration, go to Performing the Upgrade in Appendix E—Modifying and Upgrading the NetWare Operating System.

If you used the Floppy Disk run option when you originally configured NetWare, or you have deleted the files from your hard disk, see "Reconfiguring the NetWare Operating System" in Appendix E—Modifying and Upgrading the NetWare Operating System. Make sure you have a working copy of the LAN_DRV_180 disk that came with NetWare for Macintosh, then do the following:

- Review *Chapter 8—Configuring the NetWare Operating System.*

- Locate your working copies of NetGen diskettes (GENDATA, SUPPORT, NETGEN, UTILEXE-1 and -2, OSEXE-1 and -2 and AUXGEN). You will also need your other NetWare diskettes, preferably copies, not originals.

- Go to Changing the Network Configuration in the Novell SFT/Advanced NetWare 286 Maintenance Manual and follow the instructions there. Be prepared for a lot of disk swapping.

- When you are through with the NetWare Configuration go to Performing the Upgrade in Appendix E—Modifying and Upgrading the NetWare Operating System.

Installing the AppleTalk LAN Driver as Part of an Initial NetWare Installation

If you are installing NetWare for Macintosh as part of an initial installation, you should follow the instructions in *Chapter 8—Configuring the NetWare Operating System* and *Chapter 11—Installing NetWare.*

We recommend that you use the Hard Disk Run Option (described in Chapter 8). If you do, during the process of installing the NetWare configuration files on your hard disk, you will be prompted with:

```
Upload Additional Diskettes?
```

Insert the disk labeled LAN_DRV_180 into your drive A, then select "Yes."

When you are at the point of selecting your LAN drivers, select the "Load and Select Item" option in the LAN Driver Options menu. The following messages will be displayed:

> The "NetWare NL1000 & NL/2 (AppleTalk)" file was read successfully.
> Press ESCAPE to continue.

The "3Com 3C505 EtherLink Plus With AppleTalk" file was read successfully.
Press ESCAPE to continue.

Then follow the instructions to "Select Loaded Item."

Note: If you are using the 3Com 3C505 board, make sure that you select the driver "3Com 3C505 EtherLink Plus With AppleTalk."

When you are through with the NetWare configuration, proceed to *Chapter 9—Generating Workstation Shells* (for DOS workstations), and *Chapter 11—Installing NetWare*. After you have installed the NetWare OS on your file server you can continue with the NetWare for Macintosh installation.

Installing and configuring the NetWare for Macintosh VAP Files

To install the NetWare for Macintosh VAPs on your file server do the following:

- Log in as Supervisor. Insert the MACINST disk in drive A (the GATEWAY disk if you have 3 1/2" drives) and type:

  ```
  A:MACINST <Enter>
  ```

  This copies the MACSETUP files to your SYS:PUBLIC directory.

- While logged to a network drive type:

  ```
  MACSETUP <Enter>
  ```

The following screen will appear:

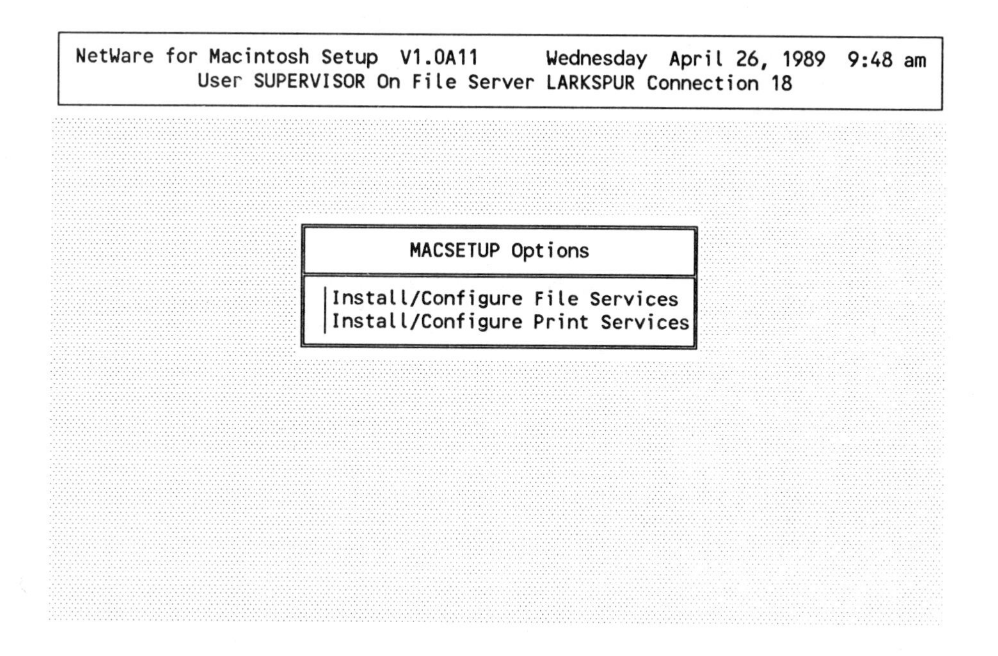

Select Install/Configure File Services.

```
File Services Options
Prepare a Target File Server
Prepare a File Service Gateway
```

Select "Prepare a Target File Server." A target file server is any file server that will be accessible to Macintosh users.

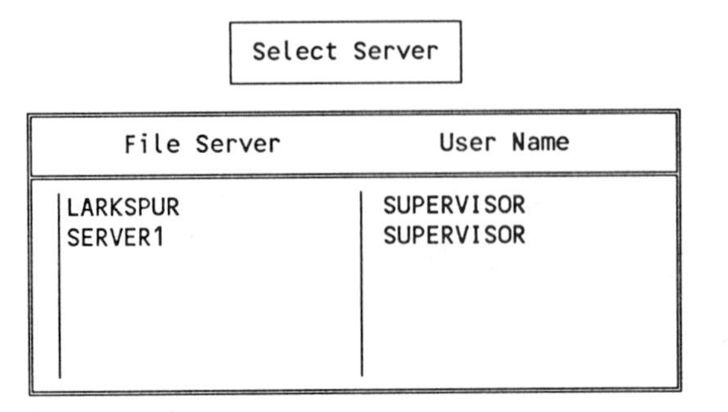

A list of the file servers to which you are currently logged in will be displayed. (To list file servers that you are not logged in to press <Ins>.) Select the file server that you are specifying as a Target Server. If you are not logged in to that file server you will be prompted for your user-name and password if needed. You must log in as Supervisor or a user with Supervisor equivalence. If you are using 5-1/4" disks, you will be prompted to put the GATEWAY diskette in drive A (unless it is already in drive A). After you put the GATEWAY disk in drive A and press <Enter> (if necessary), a message will be displayed telling you that the file server has been successfully prepared. Repeat this process for all file servers that you wish to specify as Target File Servers.

MACSETUP creates a hidden subdirectory called "DESKTOP" in the root directory of each volume on your file server. This directory contains files required by Macintosh users. Macsetup grants rights to the DESKTOP directories to the group EVERYONE.

```
Fil  Host Type     ons
Prepar              Server
Prepar File Server e Gateway
       Bridge
```

Select "Prepare a File Service Gateway." A File Service Gateway is a Host file server or bridge where the file service VAPs reside. A File Service Gateway must have the appropriate NetWare for Macintosh LAN drivers installed on it.

You will be prompted as to whether the Host is a file server or a bridge. Since you are installing on a file server, select that.

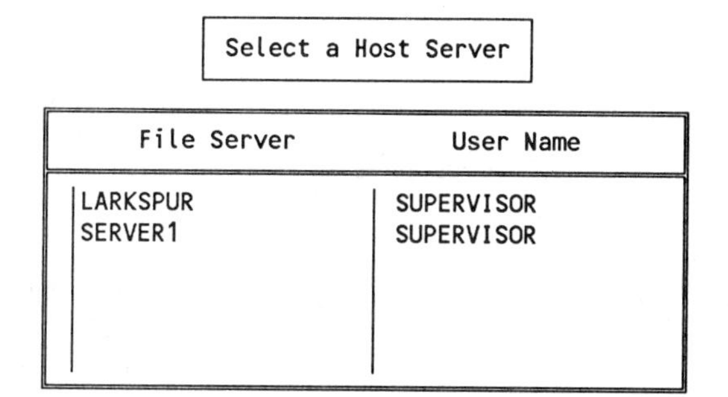

A list of file servers to which you are attached will display. (Press <Ins> to display file servers to which you are not attached.) Select the file server that you wish to use as the File Service Gateway. You will be prompted to insert the LAN_DRV_180 diskette in drive A, followed by the GATEWAY diskette.

```
Current Targets
LARKSPUR

Host Options
te Gateway Software
ct Target File Servers
```

A list of "Current Targets" will be displayed. This is a list of Target Servers (which you defined earlier) to which you are currently logged in. This list should contain all file servers, including this File Service Gateway, which Macintosh users connected to this gateway will be able to access. (Press <Ins> for a list of Target Servers to which you are not logged in.) Press <Esc> until you return to the "Macsetup Options" menu.

MACSETUP has installed the file service VAP files in SYS:SYSTEM on the File Service Gateway.

If you are not installing print services for Apple printers, Press <Esc> to exit MACSETUP. Otherwise continue.

Installing and Configuring AppleTalk Print Services

```
Print Services Options
---------------------------
Prepare AppleTalk Print Queues
Prepare Print Service Gateway
```

Macintosh and PC users can use NetWare print queues to access printers on a LocalTalk network. This requires the installation of a Print Service Gateway and the creation of one or more AppleTalk print queues.

Select "Install/Configure Print Services" from the MACSETUP Options menu, then select "Prepare AppleTalk Print Queues."

Select Server

File Server	User Name
LARKSPUR	SUPERVISOR
SERVER1	SUPERVISOR

A list of the file servers to which you are attached will be displayed. (Press <Ins> to display the file servers to which you are not logged in.) Select the file server on which you wish to create AppleTalk print queue(s). To keep network traffic to a minimum, this would usually be the File Service Gateway file server, but it does not have to be. Highlight "Prepare AppleTalk Print Queues" and press ENTER.
This option allows you to create print queues on a specified target file server.

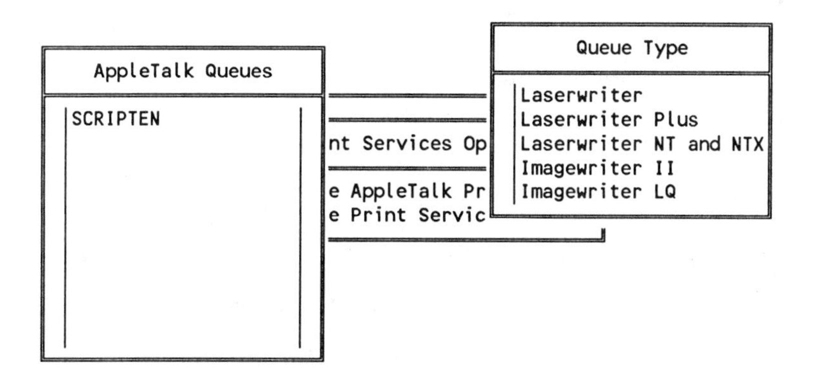

You will be prompted for a Queue name. Queue names must be different from Apple printer names. Once you create a queue name, a list of queue types will be displayed. Select the queue type that corresponds to your Apple printer. To create multiple queues repeat this process.

NetWare allows multiple queues to service a printer and multiple printers to be serviced by a single queue. In most cases you will be defining a single queue per printer.

When you have finished defining your print queues, press <Esc> to return to the Print Services Options menu and select "Prepare a Print Service Gateway."

You will be prompted for a host type, either a file server or bridge. Since you are doing a file server installation, select "File Server." A list of the file servers to which you are attached will be displayed. Press <Ins> to display file servers to which you are not logged in. Select the file server which is to be your Print Service Gateway. This would usually be the File Service Gateway file server, but it does not have to be.

You will be prompted to insert the LAN_DRV_180 diskette in drive A, followed by the GATEWAY diskette.

Served Queues	Host Type	AppleTalk Queues
	File Serve Bridge	SCRIPTEN

A "Served Queues" list is displayed. Press <Ins> and a list of the file servers to which you are attached will be displayed. (Press <Ins> again to display the file servers to which you are not attached.) Select the file server on which the queue(s) you want serviced by this gateway reside.

After you select a file server, a list of AppleTalk queues on that server will be displayed. Select the queues on that file server that you want served by this Print Service Gateway. You may select multiple queues on multiple file servers.

```
Served Queues          Host Type      Queue Options
LARKSPUR/SCRIPTEN      File Server    Queue Status
                       Bridge         Attached Printers
```

After you have selected one or more print queues, you must specify the attached printers for each queue. Highlight a queue in the "Served Queues" window and press <Enter>. Select "Attached Printers" from the "Queue Options" menu.

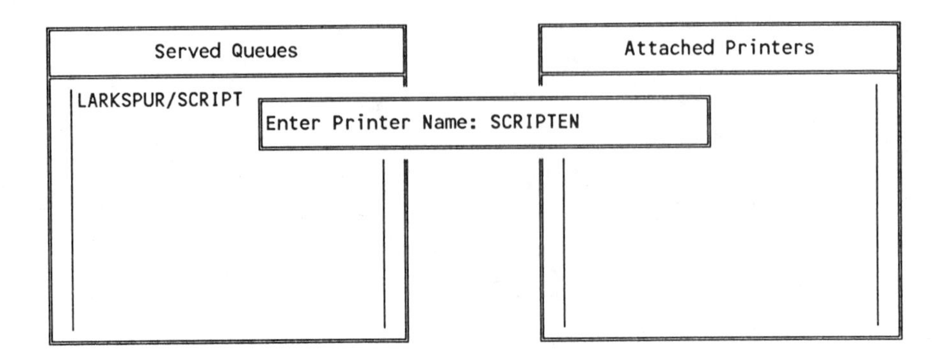

A window entitled "Attached Printers" will display. To add a printer to the list, press <Ins>. You will be prompted to enter the name of the printer that you want to attach to the queue.

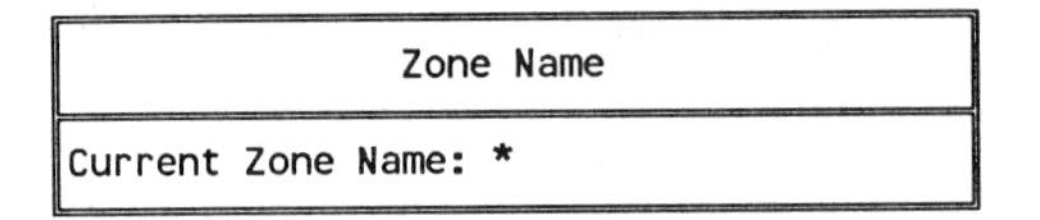

Once you have added a printer to the attached printers list, you must state which LocalTalk "Zone" the printer is in. Zones are defined by AppleTalk bridges and gateways. If your do not have any AppleTalk bridges or gateways, or your printer is attached to the local zone, enter "*." If you do need to attach a printer in another zone, the Chooser on a Macintosh can display printers and their zones.

Repeat these steps to add more printers.

When you are satisfied with your installation, press <Esc> until you get to the exit prompt. You can reenter MACSETUP at any time to edit your installation.

Setting up Macintosh Users, Groups, and Directories

Setting up usernames, groups, and directories for Mac users is like setting up directories for PC users. The basic steps are:

1. Plan your directory structure. Except for specific directories for files that can be shared between PCs and Macs, your Macintosh LAN directory structure should parallel the PC LAN directory structure, and should not overlap.

   If this is a new NetWare installation or you are creating a completely new file server directory structure you might want to consider this basic scheme:

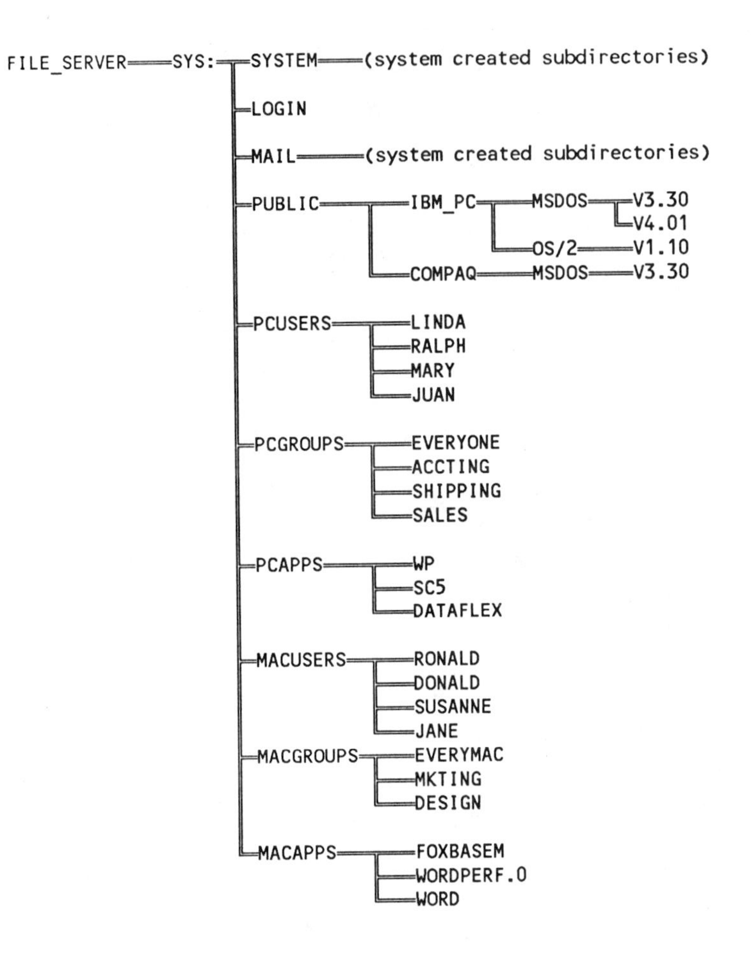
FILE_SERVER
SYS:
SYSTEM
(system created subdirectories)
LOGIN
MAIL
(system created subdirectories)
PUBLIC
IBM_PC
MSDOS
V3.30
V4.01
OS/2
V1.10
COMPAQ
MSDOS
V3.30
PCUSERS
LINDA
RALPH
MARY
JUAN
PCGROUPS
EVERYONE
ACCTING
SHIPPING
SALES
PCAPPS
WP
SC5
DATAFLEX
MACUSERS
RONALD
DONALD
SUSANNE
JANE
MACGROUPS
EVERYMAC
MKTING
DESIGN
MACAPPS
FOXBASEM
WORDPERF.0
WORD

If you are adding NetWare for Macintosh to an existing server, you might want to add a directory structure similar to the following:

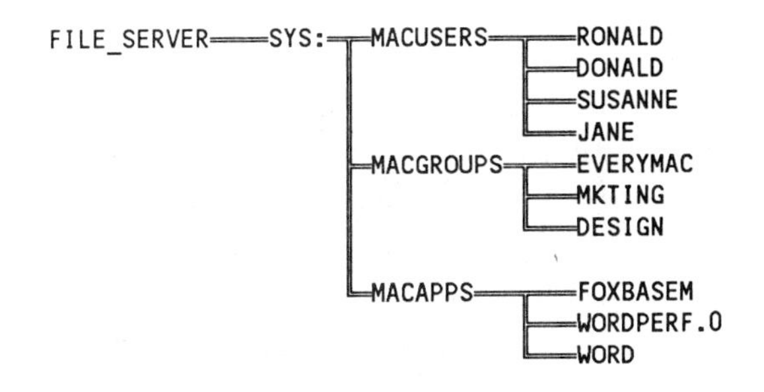

A Macintosh user sees each directory of a volume as a file folder. To keep the Macusers' "desktops" uncluttered, you can do three things:

A. Limit the number of directories in a volume's root directory.
B. Hide certain directories. Directories such as SYSTEM, LOGIN, and MAIL, which are never accessed directly by most users, could be hidden using NetWare's FLAGDIR command from a PC workstation. The FLAGDIR command is explained in detail below.
C. Use FLAGDIR to flag directories that are strictly DOS directories as private. In this case the folder is still on the desktop, but unless the Mac user has search privileges to the directory, it appears as a gray private folder and is inaccessible.

2. Plan your Macintosh Groups. Although NetWare automatically adds all new users to the group EVERYONE, you may want to consider removing Mac users from that group and creating a separate group for all Mac users. If you do this, you need to grant this group READ, WRITE, OPEN and DELETE privileges to the hidden DESKTOP directory on each file server volume.

3. Plan access for your Macintosh Users. Mac users do not need access to DOS program files, and DOS users do not need access to Macintosh program files.

AppleShare and NetWare Security

AppleShare has four levels of directory access rights, whereas NetWare has eight. To effectively map NetWare access rights to AppleShare access rights, Novell has made a change in its rights structure and added a new command, "FLAGDIR," which allows attributes to be placed on directories.

FLAGDIR

FLAGDIR allows you to flag directories with the following attributes:

NORMAL—Cancels directory attributes that have been set. Corresponds with the public folder in the Macintosh environment.

HIDDEN—Hides a directory so users cannot see it in a directory listing. Does not prevent users from accessing the directory.

SYSTEM—Used for directories required for the system to function. A directory flagged with this option will not appear in a directory search.

PRIVATE—Prevents users from viewing the contents of a subdirectory. Users can see the subdirectory flagged as Private from the parent directory, but they cannot see the contents unless they have the Search right. Corresponds to the private (gray) folder in the Macintosh environment.

NetWare Rights

Eight levels of directory rights can be granted to a PC user or group of users. Each directory has an Overall Rights Mask consisting of one or more of the eight rights. The Overall Rights Mask sets maximum available rights for any user to a directory, regardless of rights assigned to that user.

A brief description of each right follows:

CREATE allows you to create new files in the selected directory. In order to write to a newly created file you must also have WRITE privileges. You can also create new subdirectories under the selected directory.

DELETE allows you to delete files in the selected directory.

MODIFY allows you to modify the attributes associated with a file, to rename a file, and to modify the file's creation and last accessed and last modified dates. The MODIFY right also allows you to rename subdirectories and to change a subdirectory's creation date. If you have PARENTAL rights then you can also change the directory attributes with FLAGDIR.

OPEN allows you to open a file that already exists. You will also need the READ right to read from the file and the WRITE right to write to the file.

PARENTAL allows you to specify trustees in the selected directory and the rights that each trustee has. It also allows you to change the maximum rights mask of the selected directory. This right also gives you additional privileges when it is used in combination with the Create, Modify, or Delete rights.

Note: If a user has PARENTAL rights to a directory, that user can grant any user, including herself or himself, all rights to that directory and its subdirectories.

READ allows you to read from an open file.

SEARCH allows you to view the name of the files in this directory. Without this right you can not see what files are in the directory. If a directory is flagged PRIVATE, then you must have SEARCH privileges to see subdirectory names in that directory.

WRITE allows you to write to an open file.

AppleShare Rights

AppleShare has four access rights:

SEE FOLDERS allows a user to see folders inside another folder. If a NetWare folder (directory) has been flagged PRIVATE, then you must have SEARCH rights to see folders (subdirectories) in that folder. If the folder is not flagged PRIVATE, no rights are required to see folders within it.

SEE FILES allows a user to see files within a folder and to open, read, and copy those files. On a NetWare server, it allows SEARCH, OPEN, and READ rights to see files within a folder.

MAKE CHANGES allows a user to create new files and folders, delete files and folders, write to files, and rename files and folders and change non-security attributes. On a NetWare server OPEN, CREATE, WRITE, DELETE, and MODIFY rights give you rights equivalent to MAKE CHANGES.

OWNERSHIP allows a user to change access rights to the folder. The NetWare PARENTAL right is the equivalent of OWNER-

Warning: Any changes made to NetWare security from a Macintosh workstation should be made from the NetWare Desk Accessory or the NetWare Control Center (the Control Center is described below). DO NOT use the AppleTalk Access Privileges or Get Privileges programs. See the section Setting Access Rights below for a discussion of why this is important.

Setting Access Rights

Access rights to server directories for Macintosh users can be set using the FILER, SYSCON, or command line utilities GRANT, REMOVE, and REVOKE from a PC workstation. They can also be set from a Macintosh using the NetWare Control Center or the NetWare Desk Accessory (described below).

The Macintosh Get Privileges File menu option and the Access Privileges desk accessory should never be used to change access rights to a NetWare server. These utilities reset ALL security information whenever a change is made. Because the changes are based on the four AppleShare access levels, and not the eight NetWare levels, the results are unpredictable. These utilities should only be used for AppleShare file servers.

If you do not have any AppleShare file servers you might want to remove the Access Privileges desk accessory using the Mac's Font/DA mover (described below).

Macintosh and DOS File Names

Macintosh file and folder names can contain up to 31 characters, and a disk or volume name can contain up to 27 characters. The only character that cannot be used in a Mac file name is a colon (:).

DOS file names are restricted to eight characters, optionally followed by a period and a three character extension. DOS file names cannot contain any of the following characters:

."/|[]:| <>+=;'

On a NetWare file server, DOS users will see a truncated version of a Mac file name unless Mac users follow DOS naming conventions. If a truncated name is the same as another existing file name in the same directory, NetWare will add a number to the second file name.

Backing up Macintosh Files

Because of the structure of Macintosh files, most backup and archive utilities designed for DOS will not back up Macintosh files. For this reason, Novell provides MACBACK. MACBACK will backup Macintosh files to network and local PC drives. Local drives can include floppy disks, hard disks, high-capacity removable drives, and tape drives that can be addressed as local drives, such as those from ADIC.

MACBACK must be executed from a DOS workstation running a version 2.15 or above shell. MACBACK can only be used with Macintosh files. For MACBACK usage and syntax, see *Chapter 4—Archiving Macintosh Files* in the NetWare for Macintosh Supervisor Supplement.

NetBack, third-party utility from Cheyenne Software, Inc., will also back up and restore Macintosh files. NetBack will archive and restore both DOS and Macintosh files. For more information on NetBack, see *Appendix B—Network Utilities*.

Setting Up Macintosh Workstations

To access a NetWare file server, you need a startup disk that contains the Macintosh system software, the AppleShare workstation software, and optionally, some NetWare for Macintosh utilities. In addition to the NetWare utilities, the NetWare for Macintosh disks contain the latest versions of the required Macintosh system software. *Note:* If you are using Ethernet, in addition to the following you must follow the installation instructions for the particular Macintosh Ethernet interface you are using.

Installing the Macintosh System Tools

The following procedures will create a new startup disk or update an existing one. A startup disk can be an 800K floppy disk or a hard disk.

If you are updating an existing startup disk, back it up first. If you are updating a disk that has applications installed, make sure those applications are compatible with the latest system software. If they are not, then do not upgrade that disk. NetWare for Macintosh is compatible with system software version 4.2 or later.

If you have a 512K Mac or a Mac Plus, then do not upgrade to the latest system software.

If you are using a new 800K diskette as a startup disk you will need to initialize it first. To do this:

1. Eject the System tools diskette by clicking on its icon and dragging it to the trash can.

2. Insert a new diskette in the drive. A dialog box will give you three options: Eject, One-Sided, and Two-Sided. Double click on "Two-Sided." Double click on "Erase" on the next dialog box.

3. You must now give the disk a name. This name can be up to 27 characters long, cannot contain a colon (:) and cannot have a period for the first character. Move your arrow to the end of the word "Untitled" and clear it with the <Delete> key, then type in your new name and click on "OK."

A dialog box will display several messages, and will then display the disk's icon on the screen when the initialization is finished.

To install the system tools:

1. Insert the Novell-supplied Macintosh System Tools-1 disk into your Mac floppy drive and turn on the computer. If the computer is already on, eject any floppy disks and shut down the computer first.

2. Select and open the System Tools disk icon. To do this, move the arrow to the icon and double click on it.

3. Move your arrow to the System Folder and double click to open it.

4. Move your arrow to the Setup Folder and double click to open it.

5. Move your arrow to the Installer Icon and double click to open it.

6. If you are installing on a hard disk:

   The name of your hard disk should be displayed in the upper right-hand corner of the screen. If not, click on the Drive button until your disk name appears. Go to step 9.

7. If you are installing on an 800K diskette and you have two floppy drives:

   Make sure that your startup disk is in your second floppy drive. The name of your disk should be displayed in the upper right-hand corner of the screen. If not, click on the Drive button until your disk name appears. Go to step 9.

8. If you are installing on an 800K diskette and you have one floppy drive:

   Click on the Drive button until the System Tools disk name appears, then click on eject. Insert your startup disk in the floppy drive. Go to step 9.

9. If you need to update your system files and install AppleShare, then hold down the shift key on the keyboard, click on AppleShare Workstation and the appropriate system, then release the shift key. If you only need to install AppleShare, click on AppleShare Workstation. A message will appear for each selection telling you how much disk space you will have left after the installation. If you do not have enough room to install the files, see your Macintosh documentation about reclaiming disk space on your startup drive.

10. Click on the Install button. When the installation is complete, click on the Quit button.

Installing the NetWare Desk Accessory

Desk accessories are utilities that are available to you while you are working in other applications. Desk accessories include the Chooser, which lets you select printers and file servers, a calculator, an alarm clock, etc.

The NetWare desk accessory provides a convenient way to view and change file server information. It includes a rights module that lets you view and change security information.

The NetWare desk accessory must be installed using the Macintosh Font/DA Mover. Both the NetWare desk accessory and the Font/DA Mover are included on the NetWare for Macintosh Utilities Disk.

To install the NetWare desk accessory:

1. Start your Macintosh with your startup disk.

2. Put the NetWare for Macintosh Utilities Disk in the floppy drive.

3. Double click on the NetWare Utilities disk icon.

4. Double click on the Font/DA Mover icon.

5. The screen will display your currently installed fonts. Click on the Desk Accessory button.

6. Click on the Open button on screens lower right. Click on NetWare on the next screen, then click on the Open button.

7. Click on the <<Copy button to move the desk accessory to your startup disk.

8. Click on the Quit button to exit from the Font/DA Mover.

Installing the Rights Module

In order to use the NetWare Desk Accessory, you must install the Rights module in the System folder of your startup disk.

1. Open the system folder on your startup disk. If your startup disk is a floppy diskette, and you have a single disk drive, you will have to eject the startup disk after opening it.

2. Insert the NetWare Utilities disk in the floppy drive and click on its icon to open it.

3. Drag the Rights icon from the utilities disk to your system folder.

Warning: Any changes made to NetWare security from a Macintosh workstation should be made from the NetWare Desk Accessory or the NetWare Control Center (the Control Center is described below). Do not use the AppleTalk Access Privileges or Get Privileges programs.

Logging In

Since the Macintosh clock is not automatically synchronized with the file server clock on login, it is important to make sure your date and time are set correctly. To do this:

1. Click on the Apple icon on the upper left of the screen and hold down the mouse button. This will display the desk accessory menu. Move your arrow to Alarm Clock and release the button.

2. Click the lever on the right side of the clock to display the clock control panel.

3. To change the time, click on the clock icon, then move your cursor to the digits you want to change. Click on the up or down arrow to change the digits.

4. To change the date, click on the calendar icon and follow the procedure outlined in 3 above.

5. To hide the clock display, click on the Close Box in the upper left corner.

When the date and time are correct, you can log in to a file server.

1. Select Chooser from the desk accessories menu (the Apple icon), then click on the AppleShare icon.

2. Chooser will display a list of available file servers. Click on the NetWare server to which you wish to log in.

3. Move your cursor to the User Name window and enter your login name. Make sure that the AppleTalk Active button is selected. Click on the OK button.

4. Verify your login name on the next screen and enter your password if you have one. Make sure the Registered User button is selected. Click on the OK button.

5. A list of available volumes is displayed. Click on the volume that you wish to work with. You can shift-click to select multiple volumes. A cross in the box next to the volume name means that volume will be automatically selected the next time you log in. Clicking on the box will add or remove the cross.

   You have the choice of setting automatic login by selecting the Save My Name and Password option. If you select this, you will be automatically logged in to the selected file server each time you turn on your Macintosh. This also means that anyone else using your computer will be automatically logged in with your name and password.

   When you are satisfied with your selections click on OK.

6. You will return to the Chooser Screen. If you wish to select additional file servers you can do so, or you can click on the Close Box to leave Chooser.

Note: The first time a NetWare file server directory (folder) is accessed from a Macintosh, NetWare may need to do some file restructuring. This may make server access seem very slow. This is a one-time process and is nothing to worry about.

Logging Out

To log out of a file server, simply drag its volume icon(s) to the trash can.

The NetWare Control Center

The NetWare Control Center lets you view and modify detailed information about NetWare users, groups, volumes, directories, and files. A user's level of access to the control center will depend on that user's access rights to NetWare file server volumes.

The NetWare Control Center can be installed on local Macintosh disks or on a file server drive. By installing on a file server drive, one copy will be available to all Macintosh users.

To load the NetWare Control Center into a folder:

1. Open the selected folder.

2. Put the NetWare Utilities diskette in a floppy drive and double click on it.

3. Drag the NetWare Control Center icon from the NetWare Utilities disk to your folder.

4. Close the NetWare Utilities disk and drag its icon to the trash can.

To use the NetWare Control Center, click on its icon. Detailed information can be found in Chapter 6 of Novell's NetWare for Macintosh User's Guide.

Warning: Any changes made to NetWare security from a Macintosh workstation should be made from the NetWare Desk Accessory or the NetWare Control Center. Do not use the AppleTalk Access Privileges or Get Privileges programs.

Installing AppleTalk Printers

In order to access an AppleTalk printer from a Mac workstation, you must have the appropriate printing tools for your network printer(s) on that workstation. To find out if the printing tools are installed, click on the Apple (Finder) icon in the upper left corner of your screen, hold the mouse button down, drag the arrow down to Chooser, then release the button. If the icon corresponding to your network printer is not displayed, you must install it. To install the printer tools, do the following:

1. Turn on your Macintosh.

2. Open the System folder on your startup disk.

3. Insert the Macintosh Printing Tools diskette in your floppy drive, then double click on the Printing Tools icon.

4. Select the icon(s) for the printer(s) that you want to install and drag them to your System folder. You may use the shift-click technique

to select more than one icon at a time. If you are installing a LaserWriter, also select the LaserPrep icon.

5. Click on the Printing Tools Close box, then drag the Printing Tools icon to the Trash can to eject the diskette.

Warning: If you are sharing a LaserWriter printer on your network, it is important that all users have the same version of the LaserWriter and LaserPrep software. If you are not sure, install the latest version on all Macintosh workstations that will be sharing a LaserWriter.

Printing with AppleTalk Printers

NetWare for Macintosh lets both PC users and Mac users print to AppleTalk printers through the NetWare queues. Currently, AppleTalk printers must be connected to the NetWare file server or bridge with LocalTalk hardware, not Ethernet.

Important Note: If you have added or modified a NetWare for Macintosh print queue, the file server must be shut down and restarted before using that queue.

Printing from a Macintosh

As a Macintosh user on a LocalTalk network, you can print directly to an AppleTalk printer or use the NetWare print queues. Ethernet users must send jobs to the queue. By using the queues, you do not have to wait for the printer to be available to accept your job. Once a print job is sent to a queue, your workstation is free to continue with other tasks.

To use the print queue(s), do the following:

1. Click on the Apple (Finder) icon in the upper left corner of your screen and hold down the mouse button.

2. Drag the arrow down to Chooser, then release the button.

3. Select the icon that corresponds to your network printer type.

4. The name(s) of your printer(s), as well as the name(s) of the NetWare print queue(s), will be displayed. NetWare print queue names are always displayed in upper case, while printer names are displayed in upper/lower case. Click on the queue that you wish to use.

5. Click on the Close Box to exit Chooser.

You can now print to the print queue as if it were a printer.

Printing from DOS Workstations

Printing to an AppleTalk printer from DOS workstations is similar to printing to printers attached directly to a NetWare file server, with a few minor differences.

NetWare for Macintosh supports Apple LaserWriter or Apple ImageWriter printers. LaserWriter printers support the PostScript page description language. DOS applications that use PostScript can share a LaserWriter printer. In addition, you can use the LaserWriter in Diablo 630 emulation mode.

Printing with CAPTURE or NPRINT

To use an AppleTalk printer with the NetWare CAPTURE or NPRINT commands, you will need to use PrintDef to create at least one form and to import the Apple printer definition files. You will need to import one or more of the following files from the NetWare GATEWAY diskette that came with NetWare for Macintosh:

LASER.PDF for a LaserWriter in PostScript mode.

LW630.PDF for a LaserWriter in Diablo 630 mode.

IMAGE.PDF for an ImageWriter.

If you are not familiar with PrintDef, please see *Chapter 16—Managing Network Printers.*

```
                Edit Print Job Configuration "POSTSCRIPT"

Number of copies:     1              Form name:        STANDARD
Suppress form feed:   No             Print banner:     Yes
File contents:        Byte stream    Banner name:      PATRICK
Tab size:                            Banner file:

Local printer:        1              Enable timeout:   No
Auto endcap:          Yes            Timeout count:

File server:          LARKSPUR
Print queue:          SCRIPTEN
Device:               LASERWRITER
Mode:                 POSTSCRIPT
```

Next, use the PrintCon utility to create one or more print job descriptions to be used to access the AppleTalk printer(s). Your print job description must specify the following:

File Contents must be set to "Byte stream."

Queue must be set to a queue you created for the AppleTalk printer.

Device must be set to "LASERWRITER" for a LaserWriter in PostScript Mode, "LASERWRITER360" for a LaserWriter in Diablo 630 Emulation mode, or "IMAGEWRITER" for an ImageWriter printer.

If you are not familiar with PrintCon, please see *Chapter 16—Managing Network Printers.*

If you plan to use the CAPTURE or NPRINT commands for a LaserWriter in Diablo 630 emulation mode, the line

```
PRINT HEADER=255
```

in the SHELL.CFG file of each workstation using the LaserWriter in this manner will appear. Please see "Setting Up Workstation Boot Disks" in *Chapter 9—Generating Workstation Shells.*

Printing with (DOS) NetWork WordPerfect

WordPerfect network version uses the NetWare 2.0 spooler functions to send output to network printers. In order to print to an AppleTalk printer from within WordPerfect, you must map a spool number (0 through 4) to an AppleTalk print queue at the file server console. To do this, go to the file server console and type:

```
SPOOL spool# TO QUEUE queue_name
```

where spool# is the NetWare 2.0 spool number that you wish to use, and queue_name is the name of the AppleTalk print queue that you wish to attach.

If you add this line to the System AUTOEXEC File, accessed through the Supervisor Options menu of the SysCon utility, your spool mapping will be set automatically each time you bring up your file server.

```
System AUTOEXEC File

Printer 0 ADD PRINTQ_0
Printer 1 ADD PRINTQ_1
Printer 2 ADD PRINTQ_1
Spool 0 to Queue PRINTQ_0
Spool 1 to Queue PRINTQ_1
Spool 2 to Queue PRINTQ_2
Spool 3 to Queue SCRIPTEN
MONITOR
```

In order to use an AppleTalk printer from WordPerfect, you also need to install the proper printer driver(s) and select the proper WordPerfect device(s) to print to. See your WordPerfect documentation for more information.

Appendix D

Installing ELS NetWare

ELS NetWare is a low cost, limited version of NetWare. There are two versions of ELS: Level I and Level II.

ELS NetWare 286 and 286/2 Level I

ELS I is a four-user version of NetWare. ELS I is NetWare revision 2.0a, and as such lacks many of the advanced features of Advanced NetWare 2.1x. Its chief differences are:

- Only 4 users can attach to the file server at any one time, although the number of stations physically cabled, as well as the number of users and groups defined, is not restricted.

- ELS NetWare 286 Level I only supports Novell NE-1000 Ethernet, Novell RX-Net, SMC/Pure Data ARCNET, and 3Com 3C501 Ethernet cards with AT-type file servers. ELS NetWare 286/2 Level I supports the IBM PC Network II (baseband or broadband version) with PS/2 model 50, 60, and 80 file servers. Boards that are driver-compatible with these may be used also, but their operation is not guaranteed. Several board manufacturers, including Western Digital Corp., supply ELS I with drivers for their own boards.

- ELS I only supports AT or PS/2-type controllers and drives.

- ELS I does not provide for bridging to other file servers or other LANs.

- Account restrictions are not available (no encrypted or minimum length passwords, and no restriction of user disk space or allowable log in dates and times).

- No FCONSOLE utility (including all of FCONSOLE'S file server statistics).

- Printer support is limited to basic spooling service, with one printer per queue and no print job definition or print device support.

ELS I is a good choice as an entry level system for a small office on a small budget. Where standard NetWare costs $2,995 (as of this writing), ELS I costs only $695 (plus the cost of the hardware and file server.)

ELS II Installation

Preparing for an ELS II installation is much the same as preparing for an Advanced or SFT installation. Because ELS II has fewer options than Advanced NetWare 286, the installation program, ELSGEN, requires fewer steps than NETGEN.

Chapters 8, 9, and 10 cover the pragmatic issues of configuring and installing ELS II, although some of the details will vary. Use your ELS II installation manual as a guide.

ELS I Installation

Preparing for an ELS I installation is much the same as preparing for an Advanced or SFT installation. The installation instructions presented here should prove sufficient for the great majority of ELS I installations. It is nevertheless a good idea to review Novell's ELS NetWare 286 or 286 Level I Installation Manual and keep it handy.

- Before you begin, equipment locations should already have been chosen, power requirements met, and all cabling should have been installed.

- Prepare the file server (including installing the hardware and network operating system on it) in advance of installing it on the network. These tasks are best done in a quiet location where you are not being constantly interrupted and where you will be free to make mistakes (if this is your first installation, you will probably make some). This could be a private office, a back room, or even somewhere off-site.

- When you have finished the network operating system installation, log in to the network. Ideally, this would be the time to create users and directories, install applications, etc. It is also a good idea to connect at least one workstation to the file server to make sure you can establish communications.

- Perform these operations during times when technical support is available.

- Give yourself plenty of time. Many LAN installation disasters are the result of rushing.

After these tasks have been completed, you can install the server on-site and begin attaching and testing more workstations and other network devices.

To install ELS I on your server, you will need the following:

- The ELS NetWare 286 or the ELS NetWare 286/2 Level I Installation manual.

- You may want to have on hand the phone numbers of your Novell dealer and/or Novell's LANswer help line (If you don't have a Novell support contract, have your credit card handy).

Preparing the ELS I Working Disks

Before you begin the ELS I installation you should make copies of the Novell ELS I diskettes. Use the DOS DISKCOPY command to make the copies, rather than the DOS COPY command.

Note: There are several diskettes labelled OS_xxxxxx, one for each NIC type you could install. You will only use the one associated with your NIC hardware.

Preparing the Network Interface Card and Cabling

The NICs available for an ELS 286 Level I LAN can be Ethernet or ARCNET:

Ethernet

NetWare NE-1000 Ethernet
3Com 3C501 EtherLink

The NE-1000 is the Novell Ethernet board. There are many compatible boards designed to this standard by other manufacturers. For example, Gateway Communication's G-Ethernet can use the NE-1000 drivers. Gateway supplies the standard version of ELS I to their customers.

Cabling is RG-58/U 50 ohm coaxial cable.

ARCNET

NetWare RX-Net
SMC ARCNET

Many brands of ARCNET boards use the SMC driver and should work with ELS.

Cabling is RG-62/U 93 ohm coaxial cable.

The required hardware (NICs, hard disk should already be installed and configured in accordance with the parameters listed in the ELS manual. ELS I gives you no choice about configuration alternatives, unlike the Advanced or SFT NetGen program, which makes it easier to install. On the other hand, because you have no configuration alternatives, your freedom to mix and match devices that use the same PC resources is gone.

The NICs available for an ELS 286/2 Level I LAN can be the IBM PC Network II baseband or broadband cards. Please see your ELS 286/2 Installation manual for information on these NICs.

Preparing the File Server

The file server for an ELS 286 Level I network must be an IBM AT-compatible 286 or 386. The file server for an ELS 286/2 Level I network must be a PS/2 model 50, 60, or 80. Many AT compatible machines will not work properly with ELS I. Check with your dealer if you are unsure.

The file server's drives and controllers should be installed and identified with the SETUP utility for AT-type machines or the REFERENCE utility for PS/2-type machines.

Although the ELS I installation program performs a format of the disk, preformatting the disk and initializing with DOS will help isolate hard disk problems from network installation problems.

To ensure that your disk is a bootable DOS disk before attempting the NetWare installation, format it with the command:

```
A>format c: /s
```

Installing ELS I

To begin installing ELS I, first boot the file server with DOS 3.1 or above.

Insert the diskette labeled START in the file server drive A.

Locate on drive A and begin the START program:

```
A>START
```

START issues a warning and asks if you want to continue:

```
WARNING:  This procedure will destroy all data on drive
C:!  If you haven't already done so, make a backup copy
of all files on your hard disk.

Do you want to continue? (y/n)
```

Enter Y to continue.

START prompts you to insert a DOS disk. It reads from the disk, then prompts you to re-insert the START disk. Do so, and you will see the following message:

```
Your hard disk will now be tested and prepared for Net-
Ware. This procedure requires a minimum of 30 minutes to
complete, plus an additional 1 minute per megabyte of
hard disk storage.

   Drive Size      Approximate Time for disk test
   ----------      --------------------------------
   10 megabytes    40 minutes
   30 megabytes    1 hour
   70 megabytes    1 hour, 40 minutes
   155 megabytes   3 hours, 5 minutes
```

Note: This screen will remain unchanged throughout the test.

START automatically performs a test of the hard disk's track 0 and executes the Comprehensive Surface Analysis utility (CompSurf) and prepares the disk as a NetWare drive. COMPSURF provides several functions. It performs a low-level format on the selected drive; it performs a media analysis test on the selected drive; it locates the bad block table in the location required by NetWare and updates the table with any bad blocks it finds during testing.

START will report what percentage of the test is done and will update the report periodically.

The test may take longer than the times indicated. Do not exit by rebooting except as a last resort, when the test has run well over schedule and there has been no disk activity for some time.

If the disk fails the test or is unusable as a NetWare drive, you will receive an error message and start will abort the program.

Important Note for the Experienced Network Installer:

> The ELS I START utility is comprised of several installation utilities, including CompSurf, Prepare, and Install. START takes defaults for all of the parameters set by these utilities and does not display them. If you need to observe or modify the default parameters set by these utilities, you can invoke them individually from the installation disks. You might bypass the START utility, for example, to hand-enter the manufacturer's bad block table in CompSurf. You might use the Install utility to initialize a hard disk (usually the file server's second hard disk), create or edit a partition, change the file server's name, or modify volume directories, among other things.

Instructions for running CompSurf interactively can be found in the NetWare ELS I Installation Manual's Appendix B. Instructions for Prepare are in Appendix C, and for Install in Appendix D.

When the start utility completes, you will see the message:

```
The test of your hard disk was successful.
Strike a key when ready...
```

Press a key, and start will inform you that it is preparing the drive and creating the NetWare volume. You will be prompted to insert the SYSTEM and PUBLIC diskettes as they are required. When this process completes, you will receive the message:

```
System files successfully installed.
Strike a key when ready...
```

The start utility instructs you to put the START diskette in drive A and strike a key. You will be prompted:

```
This completes the ELS I NetWare Installation.
To boot the file server insert your Operating System (OS) diskette
in drive A: and strike a key when ready...
```

Your OS diskette is the diskette labelled OS_xxxxxx, where xxxxxx corresponds to the NIC hardware you have installed. For example, if you installed an NE-1000 compatible board, you would insert the diskette labeled OS_NE1000.

Booting the File Server

The file server must be booted from the OS diskette. It is important that you keep the original stored in a safe place, and use a working copy.

Logging in to the File Server

The first network drive letter is usually F: To reach the network drive, type the drive letter:

```
F:
```

The first network drive (shown as F: in the examples in this chapter) will vary depending on the version of DOS you are using, the type of workstation you are using, the hardware configuration of your workstation, and options specified in the CONFIG.SYS file.

At the prompt, type:

```
LOGIN SUPERVISOR     <Enter>
```

LOGIN finds your user profile in the bindery (the database of information about users, groups, and security) then uses your user profile to set your access rights to volumes and directories on the file server.

When you first login in as Supervisor, which is the only user defined on a brand new file server, NetWare runs a default login script to set drive maps to certain directories that you will need to set up the system.

The screen will respond with a display similar to the following. This is the "default login script" that executes for any user when there is neither a system login script nor a user login script.

```
Drive A maps to a local disk.
Drive B maps to a local disk.
Drive C maps to a local disk.
Drive D maps to a local disk.
Drive E maps to a local disk.
Drive F:= ELS_NETSERVER/SYS:SYSTEM
Drive G:= ELS_NETSERVER/SYS:LOGIN
Drive H:= ELS_NETSERVER/SYS:PUBLIC
----
```

```
SEARCH1:= Z: [ELS_NETSERVER/SYS:PUBLIC]
```

After logging in for the first time the Supervisor will set up workstation boot diskettes, modify the file server's directory structure, install applications, set up system defaults, and set up groups and users with the syscon utility. The directory structure design and implementation is much the same for an ELS I file server as for an Advanced or SFT file server, as discussed in Chapter 12. syscon for ELS I is similar to syscon as discussed in chapters 13 and 14, except that advanced features not relevant to ELS I are omitted from the program's menus.

Downing the File Server

After verifying that the file server is functioning properly, you should bring down the file server using the DOWN command, then set up your boot disks. To issue the DOWN command, you must first put the file server in Console mode with the CONSOLE command. Insert your working OS diskette in drive A and type:

```
A:CONSOLE <Enter>
```

At the console colon (:) prompt type:

```
DOWN <Enter>
```

A message will appear shortly that indicates that the file server has been shut down.

Setting up Boot Disks

You need to create a boot disk for the file server and for each workstation on the network, unless you are using Remote Reset (diskless booting) workstations. (See the ELS I Installation manual for instructions regarding Remote Reset.)

Setting Up the File Server Boot Disk

The boot disk you will use for the file server must be formatted as a DOS-bootable system disk with the command:

```
FORMAT A: /S
```

Follow the DOS instructions for switching disks. Label the diskette as the File Server Boot Disk.

With the file server boot disk in Drive A:, boot the file server.
Then place your OS diskette in drive A and type A:

At the A> prompt, type

```
BOOT      <enter>
```

The network operating system will be loaded on the file server. Connect to the network by typing F: (or whatever letter is the first network drive in your installation). Type:

```
LOGIN SUPERVISOR
```

Setting Up Workstation Boot Disks

To set up a workstation's boot disk you will need the DOS boot disk it uses and the ELS I NetWare diskette labeled SHELL-1.

Use the FORMAT command on the workstation's DOS disk (or directory) to format a new boot disk with the command:

```
FORMAT A: /S
```

Follow the DOS instructions for switching disks.

If the all of the workstations are using the same version of DOS and the same hardware, you can create one boot diskette and then make copies of it with the DOS DISKCOPY command. If workstations use different versions of DOS, you should create each boot disk at the workstation that will use it, so that the shell program records the right version of DOS.

Insert the SHELL-1 disk in the workstation's A drive. This diskette contains four directories:

```
3C501     <dir>
RXNET     <dir>
NE1000    <dir>
PCN2      <dir>
```

Change to the directory that corresponds to your hardware. For example, type

```
CD\NE1000
```

if you are using a Novell Ethernet-type card in the workstation.

Copy all of the files from this directory to the root directory of the workstation boot disk. For example, if you have the SHELL-1 diskette in drive A: and the new workstation boot disk in drive B:, simply type:

```
copy A:*.* B:
```

Warning: The SHELL-1 directory includes an autoexec.bat file. If you are using an existing workstation boot disk that contains an autoexec.bat file, it will be overwritten by this procedure. If you do not want to destroy the existing autoexec file, you should make a copy of it. You can then review the two autoexec files and incorporate the commands of one into the other.

The files copied to the boot disk are the shell file ANET3.COM, the NetBios emulator NETBIOS.COM, an autoexec.bat file, and the DOS command processor COMMAND.COM.

Logging in at the Workstation

The shell can be invoked manually by booting the workstation and typing ANET3 at the prompt, or it can be automated by using the autoexec.bat file.

When you execute the autoexec (or ANET3 manually) you will see a message similar to the following:

```
Novell IPX/SPX
(C) Copyright 1985, 1988 Novell, Inc.  All Rights Reserved.

LAN Option: Standard Microsystems ARCNET/Pure Data V1.00
(881010)
Hardware Configuration IRQ=2, I/O Base=2E0h, RAM Buffer at
D000:0

ELS NetWare 286 Level I  - Workstation Shell for PC DOS V3.x
(C) Copyright 1983, 1988 Novell, Inc.  All Rights Reserved.

Attached to Server ELS_NETSERVER
Sunday, April 16, 1989     9:03:47 am
```

If you will be running applications that require the NetBIOS emulator, you may need to type:

```
NETBIOS <Enter>
```

If you have added the command ANET3 to the autoexec file, you might want to add NETBIOS on the following line as well.

A typical autoexec.bat file might contain the following commands:

```
Echo off
Prompt $p $g $c
ANET3
NETBIOS
F:
LOGIN username
```

Now change to the first network drive, (usually F:) and execute the login program by typing

```
LOGIN
```

If F:\LOGIN> appears on the screen, you have successfully changed to the first network drive. If the message "Invalid drive specification" appears, try typing other drive letters (D or E) until you find the correct network drive for your workstation.

When the F:\LOGIN prompt appears, you have connected to the network successfully, but you have no rights to do anything.

To log in from the workstation, type

```
LOGIN SUPERVISOR <Enter>
```

or, if the supervisor has set up users and passwords, type

```
LOGIN USERNAME       <Enter>

Password: PASSWORD    <Enter>
```

LOGIN finds your user profile in the bindery (the database of information about users, groups, and security), prompts you to enter your password, if you have one, then uses your user profile to set your access rights to volumes and directories on the file server. LOGIN then runs a login script, which contains instructions to assign drive letters and search paths to selected directories (called mapping) and set other parameters for your own network environment.

ELS II

ELS II is an eight-user version of NetWare. ELS II is NetWare revision 2.12 (and should by 2.15 by the time this book is published).
The primary differences between ELS II and Advanced NetWare 286 are:

- Only 8 users can attach to the file server at any one time, although the number of stations physically cabled, as well as the number of users and groups defined is not restricted.

- ELS II only supports XT, AT, and PS/2-type controllers and drives.

- ELS II does not provide for bridging to other file servers or other LANs. (NetWare for Macintosh should be supported with version 2.15, however.)

- When installed in non-dedicated mode ELS II can be run on an XT- type file server.

Appendix E

Modifying and Upgrading NetWare

From time to time you will want to upgrade either your hardware or your network software. Sometimes you will have to do both. The programs you use to perform an upgrade are the same as those you use to perform an installation; the specific steps you take within the program depends on the kind of upgrade you are performing. Invariably the first thing you should do before beginning any upgrade is to perform a full back up of any existing files (unless there is no chance that you will want to use the files again.)

Hardware Upgrades

If you are installing new components on NetWare 2.15 (a new hard disk, a disk coprocessor, or even a new server machine) you may have to modify the configuration of your network operating system to specify the new component, generate a new operating system, and install it on the server disk. If you are installing a new disk, you may have to run the CompSurf utility to format and partition it during the installation. The instructions for generating the operating system are in Chapter 8. The instructions for installing the operating system are in Chapter 11.

Adding Disk Drives

If you are adding disks using existing disk channels you will need to do the following:

- If you are adding a drive to an IBM-Type controller, you will need to update the file server's drive table. This is done with the Setup utilities on an AT-type server. You will then need to run the CompSurf utility on the added drive. Follow the instructions in Chapter 11—Running CompSurf, then proceed to Performing the Upgrade, below.

- If you are adding a drive to a DCB, then you will need to run the DiskSet utility. Follow the instructions in Chapter 8, Running DiskSet. If the disk that you are adding is not a Novell disk or is not pre-CompSurfed, you will need to run the CompSurf utility on the added drive. Follow the instructions in Chapter 10, Running CompSurf, then proceed to Performing the Upgrade, below.

Adding or Changing Disk Channels

If you are adding or changing disk channels, proceed to Reconfiguring the NetWare Operating System, below.

Note: If you are adding an IBM-Type disk channel, then you will need to run the Setup Utility supplied with your file server PC. Only one is allowed per file server.

NetWare Upgrades

There are essentially three classes of NetWare upgrades:

Upgrading from versions prior to Advanced NetWare 2.0
Upgrading from versions of Advanced or SFT NetWare 2.0
Upgrading from versions Advanced or SFT NetWare 2.1 and above

A summary of instructions for each of these upgrades begins in the following section.

Again, before you make changes to the NetWare OS, ALWAYS back up your file server. For NetWare upgrades, it is a good idea to make two backups: one with all files and security information and one with non-NetWare programs and data only. If your backup system does not allow you to restore in this manner, or does not allow you to selectively exclude system files and security information, get a new backup system before upgrading.

If the upgrade was unsuccessful for some reason, restore the complete tape. If the upgrade was successful, use the tape without the old NetWare files, which will preclude the possibility of restoring your old network operating system on top of the new one you just installed.

Upgrading to version 2.15 from versions prior to 2.0

If you are upgrading from versions previous to Advanced NetWare 2.0, proceed as if you are installing NetWare for the first time:

Do two backups of the file server as described above.

Record the server's directory structure and security information (users and user rights, group memberships, login scripts, etc.)

Perform a complete installation, including configuring, generating and installing the NetWare OS and generating new workstation shells. This is covered in Chapters 8–11.

Before restoring your files to the file server, read "Restoring Data to Network Hard Disks" in the NetWare Upgrade Supplement.

If your backup tape has old NetWare system files on it, you must control the restoration of each file, making sure old system files are not restored.

Upgrading to version 2.15 from versions of 2.0

Do two backups of the file server as described above.

Record the server's directory structure and security information (users and user rights, group memberships, login scripts, etc.). You should not have to re-enter this information, but it is a good idea to have it just in case.

Record your current hardware configuration for file servers and workstations. The CONFIG command entered at the file server console will display your server LAN driver configuration.

Configure the operating system and shells as outlined in Chapters 8 and 9. Unless your workstation shells have been modified with DEBUG or some other utility, the Default Configuration Option of ShGen should provide the correct new shells.

Proceed to "Performing the Upgrade," below.

Note: Novell's Disk Interface Board, used for Novell's disk subsystems, is no longer supported and will have to be replaced with a Disk Coprocessor Board (DCB). In addition, OMTI and Zebec disk controllers, used in some older Novell sub-systems, are also no longer supported. If you replace these boards your disks will have to be reCompSurfed and you will have to follow the instructions on upgrading from versions previous to Advanced NetWare 2.0, above.

Upgrading to version 2.15 from versions 2.1 and above

Do two backups of the file server as described above.

Record the server's directory structure and security information (users and user rights, group memberships, login scripts, etc.). You should not have to re-enter this information, but it is a good idea to have it just in case.

Record your current hardware configuration for file servers and workstations. The CONFIG command entered at the file server console will display your server LAN driver configuration. You can also use Lan Driver Information option of FConsole to obtain this information. FConsole will also display the disk channels that you are using. Each time you load a workstation shell its configuration is displayed on the screen.

Configure the operating system and work station shells as outlined in Chapters 8 and 9. If you have recorded your shell configuration(s) the Intermediate Configuration Option of ShGen should provide the correct new shells.

Proceed to Performing the Upgrade, below.

Changing File Server Parameters

If you are doing any of the following:

Adding/changing/removing file server LAN drivers
Changing network address(es)

Changing the number of routing buffers

then proceed to "Reconfiguring the NetWare Operating System," below.

If you only doing one or more of the following:

Changing the file server name
Changing the number of open files
Changing the number of indexed files
Changing the transaction backout volume (TTS only)
Changing the number of transactions tracked (TTS only)
Limiting disk space or the number of Bindery objects
Changing volume parameters:
  Volume names
  Number of allowable file/directory names
  Caching
Changing spooled printers list or parameters

then proceed to Performing the Upgrade, below.

Reconfiguring the NetWare Operating System: Hard Disk Option

If you used the Hard Disk run option when you originally configured your NetWare OS, and the NetGen directories and files are intact, your job is easy. Do the following:

Review Chapter 8, Configuring the NetWare Operating System.

Locate your working copies of NetGen diskettes (GENDATA, SUPPORT, NETGEN, UTILEXE-1 and -2, and OSEXE-1 and -2).

Go to the \GENERATE\NETWARE directory on your hard disk and type NETGEN. Select the Hard Disk Run Option, then select the Custom Configuration option. To make your changes, follow the instructions in the "Using the Custom Configuration Method" section of Chapter 8.

If you have added or changed disk channels, see "Adding Disk Drives," above.

When you are through with the NetWare Configuration proceed to "Performing the Upgrade," below.

Reconfiguring the NetWare Operating System: Floppy Disk Option

If you used the Floppy Disk run option when you originally configured NetWare, or you have deleted the files from your hard disk, your job is a little more time consuming. Do the following:

Review Chapter 8—Configuring the NetWare Operating System.

Locate your working copies of NetGen diskettes (GENDATA, SUPPORT, NETGEN, UTILEXE-1 and -2, OSEXE-1 and -2 and AUXGEN). You will also need your other NetWare diskettes, preferably copies, not originals.

Go to "Changing the Network Configuration" in the Novell SFT / Advanced NetWare 286 Maintenance manual and follow the instructions there. Be prepared for a lot of disk swapping.

If you have added or changed disk channels, see Adding Disk Drives, above.

When you are through with the NetWare configuration proceed to Performing the Upgrade, below.

Performing the Upgrade

Follow the instructions in Chapter 11 on "Scheduling the Installation" and "Installing NetWare". If you have not performed a NetWare installation or upgrade before, you should review Chapter 11 in its entirety.

To begin your upgrade, first boot the file server with DOS 3.1 or above. Make sure your boot disk has a CONFIG.SYS file and that the files parameter is ten or greater.

Insert your working copy of the NETGEN diskette in the file server drive A. If the file server has a drive B, insert the SUPPORT diskette (working copy) in drive B. (If the server doesn't have a B drive, NetGen will occasionally prompt you to switch between the two diskettes.)

Select the Custom Configuration option from the menu.

Unless you are installing NetWare from another attached file server, choose the Floppy Disk run option.

Choose NetWare Installation from the options menu. (Note: Depending on previous actions you have taken in the NetGen program, the Network Generation Options menu may not display all of the options listed here.)

NetGen may prompt you to insert your configured NETGEN and SUPPORT diskettes several times.

At this point you will see a message indicating that NetWare is analyzing the system to determine the kinds of disk drives that are connected. This may take several minutes, depending on what kind and how many disk drives are connected to the file server.

NetGen reports the kind of disk drive(s) you selected earlier. If this information is not correct, NetWare may not function, may function incorrectly, and under certain circumstances can cause disk damage.

The information should be checked against the printout or other documentation you made while generating the operating system, and should also be checked against the actual equipment installed in the file server.

Unless the drive list is wrong, select "Drive List is Correct" to continue.

If the drive list is incorrect or incomplete, you should choose "Incorrect Drive List." You will be prompted to exit, which you should do. Then go back to Chapter 8—Generating the Operating System. Re-run NetGen, modify the disk drive selections as necessary, and re-generate the operating system. Then begin this chapter again.

After you verify the drive list, the menu for choosing default or custom installation will appear. Select Custom Installation.

Master System Drive Table stores information about all file server drives. Any changes made to drives and/or controllers can require the table to be updated.

Other options:

Miscellaneous Maintenance is used to load the operating system and the system and public files, change the file server name, modify the system configuration, view volume information, and modifying the spooled printers list.

Modify HotFix Redirection Tables is used to change the size of the area available for NetWare to redirect data from bad blocks on the disk. Un-

Unless you are trying to recover a little extra disk space, or mirror or duplex two slightly different sized drives, leave this at the default size.

Modify Partition Tables only appears on the menu if you are using AT or PS/2-type drives and controllers. The partition table allows multiple operating systems, such as NetWare, DOS and UNIX, to reside on the same disk. Modifying an existing partition will destroy the data in that partition.

Reinitialize a Disk will erase the directory and file allocation table, effectively destroying all data. Use this option with caution.

If you have two or more initialized disks, the following options, in addition to the ones shown above, will appear on the menu:

> **Remove A Disk** allows you to logically remove a disk from the file server. Once a disk has been removed the Restore a Disk will appear on the menu, allowing you restore that disk.
>
> **Modify Mirror Tables** allows you to establish, view and unmirror mirrored disk pairs. When two drives become a mirrored pair, the secondary drive will maintain a mirror copy of information contained on the primary drive. For more information about disk mirroring, refer to the Advanced NetWare 286 Installation and Maintenance manuals.

If you have added a disk that has not been initialized the option Initialize a Disk will appear on the menu. See Chapter 11—Installing NetWare, for more information.

Miscellaneous Maintenance

Load Operating System sets a flag to load the operating system onto the file server's hard disk from floppy diskettes. The operating system will not be copied until the installation session is completed, at which time you will be prompted to insert the proper diskettes.

If you have made changes to the operating system with the configuration mode of NetGen or you are upgrading from a previous version of NetWare, select "Yes" in the confirmation window.

Load System & Public Files sets a flag to load the system and public files onto the file server's hard disk from floppy diskettes. The files will not be copied until the installation session is completed, at which time you will be prompted to insert the proper diskettes. If you are upgrading from a previous version of NetWare, select "Yes" in the confirmation window.

System Configuration lets you change the file server name, numbers of open and indexed files, the transaction backout volume, maximum number of transactions to be tracked, the disk space limit, and the number of allowed Bindery objects.

Volume Information lets you review and edit the volume(s) you have created. You can change the volume name of any volume (except SYS), the number of allowed directory entries, and the caching parameter.

Printer Maintenance allows you to define file server LPT and COM ports as network printer ports. On a PC or AT-type file server, NetWare can recognize up to five printers attached to LPT1 through LPT3 and COM1 and COM2. This table shows which devices are currently being used and what their printer numbers are. The printers are numbered from 0 to 4. If you have only one printer, it must be assigned to printer number 0.

Each printer you define will either be parallel or serial, depending on the port to which it is connected.

For parallel printers you may select or edit the printer number.

For serial printers you may select or edit the printer number, baud rate, word length, stop bits and parity, and specify whether the printer uses the Xon/Xoff protocol. The serial printer parameters should correspond to the configuration of the printer.

Installing Your Changes and Upgrades

When you are satisfied with the installation parameters you have selected, return to the "Installation Options" menu, then select Continue Installation.

NetGen will now begin the installation. You will be prompted for the diskettes required to install the upgrades or changes you have selected.

CAUTION: Never attempt to abort the installation process while files are being transferred from a diskette. If you must abort the process, you may safely do so after a diskette has finished transferring files by pressing <Ctrl><Break>.

When the installation process is finished, select "Exit NetGen" from the main menu and return to DOS. You can now re-boot your file server.

If you have upgraded from a previous version of NetWare, proceed to "After the Upgrade," below.

Recreating the File Server for Upgrades from Versions Prior to 2.0

If you are upgrading from NetWare 86 or 286 below version 2.0, you will have to recreate the file server directory structure, system security and defaults, and groups and users. After that, you will restore from backup any non-NetWare application and data files you want to use on the new system.

Creating the Directory Structure

Using the documentation you created about your original file server's structure and the instructions in Chapter 12—Setting Up File Server Directories to recreate your file server directories.

Setting Up System Defaults

Using the documentation you created about the original file server and the instructions in Chapter 13—Setting Up System Defaults, set up the system defaults for the server.

Creating Groups and Users

Using the documentation you created about the original file server and the instructions in Chapter 14—Setting Up Groups and Users, recreate the users and groups on the original file server.

Restoring Files from Backup

Restore any needed files from the file server backup you performed at the beginning of the upgrade procedure. Do not restore any files from the SYS:SYSTEM (formerly SYS:SUPER), SYS:LOGIN, or SYS:MAIL directories. Make sure that you only restore non-NetWare files from the SYS:PUBLIC directory.

After The Upgrade

Now that the server upgrade is done, you still have several tasks to accomplish:

- Generate new workstation shells and boot files. See Chapter 9—Generating Workstation Shells.

- Modify batch files and login Scripts to reflect command name changes. For example, the SPOOL and ENDSPOOL programs of versions 2.0a and before are replaced by CAPTURE and ENDCAP in current versions.

- Create print job configurations and set up network printers. This should be done if you are upgrading from versions 2.0a and previous. See Chapter 16—Managing Network Printers.

- Test your applications. Applications that worked fine with earlier NetWare versions may need upgrading or modifying.

- Test your backup system(s). Make sure your backup hardware and software functions properly with the new operating system.

About the Authors

Patrick H. Corrigan

Aisling Guy

Patrick H. Corrigan, a nationally recognized authority on local area networks, is the director of The Corrigan Group—Information Services, a consulting firm based in San Francisco, California. Mr. Corrigan lectures and teaches extensively in the areas of LAN system design and implementation and has written numerous articles on LAN-related topics.

Aisling Guy, co-author of the best-selling book *Mastering 1-2-3* (Sybex 1988), is a freelance writer and consultant based in San Francisco, California. Her consulting firm designs and supports office and departmental LAN systems and applications.

Index

More Management and Business Resources from M&T Books

Public-Domain Software and Shareware, Second Edition

by Rusel DeMaria and George R. Fontaine

Why pay $150 or $300 for software when you can buy a comparable package for only $15 or $30? This book critically reviews the public-domain and Shareware gems that are available, and provides all the information you'll need on how and where to find them. The new 498-page second edition contains twice as many program reviews, with expanded software categories. You'll find accounting, database, graphics, and entertainment software, as well as editors, utilities, DOS shells, desk managers, menu programs, and much more. Sample public-domain programs are available on disk.

Book & Disk (MS-DOS)	***Item #014-1***	***$34.95***
Book only	***Item # 011-7***	***$19.95***

SQL for dBASE Programmers

by Edward Dowgiallo

SQL for dBASE Programmers provides a detailed introduction to the Structured Query Language (SQL) world. Written specifically for the dBASE programmer, this book is an invaluable resource that serves as a bridge between dBASE and SQL. Chapter topics discussed in detail include the anatomy of the SQL language, facilities for constructing database structures, an advanced discussion of database views, set manipulation aspects, overview of SQL implementations, SQL kernels, application generators, multiple-user environments, SQL and SAA, and more!

SQL for dBASE Programmers is the reference you need to make design decisions. It will provide the information required to make your next project a success.

Book & Disk (MS-DOS)	***Item #035-4***	***$39.95***
Book only	***Item #034-6***	***$24.95***

More Resources ...

PC Accounting Solutions

by the Editors of *PC Accounting* (formerly *Business Software*)

PC Accounting Solutions is a well-rounded collection of articles written by accounting experts and is an excellent source of information for managers who want to implement a PC-based accounting system or gain better control of their existing system. From choosing and maximizing your accounting systems and software to building better spreadsheets and budgets, you'll find that ***PC Accounting Solutions*** is an immensely valuable source that will improve your ability to analyze the information that is critical to the success of your business.

Additional topics include choosing and maximizing PC-based accounting systems, generating and using management accounting reports, developing vertical applications and accounting solutions, forecasting with regression analysis, and more.

Book & Disk (MS-DOS)	***Item #008-7***	***$37.95***
Book only	***Item #009-5***	***$22.95***

PageMaker 3 by Example

by Tony Webster and David Webster

PageMaker 3 by Example is an excellent, hands-on tutorial designed to make this versatile program easy to understand and use. Its contents and approach are based on over 1,000 hours of training users on desktop publishing.

The book is broken up into modules with each progressive module covering more detailed operations of PageMaker. Each module contains an information section designed to introduce and outline the associated concepts. Provided are numerous examples of how different concepts are utilized. By making use of these exercises and screen illustrations, the learning process is reinforced. Topics include loading files, manipulating PageMaker text blocks, text editing, internal graphics, advanced picture formatting, templates, setting defaults, printing, and much more. ***PageMaker 3 by Example*** is available for both the Macintosh and IBM PC compatibles.

Book (PC version)	***Item #050-8***	***$22.95***
Book (Macintosh version)	***Item #049-4***	***$22.95***

More Resources ...

Building Local Area Networks with Novell's Netware

by Patrick H. Corrigan and Aisling Guy

Building Local Area Networks is a practical guide to selecting and installing PC local area networks (LANS). The specifics of building and maintaining PC LANs, including selection criteria, cabling, installation, and on-going management are described in a clear, concise, step-by-step manner. This book is designed to help you make effective and informed LAN planning, purchasing, and operating decisions.

Book & Disk (MS-DOS) ***Item #025-7*** ***$39.95***
Book only ***Item #010-9*** ***$24.95***

To Order: Return this form with your payment to: **M&T Books**, 501 Galveston Drive, Redwood City, CA 94063 or **CALL TOLL-FREE 1-800-533-4372** Mon-Fri 8AM-5PM Pacific Standard Time (in California, call 1-800-356-2002).

❑ **YES!** Please send me the following:

❑ Check enclosed, payable to **M&T Books**.

Item#	Description	Disk	Price

Subtotal ______

CA residents add sales tax __% ______

Add $2.99 per item for shipping and handling ______

TOTAL ______

Charge my ❑ Visa ❑ MC ❑ AmEx

Card No. ______

Exp. Date ______

Signature ______

Name ______

Address ______

City ______

State ______ Zip ______

7029

M&T BOOKS